A Leatherstocking Companion

Novels and Narratives as History

By James M. Volo

THE TRADITIONAL AMERICAN HISTORY SERIES
NUMBER 13

To my nephews and their children
So they might know the America that I have known.

The Traditional American History Series
Affordable books dedicated to the History of American Exceptionalism
By James M. Volo, PhD

The God of Democracy,
Religion in Revolutionary America, No. 1

Stand Alarmed,
Militia in America, 1608-1783, No. 2

From Whence the Silver,
The Role of Money in Colonial America, No. 3

They Came to Sing,
Music in the Colonies, 1607-1787, No. 4

Slow But Deadly
The Dive-bombers of World War II, No. 5

To Bend the Bow of Ulysses
Wade Hampton's Southern Cavalry, No. 6

Soldiers of the Press
Civil War Journalism, 1861-1865, No. 7

Custer's Civil War Cavalry
Forged by Fire, United By Will, No. 8

Railroad Raiders of the Civil War, No. 9

Antebellum America
Cultural Connections through History, 1820 – 1860, No. 10

To Starve, Die & Be Damned:
The Delaware Blues of the American Revolution, 1776-1783, No. 11

Blow Ye the Trumpet in Zion
Religion in the Civil War Era, No. 12

This book DOES NOT promote, encourage, or condone ethnic, racial, religious or sectional animosity or stereotyping. It DOES uphold traditional values of patriotism, personal ethics, honor, and devotion to the production and representation of authentic American history.

EZ-Read format

A Leatherstocking Companion

Novels and Narratives as History

By James M. Volo

It is hardly possible to imagine a more picturesque field for the novelist as well as the historian, than the wilderness farms of the heroic settlers and their families who planted their crude homes in the new country.
- Emanuel Spenser, 1890

I've heard it said that there are men who read in books to convince themselves there is a God ... but never could raise within me the solemn feelings and true affection that I feel when alone with God in the forest.
- James Fenimore Cooper

I. Introduction

American frontier narratives of the 19th century in the form of novels, reports, diaries, histories, and journals draw a unique portrait of an American identity and contribute to the cultural myth of the frontier hero. The historic novels of the Central New York frontier by James Fenimore Cooper known as the *Leatherstocking Tales* figure prominently in this role. The concept of the leatherstocking frontiersman seemingly exemplified the human being in the State of Nature so prized by the Founders of America and so well rationalized by political philosophers like Thomas Hobbes and John Locke — a unique American character: rugged individualism, self-reliance, indomitable persistence, moral certitude, crude border courage, freedom from the stifling protocols of urban society and palpable unease at being too near to the civilized world. These characteristics were portrayed through physical acts of valor — the struggle against nature, the rescue of captives, an unrivaled strategic sensibility and ability with weapons, and success against countless enemies on the frontier. There were enough genuine frontiersmen of this character – Boone, Kenton, Crockett, Gist, Rogers – to support the literary myths. Herein, the 18th century frontier hero becomes a symbol of God's providence and the nation's manifest destiny.

The Scene

It may seem odd for some readers to associate the State of New York with the frontier. New York seems too familiar and well civilized to support a series of wilderness adventures. Yet, even in the 19th century, much of this rugged region was not thought completely safe. There were settlements on the shores of the Hudson River, in the advanced frontier neighborhoods of the Palatine on the Mohawk and in the valleys of the Schoharie, the Delaware, and the Susquehanna, on the shores of the inland seas and the many lakes of the region, and along the Niagara escarpment where enemy incursions had not faded from living memory. "It became, emphatically," wrote Cooper, "the bloody arena, in which most of the battles for the mastery of the colonies were contested." The surrounding Catskill, Pocono, and Blue Ridge mountains (usually grouped with vacation resorts of the northeastern extension of the Appalachians today) formed the barrier between white settlement and Native American lands in this region, and defiles like Grand Gorge, Lockwood Gap, Wind Gap, and Indian Town Gap served as corridors into the wilderness. Imaginary boundaries, set by the government surveyors of the several colonies as lines on a map, crossed a unique region that was heavily forested, well watered, and incredibly fertile. This was the early America that Cooper knew as a boy. [1]

Cooper himself noted in the introduction to *The Last of the Mohicans*: "In point of fact, the country which is the scene of the following tale has undergone as little change, since the historical events alluded to ... as almost any other district of equal extent within the whole limits of the United States. There are fashionable and well-attended watering places at and near the spring where Hawkeye halted to drink, and roads traverse the forests where he and his friends were compelled to journey without even a path. ... But, beyond this, the enterprise and energy of a people who have done so much in other places have done little here. The whole of that wilderness, in which the latter incidents of the legend occurred, is nearly a wilderness still." It is possible in this region, even in the 21st century, for a person to evade the detection of hundreds of searchers armed with helicopters and infrared seeking devices for weeks or months. Recent manhunts in northeastern Pennsylvania and northern New York have strengthened this statement.[2]

The so-called Leatherstocking region of Central New York was named for the unique leather leggings worn by many frontiersmen and Natives made famous by the work of Cooper. Hence is the genesis of the name of this selection. Called by many names such as spatterdashers, mitasses, or Indian gaiters, all were essentially the same item of clothing. Leatherstockings – more like close-fitted cowboy chaps then hosiery – were worn for protection against thorns or brush, as a defense against insects and the elements, and may have helped in avoiding snakebites of which frontiersmen and Indians had great apprehension. Unlike trousers they have no seat and are not joined at the crotch. Whites quickly recognized the utility of these garments and adopted them in leather, wool, and canvass. Even the great armies of Europe made the leggings, somewhat modified into button festooned gaiters fitted to the lower leg, part of their standard kit. Cooper noted: "Whoever comes into the woods to deal with the natives, must use Indian fashions, if he would wish to prosper in his undertakings." Many tribes commonly wore moccasins, a buckskin shirt that hung free over the hips, a breechcloth and separate leatherstockings fastened to a waist belt (rather than one-piece trousers). Cooper noted of Hawkeye in *The Last of the Mohicans* (1826): "The only part of his under dress which appeared below the hunting-frock was a pair of buckskin leggings, that laced at the sides, and which were gartered above the knees, with the sinews of a deer." [3]

Scraped raw in the last Ice Age a dozen millennia ago, the Allegheny Plateau, a large area in western and central New York and northern and western Pennsylvania, was the home to many Native nations attracted to the annual shoals of river herring (a.k.a. shad) that swam hundreds of miles upstream to their spawning grounds. It was these fish rather than the animals of the forest that provided much of the end-of-winter foundation of the Native American diet in this region. Shad has been described as "the fish that fed the nation's founders." During the spawning run, multiple species of shad can be found together. A 17th-century observer, Thomas Harriot, reported in his journal that the Indians caught a wide variety of fish in their weirs, including "very many other sorts of excellent good fish, which we have taken and eaten, whose names I know not but in the country language. ... For four months of the year, February, March, April and May, there are plenty of sturgeons. And also in the same months of herrings, some of the ordinary bigness of ours in England, but for the most part far greater, of eighteen, twenty inches, and some two feet in length." The starving time was always in Spring when stockpiles of winter food were exhausted and new growth had not yet appeared in the fields. These fish literally staved off death. This river species is distinct from other herrings by having a deeper body and can be found on both sides of the Atlantic Ocean and in the Mediterranean Sea. Many of the rivers across the historic range of shad are now heavily dammed, eliminating many of its historic spawning grounds. [4]

The fleet-footed deer and stately elk, meadow rabbit and stalking turkey were the common targets of the aborigine arrow, but it is clear that nearly anything that walked, crawled, swam, flew or grew in the region was regarded as a potential food resource. The Indians hunted and gathered wild grapes and berries in the forests and meadows; they maintained plum, peach, and apple orchards, and immense fields of squash, beans, and corn – the three "sisters" of Native tradition. Daniel Brodhead recorded in the late 18th century, "I never saw finer corn although it was planted much thicker than is common with our farmers."[5]

Mild in summer, if a bit snowy in winter, the lofty crags of the Adirondacks and Allegheny Mountains that surrounded this virtual "breadbasket of nature" were all but impassable except along so-called Indian trails or on the natural waterways that crossed the plateau. The retreating glacier often left behind large hollows between drumlins or hills, and as the ice age ended, these created lakes and elongated ponds, especially the Great Lakes and Finger Lakes. Lake Winnipeg, Lake Manitoba, and Lake of the Woods in Canada, and Lake Champlain, Lake George, Lake Placid, and Saranac Lake in eastern New York, are also notable relics of the ancient ice sheet. Among the minor lakes formed in this manner, one of these, just eight miles long and one wide, was Lake Otsego, the Glimmerglass upon which Cooper grew as a boy.

It is among the fertile hills of the plateau that the Mohawk River finds its source, and the Delaware and Susquehanna pass to the sea flowing south from the watershed of this region. Some streams passed along the folds and faults of the mountains. Others flowed so rapidly in freshets and cascades that they cut right across the rock strata, carving canyons and gorges through the layers of sediment and exposing the nodules of glassy chert and flint from which to make razor sharp tools and weapons. Still others meandered from side to side across incredibly fertile valleys that had entertained glaciers in the mists before history.

At a time when the line of mountains was the boundary between the English settlements and the wilderness, there were three significant water routes open through their fastness into the interior. Besides the Hudson / Mohawk River system, the major rivers of the northeastern Atlantic seaboard in this region were the Delaware and the Susquehanna. The tributaries of the Delaware and Susquehanna rivers are almost completely entangled in the plateau region. For almost their entire length these rivers were navigable by canoes with only short *portages* between entering and exiting points around small falls and rapids. The lower Great Lakes, Erie and Ontario, were separated by the impressive cataract of Niagara and a difficult portage of seventeen miles. Frontier fur trader Pierre Esprit Radisson reported that the Indians could paddle 50 miles in a day making one stroke every second. The stroke itself was short with the back and shoulder put into every one. Only effort and coordination could drive canoes upriver against the flow of the water.⁶

Shooting the rapids from a 19ᵗʰ century edition of Cooper's works.

The key to the inland waterways of North America proved to be a pattern of these short land bridges where goods and boats (bateaux) could be manhandled overland from one water route to another. As an example, a traveler ascending the Hudson from Manhattan could transfer to a canoe at the falls at Troy and go west on the Mohawk. There was a portage at the Great Carrying Place (Rome, New York) between the Mohawk River and Wood Creek, which stream flowed to Lake Onondaga (the center of Iroquois governance), thence to the Onondaga River, and finally to Lake Ontario at Oswego. Much of this was the general route followed by the Erie Canal, and this coincidence favors the intelligence and technology of the Native Americans in this region.

Nonetheless, neither the Indian canoe nor the traders' bateaux guaranteed unimpeded passage at all seasons of the year. Inland streams swollen by melt water and heavy rains were just as impassable as those that turned into a long wet puddle of boulders in the dry seasons. Travelers often had to exit their vessels and drag them through shallow water and across bars of gravel and sand. The Native Americans had discovered these interconnections through centuries of travel. Most Indians kept in their heads the course of the waterways that Europeans so carefully recorded on paper maps without the associated errors or misalignments of the latter.

A replica of the common bateaux is on display at the National Park Service museum at Fort Stanwix in Rome, New York.

The Hudson River is a tidal estuary north to Troy. Strong tides make parts of it difficult and dangerous to navigate. During the winter, ice floes drift south or north, depending upon the tides. The Mohican name of the river *Muhhekunnetuk* means "the river that flows both ways." Moreover, at the narrow point of the river upstream of Tappan and below West Point were the "horse races" named for the daily cycle of tidal waters that affect the estuary. The races could be formidable obstacles to the navigation of the river in either direction, but they were not particularly dangerous except in late autumn or when the river was otherwise carrying an unusual amount of run-off. Later in the season large ice flows and whole sheets of ice made winter navigation of the river all but impossible for wooden ships. A contemporary observer noted of the winter of 1779-1780, "The North [Hudson] River was wholly frozen over and the East River had an astonishing quantity of floating ice. As, in spite of this, many people ventured out in boats, sad accidents happened almost daily ... on account of the ice." Even in Cooper's day, the steamers would anchor in the wide expanse of the Tappan Zee awaiting an upriver run with the tide.[7]

As the name suggests, the Northeast woodlands region was generally covered with trees ranging from conifers (evergreens) in the Canadian North to deciduous (leaf shedding) trees in the American Midwest. Meadows, flatlands, and treeless (subarctic) regions could be found, but only in the western sections were there significant patches of open plain that might be classified as prairie. The region north of the Great Lakes was covered mostly in pine and spruce as were the mountainous regions elsewhere. At high altitudes it is often too cold and dry for organic matter to decay rapidly into soil. These conditions favor the growth of the more persistent evergreens and make it more difficult for deciduous plants to establish themselves. From Illinois to southern New England there was a wide belt of predominantly deciduous oak and hickory trees; from Wisconsin to central New York was a band of northern hardwoods, such as birch, beech, maple, and ash. The distribution of these species was not uniform, and individual examples could be found almost anywhere that environmental conditions proved favorable. Local native culture was greatly affected by the type of woodland and its distribution in the immediate area.[8]

Frontiersman and guide Conrad Weiser noted that the woods were so thick, that for a mile at a time the sunshine could not penetrate, even on the clearest day. Yet a man afoot could transverse them with care. "The forest, as usual, had little to intercept the view below the branches but the tall straight trunks of trees," wrote Cooper. "Everything belonging to vegetation had struggled towards the light, and beneath the leafy canopy one walked, as it might be, through a vast natural vault, upheld by myriads of rustic columns. These columns or trees, however, often served to conceal the adventurer, the hunter, or the foe."[9]

The People

The place names found in Central New York seem like whispers among the shadows of the early Native nations that had once occupied the region: Unadilla, Chemung, Canandaigua, Otsego, Tioga, Canajoharie, Onondaga, Ticonderoga, Oswego, Niagara. Archaic humans (8,000 - 1,700 BC) had long resided in these forests, but those found herein by Europeans were not their original occupants. The Iroquois have often been mistakenly suggested as the perpetrators of the demise of these archaic people. Rather, before the Iroquoian invasion, the region between the Cumberland and Ohio Rivers had seemingly been an empty land for many generations. The Indians first contacted by Europeans seem to have been as much in the dark as they with regard to the identity of the Archaic people.

Although most of the Northeast woodland region was dominated by a type of lifestyle characteristic of its post-contact forest residents, the presence of physical evidence suggests the existence of a prehistoric and mysterious mound building culture in the heartland of America that may have been significantly different. The lack of any written record among these pre-contact residents has obscured the actual pre-history of this region drained by the Ohio and Tennessee Rivers and the motivation behind raising so many large and small mounds. In 1775, one of Anglo-America's first naturalists, William Bartram, could not fathom why the natives had raised such "heaps of earth." There may have been more than 200,000 mounds in the eastern woodlands representing a total amount of work greater than the sum of all that done on all the pyramids in ancient Egypt.

Major sites at Cahokia (Illinois) and Moundville (Alabama) appear to be at the core of the abandoned so-called Mississippian cultural area, which extended through the lower Ohio River valley including western and central Kentucky, western Tennessee, and northern Alabama and Mississippi. There is no archeological or historical evidence that the region was used for anything other than hunting at the time of European contact. The development of an archaic culture from independent roots is less of a problem for historians than explaining its sudden collapse. The minimal evidence of four different language groups occupying this key region of the Northeast woodlands has led researchers to propose each language group as its original residents at one time or another.

A hypothesis, supported by Iroquois tradition, claims that a large mass of Iroquoian speaking peoples (including Five Nations Iroquois and the cantons of Huron, Petun, Erie, and Neutrals) migrated from the geographical center of the region east of the Mississippi

River Valley as invaders of the Northeast woodlands in the 15th century, pushing aside the more numerous but less fierce Algonquian-speaking nations of the region and leaving behind the Iroquoian Susquehannock, Cherokee, and Tuscaroras, to split off and push down the coastal plains of Maryland, Virginia, and the Carolinas. The Huron and their associated cantons, thereafter, moved into the inter-lake region of present-day Ontario, while the Five Nations Iroquois settled in the Finger Lake region of central New York. In the 17th century, these Iroquois waged a near-genocidal and well-documented war on their cousins in the Great Lakes, while they further consolidated their own confederacy. Annually some among the Seneca and Cayuga sent parties south to war among the Susquehannock, Cherokee, or Catawba, and the Mohawk constantly harassed their neighbors to the north and east. Consequently, Europeans could not befriend one tribe without inviting the enmity of some other.[10]

The trapping of fur-bearing animals, which had supplemented the acquisition of food as the primary purpose of hunting, quickly became an activity with some of the characteristics of an addiction. By the middle of the 17th century, Father de Brebeuf noted that the Indians seemingly "spent the entire year in the act of [fur] trading or in preparing for it." Although this development failed to change the alternation of compact (tribal) and diffuse (familial) times among tribal groups significantly, it changed radically the nature of the tasks carried out by individual families when separated from their tribal groups as a whole. Family units became fixated on trapping and accumulating furs. The enforcement of tribal hunting boundaries and the need to pass down certain rivers to trading posts established by Europeans became, for the first time, major stumbling blocks to native cooperation and the cause of violence, murder, and war.[11]

The entire region from Lake Champlain in the east, along the Mohawk River Valley to the Genesee River in the west was generally known as *Iroquoia*. The Five Nations Iroquois Confederacy had occupied this headwaters region for several centuries. The Iroquoians were clearly clan-like, not only in their living style, but also in their social, military, economic, and political structure. Generally known as "the Iroquois," the Iroquois Confederacy included the Seneca, Cayuga, Onondaga, Oneida, Mohawk, and later the Tuscarora. These tribes were formed into the strongest of the political and military confederacies in the region, known either as the Five Nations, or Six Nations (after 1722). Many of the political thinkers of Cooper's day looked to the concept of the Iroquois Confederacy as a forerunner of the representative government of the United States with its checks and balances and powers of veto.

The region south and west of Georgian Bay and centered on Lake Simcoe was appropriately called *Huronia*. At the time of the first European contact in the 17th century, the Huron natives called Lake Simcoe *Ouentironk* (Beautiful Water). A portage running between Lake Ontario and Georgian Bay that passed through Lake Simcoe was called the Toronto Passage, which in turn was used as the name for an early French fort located nearby. The Huron and Petun of the Wendat Confederacy inhabited the islands and shoreline along the coast, having migrated from the northern shores of Lake Ontario.

Located between the Ottawa River and Georgian Bay was Lake Nipissing home of the eastern Ottawa (Nipissing) Nation. The residents of Nipissing were so successful in taking whitefish from the lake that they traded the dried white flesh for furs to other nations as a commodity, and then traded the furs to the French in Montreal. During much of the 17th century, *Ottawa* was a generic term used by the French for any western Indian who traveled east to trade at Montreal or Quebec on the St. Lawrence River. These often included, besides the Ottawa themselves, any of the Ojibwa, Nipissing, and Pottawatomie of the Three Fires Confederacy. They also dealt "in cornmeal, sunflower oil, furs and skins, rugs and mats, tobacco, and medicinal roots and herbs" at Detroit. The name Ottawa was reported to have come from *Outaouacs* supposedly from the Anishinaabe word meaning "to trade," or "to buy and sell." It is a term commonly applied to a number of western nations. A Jesuit observer, François Le Mercier noted, "All who go to trade with the French, although of widely different nations, bear the general name Outaouacs, under whose auspices they make the journey." In the Jesuit Relations for 1665 the same priest says of the Ottawa that they were better merchants than warriors. The Relations of 1667 report three tribes living in the same town among the bulrushes along the Ottawa River: the Ottawa, the Kiskakon, and the Sinago – all three tribes speaking the same language. Le Mercier added that the ancient habitat of the Ottawa had been a quarter of Lake Huron, "whence the fear of the Iroquois drove them." Le Mercier compiled nine of the annual Relations, 1653 to 1655, and 1665 to 1670 inclusively, besides the two written by himself on the Huron mission in the years 1637 and 1638. [12]

Further to the south the riverbanks of the Delaware and Susquehanna to the sea were lined with the homes of many sub-tribes of the Delaware, Shawnee, Nanticoke, and Susquehannock nations, making the watershed one of the most densely populated centers of Native American life east of the Mississippi River. The Algonquian-speakers among these had been in possession of the coastline, the bays, and the sounds for at least 1,000 years before white contact. Major centers of Native American settlement were located near these watercourses in the present-day states of New York, New Jersey, Pennsylvania, and parts of Maryland, Delaware, and Virginia. The Iroquoians seemingly formed wedges of invasion among the other tribes pushing the Algonquians onto marginal farming lands along the coast and forcing the northernmost Muskhogean-speakers south into Georgia and Alabama. Many outnumbered minor nations simply retreated into uninhabited pockets in the woodlands to hunt and fish. It is not known with confidence from whence the Iroquoians originated. Archaeologists refer to the Erie, Neutrals, Huron, the Six Nations and others who spoke the same language as Iroquoians of the same original bloodline. All modern archaeology digs show a south to north movement of these people.

The archaeology, however, sometimes flies in the face of Native tradition, which states that many Iroquoians lived to the north at Montreal under the subjection of the Adirondacks, a defunct branch of the Algonquians, the former having disappeared by the time of white contact. They fought the Adirondacks for their independence, but lost. Forced to flee Canada to escape extermination, they traveled south down the St. Lawrence River, Lake Ontario and entered Central New York by the Oswego River and settled near Onondaga Lake expelling the small family tribes living there. A tradition among the Iroquois that they lost a war in the pre-contact period is highly unusual because they admitted to it, and this characteristic seems to give it added credence. Historian Scott Stevens notes that the Iroquois began to influence the writing of their own history in the 19th century, including the Mohawk Joseph Brant, and Tuscarora David Cusick. Notable women historians among the Iroquois emerged in the following decades, including Laura "Minnie" Kellog (Oneida, 1880-1949) and Alice Lee Jemison (Seneca, 1901-1964).[13]

Lewis Morgan, a wealthy lawyer and intellectual, met Eli Parker, a well educated Seneca, in a bookstore in Albany in the 1840s. Morgan was very interested in Iroquois history. Parker told Morgan that he would like to have the Iroquois history put into writing. Both were prolific writers and many of their papers are located in the library of the University of Rochester. Parker immediately began to search the memory of living tribal elders whose duty it was to remember the past history of the Iroquois, which he had learned from former elders, from artifacts, wampum belts, etc. This history of the Iroquois was put into writing, finished in about 1848 and published in 1851, after the death of Cooper and long before the present conflict over Iroquois origins erupted. The Parker home also became a meeting place of non-Indian scholars, such as Henry Rowe Schoolcraft and John Wesley Powell who were connected to the studies that formed Native American anthropology as an academic discipline.

There are a number anomalies that fuel this conflict such as a tribe called the Laurentian Iroquois that seemingly entered New York in 1536, another listing the Owasco as possible forerunners of the Iroquois entering New York in 800, and the Oak Hill Iroquois of 1300, suggested by a dig completed nearby. The evidence may be confounded by several migrations of related peoples moving across the region like a series of flooding and ebbing tides. Other Iroquoian-speaking peoples had lived at various times along the St. Lawrence River, around the Great Lakes, and in the American Southeast. The Laurentian Iroquois appear to have disappeared from the St. Lawrence valley some time prior to 1580. Based in part on material from the 18th century, a theory emerged that the Mohawk (and in some cases also the Onondaga and Oneida) had migrated from the south and had settled for a brief time in the St. Lawrence River valley before relocating to their historic territory of present-day New York. This theory fit well into the oral traditions already mentioned concerning the mysterious Adirondacks.

Chronology in absolute terms, however, was not a Native strong point, nor did it figure greatly in their oral histories. It has been pointed out that there is no word in the Native American tongue for time, or for the reckoning of it, and the concept of duration was based solely on a relative separation between visible events that would have made a man like Albert Einstein pleased. There simply was no description of time in isolation from events. "There are words for day, and night, one for sunrise, sunset, for the lunar cycle, one for the yearly cycle, youth, adulthood, and old age, but no word for absolute time which measures the universe from outside of it." Indians reckoned time in cycles like the passing of the seasons, of which they recognized several: Spring, Summer, the Earing of the Corn, Harvest, the Fall of Leaves, and Winter. The concept of *when* could be expressed in images, as in "the winter of the deep snows," but not in numbers, as in "7 years ago." There were no birthdays, no anniversaries, and no holidays in the European sense. Feasts were organized to celebrate things in the *now,* or *neegeh.* A new year, for instance, was determined by the first new moon after the freezing of the local creek — an actual event that happened earlier in the north than it did in the south — or by the moving of a village as in the case of the Ceremony of the Dead.[14]

The Christian inhabitants of Maryland regarded the residents of the Susquehanna Valley the most noble and heroic nation of Indians that dwelt upon the confines of America, and that the other Indians "by a submissive and tributary acknowledgment" held them in like esteem. In the writings of Swedish and Dutch authors of the 17th century many references are found to a people called Minquas, Minquosy, or Mingo, names that were evidently bestowed on them by the Algonquians of the lower Delaware River and bay. "Mingo" was a Lenni Lenape word meaning "stealthy" or "treacherous" possibly better applied to the Huron-Petun or Erie nations of the lakes. Subsequent to the early period the names Wyandot, Susquehannock, and Minqua, especially the last, had acquired a broader or more comprehensive significance.

It would be impossible herein to describe in detail the many nations that peopled this vast region. Suffice it to say that they resembled their Iroquois neighbors to the north, for whom there were many descriptions by contemporary observers, and that they shared many of their religious and cultural characteristics. There were at least sixteen different groups of Iroquoian speakers including the Huron, Wyandot, Seneca, Mohawk, Onondaga, Oneida, Cayuga, the Susquehannock, the Nottoway, the Tuscaroras, the Petun, the Erie and several others. The Eastern Algonquians were comprised of approximately twenty language groups. These included the Micmac, Maliseet, Passamaquoddy, Eastern and Western Abenaki, Massachusetts, Mohegan-Pequot (of Connecticut), Unami, Munsee, Montauk, Mohican, and others. The equally numerous Western Algonquians were generally outside the scope of Cooper's writing. The aggregated Algonquian dialects of Ojibwa comprised the second most commonly spoken First Nations language in Canada after Cree. The Susquehannock were called "Minguas" by the Delaware, from whence comes "Mingo," a generic term often used by Cooper. The Delaware (a.k.a. Lenape) spoke Unami or Munsee languages.

From the outset, it is clear that Cooper was a novelist and not all that interested in, nor capable of, presenting an accurate historical or anthropological rendering of the region, nor has any responsible person ever claimed he did. In *The Pioneers* Cooper first confronts the Indian as a representative of a traditional life in familiar surroundings. In other novels set in various places and historical events, Cooper shows his fascination for Indians with heroic traits, and in *The Oak Openings* (1848), his last Indian novel, he envisions a brotherhood in the Christian faith for the Indians as vanishing Americans.

Cooper's early interest in Native Americans, based on available writings, was informed through contact with the few Indians that passed through Cooperstown in his childhood – especially one old Mohican cave dweller, and the brief encounters with Indians on Lake Ontario while he was in the Navy. He also seems to rely on other historical or anthropological texts like Jonathan Trumbull's papers as governor of Connecticut or John Heckewelder's book *History, Manners, and Customs of the Indian Nations* (1818). Moreover, besides the term Mohican (rather than Mahican), Cooper used a limited palette of nations in his books referring to the Huron, Delaware, and Iroquois, each more than 100 times, the Lenape and the Mohawk sub-tribes 30 times, the Wyandot 7 times, and other nations hardly at all. He thereby fashioned a simplified catalogue of nations into which he might insert his fiction. The three Indians of import and focus in the *Leatherstocking Tales* are Uncas, Chingachgook and Magua. The first two are identified as Delaware (Mohican), while Magua is a Huron. In *The Pathfinder*, the character Arrowhead is a Tuscarora as is Wyandotté in the novel named for him. In *The Wept of Wish-ton-Wish* set in New England, Canonchet is the heroic chief of the Narragansett. In *Oak Openings* set in the prairies and open groves of southern Michigan, the hostile primitive Pottawattamie are appropriately opposed to a few American Whites and their Chippewa ally Pigeonswing. Cooper's catch-all for other tribes seems to be Mingo, which he uses more than 100 times. This is not altogether inappropriate as the term suggested a landless or displaced person. Cooper often called the resident tribes of the Great Lakes region "Canadian."

The Delaware and Susquehanna rivers provided the indigenous populations of this region with the best water routes from Central New York to their respective bays and the Atlantic to the south. The Delaware River rises in two main branches that descend from the western flank of the Catskills. The West Branch begins in Schoharie County. The river's East Branch begins at Grand Gorge in Delaware County. In 1609, the lower river was first visited by a Dutch East India Company expedition led by Henry Hudson. Early Dutch and Swedish settlements were established along the lower section of the river and Delaware Bay. The colonials called the river the *South River* compared to the Hudson River, which was known as the *North River* through to the American Revolution. The region between these was the site of early Dutch colonization.

Cooper believed that the headwaters of the Susquehanna in New York were at Lake Otsego on the shores of which Cooperstown was to be found. The North Branch of the Susquehanna comes out of the south end of the lake in a baptismal trickle immortalized in Cooper's books. The West Branch, however, is entirely within the state of Pennsylvania, draining a large mountainous area within the Allegheny Plateau and serving as the principal canoe route across the Alleghenies connecting the Susquehanna and Ohio valleys. It should be noted that the Ohio country of colonial times was considered a much more extensive region than that drained by the river of that name today extending well into western Pennsylvania and Virginia.

In the 18th century, William Penn, the founder of the Pennsylvania Colony, negotiated with the Lenni Lenape to allow white settlement in the area between the Delaware River and the Susquehanna, which was then part of Lenape territory. In 1735, Penn's descendants took advantage of the lack of precision in the agreement to vastly expand the grant to the disadvantage of the native population. So extensive was the expansion of the original agreement, that by 1737 the Delaware were left virtually no land in the province of Pennsylvania at all. Six major "towns" were identified in this region in the 17th century, but it is difficult to locate these towns correctly on a modern map, the names evidently being highly conventionalized forms of the native originals. [15]

One of those that have been located was the Indian town at Minisink. The Lenape used the great Esopus-Minisink trail that crossed the Delaware at Minisink Island for travel and trade between the Delaware and Hudson Rivers and then continued north to Goshen and the Schoharie. During the French and Indian War, this region was considered the frontier. The area south of Marbletown, New York was particularly vulnerable, as evidenced by the burning of nearby Kingston by Native Americans. The Revolutionary years were also a tough time for the settlers living in this frontier region. Joseph Brant's Mohawks and Tories attacked settlements near what is today the city of Port Jervis in July 1779. In the process, they burned Fort Decker, which had been a refuge during the French and Indian War. The raiding parties ended when Major General John Sullivan marched with thousands of soldiers on the Iroquois, to avenge the defeat of the militia at the earlier engagement at the Battle of Minisink. Historically, the name Minisink applied to a much larger area than the current town, running as far as thirty miles north of the Delaware Water Gap to Lackawaxan and from the Kittatinny Ridge to the east to the Poconos to the west. It generally follows the Delaware River, and centers on the geographical nexus of the States of New York, New Jersey, and Pennsylvania – all today within a two-hour drive by car from Manhattan or Philadelphia!

The Leatherstocking Series

In 1823, Cooper began the Leatherstocking Series: the first appropriately called *The Pioneers: Sources of the Susquehanna*. This was followed by *The Last of the Mohicans: A Tale of 1757* (1826), which setting was moved east to Lake George, *The Prairie: A Tale* (1827), *The Pathfinder: The Inland Sea* (1840), on Lake Ontario, and *The Deerslayer: The First Warpath* (1841), which took place again on Lake Otsego. The author located all these novels except *The Prairie* on the New York frontier, the latter novel being set in Kansas. Very early on, editors and critics began to rearrange the published order of the Leatherstocking novels into the chronological order of the hero Natty Bumppo's fictional biography, the order that Cooper finally authorized. The order happens to be alphabetical with the titles. *The Spy* and the *Leatherstocking Tales* form the basis of his fame.

Consequently, Cooper's works follow, from virulent youth (*The Deerslayer*) to old age (*The Prairie*), the fictional life of the heroic frontiersman Natty Bumppo, "a valiant, a just, and a wise warrior" and his Native allies, the embodiment of the 19th century concept of the Noble Savage. The period covered ranges from about 1740 to 1804, and Natty Bumppo is seen in stages of his life from his 20s to his 80s. Continuity with *The Last of the Mohicans* is indicated by the appearance of the grandson of Duncan and Alice Heyward (Captain Duncan Uncas Middleton) in the later part of the chronology. Chingachgook eventually dies, representing fears of the race of "vanishing Indians," and Natty himself vanishes into the sunset. While in Europe, the idea of an additional Indian narrative, connected with the falls at Niagara, occurred to Cooper; but he would have had to carry a party of believable characters through the whole adjoining country while it was still a forest. "Would that the book had been written!" wrote his daughter Susan Fenimore Cooper. "What varied pictures of Niagara should we have had in its pages; what wild interest of adventure would he not have thrown over its scenes!"[16]

Historical fiction rose to prominence in the early 19th century largely through the influence of the British writer Sir Walter Scott's *Waverly* (1814), *Rob Roy* (1817) and *Ivanhoe* (1820). Scott strongly influenced Cooper. There is not a word about other writers in Cooper's correspondence other than references to Scott, but other adventure novels and historical novelists following similar "manly themes" were equally successful throughout the century. Each of these evoked a historical response from the reader, was set in an exotic location, and was filled with foreign characters: swordsmen, Cossacks, pirates, rebels, bandits, and knights in armor. This gave them an additional appeal for the reader beyond the story.

The *Leatherstocking Tales*, however, were clearly rooted in the reality of colonial America, and, rather than being familiar, they painted the nearby wilderness with the varnish of romance – each frontier cabin a castle, each glimmering pond or lake an ocean, each bark canoe a frigate. Rifle and tomahawk replaced sword and buckler, the line of militia turned into a broadside, and the woodsman became the knight-errant of the American wilderness. *The Last of the Mohicans*, with Bumppo as Hawkeye the frontier scout, has always been the most popular of the "Leatherstocking Tales" because it is, at heart, a piece of genuinely good adventure literature.

The Deerslayer is actually the last "Leatherstocking Tale" published but the first in the chronology; and the reader sees, therefore, the character Bumppo that the author developed at a late period of his own life – in reverse, if you will, the old man creating the younger. Cooper realized this problem about *The Deerslayer* and addressed it in the preface to the compilation of the *Leatherstocking Tales*: "Whether these progressive years have had a tendency to lessen the value of the last-named book [of the series], by lessening the native fire of its author, or of adding somewhat in the way of improved taste and a more matured judgment, is for others to decide." [17]

Before 1820, the majority of books on any topic found in America, and hence the attitudes that they conveyed, were largely rooted in reaction to those cultural ideals held by the educated classes of Boston or Charleston and the better society of London or Paris. These readers were firmly focused on the recent decades-long European struggles with Republican and Napoleonic France, which did not end until 1815. Tolstoy's monumental *War and Peace* (1865-1869), often celebrated as the greatest historical novel ever written, offered an example of fiction used to critique society. Yet the literary left received the historical novel coldly. They saw it as totally devoid of social consequence. On the other hand, Victor Hugo's *The Hunchback of Notre-Dame* (1831) or *Les Misérables* (1862) were admired for their beauty and earned widespread respect for championing social causes.

Colonial history set in wilderness America, therefore, was initially not high on the reading list of the literate public except as a reminder of the continued embarrassment of the British since 1775. The American Revolution was the only war in Britain's recent history that it fought without European allies. It therefore enlisted the support of the native nations of America against the colonial revolutionaries. This had two significant effects. The British were roundly disparaged for having set the Indians on the warpath, and the Indians became the targets for a widespread retribution by the nascent United States. Many Americans believed that it was necessary to discard the previous history of the colonies as being British in order to underpin a new Americanism. The continued conflict with Britain, which remained largely unresolved until 1815, added to this attitude. In 1800, only five historical societies existed in the United States – the oldest in operation for just six years, founded in Boston in 1794. By 1860, however, the country had produced 111 such organizations, at least 90 of which published their annual proceedings, and a new interest in America's colonial roots was undertaken.

Cooper's *The Spy* (1821) was once described by a biographer as unmistakably American and at the same time straight out of Sir Walter Scott. Of course, between 1815 and 1830, Scott dominated historical fiction in the international market. Scott, the novelist, developed his stories from documentary sources as any historian would have done, but as a romantic he gave his subject a deeper imaginative and emotional significance. *The Scarlet Letter* (1850) by Nathaniel Hawthorne is perhaps the most famous 19th-century American historical novel, but its social theme outweighs its history for most readers. *Moby Dick* (1851), the sixth book by American writer Herman Melville, was initially received with mixed reviews, a mere tale of a madman chasing a whale; and at Melville's death four decades later was accounted a sea fable for children. It is now considered one of the leading works of American Romanticism. The opening line, "Call me Ishmael," is one of the most recognizable opening lines in Western literature.

Cooper made use of both the historical and social themes used by other novelists, but his purpose was always to illustrate the moral courage of the American individual, and not just to justify a social conscience. For Cooper, evil proceeded not from a broken system of social hierarchy, but from too many systems operating at cross-purposes or competing for dominance. "The primacy of this moral thesis over a social thesis is what defines Cooper's establishment of the American novel."[18]

The *Leatherstocking Tales* have a peculiar appeal. They fail every modern literary test. They appear on few lists of great novels. The writing is verbose and overly flowery, the conversations between characters come across like sermons, and the plots meander and are sometimes just downright bizarre – especially in *The Prairie*. Yet the magic is in the archaic formalism, the language, the vocabulary, and the rhythm and setting of the scenes. The tales conjure up a culture, a mind-set, a landscape, and a history. Once the sermonizing and editorializing have ceased, the woodland pursuits and evasions begin, arrows silently announce the presence of certain death, tomahawks flash through the darkening air, rifles discharge from the shadowed underbrush, and canoes glide stealthily across lakes of impossible beauty and shoot impassable rapids, all among impenetrable forests. "Literature is not, finally, its medium; not words at all, but something beyond … words." Whatever the quality, it has insured Cooper's survival as a producer of Great Literature.[19]

James Fenimore Cooper – "The poet of rural life in Early America." Cooper's personal appearance was in accord with the strong individuality of his character. He was of massive form, six feet in height, over two hundred pounds in weight and rather portly in later years, of firm and aristocratic bearing; a commanding figure; "a very castle of a man" was the phrase which Washington Irving applied to him.

II. Purpose

The writers and journalists of the first half of the 19th century offered a snapshot of American history, oftentimes as they themselves were then living it. Yet, in many cases, the novels, diaries, and journals concerned societies and institutions that were changing and evolving even as the authors sought to capture their characteristics on paper. As such, each can serve as a history inside a history in a specific place and at a critical time. There is a value in these sources hidden in the fact that their authors could not foresee the outcome of their present circumstance or situation.

The frontier journals of Conrad Weiser (1748), George Croghan (1750-1765), Christian Frederick Post (1758), Thomas Morris (1764), and Jolicoeur Bonin (1755-1763) are among the most important to record the frontier of the French and Indian War period. The narratives of Mary Rowlandson (1682), Elizabeth Hanson (1728), or Mary Jemison (1824) provide a unique insight into the frontier life of women and children. There were a number of other white captives and adoptees among the tribes who recorded the details of family life among the Indians of the Northeast woodlands. Among these were Harmen van der Bogaert, Peter Kalm, Henry Timberlake, Pierre Pouchot, Pierre Esprit Radisson, John Williams, Elizabeth Hicks, and many more.

The formal reports that the black robed Jesuit fathers sent home to France from North America are particularly important. The Jesuit devotion and self-sacrifice, the hardships they endured, and their triumphs or martyrdom were all set down in meticulous detail. In the 19th century, the individual reports were combined into 70 massive volumes known as *The Jesuit Relations* (1610-1791). Full English translations of the *Relations* can be found in most college libraries or on the Internet. Although written with the obvious bias of Christian churchmen serving among people they considered heathens, pagans, and savages, the *Relations* serve, nonetheless, as a major source of information about Indian life in early America especially among those nations living north of the Tennessee River. There are also numerous reports written by the officials of the Crown in New France. However, these tend to deal with the political environment of the French colony rather than Native American life. British and American colonial documents have similar value.

The colonial history of North America has also had much written about it by early professional historians and academics particularly Francis Parkman, John Heckewelder, and Timothy Dwight, but the view of the period imparted by others of them has often been one of a simple prelude to the revolutionary climax that was to come in the English colonies. The equally important French colonies and Native American nations are often treated as a simple background to Anglo-American development. Much of the serious research in this area has rightly dealt with colonial governments, battles, commanders, and military personalities. However, the lives of the civilians who populated the frontier have been largely left to the more dramatic, if less authentic, pens of the romantics who write adventure stories and screenplays. One modern historian has noted; "Instead of dauntless, adventuresome woodsmen of high moral character, they were mainly ordinary people drawn to the frontier solely for the possible gain it might net them. Many, in fact, were outright scoundrels ... basically an uncouth, obscene and filthy lot given to excesses in drinking, gambling and bedding down with the few available harlots.[20] Cooper noted, however, "Rigid adherence to truth, an indispensable requisite in history and travels, destroys the charm of fiction; for all that is necessary to be conveyed to the mind by the latter had better be done by delineations of principles, and of characters in their classes, than by too fastidious attention to originals."[21]

A Leatherstocking Companion is essentially a book about James Fenimore Cooper, but not about him alone. It is a social, literary, and military history whose contents are dictated by following the strands of Cooper's life and works. It is designed to dovetail the wealth of sources contemporary with the author to those within the colonial period of which he wrote. The frontier period has consistently been the setting for American authors from the captivity narratives of the earliest times to the series and histories of recent writers. These popular histories, novels, and narratives are visited in order to provide a more complete and precise picture of life on the frontier and of the environment in which Cooper and his contemporaries wrote. There is a growing necessity for this to be done, as the future generations of Americans become further removed from the foundations of the nation, and history courses increasingly focus on America's shortcomings and prejudices. There is an active and pernicious crusade among some in social and academic circles to cleanse American history of some of its discomforting facts and rewrite it with respect to more "modern" or "enlightened" ideologies. It is also an objective of this work, therefore, to provide evidence of the environment in which these sources were written and read in order to give context to the social life of the early antebellum period.

Among these sources are, of course, the works of James Fenimore Cooper; but also the diaries, journals, letters, colonial and military documents, maps, tracts, narratives, and personal reminiscences of many other persons. Cooper's own daughter, Susan Fenimore Cooper has left a great deal of written material concerning her father and the details of his career as a writer. Susan became his literary executor and the caretaker of his literary legacy after his death (1851). She was very devoted to her father, faithfully striving to protect his accomplishments and values. She oversaw the posthumous publication of some remaining manuscripts, and edited *Pages and Pictures, From the Writings of James Fenimore Cooper* (1861), a beautifully illustrated book containing excerpts from his writings along with her very warm and personal commentary.

The reports of missionaries and the anecdotal narratives of captives serve to record much about the Native American lifestyles and cultures that would otherwise be lost. The hazards of frontier life are reported in the manner the participants would have experienced them in their own microcosm rather than in a grand overview of colonial history. In this regard, the reports of average citizens, traders, and militiamen, available in period newspapers, letters, and journals, have been incorporated wherever possible into the discussion of military and political events. The reader is warned that the narrative may sometimes seem to wander due to the nature of these sources – many of which were meant by their authors to be personal rather than public documents, but be assured that the digressions are made to insure the ultimate progression of the text. The reader should remain aware of the interconnection of personalities, the apparent web of familial and social connections especially among persons of the same class or station.

The main historical theme that runs through much of Cooper's *Leatherstocking Tales* is the great struggle between France and England for control of the North American trading empire from 1688 to 1763. The desire to establish a fur trade monopoly, shared by both the Europeans and the Native Americans, and the consequences of fur trade on the culture and society of each, are closely scrutinized from the days of early European - Native American contact to the end of the French and Indian War and somewhat beyond.

An attempt has been made to study the later impact of European contact on the early United States in the areas of society, culture, economics, and religion during the period of Cooper's greatest output. Nonetheless, the details of the earlier military struggle remain of great weight and importance, and it is hoped that this work will integrate into the body of military and political knowledge the details of the lifestyles of the frontier population and of the principal Native American communities with whom they were to interact.

Amid all the printer's ink and historical speculation, the Antebellum Period (approximately 1820-1860) of which Cooper was a significant personage has largely been ignored until recently. It often gets lost between its better-documented Federalist and Victorian "bookends," or overwhelmed by the tragedy of the American Civil War. Well-educated adults are often unsure of the meaning of the term "antebellum." These pre-Civil War Americans did not live in a box sealed off from the rest of the world, or conveniently segregated as American rather than British or Asian History in a modern collegiate course catalog. As will be seen, there is ample evidence that Americans affected and were affected by occurrences that took place oceans away.

Native American terms and place names have many spellings in different dialects. Those attempting research in this area can find consistency in spelling daunting. For instance, the term *Caughnawaga* has 17 spelling variations recorded by European of the Mohawk *Kachnawage,* the Tuscarawa *Kahnawake*, or *Gandaouage* some meaning "at the rapids" and others suggesting a fortified place or village, and still others describing a band of people – Iroquois living at the Jesuit mission at the rapids across from Montreal.

Statistical information about the period and its people has been presented wherever it has been found to be reliable. Many significant historical sites have been visited to provide photographs and illustrations that are intended to add authenticity to the text.

D.H. Lawrence enjoyed poking fun at Cooper. Lawrence noted that in Cooper's novels: "Of course, it never rains: it is never cold and muddy and dreary: no one has wet feet or toothache: no one ever feels filthy, when they can't wash for a week … which isn't quite fair. You need only go camping for a week, and you'll see. But it is a myth, not a realistic tale." It must be remembered when reading this *Companion*, however, that the real settlers and native residents of America ran all manner of risks to accomplish their purposes, even those of starvation, exposure, and sudden violent death.[22]

For archaic man the wilderness universe was wholly sacred, and he but a part of it.[23]

III. An Unlikely Scribbler

Sidney Smith, an eccentric Scottish clergyman, wrote in 1820 in the *Edinburgh Review:* "In the four quarters of the globe, who reads an American book? Or goes to an American Play?" This article, immediately after its publication and for many years thereafter, led to intense indignation in the United States. "Thus far," continued the reverend gentleman, "we are the friends and admirers of [Brother] Jonathan [an early incarnation of Uncle Sam]. But he must not grow vain and ambitious; nor allow himself to be dazzled by that galaxy of epithets by which his orators and newspaper scribblers endeavor to persuade their supporters that they are the greatest, the most refined, the most enlightened, and the most moral people upon earth. ... During the thirty or forty years of their independence, they have done absolutely nothing for the Sciences, for the Arts, for Literature, or even for the statesman-like studies of Politics or Political Economy. ... Finally, under which of the old tyrannical governments of Europe is every sixth man a slave, whom his fellow creatures may buy and sell and torture?"[24]

American authors in the early 1800s struggled to attract an audience away from their English counterparts. It has been observed, strictly as a matter of anecdote, that six of America's greatest authors were born within 16 years of one another during the first decades of the nineteenth century: Ralph Waldo Emerson (1803), Nathaniel Hawthorne (1804), Edgar Allan Poe (1809), Henry David Thoreau (1817), and Herman Melville and Walt Whitman (1819). None of these was projected to be a great writer when Rev. Smith cast his jibe. Perhaps the literary stars and planets were correctly aligned during this mythological period. However, the observation can be drawn so narrowly or so broadly that any conclusion can be made. James Fenimore Cooper (b. 1789) was producing a form of American literature popular at home and in Europe before these authors were adults. Certainly the list of births could be lengthened to include other authors, male and female in similar circumstances, like Washington Irving (1783), William Cullen Bryant (1794), Sarah Josepha Buell Hale (1788), or even Harriet Beecher Stowe (1811), who produced the bulk of the printed work enjoyed by the common population of American readers or are noted more for their specific significant contributions. Yet the statement does indicate that America was not ready to produce its own literature until its spirit of democracy and nationalism had had time to coalesce and take root.

Cooper like many other writers in the American nature-writing tradition, possessed a profound sense of loss that was expressed throughout their descriptions. Nineteenth-century writers, like landscape painters, celebrated the glories of the American creation in their work partly because it was being destroyed and Europeanized before their very eyes. They sought to capture it or at least to retard its demise. To some extent they were successful. The very genre of the frontier novel arises only in reaction to the destruction of the wilderness environment.

Many Europeans described America as a wilderness, but most areas of the world considered wilderness today are more remote, inhospitable, or bereft of natural resources. Regions filled with wildlife, timber, fresh water, and fertile soil, as was America in the seventeenth and eighteen centuries, generally do not evoke the necessary quality of desolation associated with a wilderness tract. Yet for most European immigrants the concept of wilderness was heavily freighted with a myriad of personal meanings and symbolic devices. In Europe the mountain peaks and cliff sides were the only landforms that had not been put into production by the sixteenth century. Possibly for these reasons many Europeans tended to link the concept of wilderness with uncultivated land that was rocky, heavily wooded, and inhabited only by wild beasts – a combination of forests, crags, and cliffs not uncommon in North America. For the Europeans, the thought that North America was a wilderness was a great advantage to the newcomer who wished to establish a claim on supposedly vacant land by dispossessing its native overlords.

Throughout the first half of the 19th century, artists and painters attempted to record on canvass and paper the unsullied beauty of America. Many of their paintings depicted the Hudson River Valley and the surrounding area, including the Catskill, Adirondack, and the White Mountains. Eventually works by a second generation of artists associated with the school expanded to include other locales. Yet it seems that the hillsides of the Hudson Valley in Cooper's time must have teemed with painters carrying brushes and palettes rather than muskets or tomahawks. Tongue firmly set in cheek, Cooper once had allowed his character Natty a simple double entendre in this regard involving the pronunciation of *panther* (the animal) as the colloquial *painter* (the artist): "Up on the Catskills, I used often to go up into the mountains after wolves' skins, and bears; once they bought me to get them a stuffed *painter*." Certainly Cooper was poking fun at some among his best friends and acquaintances, but he was a serious admirer of the region also. "If being the best part of a mile in the air, and having men's farms and houses at your feet, with rivers looking like ribbons, and mountains bigger than the 'Vision,' seeming to be haystacks of green grass under you, gives any satisfaction to a man, I can recommend the spot. ... To my judgment ... it's the best piece of work that I've met with in the woods; and none know how often the hand of God is seen in a wilderness but them that rove it for a man's life."[25]

Just how wild a region needed to be to qualify as a wilderness to the minds of Cooper's readers is not certain. Some small amount of civilization seems to have been permitted, while any form of architecture or human construction that failed to demonstrate its influence in European terms of fences, buildings, or roadways seems to have been dismissed. Certainly Cooper used his share of forests, crags, and cliffs as settings for his stories, and he added in the racing rivers, expansive lakes, turbulent cascades, and immense caverns for good measure. The Hudson River School landscapes of many among Cooper's friends were characterized by their realistic, detailed, and sometimes idealized portrayal of nature, often juxtaposed with peaceful agriculture and the remnants of wilderness, which were fast disappearing from antebellum America.

Cooper was an unlikely candidate to become a professional "scribbler." At age 17, Cooper had withdrawn from Yale, having failed to curb his independent spirit to the liking of his instructors, and taken to the sea. His first voyage, taking forty days, brought him to an English port with a cargo of flour. Britain was in the midst of war with France at the time, and a British man-of-war approached their ship and impressed a member of the crew into the Royal Navy. The next voyage took Cooper to the Mediterranean. It was in the merchant service and in the US Navy that Cooper learned shipbuilding, shipyard duties, and the details of a seaman's life that would fill his maritime novels. During this period at sea, he started to seriously think of himself as a writer. After the death of his father, he resigned from the Navy and went back to the land to try his hand at farming and estate management.

Unfortunately, he proved a poor hand as a gentleman farmer or in managing the portion of the estate that his father had left heavily indebted. A large family of his own increased his expenses. His brothers having spent most of their share of the estate – a significant fortune, each having received $50,000 in cash and rents from tenanted farmsteads, the equivalent of 1 million dollars in 2015 – they then borrowed considerable sums from their youngest brother. Cooper's own business ventures did not turn out as successfully as he hoped. In 1819, he had invested in a whaleship, *The Union*, but it did not prove very profitable. He himself commanded this whaleship at times in the years when he was just launching his literary career, but the vessel seems to have avoided lengthy and more profitable voyages passing in and out of Sag Harbor, New York and Newport, Rhode Island several times (1819-1822).

It should be remembered that Cooper was a typical landlord, like his father, and that the bulk of his income was derived from rents and fees wrung with some difficulty from his tenants. Cooper drew extensively on his father's experience in his representation of Judge Temple, the chief landlord and governmental official of post-revolutionary Templeton in *The Pioneers*. A kind of squirearchy prevailed – the gentry, the benevolent proprietors of a pastoral world. Yet the spectacle of a landed gentleman living in semi-feudal splendor among his tenants was an anachronism to a post-revolutionary generation that had supported popular democracy. The number of small independent farmers that Cooper called "yeoman" freeholders was increasing. A tenants' revolt in upstate New York finally exploded with the death of Stephen Van Rensselaer III in 1839. In the late 1840s, Cooper would write the *Littlepage Trilogy* where he defended landowners along the Hudson River, lending them social and political support against rebellious tenant farmers in the anti-rent wars that marked this period.

By the 1820s Cooper was rapidly overreaching himself in an effort to salvage his father's estate. What he seemed to lack was his father's ability to make money, if not to manage it. Judge Cooper appears to have first worked as a wheelwright, and then as a storekeeper in Burlington, New Jersey, located along the Delaware River, and by the end of the 1780s, he was a successful land speculator and wealthy frontier developer. He acquired a tract of land of several thousand acres within the borders of New York State among the headwaters of the Susquehanna River and Otsego Lake.[26]

With all of his older brothers prematurely deceased by 1819, leaving widows, children, nephews and nieces behind, Cooper, the author was the titular head of a devastated family that had once been composed of seven adult brothers and sisters. Three other brothers and two sisters had died in infancy. This was not unusual. A typical grave from the 19th century might be that of a mature husband aged 60 or more flanked by two or even three wives each but the last having died in her 20s or 30s. The leading cause of early death among adult women was childbirth or accident (especially from burns in kitchen fires). Certainly many of these women died in childbirth, because their death dates match the birth dates on the children's stones nearby. Several children might be named alike. Judge Cooper had two sons named Abraham who failed to survive infancy. The anecdote that persons did not live as long in the past as they due today is not quite true. While the modern average life expectancy has gone up, the former shorten life reflected a large number of early deaths. An adult male in the 19th century could expect to live the biblical 70 years or longer. "The days of our years are three score years and ten; and if by reason of strength they be fourscore years, yet is their strength labor and sorrow; for it is soon cut off, and we fly away." (Psalms 90: 10)

Infant deaths would strike James and Susan twice among seven children, and both the De Lancey and Cooper clans suffered many infant and accidental tragedies. The accidental death of his oldest sister Hannah (age 23) from a fall from a horse in 1808 had deeply affected an adoring Cooper, who was just 18 at the time. The Judge, his father, was killed in Albany in December 1809 by a blow to the head delivered by a political opponent in a tavern brawl after a heated public meeting. Amazingly no one was indicted or prosecuted for Judge Cooper's death. This was followed in the next decade by the near simultaneous deaths of all his adult brothers: Richard Fenimore (d. 1813), Isaac (d. 1818), William (d. 1819), and Samuel (d. 1819). Richard, the eldest, was just age 48. Each brother had left between 3 and 10 children. Eventually, only James and a sister Ann Cooper Pomeroy (1784-1870) were left from their generation. He lived to be 62, she an amazing 86. The sense of loss often comes through Cooper's writing. The young James and his brothers had roamed and explored what was then a frontier village with a freedom that most children today would find enviable. Cooper's sister Hannah had written of her brothers, "They are very wild and show plainly they have been bred in the woods." In a way, James Fenimore was virtually as much the last of the Coopers as his character Uncas was the last of the Mohicans.[27]

Cooper knew perfectly well that the entire tribe of Mohicans was not on the verge of extinction, just as his own bloodline was all but assured of continuation. Yet his only son Paul was in his infancy when Cooper was writing the novel. It was strictly true that towards the close of the last century the noble warrior and sachem had died out among the Mohican. The Mohican were a defunct nation because, according to Cooper, there were no fertile women left among their nation to continue the line of the Sagamores (Sachems). Here it is best possibly, before continuing with the list of Cooper family tragedies, to explain why Uncas might be considered the last of his people while his father still lived and was young enough to have more children.

In many societies where kinship connections are important, there are rules of descent, though they may be implied or be taken for granted. *Unilineal* rules determine the kinship of an individual through the descent of one gender only, that is, either through males or through females. These are subdivided into either *patrilineal* (male) or *matrilineal* (female) kinship systems. With few exceptions, European descent is usually decided through the bloodline of the acknowledged father, if not the actual one. Hence, a single surviving male can continue the bloodline. In its use by Continental hereditary monarchies since the 15th century, aiming at the justification of succession to the throne or noble estate, the Salic Law – made famous by Shakespeare in *Henry V* – is regarded as excluding all females from the succession as well as prohibiting succession rights to transfer through any woman although the bloodline of the mother could not be contested. Ultimately, the law was amended to permit inheritance of land by a daughter if a man had no surviving sons.

One of the consequences of the plagues that affected Europe in the 14th and 15th centuries may have been a new appreciation for the role of male children as conduits of continuity. Ironically, it also became more difficult for the nobility to produce an adult male heir in the post-plague era. In England, three-quarters of all noble families failed to produce a male heir through two generations after the plague. In France, many old aristocratic families disappeared, and new ones replaced them. It took 150 years for Europe's population to recover. By the 16th century, many Europeans came to focus on having large families with several surviving sons as repositories of family bloodlines and symbols of earthly immortality.[28]

Among many Native American nations, however, descent is traced through the female. Hence, a single fertile female and a live birth are needed to continue the bloodline. In some cases, even when the lineage was counted through the father, a son approaching adolescence moved to live with his maternal uncle. This type of living was known as *avuncular*. In these cases, men took to their maternal uncles in much the same way as patrilineal men took to their fathers. Each child among matrilineal tribes belonged to the clan of his mother and lived in a clan house or a group of wigwams with his mother's relations.

While this did not disqualify the father from taking a critical role in the life of his children, the most important males in a boy's upbringing were undoubtedly his mother's brothers, or his maternal uncles. These would be the ones who instructed him in the skills that he would need as an adult, and it was they who would decide if he was ready to move forward through the events that led to manhood, such as the *vision quest*. This freed the biological father from having to make life-altering decisions in his son's life and insured a more unbiased judgmental process. His uncles "taught him keenness of observation and how to bear pain without grimace, loss without depression, danger without fear and triumph without pride. He taught him mastery of self, the need to control and direct his passions and not let them rule him." With regard to marriage partners, the primary candidate for a wife under this system was a young man's mother's brother's daughter. Female children remained with their mother to be taught their role as women by the clan matrons. This form of matrilineal kinship seems to be more common among tribal societies that are arranged in clans, but many in India, China, Africa, Malaysia, and the Middle East also follow it. [29]

Cooper's own mother, having no living brothers, had sought to ensure the continuance of her family's name by offering her youngest adult child (then named simply James Cooper) some properties near Cooperstown that she owned in her own right if he would legally take her family name "Fenimore," his eldest brother Richard Fenimore Cooper having died in his own home in 1813. He applied to the Legislature to change his name to James Cooper Fenimore, but the request was denied as too extreme. The change was made instead to James Fenimore-Cooper with a hyphen in 1826. He soon dropped the hyphen.

Susan Fenimore Cooper, James' daughter, was a writer of some note in her own regard. In 1883, Susan Fenimore wrote about her uncles:

The only one of my Uncles of whom I have any recollection was my Uncle Isaac. ... My Mother was much attached to him; he was very warm-hearted and affectionate, and very benevolent. ... Uncle Isaac ... wrestling in fun with his brother-in-law Richard Morris ... was thrown with some force against the railing of the piazza, injuring his spine. He lingered for a year or more, but abscesses formed, and he died at last of exhaustion. ... Mother always spoke kindly of her brothers-in-law. My Uncle William was wonderfully clever, quite a genius, a delightful talker, very witty. My Uncle Richard was a handsome man with remarkably fine manners; my Grandfather De Lancey, who had seen the best society in England, said he was "a very well bred man." ... My Uncle Sam was clever, but undersized and eccentric. My Mother has often said they were all fine tempered men. ... In winter there was a great deal of skating. My Uncle Richard and my Uncle William were particularly accomplished in that way, very graceful in their movements, and cutting very intricate figures on the ice. So I have been told.[30]

Cooper, the last adult male of his generation, was now dedicated to resurrecting his father's world – if not in fact, then in fiction. Cooper began searching for more than work; he needed wealth to underpin his family. He, therefore, decided to become a writer; but the explanations for this decision remain unclear. Prior to the age of thirty, Cooper had never composed a serious work of literature. Yet his own mother was a dedicated reader of romances, and he a fan of military works, travelogues, biographies, histories, and novels. According to some sources, he regarded the writing of letters and outlines as onerous tasks. One reason for his decision may be, of course, his financial position. His marriage in 1811 to Susan De Lancey, the daughter of a very rich and influential family from Westchester County, just north of New York City, certainly placed him among a group of peers who worked at their desks and not with their hands. However, one reason for his decision is often mentioned: Cooper, reading a mediocre English romance one evening, said casually to his wife that he could write a better book, and she challenged him to do so. Cooper was never reticent concerning challenges either implied or explicit. Cooper's first novel *Precaution* (1820) was written in imitation of contemporary English domestic novels like those of Jane Austen, Maria Edgeworth, or Amelia Anderson Opie.

During this interval he rented a small farm, appropriately named Closet Hall, in New Rochelle, about five miles from Susan's family home. His wife's persistent desire to live near her family had pinned Cooper to New Rochelle. His daughter, Susan described the critical moment in her "Small Family Memories," written as an introduction to *Correspondence of James Fenimore Cooper*:

> A new novel had been brought from England in the last monthly packet; it was, I think, one of Mrs. Opie's, or one of that school. My mother was not well; she was lying on the sofa, and he was reading this newly imported novel to her; it must have been very trashy; after a chapter or two he threw it aside, exclaiming, "I could write you a better book than that myself!" Our mother laughed at the idea, as the height of absurdity – he who disliked writing even a letter, that he should write a book! He persisted in his declaration, however, and almost immediately wrote the first pages of a tale, not yet named, the scene laid in England as a matter of course.[31]

Nothing of this kind is *now* read

First used in English in 1710, the concept of "authorship" whether amateur or professional for men or women was a relatively recent one. The tacit acceptance of this concept in the antebellum period was reflected not only in the academic search for the creators of literature, as with a Homer or a Shakespeare, but also in the innovative concept of intellectual property, of getting paid just for writing! Yet most of Cooper's social peers, who willingly put pen to paper to write a political thesis or a monograph on farming techniques, would not dare to venture a novel into print as a commercial vocation. There was apparently something thought sordid about throwing ones inner musings out to the masses in return for mere money.

The variety of topics characteristic of the novel may be one reason for the initial attraction of this literary form for Cooper. Romance, horror, adventure, conduct, mystery, detective, or history, the novel was among the youngest of literary genre – the frontier novel not being listed even among these at this point. The English term "novel" derives from the Italian "novella," a short tale in prose very popular in the 14th century. The "picaresque," the "caricature," and the "romance" are also said to be predecessors of the novel. All these literary forms contributed to the genesis of the genre, but it was not until the 18th century that books could be written which today most people would consider novels. The novel permits the author to develop a complicated plot, to introduce many characters and motifs, to portray the characters in detail and to show how they change their opinions and attitudes during the story.

The novel was also the literary genre in which women writers had been most successful. Women, especially in Britain, wrote many novels and bluebooks in the antebellum period, and a number of them were successful in the 19th century even though they often had to publish under a masculine pseudonym. Charlotte, Emily, and Anne Bronte were published under their male names (Currer, Ellis, and Acton Bell) because they had to hide their newfound profession from their father who was an Anglican preacher. Their publishers were deceived having no idea these three were actually women. The author of *Silas Marner* (1861) and six other English provincial novels, Mary Ann Evans famously wrote as George Eliot because she wanted to escape the stereotype of women only writing lighthearted romances. An additional factor in her use of a pen name may have been a desire to shield her private life from public scrutiny and to prevent scandals attending her long-time relationship with a married man. American Louisa May Alcott – ironically the author of *Little Women* (1869), a book about the trials of a female author – wrote under the androgynous name of A.M. Barnard and Miss Oranthy Bluggage, acknowledged to be an accomplished strong-minded lecture on women's rights; but also as Aunt Weedy, Flora Fairfield, and Minerva Moody. In the mid-1860s, Alcott wrote passionate, fiery novels and sensational stories as A.M. Barnard. Among these are *A Long Fatal Love Chase* (1866) and *Pauline's Passion and Punishment* (1863) winner of the $100 prize for writing offered by *Frank Leslie's Illustrated Weekly*. Herein the protagonists were willful and relentless in their pursuit of those who had humiliated or thwarted them. Alcott seemingly saved her feminine pen names for her less dramatic juvenile literature.

Although British works dominated in popularity, over half of English-language novels from the period written in America were by women. The widespread popularity of sentimental and often formulaic domestic novels written in this period caused Nathaniel Hawthorne to complain, "America is now wholly given over to a damned mob of scribbling women." Writing was an acceptable female hobby, and women who practiced the profession of letters seem to have been viewed with less disapprobation than those who became teachers, nurses, or lawyers.[32]

The majority of the readers of romantic novels were, of course, women. Like no other literary form, these readers seemingly devoured novels "as a means of escaping that life by women who knew its gender constraints only too well." In the absence of modern technologies, reading served as the main source of individual and small group entertainment. A noteworthy aspect of both the 18th and 19th century novel was the way the novelist directly addressed the reader as a personal narrator.[33]

The Romantic era in literary history generally runs from the late 18th century until the beginning of the Victorian era in 1837. The phrase today is often used to refer to the popular genre that focused on romantic love. These documented in a fictional format the hardships of middle and upper class women, who usually did not inherit money, could not work and depended largely on the man they married for their lifestyles. These works revealed not only the difficulties of women under the strictures of the Cult of Domesticity, but also what was expected of men and of the careers they had to follow as members of proper society. Such gender differentiation of obligations ruled not only Victorian Britain but also Antebellum America.

Prompted by a general recognition of women's historical contributions to events and culture today, various academic disciplines such as the history of women writers have developed in response to the belief that women's lives and contributions have been largely underrepresented as areas of scholarly interest. The so-called "ladies of the salon" had been writing impossibly long stories for many decades since the opening of the Enlightenment. It has been noted, however, that there was also "a concerted attack by many male writers on the capacity of women in general to contribute to the store of ideas and discussions." Although women began writing novels around the same period as many men (Daniel Defoe, *Robinson Crusoe* (1719); John Bunyan, *The Pilgrim's Progress* (1678); or Jonathan Swift, *Gulliver's Travels* (1726), for example), they failed to gain the same reputation as possible inventors of the English novel format. Even narratives with females as protagonists written by male authors like Samuel Richardson, *Pamela: Or, Virtue Rewarded* (1740) or Defoe, *Moll Flanders* (1722) have been largely ignored.[34]

When Eliza Haywood's novel *The History of Miss Betsy Thoughtless* was published in 1751, Haywood finally won success and recognition as an author but was still something of a curiosity although she had been writing for three decades. Haywood's prolific fiction developed from titillating romance novels and so-called amatory fiction during the early 1720s to works focused more on women's rights and position in society in the 1740s. Haywood's first novel, *Love in Excess; Or, The Fatal Enquiry* (1719) concerned themes of education and marriage. Known as part of the "Fair Triumvirate of Wit" with other early professional authors Aphra Behn, *Oroonoko* (1688) and Delarivier Manley, *New Atalantis* (1709), Haywood was one of only a handful of popular authors of her time acknowledged as females. Rev. James Sterling coined the term "Fair Triumvirate of Wit" in dedicatory verses to these three in 1751 as the most influential women writers of his time.

Haywood wrote and published over seventy works during her lifetime including fiction, drama, translations, poetry, conduct literature and periodicals. Haywood's writing career began in 1719 with the first installment of *Love in Excess* and ended in the year she died with conduct books *The Wife* and *The Husband*, and the biweekly periodical *The Young Lady* (1756). Manley was derided for the pointed political attacks that were contained in her "fiction," but Behn was one of the first English women to earn her living by her writing. These female authors broke many cultural barriers and served as literary role models for later generations of women authors. By the 19th century, the British literary landscape was filled with women writing in virtually every genre, many as professionals.

The first novels were too lengthy to be printed profitably as finished books. Most were released as serializations. Publishers then took a chance on the most popular works in hopes they would become steady sellers and need to be reprinted. The upper classes generally avoided the earliest novels as below their interest. "A novel! Nothing of this kind is *now* read, I assure you," wrote one publisher of fine literature. "Novels are a drug; a mere drug: they are as dead a weight upon our hands as *sermons*." Full-length versions sold poorly and abridgements carried small royalties. Due to the economy of publishing in the 18th century, novels often ran to multiple volumes or episodes. Authors were paid only once for a book and received no royalties; a second volume or episode meant a second payment. In 1803, a curiously pathetic account was appended to a short Gothic tale that appeared in London. It was written anonymously by the author of the work (actually by Sarah Carr Wilkinson) and narrated the distressing and dismal "Life of an Authoress, Written by Herself." It was published as a "warning to every indigent woman, who is troubled with the itch of scribbling, to beware of my unhappy fate and beg her to take this advice; that, whatever share of learning or wit she may have, if she has nothing better [than writing] to recommend her to public favor, she must be content to hunger and thirst all her days in a garret, as I have done." Nonetheless, the genre ultimately gained the interest of the public.[35]

Amelia Anderson Opie – referenced by Susan Fenimore Cooper as the proximate cause of her father's writing career – wrote *The Dangers of Coquetry* (1790) anonymously at age 18. Her novel *Father and Daughter* (1801) was about misled virtue and family reconciliation. Encouraged by her artist husband John Opie to continue writing, she published *Adeline Mowbray* (1804), an exploration of women's education, marriage, and the abolition of slavery. The latter novel is noted in particular for revealing the history of Opie's former friend Mary Wollstonecraft, whose relationship outside of marriage with the American Gilbert Imlay (known in his day as a shrewd but unscrupulous businessman involved in land speculation in Kentucky) and her later marriage to the philosopher William Godwin caused some scandal. A daughter, Mary Wollstonecraft Godwin, would become an accomplished writer herself, as Mary Shelley, the author of *Frankenstein*. Amelia Opie, considered a radical and activist, was a friend of Walter Scott, the playwright Richard Sheridan, and many other notables. Her husband had painted portraits of many great men and women of his day, most from the artistic and literary professions.

Maria Edgeworth was a significant figure in the evolution of the novel and had a profound impact on the portrayal of Irish culture in literature. She generally mixed with the Anglo-Irish gentry, particularly with Kitty Pakenham (later the wife of Arthur Wellesley, 1st Duke Wellington). Raised in England as a child, she used her fiction to address the problems inherent in religious, racial, gender, and class-based identities producing a half-dozen novels over two decades beginning at age 32. In *Letters for Literary Ladies* (1798), Edgeworth satirized, from the perspective of an unmarried woman of 30 years of age, much of the nascent pattern of feminism underlying the novel of manners (conduct) for which Jane Austen was so well known. In *An Essay on the Noble Science of Self-justification* (1787 published in 1795), Edgeworth wrote to her readers:

> Candid pupil, you will readily accede to my first and fundamental axiom – that a lady can do no wrong. ... Your general ideas of the habits and virtues essential to the perfection of the female character nearly agree with mine; but we differ materially as to the cultivation, which it is necessary or expedient to

bestow upon the understandings of women. You are a champion for the rights of woman, and insist upon the equality of the sexes: but since the days of chivalry are past, and since modern gallantry permits men to speak, at least to one another, in less sublime language of the fair; I may confess to you that I see neither in experience nor analogy much reason to believe that, in the human species alone, there are no marks of inferiority in the female. ... For the advantage of my subject I address myself chiefly to married ladies; but those who have not as yet the good fortune to have that common enemy, a husband, to combat, may in the mean time practice my precepts upon their fathers, brothers, and female friends; with caution, however, lest by discovering their arms too soon, they preclude themselves from the power of using them to the fullest advantage hereafter. ... Fair idiots! Let women of sense, wit, feeling, triumph in their various arts: yours are superior. ... Let him go on to prove that yours is a mistaken opinion: – you are ready to acknowledge it long before he desires it. You acknowledge it may be a wrong opinion; but still it is your opinion![36]

Jane Austen addressed her own readers directly in parts of her works by giving a lengthy opinion of the value of novels, and of the contemporary social prejudice against them in favour of drier historical works and newspapers:

Let us leave it to the reviewers to abuse such effusions of fancy at their leisure, and over every new novel to talk in threadbare strains of the trash with which the press now groans. Let us not desert one another; we are an injured body. Although our productions have afforded more extensive and unaffected pleasure than those of any other literary corporation in the world, no species of composition has been so much decried. From pride, ignorance, or fashion, our foes are almost as many as our readers. ... There seems almost a general wish of decrying the capacity and undervaluing the labor of the novelist, and of slighting the performances, which have only genius, wit, and taste to recommend them.[37]

Cooper's first novel *Precaution* was a failure. Even in later years when its author had reached acclaim, there was no call to put it back in print. This is not surprising. At the time, Cooper knew nothing of "manners" as practiced in Britain. His world was a derivative of England – a polite gentry with whom he had no real contact, only the examples served up by his in-laws and acquaintances, and information gleaned from his reading. Yet he had seemingly found pleasure in the freedom of writing fiction. His second novel, which largely abandoned British literary protocols, was a hit.

Home Sweet Home

The Cooper's were seemingly in constant motion with regard to their residences. The initial move to Cooperstown about this time was accompanied by tragedy: the Coopers' first child, two-year-old Elizabeth, died within a month of the arrival and was buried in a private spot on the property in the family ground. His father, and his sister Hannah, whom he had loved so much, were already placed in the local churchyard. The enclosure was intended for the family burying-ground. It was a general custom in those days for all families living in the country to have private places of burial on their own grounds. This circumstance may have added to his wife's dislike of the place. Some years later, when the property was sold, the remains of Elizabeth were removed to the local churchyard.

There seems to have been a disturbing dynamic between Cooper and his wife regarding the location of their home pitting one against the other – she favoring Westchester, he Cooperstown, but not all of their moves were willing ones. While on an extended visit to Susan's parents, Cooper's own mother died. His father's house, Otsego Hall, was condemned to be sold to satisfy debts against the estate. Instead of returning to Cooperstown after a six months' visit with his in-laws, it was decided that Cooper should occupy a country-house on a property that was destined for his wife by her own father, Mr. De Lancey. This was on a hill in Scarsdale. A new farm at Cooperstown, now the location of the Fenimore Art Museum, begun by James and called Fenimore burned down before its completion. "In that house James and Susan expected to pass their lives. But in fact it was never inhabited," wrote their daughter. "The position of that house was charming, on a rising knell, commanding a lovely view of the lake and village. The grounds reached to the brook, southward, and the principal entrance was to have been at the point where the road crosses the brook." [38]

The De Lancey's had provided a temporary farm at Scarsdale called Angevine after its former tenant. Cooper became deeply interested in the subject of planning a lawn, building decorative fences, setting out trees, and generally playing the role of country gentleman. Nonetheless, leaving Cooperstown was a severe blow to Cooper. A quarrel with the De Lancey family over the management of both his own money and his wife's properties led Cooper to abandon Angevine and take his family to live in a rental property in Astoria, Queens County in New York City.

Otsego Hall was completed by Judge William Cooper in 1799.

Manhattan at that time was an island of villages and small towns, as was the western end of Long Island. The five boroughs – Brooklyn, Queens, Manhattan, the Bronx, and Staten Island – were not consolidated into a single city until 1898. In those days, Fordham, Bloomingdale, Inwood, Flushing, Bushwick, Richmond, Harlem (a modification of the Dutch Haarlem), and other areas of the city were small clusters of country homes and shops. Joseph R. Drake described the village of Fordham, for instance, in his 1817 poem "Bronx" as filled with rocks and clefts full of loose dangling ivy and sumac of the liveliest green. "Yet I will look upon thy face again, my own romantic Bronx, and it will be a face more pleasant than the face of men." The poem "Annabel Lee," which explores the theme of the death of a beautiful woman, was written at Poe Cottage in Fordham and is thought to describe the fate of Poe's young wife with whom he moved their for her health. Written in 1849, it was not published until shortly after Poe's death that same year. Fordham was then a stop on the daily coach from the tip of Manhattan to Westchester and later for the railroad. "From the railroad station the road winds up the Fordham hill to the cottage, with the native rock as a pavement," wrote historian J. Thomas Scharf. "The cottage seems no more than a little paint-box, shingled on the sides as well as the roof, and covered with vines." The stages originally started from Cortlandt Street downtown; the route, of course, was over the Boston Road from that point to Kingsbridge just below Fordham. The water of the nearby Bronx River was considered so "pure and wholesome" that during the 1820s and 1830s the Board of Aldermen debated ways to tap into it to supply the growing city with drinking water. Only later in the century did areas of the city named for their industry or their residents such as the garment district and the meatpacking district, or China Town and Little Italy come into use.[39]

Beginning in the early 19th century, affluent New Yorkers constructed large residences around 12th and 14th streets in Queens County, an area that later became known as Astoria Village (now Old Astoria), a noted recreational destination and resort for Manhattan's wealthy. Originally called Hallet's Cove, after its first landowner William Hallet, the area was renamed after John Jacob Astor, then the wealthiest man in America with a net worth of over $40 million, in order to persuade him to invest in the neighborhood. Astor's fur trading ventures were disrupted during the War of 1812, when the English captured his trading posts. In 1816, he joined the opium-smuggling trade to China. Astor's commercial connections extended over the entire globe, and his ships were found in every sea. In 1830, Astor had abandoned the fur trade in which he had made his fortune diversifying his business holdings by investing in New York City real estate and later becoming a famed patron of the arts. From Astor's summer home in Manhattan — on what is now East 87th Street near York Avenue — he could see across the East River the new Long Island village named in his honor. In 1836, Washington Irving gave a lengthy description of Astor's empire based on documents, diaries, etc. in his travelogue *Astoria*.

Cooper had a romantic hostility toward the city, but he was willing to come to an accommodation with it. Here he was nearer his publisher and was able to establish himself among the city's congenial cultural surroundings. Yet he neither accepted nor understood this new order and staunchly defended the agrarian order to the last. In later years, he would call the city environment a "social bivouac."

In 1826, however, Cooper, now famous, took his family to Europe for seven years. It was in Europe that his novels had the greatest success. He returned to Cooperstown in 1834 and repurchased his father's house; and he and his wife lived in Cooperstown for the rest of their lives. During the 1830s while the Coopers sojourned in Europe, the race for success had given a speculative and morally bankrupt tone to America's commercial classes. During Cooper's absence, however, the successful men on the make in New

York in the previous decade were consolidating their wealth and social position. They had transcended established family and antique inheritance; they now wanted to stabilize their place in society. To Cooper, New York was the only American city that rivaled those in Europe. Cooper declared on his return that the city showed signs of an improving taste.[40]

IV. Old Money, New Fame

In 19th-century America, life was seemingly filled with opportunity, and the successful man was expected to aspire to a level of achievement commensurate with his class and abilities. Money in sufficient quantities was considered the ticket to social prominence. Nonetheless, being born of a prominent family was no simple indicator of futurity. Even great wealth, if newly found, "needed aging," and a generation of family philanthropy was needed to guarantee a place in the carefully guarded social circles of the uppermost classes. A man's personal manner, dress, voice, style, and bearing were all part of the standards by which success was measured. Moreover, these qualities could not be artificial, affected, or insincere. During the Jacksonian period, the landed gentry were in decline being replaced by an urban aristocracy rooted in commerce. Richard Henry Dana of New York, who was something of a social snob, noted that "inferiority of caste is noticeable as soon as you get out of the aristocracy and upper gentry with hereditary estates and old names."[41]

While resident in New York City, Cooper had founded the Bread and Cheese Club and became the center of a circle that included notable painters of the Hudson River School as well as writers and others. An outgrowth of "Cooper's Lunch," an impromptu gathering of Cooper's network of intellectual friends, the club's membership consisted of about 35 individuals, including Charles Wiley, who had made Cooper a national celebrity when he published Cooper's second novel; painters Thomas Cole, William Dunlap, Asher B. Durand, Henry Inman, and John Wesley Jarvis; friend, painter, and inventor Samuel F.B. Morse; poets and writers William Cullen Bryant, Fitz-Greene Halleck, J.A. Hillhouse, James K. Paulding, J.G. Percival, and Robert Charles Sands; editors Gulian Verplanck and Charles King; naturalist James Ellsworth De Kay; physician John Wakefield Francis; and jurist James Kent.

Included as a member of the Bread and Cheese Club was merchant, diarist, and Mayor of New York, Philip Hone, who is known for popularizing the phrase, "The Good Olde Days" in the 1840s. Hone was also a founder of the Mercantile Library Association and was the first president of the Delaware and Hudson Canal Company in 1825. Hone's diary records not only his social engagements and the major events and spectacles in the city in the first half of the century, but also his views of a changing city; his disapproval of Andrew Jackson; the disconcerting effects of the city's constant construction; and his utter disgust with most of the Irish, although he himself was the son of German immigrants.

In 1824, Washington Irving, a member of the club who was then living abroad, was made the honorary chairman in absentia. That same year, the Bread and Cheese Club greeted the Marquis de Lafayette during his historic visit to the United States. Clearly as the club's founder, Cooper was at least part of the cement that held it together. The list of club members suggests Cooper's prominence in antebellum society. This rested both on his father's former wealth and status as a judge and congressman, and on his own marital connection to the powerful De Lancey family through his wife Susan. The club dissolved soon after Cooper moved away from New York City in 1826, some of its members branching off to form other literary associations. The Bread and Cheese Club predated by almost 100 years the similarly formed Algonquin Round Table, a celebrated group of New York City writers, critics, actors and wits founded in 1919.

The squirearchy of country gentlemen

Social life in the colonies was both burdened and charmed by its patrician ways. The south had its well-documented plantation aristocracy to undergirth the social position of its families, but the north had its less renowned squirearchy of country gentlemen that served a similar purpose. "The early social classes of the colonies were counterparts of the European social classes, except for an overabundance of middle class elements in New England and eastern Pennsylvania. ... The more one learns about the colonial age, the less can one detect any signs of increasing equality or open opportunity or ... intensive social mobility." In order to maintain their social hegemony, family matrons might gather periodically to recount the lineage of their aristocratic houses back to the Royalists who fought at Naseby or the Roundheads who supported Cromwell.[42]

Prior to the American Revolution, two fairly distinct social and economic classes had developed in colonial America among free whites. One of these, composed of the rich and the well-born – merchants, large landholders, and moneylenders – dominated almost every conceivable phase of colonial life. Socially, its members considered themselves superior to the common people, toward whom they generally assumed a snobbish attitude. Indeed, unless one had money or was a member of an "old respectable" family, or was well educated, or had served the state in some prominent capacity, he was regarded as socially inferior. At many universities prior to the Revolution, the student's names were ordered with respect to the social position of their families rather than alphabetically, by academic rank, or some other objective metric.

Bonds of blood or biological kinship linked all so-called primary relatives with one exception, that of husband and wife, who were normally linked only by the contractual marital bond. Mathematically, any person with seven primary types of relatives (father, mother, sisters, and brothers in their childhood family, and their husband or wife, sons, and daughters in their family of procreation) will have 83 secondary types, 151 tertiary types, and so on geometrically. Within just a few generations in an isolated population, it would be almost impossible to marry with a person totally unrelated by blood. Imagine the result in an antebellum society, where marriages were relegated to the sub-category of a limited upper class. Yet in most societies marriages are accomplished only within the same generation, and unions between primary relations of widely different ages are considered incestuous. Only among cousins are the concurrent generations generally available for marriage partners. Hence, eyebrows can be raised among those ignorant of the underlying mathematics. The biblical categories of prohibited relationships does not entirely match the antebellum definitions of prohibited incestuous relations then in force. Cousin marriage was legal in every state before the Civil War. However, the practice between close cousins, though more common in Britain and the American South, was almost unheard of among Northern families.[43]

The squirearchy in New York was relatively less numerous at the beginning of the 19th century then later in the Antebellum Period but individual families were larger. As proper society was comparatively limited, intermarriage among its members became increasingly frequent and everywhere added its weight to the build up of the local pool of consanguineous squirearchy. For instance, Elisabeth Livingston Ludlow, of the powerful Livingston family of New York and married into the important Ludlow clan of neighboring Connecticut, was the grandmother of Eleanor Roosevelt, who would be First Lady of the United States when she married her fifth cousin once removed, Franklin.

Nonetheless, parents hoped to marry-off their daughters to any husband with appropriate social background and financial bono fides. The eldest son would inherit his place, but his younger brothers might be sent off to learn a profession, to serve in the military, or take up a benefice at a small parish. Because the oldest son commonly inherited everything else, the younger sons had to find a profession where they could maintain their social status.

The youngest of five males, James Fenimore Cooper needed more than family connections to maintain his place in proper society. He needed money. Yet there was no standing army to officer worth mentioning. The country parson carousing among the servants and ladies' maids was at least suggestive of the lack of social dignity among frontier churchmen. The legal bar was extremely expensive, barely remunerative, and much more the resort of academics than of easily distracted younger sons. The badge of the patrician had always been land, and access to official society was a prerequisite to the securing of influence in receiving grants and patents. The sinister effects of a great grasping for land had long permeated the whole fabric of frontier society and were prominent before and after the Revolution.

As will be seen, Judge William Cooper was the quintessential self-made man in this regard, but the author's mother Elizabeth Fenimore came from a wealthy family. Her father, Richard Fenimore, a substantial Quaker, was in 1759 the second richest taxpayer in Willingboro Township, New Jersey, just south of the Delaware Water Gap. Her mother was Hannah Allen (Fenimore). She was related to William Allen, a wealthy shipping merchant, former mayor of the city of Philadelphia and Chief Justice of the Province of Pennsylvania. In 1771, William Allen's daughter Margaret married James De Lancey, the eldest son of the former New York provincial governor. Hence James Fenimore Cooper was related by marriage to his future wife by way of his grandmother. The Fenimore's owned an especially large and prosperous farm in an old, fertile, and populous county. Her father was also working at the time as an inn and tavern operator, and was accepted as part of the wealthy aristocracy of the region.

The De Lancey wealth had been founded on the fur trade of Etienne De Lancey, a Huguenot who had arrived in 1687. In 1700, Etienne, now known as Stephen, married Anne Van Cortlandt, one of almost two dozen children. This was very old "Dutch" money. The first Van Cortlandt had arrived in 1637 in New Amsterdam. Originally a soldier and bookkeeper, he rose to high colonial ranks in service of the Dutch West India Company. Cortlandt Manor derives from the history of Westchester County from before the Revolution.

The only male heir of the Manor of Scarsdale, having died during his minority in 1727, the lands of the Manor were partitioned among his heirs and deeded away to purchasers, thus the Manor of Scarsdale ceased to exist. The Heathcote male line having run out, Anne Heathcote married James De Lancey I. The De Lancey family of Scarsdale was considered minor French nobility who had served the French Crown as administrators and bureaucrats for over two hundred years. Susan Cooper's aunt Susannah De Lancey (1707–1771) was the wife of Admiral Sir Peter Warren, hero of King George's War and uncle to Sir William Johnson. Susan's uncle, Col. James De Lancey of New York was, with the possible exception of Frederick Philipse, the wealthiest man in the province for some years before the Revolution, and he was probably the best-known American-born Tory from the Revolution. Members of the De Lancey family appear to have formed some of the characters in Cooper's *The Spy*.

The grandson of the judge of the same name who had presided over the freedom of the press trial of John Peter Zenger in 1735, James De Lancey II (Susan's grandfather; her father, his son, John Peter De Lancey was referred to as Mr. De Lancey) was the county sheriff of Westchester under the British regime. Reaching the rank of captain in the French and Indian War, De Lancey II served as an aide to General Abercrombie in the Lake George campaign of 1758 and was involved in the capture of Fort Niagara in 1759. He died in 1760. Her father Mr. De Lancey took over the family dry goods business and was active in New York provincial politics. On the death of their father, Col. James De Lancey purchased the family property and flourmills in Westchester. Between the French war and the revolution they amassed a great deal of property, importing the first English racehorses, or thoroughbreds ever brought to New York. Apparently Mr. De Lancey's position against the Stamp Act in the 1760s left him in good standing with the masses, but he had refused to join the revolution. While the De Lanceys used the uproar to better consolidate their own power in the colonial assembly, their political rivals, the Livingstons, held the true support of the mob.

In 1683, New York colony had been divided into twelve counties: Albany, Cornwall, Dukes, Dutchess, Kings, New York, Orange, Queens, Richmond, Suffolk, Ulster, and Westchester. Albany County was an enormous county, including the northern part of New York State as well as all of the present state of Vermont and, in theory, extending westward to the Pacific Ocean. This vast county had fewer than 2000 residents when it was created, but it was reduced in size beginning in 1766, by the creation of almost five dozen other counties from within its borders as settlement continued. Westchester County, the larger setting for *The Spy,* was split into 6 familial manors. Some of these were sold off piecemeal, while others were later incorporated into Bronx County (c. 1874-1898). The manors and their associated families were those of Cortlandt (Van Cortlandt), Scarsdale (Heathcote), Pelham (Pell), Morrisania (Morris), West Farms (Archer/Hunt), and Philipsburg (Philipse). Of these, Cortlandt and Philipsburg were much the largest. The Bronx River that ran through much of Westchester was named after Jonas Bronck and his Dutch wife, Teuntje Joriaens, who created the first settlement as part of the New Netherlands colony in 1639, and eventually lent its name to the entire borough. Bronck purchased a tract of five hundred acres from Ranachqua and Taekamuck, Indian chiefs, lying between the Harlem and Bronx Rivers part of which is now included in Morrisania.[44]

In 1790, Livingston Manor was divided among the heirs of the last lord of the manor, Robert Livingston, rather than passed down through primogeniture, as Robert disapproved of his eldest son. These four heirs subsequently divided the land among their own families, and the power of the Livingston family was slowly diminished. Yet it had asserted itself in the Revolution. The Livingston territory among the squirearchy was in upstate New York, which they shared with the Van Rensselaer, Van Cortlandt, and Philipse families. Their manors, and the lands of their satellite relations like John Jay, Philip Schuyler, and Isaac Van Wyck, represented more than half of the colony's undeveloped land. Added to these were a number of notable but smaller country estates, particularly those of the offshoots to the major families. To the South were the Axtell, Beekman, Cruger, Morris and the De Lancey properties. Besides ships, wharves and other real estate in New York City, the De Lancey estate also contained large country landholdings, mostly in Westchester County, the setting for *The Spy*. There are speculations with supporting evidence of tombstone inscriptions that the De Lancey's had a previous union, possibly outside of marriage, with a connection to the Livingston family.[45]

The Van Wycks were an aristocratic family, originally from Holland, who were a prominent part of Dutchess County history. Their home, which still stands in Fishkill, New York, is the likely setting for Cooper's novel, *The Spy,* which was based on Enoch Crosby's story. The genuine mock trial of Enoch Crosby (the basis for the character Harvey Birch), who was to infiltrate a loyalist group as a secret agent of the United States, was held in the home's parlor. The picture of self-sacrifice and patriotism by this real cordwainer (a shoemaker) from Kent near Lake Carmel, New York turned secret agent as portrayed by Cooper's imagination was not overdrawn. Cornelius Van Wyck built the house in Fishkill on nearly 1000 acres in 1732. During the American Revolutionary War, the property was the home of Isaac Van Wyck. Seventy acres of land surrounding the house were used for a large encampment of over 2,000 Continental soldiers and many facilities such as an artillery park, a blacksmith shop, barracks, a storehouse, and stables were set up. Moreover, the story of *The Spy* opens at "The Locusts," inspired by the Rye home of the same name that belonged to Cooper's close friends and neighbors, the Jay family.

Cooper may have heard of Crosby's story from Judge John Jay at his home, although Jay (author of five of *The Federalist Papers* and later Justice of the Supreme Court) apparently did not reveal Crosby's name. To the public, Jay was also silent on all the coincidences with reality in Cooper's novel. He was especially quiet about the names of all his informants. But readers continued to press both Jay and Cooper for the real identity of the central character of *The Spy*. In 1838, John Jay's eldest son built the Peter Augustus Jay Mansion on the site in Rye of his father's childhood home, and "The Locusts" was no more. However, John Jay's homestead in Katonah, New York survives. This land, where John Jay lived in his later years as a gentleman farmer, was purchased in 1703 by his maternal grandfather, Jacobus Van Cortlandt. Hence the web of intermarriage continues.[46]

John Adams once calculated that one third of Americans were Tories, another third Whigs, and the rest undecided. These great families that made up the squirearchy in New York were quite as divided over the revolution, as were the people, some taking sides simply because another family did so or in reaction to a political enemy. There may have been as many as 100,000 loyalists in New York colony alone. In New England, Loyalism was all but exterminated by 1776, and the absolute number of loyalists in the less populous southern colonies, though considerable, was never as great as the Crown's best estimates. It seems certain, in fact, that the radicals among both patriots and loyalists were a minority of positive and determined men and women who represented the extremes of either position. Between them lay the "wavering neutral masses ready to move unresistingly in the direction given by the success of either Whig or Tory." Col. James De Lancey, known in some circles as the Outlaw of the Bronx, was one of the extremists on the Tory side. Related also to the revolutionary patriot John Jay, James De Lancey was connected by blood and marriage to the elite on both sides of the political divide.[47]

First associated with his uncle, General Oliver De Lancey, in raising volunteers from among the Loyalists of Long Island for De Lancey's Brigade, in 1777 James De Lancey was appointed captain of an elite Troop of Light Horse known as the Westchester Chasseurs. The troop was issued arms and equipment and harassed enemy depots and outposts. Driven from the county by the Patriot party, De Lancey and his like-minded loyalists now known as De Lancey's Refugee Corps occupied the Morrisania area of the Bronx. These men formed one of the most effective loyalist militia units to serve during the rebellion, and De Lancey was made a lieutenant colonel in the British army hierarchy. De Lancey was "attainted" and his estate confiscated in 1779 by the Patriot Committee of Safety. Taken prisoner late that same year, he was soon released on parole.

The Morris's were by birth, breeding, position and wealth, aristocrats among other aristocrats. The first of them to emigrate to America was Richard Morris, who is said to have been an officer in Cromwell's army. The Cooper's, through James Fenimore's brother Isaac, would ultimately become connected to this powerful family through marriage. The influential Morris family, who at one time owned all of the Manor of Morrisania as well as much of New Jersey included Lewis Morris, a signer of the Declaration of Independence, and Gouverneur Morris, a penman of the New York and national constitutions. The latter was likewise a proponent of the Erie Canal. His *Letters* present a vivid and invaluable picture of life in Paris where he was Minister Plenipotentiary to France in 1792, being the only foreign diplomat who remained at his post through the Reign of Terror. In 1809, he married Anne Carey Randolph of Virginia creating an interconnection with that family. His brother Robert Hunter Morris was governor of Pennsylvania at the time of Braddock's defeat (1755).

The Morris family estates covered tens of thousands of acres along the Hudson River as well as much of New Jersey. The Manor of Morrisania eventually included part of the manors of Fordham and Scarsdale, having been greatly added to after the war. About 1790, Lewis Morris memorialized Congress that Morrisania would make an ideal spot for the seat of the Federal government, but they seemingly preferred the insect infested banks of the Potomac in Maryland. The manor descended in the family with few alienations of land till the end of the nineteenth century many of these through intermarriage with the Valentine and Varian families who also owned land along the Bronx River. The Varian's later became important members of the Tammany Hall political machine. The Bronx was hardly an urban wasteland in those days. Today the reader will still find therein Bronx Park, Crotona Park, Randall's Island, the Bronx Zoo, the New York Botanical Gardens, the cottage rented by Edgar Allan Poe, the Valentine-Varian House (the second oldest residence in the Bronx), Fordham University, Lehman College (CUNY), and Yankee Stadium.[48]

There were substantial similarities between the Morris family of Morrisania and the Livingston's of Livingston Manor. Both families were among the richest landowners in colonial New York; both were prolific clans with many links to other aristocratic dynasties. The Morris and Livingston families were prominent in both colonial politics and the independence movement, and both families were pioneers in trade and industry in their respective areas of influence.

The hostile Loyalists had soon spread desolation over the beautiful and fertile manor of Morrisania. Almost all the Morris property and nearly all of the family wealth were destroyed in the revolution – much of it under the authority of De Lancey. Morris' tract of woodland of more than a thousand acres in extent closest in its proximity to the city and of incalculable value was destroyed; his house was greatly injured; his fences ruined; his stock driven away; and his family obliged to live in a state of exile. Morrisania was sparsely settled during the Revolution, its forests abound in wildlife and formed a secure hiding place for Loyalist refugees. The Loyalist refugees resorted to living in shacks, huts, or other improvised shelters in the "camps" in the Bronx overlooking the Harlem River and the Kings Bridge. The camps were described as "wretched" and "deplorable," but they did have a dependable supply of firewood and fresh water.[49]

Until the British evacuation of the city in 1783, James De Lancey lived in relative comfort on the rents from his lower East Side properties. The Great New York Fire of 1776 had destroyed up to 25 percent of the city and some unburned parts of the city were plundered. Almost all the damage was on the West Side making the De Lancey properties more valuable. The wartime population of the city rose from 2000 to 11,000 with the influx of loyalists, and rents soared. Meanwhile, he wisely took steps to realize as much money as he could from his holdings while the British still held the city. Some 275 individual owners purchased properties on Manhattan from the De Lancey estate at this time suggesting the extent of his wealth.

It seems clear that the patriots were unprepared to found an entirely new form of government when the war ended. The immediate reaction to victory was one of sometimes-violent retribution directed at the loyalist population. Yet these were more likely to be wealthy families who had prospered under the British rule. At least 100,000 loyalists fled to England or Canada during the course of the Revolution. Many waited until 1782 to take ship with the last of the redcoats to leave New York City, hoping in vain for a positive turn in British fortunes. One historian has noted, "The ... banishment or death ... of these most conservative and respectable Americans is a tragedy but rarely paralleled in the history of the world."[50]

With the hostilities coming to an end, Colonel James De Lancey knew that he had to leave New York, the place of his birth. He sailed for England on 8 June 1783, and there he remained for a year while pressing his claims against the British government for compensation. In the fall of 1784, he sailed for Halifax and from there proceeded to Annapolis Royal. Many of the De Lancey clan, however, decided to remain in America. This included the colonel's brother (Susan's father) John Peter De Lancey. The family, like the Morris's, had had sons, brothers, and cousins on both sides of the conflict or had remained conspicuously neutral. After the revolution James De Lancey made claims for compensation from the Crown amounting to almost £57,000 of which he was finally paid £29,842, second only to Frederick Philipse of Sleepy Hollow near Tarrytown in awards made to New Yorkers.

In a similar circumstance, Cooper's novel *Wyandotté* undoubtedly owes something to the history of the Morris family. The action of this novel is set in central New York near Unadilla Creek where the British character Captain Hugh Willoughby has just taken possession of a 7,000-acre patent. Captain Hugh and his wife, Wilhelmina, move to this new home with a number of workers, some slaves, and some regular employees. Among the latter is Saucy Nick, an outcast Tuscarora who had introduced Willoughby to the area. A Colonel Beekman visits them in an extended attempt to court their natural daughter Beulah. Beulah marries Beekman, and is killed by a stray bullet during an Indian attack. The name of the colonel should not be lost on the reader. An adopted daughter, Maud is courted by several eligible young men in Albany society, but takes no interest in any of them except Captain Robert her pro-patriot brother by adoption. Nineteen years later, in 1795, this same couple, now Lieutenant General Sir Robert Willoughby and his lady wife Maud visit America, their main objective being a pilgrimage to their old home in upstate New York.

The historical circumstance well parallels the novel. In 1769, the genuine Staats Long Morris, an officer of the crown, took out a patent of some 30,000 acres along Butternuts Creek southwest of Lake Otsego, New York. A year later, Morris and his wife, the Duchess of Gordon, visited his wilderness tract and then managed to persuade a number of families to settle in the area. In 1785, the Morris Patent was reassigned to his brother and uncle, Lewis and Richard Morris of Morrisania, to indemnify them for the losses incurred during the Revolution. The wilderness estate then passed into the hands of Lewis Morris' son, General Jacob Morris (1755-1844), a patriot veteran of the Revolution, who in 1787 settled the site of the village of Butternuts (now Morris). Jacob Morris, for years one of the foremost citizens of Otsego County, became the social and political intimate of Judge William Cooper, and his friendship with the Cooper family remained unimpaired down to the time of his death. James Fenimore Cooper's older brother Isaac had married into the fabulously aristocratic Morris family in 1804, but had died in 1818. His wife was Mary Ann Morris, a granddaughter of the Morris's of Morrisania and daughter of General Jacob Morris.

By comparison to these, Judge William Cooper was a recent addition to the pantheon of aristocratic New York families. His was so-called "new money" earned in the current financial obsession of land speculation. Post-revolutionary America was a rich nation temporarily inconvenienced by a severe lack of "hard" money. The immense stockpile of real wealth in America resided in large part in its vacant western lands, its timber and naval stores, its fisheries, its agricultural produce, its furs, and its laborers, mechanics, and artisans (free and slave). There was a necessity to transform these tangible riches into negotiable funds in a deliberate and methodical manner – a formula adopted by Alexander Hamilton for the federal government as Secretary of the Treasury in the 1780s and 1790s.[51]

The elder Cooper was originally from Burlington, New Jersey, where he became interested in land speculation in nearby Pennsylvania. Members of the Cooper family had settled on both sides of the Delaware River and in nearby Philadelphia. All the Coopers were seemingly prolific with regard to children, and the number of Cooper cousins was legion. Wealthy Loyalists had been obliged to liquidate their holdings and claims on whatever terms were offered or else suffer total loss. It was decidedly a buyers' market. His first known operations as a land promoter were in the Wyoming Valley and near Pittsburgh. He then became interested in mortgages that had been foreclosed on large tracts of land around Lake Otsego in Central New York. This was Iroquois country. Cooper had heard that George Croghan, the Indian agent and scout, had attempted a settlement there in 1769. The lake itself appears on Dutch maps as early as 1650, but the Dutch were interested in the fur trade not settlement. To investigate these lands, Cooper went out to Otsego in 1785 and finally concluded to remove there with his family in 1790.

Initially nothing was there save a dilapidated forester's hut loosely attributed to Croghan and the conspicuous remnants of a dam General James Clinton's soldiers had constructed and then broken at the mouth of the lake in order to float their supplies down the narrow upper reaches of the Susquehanna. There was only one major military engagement during the Sullivan-Clinton campaign against Iroquoia of 1779. This was at Newtown (Tioga), New York. Colonel Daniel Brodhead, generally lacking restraint with regard to Indian fighting, set "a high standard for murder" during this phase of the operation. With the loss of only 60 men from all causes, including sickness and snakebite, Sullivan had crossed Central New York and part of Pennsylvania in just 35 days, leaving behind burned villages and charred stands of Indian corn but also a number of new roads and bridges, which helped to facilitate white settlement in the region after the war.[52]

Many land speculators in this period held a dream of baronial grandeur for themselves. The leading principle of all land speculation was the reservation of choice tracts, mill sites, fords and roadways to the promoter, who would later charge tolls and fees for their use. To the poor settler, who generally took up 100 acres, he offered a fee simple deed, and secured the purchase money by a mortgage. Owners of real property in fee simple have the privilege of interest in the property during their lifetime and typically have a say in determining who gets to own an interest in the property after their death. Yet a tenant even with a deed might be required to pay a fixed annual sum of money closely resembling rent. Where similar systems of tenancy were attempted in New Jersey riots followed. Consequently, there developed in New Jersey a more evenly dispersed pattern of landholding. Thus were the poor but independent settlers in the colonies driven off to areas where more liberal land policies prevailed.

In New York huge land grants were made to influential individuals instead of to disparate groups. The resulting *patroon* system, left over from the Dutch regime, was followed up and down the western boundary created by the Hudson River, and powerful families like the Livingston's, the Van Rensselaer's, and the Warren's preempted individual ownership through an almost feudal system of tenancy and rents populated by German-speaking Europeans recruited for the purpose. The lands granted by the Dutch were to extend sixteen miles along the shore on one side of a navigable river, or eight miles on both sides of a river, and so far into the country as the situation of the colonies and their settlers permitted. Any colonist who should without written permission enter the service of another patroon or "betake himself to freedom" was to be proceeded against with all the available force of the law. The patroonship most successful, most permanent, and most typical was Rensselaerswyck.[53]

How hard the near-feudal terms were on which the tenants held their leases is apparent from a report written by the guardians and tutors of Jan Van Rensselaer, a later patroon of Rensselaerswyck:

> The patroon reserved to himself the tenth of all grains, fruits, and other products raised on the *bowery*. The tenant was bound, in addition to his rent of five hundred guilders or two hundred dollars, to keep up the roads, repair the buildings, cut ten pieces of oak or fir wood, and bring the same to the shore; he must also every year give to the patroon three days' service with his horses and wagon; each year he was to cut, split, and bring to the waterside two fathoms of firewood; and he was further to deliver yearly to the Director as quitrent two bushels of wheat, twenty-five pounds of butter, and two pairs of fowls.[54]

A large number of Palatine Germans, who originally settled the Mohawk Valley and the Schoharie Lands of Central New York, came to America in ten ships under contract as indentures in 1710 to Robert Livingston, who planned for them to establish a forest products industry along the rivers and streams of those regions. However, the initial sites selected for their settlements on the Hudson were not desirable. The native pine was found unsuited to the production of tar and naval stores in large quantities. They soon discovered that they would never be able to pay for their maintenance by such unprofitable labor. Moreover, the provisions given them were of inferior quality; and they were forced to furnish men for an expedition against Canada while their women and children were left either to starvation or to virtual servitude. In this desperate situation some of the Palatines turned from their fellow Christians to the natives. The Indians gave them permission to settle at Schoharie, and many families moved there in defiance of the landlord, who was still bent on manufacturing tar and pitch.

The great majority remained in the Hudson valley and eventually built homes on lands, which they purchased. Others who had quickly become disgruntled with being tenants migrated down the Delaware and Susquehanna Rivers to Pennsylvania or west along the Mohawk River to form discreet German language communities like Palatine Bridge, Blenheim, Catskill, Bushkill, or simply Germantown. The family of Conrad Weiser, colonial Indian Agent in Pennsylvania in the 18th century, had been one of these moving when he was an adolescent from Schoharie Creek near Schenectady to the Schuylkill River near Reading. By this means many scattered German-speaking settlements were established on the frontier early in the 18th century, but the overall growth of the New York colony was somewhat retarded.

Admiral Sir Peter Warren, who was on station in the Atlantic, sent for William Johnson to come to North America and aid him in the development of a real estate venture. A large tract of land near the Mohawk River had come into Warren's possession, and as a sailor Warren naturally found difficulty in superintending land at what was then a week's journey from the seacoast. Warren was less than a dozen years older than his nephew, whom he regarded with affectionate interest. The young man, who was then twenty-three years old, left Ireland and in 1738 reached the new plantation where his life work lay before him. For this he was admirably equipped by his Irish inheritance of courage, tact, and humor, by his study of English law, and by a facility in acquiring languages, which enabled him to master the Mohawk tongue within two years. The business arrangement between Warren and his nephew provided that Johnson should form a settlement on his uncle's land known as Warrensbush, at the juncture of Schoharie Creek and the Mohawk, that he should sell farms, oversee settlers, clear and hedge fields, purchase supplies, and establish a village store to meet the necessities of the new settlers and to serve as a trading station with the Indians. A few years after his arrival, he married and lost to illness a young Dutch or German woman named Catherine Weisenberg, who gave him three children. He next installed as head of his household Caroline, niece of the Mohawk chief Hendrick, and later Molly Brant, sister of the native war leader, Joseph Brant. Molly Brant and Johnson had eight children.

In compensation for his services to his uncle, Johnson was to be allowed to cultivate a part of the land for himself, which he did on the other side of the river establishing his own manor house known as Johnson Hall, which was free of Warren's oversight. On one side of the house lay a garden and nursery described as the pride of the surrounding country. Here Johnson lived with a frontier opulence, which must have amazed the simple settlers around him, especially those who remembered his coming to the colony as a poor youth less than thirty years earlier. Mohawk chiefs, Oneida braves, Englishmen of title and influence, and distinguished colonial guests of every kind thronged the mansion. Johnson was one of the fortunate few whose characters and careers fit exactly. He found scope for every power that he possessed and he won great rewards. The English therefore were peculiarly fortunate in finding at the most critical stage of their political dealings with the Iroquois a representative endowed with the wisdom and insight of Sir William Johnson.

Hardly baronial splendor

Colonial and early American investors entered business to make a profit, not for any other reason. They bought and shipped anything they thought would sell. Tobacco, furs, grains, flour, fish, and timber/lumber made up about ninety-five percent of the value in all colonial exports. This trade kept many of the shipbuilders and shippers of New England flush with profits. Yet many of the Scots-Irish and German immigrants that arrived late in the process of land acquisition with little money moved through the settled areas to the frontier where they simply squatted on the land. It has been estimated that two of every three acres occupied on the frontiers were held with no legal rights other than the improvements made on them. [55]

Many families known as subsistence farmers had a roof over their heads, farmed and hunted for food, and were debt free, but they were also essentially penniless. A more enterprising man might gather furs or skins in winter or split out a cartload of shingles for sale in town in order to make a few dollars each year. Others scoured the ground and streams for silver and gold without profit. Nonetheless, simple potash was lying at their feet and virtually worth its weight in gold in the Revolutionary Period.

Potash was among America's first industrial chemicals, used both domestically and as an export item. Only the burning of clam and oyster shells in order to make quick lime (an ingredient in cement) may be an older American chemical industry. Potash and lime were among the first export items from both Jamestown and Plymouth, although neither location was rich in hardwoods. Soft woods like pine has very little potassium in it. A glassworks was one of the first things attempted at Jamestown. Sand, lime, potash, mineral additives for color, and heat are the five basic ingredients needed to make glass. This commerce in ash products and other so-called extraction trades also kept busy the iron founders (who cast kettles) and the barrelmakers (ironically called coopers).

Caustic potash was also an ingredient, along with nitrate-rich animal manure, in the process for making saltpetre (potassium nitrate), an ingredient with sulfur and carbon in gunpowder. Saltpetre could also be added to dried meats like sausage and bacon as a preservative in place of common salt. Saltpetre rarely occurred in a natural state in the Atlantic states. Their climate was just too damp. The Great Saltpetre Cave, a notable limestone cave located in southeastern Kentucky visited by Daniel Boone, did not serve as an important source of saltpeter until the War of 1812. At this cave and a few others, calcium nitrate, also called niter, was leached naturally from the dry soil covered in bat and bird droppings. By boiling niter with minimal water (and using only the hot solution), potassium nitrate could be formed by adding potassium carbonate (in the form of the leachings of wood ashes) to remove calcium leaving a solution of purified saltpetre, which could then be dried into crystals. During the American Revolution, Congress had become dedicated to the idea that the united colonies could render themselves independent of foreigners for the supply of military stores (i.e. gunpowder) by this process known as the French Method. The Swiss Method, using only urine and not dung, collected urine in a sandpit installed under a stable. The sand itself was then leached for nitrates which were converted to potassium nitrate via potash.

The delegates to Congress advanced schemes of every sort for the erection of artificial nitrate works, some of them without justification as to their practicality or economy. Carbon could be had by grinding charcoal, but the discovery of major sources of sulfur at certain springs in New York and in Virginia added to their enthusiasm. As reported in the New York Times one hundred years later (30 August 1875), "So prodigious was the amount of sulfur-gas in the Gardner Spring [Sharon Springs, Schoharie County, NY] that the waters of this creek are rendered as white as milk, and the stones are covered with a thick deposit." The Committee of Safety in Philadelphia issued a pamphlet detailing the home manufacture of saltpetre, titled "Several Methods of Making Salte Petre: Recommended to the Inhabitants of the United Colonies by Their Representatives in Congress." The New York committee issued another pamphlet, "Essays upon the Making of Salt-Petre and Gunpowder." John Adams, who was particularly enthusiastic about the project, wrote, "Every stable, Dove House, Cellar, Vault, etc. is a mine of salt petre. Mould under stables, etc. may be boiled soon into salt petre." The first reference to the establishment of a gunpowder mill in America dates to 1639. A mill near Rhinebeck owned by the Livingston's, in 1775 supplied gunpowder at £20 per hundredweight.[56]

It should be obvious to the reader that Judge William Cooper came late to the process of land speculation, but he was no blindsided amateur at making money. In 1786, Judge Cooper's first profit of $9000 (almost $175,000 in 2015 dollars) was realized from a large quantity of maple sugar and potash produced in cooperation with his tenants at Cooperstown. The cast-iron kettle was the key implement in the production of both maple sugar and potash. Bulky and expensive, about an inch thick and several feet in diameter, a potash kettle contained from 400 to 1,000 pounds of metal, and had a capacity of 65 to 90 gallons. Extensive production required several such kettles, which were presumably provided by the Judge. The kettles could also be used to make common salt (NaCL). Salt had been made by the evaporation of seawater near the shore for decades. However, Jesuit missionaries visiting the region of Central New York in 1654 were the first to report the existence of salty brine springs especially around Onondaga Lake. A thick layer of mineral salt underlay the geology of the Allegheny Plateau. After the Treaty of Fort Stanwix (1784), these upwellings provided the basis for commercial salt production from the late 18th century through the early 20th century. An early entrepreneur named Asa Danforth noted that the first time he made salt at Onondaga (c. 1789), he used a 15-gallon kettle and in nine hours he had "boiled down" about 30 pounds of salt.

Potash production provided most settlers in North America with a way to obtain badly needed cash and credit as they cleared wooded land for crops. To make full use of their land, settlers needed to dispose of excess wood. The easiest way to accomplish this was to burn any wood not needed for fuel or construction. Ashes from hardwood trees could then be used to make potassium lye (caustic potash) that could either be used to make soap or boiled down to produce a valuable chemical. Water was allowed to slowly leach through hardwood ashes and the effluent was collected. This was a form of lye (alkali), which when added to animal fat made a tolerable soft soap (a metallic stearate). Depending on the nature of the lye used in their production, soaps have distinct properties. Sodium hydroxide (Na OH) gives "hard soap," which can also be used in water containing mineral salts. When potassium hydroxide (K OH) is used, a soft soap is formed. This form of soap cannot be used with good effect in mineral laden water, but it is less harsh than hard soap and perfect for washing raw wool without damaging the fiber.[57]

The potassium lye could also be further refined into a less dramatic potash. An intense, hardwood fire heated the kettle, boiling off the water and leaving a dark, crude, crystalline residue of so-called "black salts." Adding more fuel to the fire, the maker heated the kettle to a crimson glow that burned off organic impurities to leave the pink-and-gray-colored alkali grit known as potash. The larger, better-capitalized makers further refined the potash by baking it in a kiln. The firewood used for heating provided additional ashes to renew the cycle of production. Once the kettle (or kiln) had cooled, the maker tightly packed and sealed the potash into barrels made of white-oak staves for storage or shipment. Village storekeepers ran many potash works. Along with her excess eggs and butter, a frontier wife might sell her clean ashes for as much as fifteen cents a bushel, payable partly in cash, partly in trade. Those farmers still making potash at home could sell their "black salts" to a commercial works to be refined into the purer commodity.

Potash was used in fullering wool, bleaching textiles, making glass, and making soap. In the colonial period, British-capitalized American potash works had been established in port cities such as Boston, New York, and Philadelphia and were equipped with elaborate leaching vats, large furnaces for evaporation, and other equipment. Virtually everyone in America heated and cooked with wood, and the enormous volume of ashes became the object of one of the first recycling ventures undertaken there. As more American fullering mills using local wool began to open in the Northeast, they relied on barrel after barrel of soft soap from local commercial asheries.

The proceeding discussion is no mere tangent. In 1790, Samuel Hopkins received Patent No. 1 from the US Patent Office for an improvement in the making of potash and pearl ash by a new apparatus and process. Hopkins's key advance lay in burning the raw ashes in a furnace before they were dissolved in water. President George Washington, Attorney General Edmund Randolph, and Secretary of State Thomas Jefferson signed the patent. In addition to his first patent, Hopkins took out two later ones, both for the preparation of flour of mustard. The ash industry declined in the late 19th century when large-scale production of potash from mined mineral salts was established.[58]

In a similar manner, boiling off the water from the sap of the maple tree made maple sugar or a thick maple syrup. The sap runs best in the spring of the year when nighttime temperature and daytime temperature pass back and forth over the freezing point. This fluctuation in air temperature is vital to the flow of sap in sugar maple trees, and there was a short season for making maple sugar of about six weeks. While there are written accounts of maple sugaring in North America dating back to 1557, the exact origins of sugaring are unknown. Seemingly, the Indians of the Lake States, southeastern Canada, New England, and the Appalachian Mountains knew and used maple syrup long before the first explorers and colonists came to America. Maple products could be used as an alternative to expensive cane sugar from the islands of the West Indies. The second ocean-going merchant ship built in the English colonies, carried maple sugar from the Massachusetts Bay Colony to New Amsterdam as early as 1631. Maple sap could be molded into a granular, solid block of maple sugar that had a long shelf life and could be easily transported. Many among the Quakers and early abolitionists promoted maple sugar as an alternative to West Indian "slave-produced" cane sugar. Thomas Jefferson even started a maple sugaring plantation at Monticello in 1791, but it never took off as an industry until the Civil War.

Sugaring and soap making were hard work often dome by frontier women as part of their annual chores.

Cooper clearly referenced the sugaring process in his novel *The Pioneers*. Judge Marmaduke Temple (sometimes called cousin Duke) has a conversation with Squire Richard Jones, his cousin who he had named county sheriff: "As each night brought with it a severe frost, which the heat of the succeeding day served to dissipate. ... 'This is your true sugar weather, Duke,' he cried; 'a frosty night and a sunshiny day. I warrant me that the sap runs like a mill-tail up the maples this warm morning. It is a pity, Judge, that you do not introduce a little more science into the manufactory of sugar among your tenants. It might be done, sir, without knowing as much as Dr. Franklin— it might be done, Judge Temple. ... Now, sir, I assert that no experiment is fairly tried, until it be reduced to practical purposes. If, sir, I owned a hundred, or, for that matter, two hundred thousand acres of land, as you do. I would build a sugar house in the village; I would invite learned men to an investigation of the subject — and such are easily to be found, sir; yes, sir, they are not difficult to find — men who unite theory with practice; and I would select a wood of young and thrifty trees; and, instead of making loaves of the size of a lump of candy, damn me, 'Duke, but I'd have them as big as a haycock.'"[59]

Clearing the ground of its forests was an essential first step to successful farming, but it had unexpected consequences for those on the extreme fringes of civilization. As the frontier settlers wiped out the major predators who afflicted their livestock, they unwittingly exposed their grain crops to increased attacks from mice, squirrels and chipmunks. The price of grain having soared in Albany one year, all the Mohawk was swept clean of the makings of fine bread, and Judge Cooper provided his tenants with a meager ration of corn packed in by horseback from the capital and salted herring captured in the Susquehanna. In less than ten days, each family had an ample supply of salted fish and meal to grind by hand. Nonetheless, the settlers "had no mill to grind within twenty miles distance; not one in twenty had a horse, and the way lay through rapid streams, across swamps, or over bogs. ... If the father of a family went abroad to labor for bread, it cost him three times its value before he could bring it home, and all the business on his farm stood still till his return." Judge Cooper had cooperated in building wagon roads and bridges ultimately converting upwards of 750,000 acres from forest into farms, homesteads, and villages.

A hardwood forest could generate ashes at the rate of 60 to 100 bushels per acre. In 1790, ashes could be sold for $3.25 to $6.25 per acre in rural New York State – nearly the rate required to hire one laborer to clear the same area. Groups of men working together thereby produced a great deal of potential wealth.

From his own "Guide in the Wilderness," written in 1806 and published in Ireland in 1810 shortly after his death as a recruiting instrument, the Judge had noted:

In 1785 I visited the rough and hilly country of Otsego, where there existed not an inhabitant, nor any trace of a road. ... This was the first settlement I made and the first attempted after the revolution; it was, of course, attended with the greatest difficulties; nevertheless, to its success many others have owed their origin. ... I began with the disadvantage of a small capital, and the encumbrance of a large family, and yet I have already settled more acres than any man in America. [sic] There are forty thousand souls now holding [land] directly or indirectly under me, and I trust, that no one among so many can justly impute to me any act resembling oppression. I am now descending into the vale of life, and I must acknowledge that I look back with self-complacency upon what I have done, and am proud of having been an instrument in reclaiming such large and fruitful tracts from the waste of the creation. ... In May 1786, I opened the sales of 40,000 acres which, in sixteen days, were all taken up by the poorest order of men. I soon after established a store, and went to live among them, and continued so to do till 1790, when I brought on my family. ... When I contemplate all this, and above all, when I see these good old settlers meet together, and hear them talk of past hardships, of which I bore my share, and compare the misery they then endured with the comforts they now enjoy, my emotions border upon weakness."[60]

Others had operated on a larger scale than Judge Cooper, but many had failed. Land speculation swallowed up the fortunes of Robert Morris, William Duer, Oliver Phelps, and even the great Holland Land Company. Yet the character of the people seems to have been more important to success than money. Lt. Governor George Clarke, land speculator extraordinary, had carried out a successful project at Cherry Valley, New York in 1738 with experienced settlers drawn largely from a colony of Scotch-Irish in Londonderry, New Hampshire. New Hampshire men were noted for their pioneering spirit and frontier fighting abilities.

In 1788, as an agent for the Holland Land Company, Oliver Phelps had purchased 2 million acres of land in the Genesee from the Iroquois who were under duress having been on the losing side in the war. During the next two years, the Company sold 500,000 acres at a higher price to a number of buyers, but the land sales failed to raise enough capital to meet their payment requirements. Robert Morris had stepped in and paid about half of what Phelps had given the Indians. The initial sales went very well, netting him roughly $350,000 unadjusted for inflation. If Morris had quit the business right then and there, he might have lived the rest of his life among the richest men in America. But changing money values affected the mortgages held on the tracts of land and a depressed land market caused him also to get into financial difficulty. The richest man in America suddenly was locked in debtor's prison, $12 million in debt. While in prison, he reduced that sum to $3 million, and got released under a new bankruptcy law he helped devise. High among the leaders of American society, he was the only man beside Roger Sherman to sign the Declaration of Independence, the Articles of Confederation, and the Constitution. Morris spent his final five years in secluded disgrace. The life of Morris is an epic history of a man who clearly rescued his country from fiscal destruction while being constantly and unfairly suspected of self-interest.

As assistant to Treasure Secretary Alexander Hamilton, William Duer was already significant in the New York financial markets. He hooked up with a land speculator (Alexander Macomb) on a scheme to corner the market in government bonds and bank shares. He borrowed massive amounts of money to finance his deals, drawing other players into his "Six Per Cent Club," named for the 6 percent government securities he was attempting to control. A number of new banks were started to help finance these schemes, with their bank shares selling at unsustainable values. His blatant speculation and that of several other members of the Livingston clan with regard to the National Bank unleashed the Panic of 1792. A year later, he was languishing in debtor's prison, and he would remain there until death released him in 1799, seven years later.

Debtors in these prisons frequently found themselves quite literally dying of debt. They could end up in such circumstances for trivial sums. In 1787, of the 1,162 jailed debtors in New York City, 716 owed less than twenty shillings or one pound. A third of Philadelphia's inmates in 1817 owed less than $5, and debtors in the city's prisons outnumbered violent criminals by 5:1. In Boston, 15% of the debtors were women. Morris, who had owed $12 million, invited George Washington to his well-furnished cell for dinner. Washington attended!

Squire James Cooper

A former U.S. Congressman and Judge, William Cooper had easily secured a naval commission for his youngest son in 1808 through his long-standing connections with various politicians and naval officials. The blue water navy was mostly composed of rough sea dogs and near pirates at this time, but a naval officer was considered acceptable to most of proper society if he came from money. After completion of one year on Lake Ontario in 1809, the year of his father's death, James Fenimore Cooper was ordered to Lake Champlain to serve aboard a gunboat until the winter months when the lake froze over. He also took frequent cruises among the Thousand Islands where he later often spent time fishing.

Although commissioned a midshipman in the United States Navy, by 1811 Cooper had decided that life at sea was not meant for him. Though in the flush of youth at 22 and seemingly positioned to gain military preferment or advancement as owner of a wilderness manor, he missed the entire War of 1812. In a letter to a friend Cooper reveals that Susan De Lancey's acceptance of his marriage proposal was contingent on his resignation from the service. The navy was no place for a country gentleman. *The Pilot* was the first American novel worthy of its classification as maritime fiction. Herein Cooper made excellent use of his naval training on the Great Lakes as a young man. In his own words from *The Pathfinder*, Cooper "had a profound deference for a mariner of the ocean, on which he had often pined to sail; but he had also a natural regard for the broad sheet on which he had passed his life, and which was not without its beauties in his eyes."[61]

As a gentleman, he was involved with the local militia in suburban New Rochelle, but to no greater extent than his involvement with the local political or Bible societies. Hence one of the men who most helped to define woodlands warfare for generations of Americans and other readers had no personal experience with combat. His daughter Susan Fenimore Cooper notes: "Our Father figured also as a military character at that time; Governor [De Witt] Clinton made him his aide-de-camp, with the rank of Colonel, and more than once we little girls had the pleasure of admiring him in full uniform, blue and buff, cocked hat and sword, mounted on Bull-head [his horse] before proceeding to some review. He was thus transferred from the naval to the land service. To the last days of his life … one of his New York friends, never omitted giving him his title of 'Colonel.' He thus became one of the numerous army of American Colonels, *though not one of the ordinary type certainly.*"[62]

Cooper's visions of America's social progress were very much affected by the changes he perceived in its culture. His reading of the historic record suggested that proper society, of which he wished to be a part, was remarkably fragile. *The Pioneers*, also written in 1823, was dedicated to the proposition that the American republic was poised on the verge of "demagoguery, deceit, hypocrisy, and turmoil." Cooper's mocking and critical tone is seen throughout the novel. The dialogue of the settlers displays the carelessness of their society towards the wilderness and its residents. Yet it could be transformed into a stable, prosperous, and just society and thereby saved.

Cooper, the author, favored the man on the land, and, like Thomas Jefferson and like his own deceased progenitor the Judge, he believed that the leading citizens in the United States would be an agrarian elite, a class of gentleman farmers who would inevitably exceed their peers to form a natural aristocracy, an aristocracy of worth or merit rather than one of birth or title. Agrarianism is a philosophical concept that clearly reflects these ideas of honesty, innocence, and virtue. The concept of agrarianism has occupied an important place in American life and culture. In 1769, Benjamin Franklin had noted that the "great business" of America was farming, "the only honest way, wherein man receives … a reward for his innocent life and his virtuous industry." Certainly by the year of his death (1851) Cooper had realized that his self-defined form of agrarian aristocracy no longer existed. [63]

Equality before the law was Cooper's universal device against the excesses of mass-society and mass-democracy. Cooper also thought that excessive emphasis on property, money, and commercialism among the lower classes threatened to corrupt the masses and could lead to what Jefferson called "elective despotism." Cooper's open politics, unfashionable conservatism, and tendency to self-promotion often engendered an ill feeling between the author and certain sections of the public. When he passed along the street without acknowledging people who expected a greeting from him, his friends averred that it was because his mind was engaged in the development of some dramatic scene in the forest or at sea. In 1837 after Cooper published a notice decrying trespass on his land – a picturesque spot on the lake called Three Mile Point – the citizens and the press of Cooperstown organized a protest against him. Cooper himself was entirely unconscious of any arrogance in his attitude, and, when it came to his knowledge that some accused him of posing as an aristocrat in Cooperstown he resented the imputation with bitterness. Nonetheless, there is a detectable string of other authors who Cooper considered rank imitators and inferior writers. Yet he often put himself in the position of taking up a project quite similar to that already completed by others in an effort to outdo them.[64]

Alexis de Tocqueville described his impressions of a New York clearing: "Some trees cut down, trunks burnt and charred, and a few plants useful to the life of man sown in the midst of the confusion of a hundred shapes of debris, led us to the pioneer's dwelling."[65]

The frontier farm was not a pretty sight. Prosperity required at least twenty acres of cleared land, equally subdivided into three components: grain tillage, hay fields, and pastures. At four acres a year, twenty acres was five years of work. Basil Hall, a visitor to the New York frontier, found the settlers struggling to subdue a daunting mass of primeval wood. In 1829, Hall, son of the geologist Sir James Hall, published *Travels in North America*, which caused some offence due to his criticisms of American society. Hall was clearly not disposed to think favorably of the country, even though he represented himself as doing just that in America and in print. So harsh was his critique of America that Hall became known as the "arch-traitor" to American hospitality:

> Some of the fields were sown with wheat, above which could be seen numerous ugly stumps of old trees; others allowed to lie in [the] grass, guarded, as it were, by a set of gigantic black monsters, the girdled, scorched, and withered remnants of the ancient woods. Many farms were still covered with a most inextricable and confused mass of prostrate trunks, branches of trees, piles of split logs, and of squared timbers, planks, shingles, great stacks of fuel; and often in the midst of all this, could be detected, a half-smothered log-hut without windows or furniture, but well-stocked with people.[66]

In early America many settlers, disgusted with the machinations of the various land companies, agents, and politicians, avoided the practice of surveying their land claims altogether and simply marked boundaries themselves by cutting notches in trees or making piles of stones at the corners of boundaries. Indian paths and streambeds continued to be used by the whites to define the boundaries of purchases and land grants, sometimes creating difficulties in future years when assessing the legitimate limits of ownership between those who had conflicting legal interests. This ad hoc system of land division was plagued by mistakes and conflicting claims.

V. Cooper, the Author

The emergence of a new popularity of reading and writing among the American middle class between the War of 1812 and the Civil War underpinned a new national interest in publishing and professional authorship. In 1821, Cooper published *The Spy,* critically acclaimed as the first important historical novel in American literature. Cooper described the adventures of a romantic hero, Harvey Birch, during the American Revolution in and around Westchester County, the "Neutral Ground" of Cooper's in-laws and of his own residence during the War of 1812. Cooper then exploited this winning formula by writing two more books in 1823: *The Pioneers* and *The Pilot*. The former of these had been all but complete when *The Spy* made its debut. *The Pioneers* sold out on the first day of its availability. These successes encouraged him, and he quickly published *Lionel Lincoln* (1825), which dealt with the Battle of Bunker Hill and the beginnings of the American Revolution, the first of a planned series ultimately abandoned by the author. Oddly, Cooper wrote *The Last of the Mohicans* in 1826 overlooking Manhattan hundreds of miles from the wilderness that he sought to immortalize. This stunning success may have distracted him from further writing in the genre of the revolution.

In the first decade as an author between 1820 and 1830, Cooper wrote 10 novels, including some of his best known. During this decade he also improved his skill in terms of moving his plots ahead more briskly and trimming the labored prose of his earliest works. In 1831 while in England, Cooper seized the opportunity presented by an advantageous business relationship with Richard Bentley, one of London's leading publishers, to revise the texts of no fewer than six of his early novels. This was a major undertaking as it took place a decade before the steam powered rotary printing press, invented in 1843 in the United States by Richard M. Hoe. The latter technical advance, which allowed the printing of thousands of pages in a single day, ultimately decreased the cost of the republication of established works, but it also opened the literary market to less well-known and formerly less profitable American authors. In 1830, there were 500 titles by American authors published annually; three decades later there were 4000.

Partly because of the magnitude of Cooper's fictional compendium – his thirty-two novels average more than 500 pages in length – few people besides specialists in early American literature have read all of his works. Each of his novels is either absolutely good or is possessed of at least a modicum of merit; but deficiencies occur in all of them, so that every one of them is remarkable in its episodes rather than as a whole. *The Last of the Mohicans*, viewed as a chain of brilliantly executed episodes, is certainly the best because of the sustained excellence of its execution. Except when writing history, he is not known to have ever drawn up a written outline, and in one or two instances there were only a few brief notes thrown on paper regarding some particular chapter. In all the details he depended in a great measure on the thoughts and feelings of the moment. In the early morning, when Cooper shut himself in his library, he set down on paper in its final form the portion of narrative that he had worked out while pacing the hall the previous afternoon. Cooper reportedly wrote rapidly in a fine, small, clear hand, upon large sheets of foolscap, and seldom made an erasure. Cooper himself had become aware before his death that only five of his books – one tenth of his entire literary production – were worth celebrating. In a preface he wrote for an 1850 edition of his most famous novels, Cooper wrote: "If anything from the pen of the writer of these romances is at all to outlive himself, it is, unquestionably, the series of 'The Leatherstocking Tales.' To say this, is not to predict a very lasting reputation for the series itself, but simply to express the belief it will outlast any, or all, of the works from the same hand." He died within a year.[67]

Sojourn

Beset by debt, Cooper had made plans for a trip to Europe as early as 1823, when his family began lessons in French. One could live as well in Europe and as cheaply as in America, and the facilities for continuing the education of his children were unequalled. Moreover, in Europe he might be able to enforce his copyrights. He asked DeWitt Clinton, then governor of New York, to exert his influence with the federal government in securing him a diplomatic post on the Mediterranean, as a support for a projected European residence of three or four years. John Quincy Adams promptly signed Cooper's commission as consul without portfolio at Lyons. Such an appellation is completely unofficial and merely serves to underscore the extent of the individual's already-existing influence. Nonetheless, the Senate approved it, and, after attending an elaborate farewell banquet given by his club, Cooper and his family left for France. The group included his wife, four daughters, a toddler son and his nephew, William Yeardley Cooper, just sixteen, who was to act as his secretary and copyist.

The family spent just three months in London because Cooper did not like English society. His English hosts carefully noted this attitude with some resentment. He also involved himself in print in the July Revolution of 1830 in Paris and on the side of republicanism in the French finance controversy of 1831-32. Made an object of attack in the journals of his political enemies in Europe, the Whig newspapers of New York and the editors he had long regarded as his friends fell into the habit of treating Cooper as if he had betrayed his birthright and alienated himself from his homeland.[68]

There were personal matters to attend to in Europe, like the sudden illness and death of young William in late 1831 and the need to fend off European offers of marriage to his eldest daughter, Susan, now grown to young womanhood at 18. The author's primary task throughout the years in Europe, however, was that of writing. The list of works written during the seven years abroad supplied convincing evidence of the fact that Cooper was a tourist only in the off hours. Five of the books that he wrote on this trip were lively accounts of places and manners. Taken together, in *Gleanings in Europe,* the first two volumes of which appeared in 1835, Cooper concerned himself largely with the relation of political institutions and social and domestic behaviors. Nonetheless, a brief visit to France or Italy turned out to be something considerably more, and with money in his pocket, the trip had taken on the characteristics of a Grand Tour.

The epitome of touring for upper-class American families was the Grand Tour of Europe. To winter in Rome had been the fashion among Europe's social elite since the 17th century, and Americans had followed their lead and extended their trips to include their historic roots in England, cosmopolitan and modern continental cities like Paris, romantic and artistic centers like Venice or Florence, enigmatic Egypt, and often the Holy Land. Many well-known Americans had toured Europe with their families or lived there for extended periods. Among them were the politicians Thomas Jefferson, James Monroe, Martin Van Buren, John Adams, and John Quincy Adams; the writers Washington Irving, Nathaniel Hawthorne, and later Henry James; and the painters John Frederick Kensett, Jaspar Francis Cropsey, and Thomas Cole, whom Cooper knew from the Bread and Cheese Club.

Writer and novelist Henry James visited Europe at age 24. He wrote that Americans were "forever fighting against the superstitious valuation of Europe. We feel that whatever it is we are lacking here can be found in Europe. There one finds royalty, foreign languages, high fashion; philosophers, anarchists, and artists; Neanderthals, pagan temples, and castles. Those who read a lot can easily become infatuated with Europe, and it becomes a projection of what it is they most desire."[69]

Historian Henry Adams, a grandson and great-grandson of two presidents, wrote that his father (Charles Francis Adams, U.S. Minister to London) felt that too strong a love of Europe "unfitted Americans for America," but Europe remained a pilgrimage site for many of his countrymen throughout the century. The flow of socially elite families to the Continent between 1820 and 1890 was interrupted only by the wars of European nationalism in the 1840s and America's own Civil War.[70]

Available to only the richest of the antebellum plantation aristocracy, the wealthiest of the old-money families, or the most fortunate of the *nouveau riche,* the Grand Tour could last for more than a year – sometimes several years – as families took in all of Europe's major cities, sights, museums, and vacation spots. Many fathers resorted to such once-in-a-lifetime trips in order to expose their children to the ways of the world and provide a polish that was thought to be missing from America's upper-class youth. Moreover, the stay was thought infinitely superior to an equal time spent in the colleges or female seminaries of America. The cost could run into thousands of dollars, but the tour was a priceless introduction to Europe's history, art, society, and culture for the entire family. "To lives made wealthy by the whirring wheels of northern industry or bumper harvests of southern cotton ... the Grand Tour seemed the quickest and surest method of absorbing something which America lacked but which time-mossed Europe possessed in ample measure." [71]

American families often took rooms that were near each other in European cities. There were rarely less than 1000 Americans in a city like London or Paris at any time, many of them from the plantations of the South or West Indies. They thereby formed enclaves of Americanism generally in the better areas of town. They enrolled their minor children in the same schools, congregated in the same restaurants, attended the same social events, and sought out possible marriage partners for their older children from among the touring families. The height of the tour might be the passage close by of royalty, and Americans gathered in Kew Gardens, along Whitehall, or in St. James Park with Buckingham Palace standing across the green or any other venue where the royal family was known to pass in the hope of catching a glimpse of their carriage. The gossiping buzz of the London drawing rooms and Parisian salons, the elegance of the fine houses and the fashions, and a passing glance at the royal coach on the way to the opera were thought to leave a metropolitan polish on those who experienced them. The Grand Tour was, for most upper-class families, "at once the fulfillment of a lifelong ambition and a flamboyant way of letting neighbors know that they had arrived."[72]

As Mark Twain pointed out, the Grand Tour was "a brave conception; it was the offspring of a most ingenious brain. It was well advertised, but it hardly needed it: the bold originality, the extraordinary character, the seductive nature, and the vastness of the enterprise provoked comment everywhere and advertised it in every household in the land." [73]

The Return from Europe

The novelist who left New York in 1826, fresh from the triumph of *The Last of the Mohicans*, was by the early 1830s the object of attack in the Whig newspapers of that city, the editors of which he had long regarded as his friends. When Cooper returned to America from his sojourn in Europe, Hone noted: "James Fenimore Cooper and his family arrived to-day in the ship *Sampson* from London. This gentleman has acquired a high literary reputation during his residence in Europe as the author of several novels, but I doubt very much if the works which he published before he went away do not form a foundation for his fame, of which the superstructure he has subsequently erected is scarcely worthy. His late works have certainly not added much to his reputation on this side of the water."[74]

Cooper never was the man to win disciples, and both privately and publicly he antagonized many of those he encountered. He seems never to have forgiven his former acquaintances for their attitudes toward him in his absence. "Of all social usurpations," wrote Cooper in the year before his death, "that of mere money is the least tolerable — as one may have a very full purse with empty brains and vulgar tastes and habits. ... No one can better understand the vast chasm which still exists between London and New York, and how much the latter has to achieve before she can lay claim to be the counterpart of that metropolis of Christendom. ... It is now just three-and-twenty years since, that, in another work, we ventured to predict the great fortunes that were in reserve for this American mart, giving some of the reasons that then occurred to us that had a tendency to produce such a result. These predictions drew down upon us sneers, not to say derision, in certain quarters, where nothing that shadows forth the growing power of this republic is ever received with favor. The intervening period has more than fulfilled our expectations."[75]

In 1833, Cooper noted that he was shocked because of the dramatic changes that had taken place in America during his absence: the hypocritical passage of the Indian Removal Act, the imperial spirit in the Executive Mansion under President Andrew Jackson, the explosion of popular culture, and the low standard of sensationalism in the newspapers. The demise of the Indian seemed inevitable: the advancement of settled life and the displacement of the first nations in Cooper's northeast woodlands; Indian tribes driven to extinction in New England; Indian hunting grounds replaced with white family farms; and state laws replacing traditional tribal customs. From not only pure fiction, but also through outraged exposé, Cooper turned again and again to the combination of "word art" and controversy. He drew on his experience growing up in the frontier village of Cooperstown to investigate and document the history of conflict over possession of the landscape, setting the claims of Native Americans, British Loyalists, American Patriots, roaming hunters, and forest-clearing farmers against each other. His openly conservative ideas about society were reflected in many of his writings. His writing was his way of coping with America's shift of power from the landed genteel class to the urban factory owner class.[76]

In *Home as Found* (1838), Cooper portrays a society that smugly proclaims itself to be perfect, while many of its most highly placed members are actually discontented with their position in it. Cooper's picture of American life was not entirely new to Americans.

There were equally bitter descriptions in the books of English travelers like Frances Trollope and Charles Dickens, who ascribed American faults to American political institutions. Published in 1833, *Men and Manners in America* by Thomas Hamilton had served as a thorough study of the beginnings of American democracy, and as an unintended example of the prejudices natural to a nineteenth-century Englishman. If occasionally extravagant, Hamilton was never unfair, nor were his criticisms ill natured. What was new in Cooper's case was the unforgivable fact that the critic was himself an American. To Cooper, the press in particular had become an unfortunate manipulator of public opinion. Newspapers were no longer concerned with facts but with facts as news and as catalysts for subscriptions and advertising revenue. "Cooper believed that the press … had outlived in part its historical function. The press had been useful in the struggle for political liberty, for it could help arouse public opinion against tyrannical governments. But after political democracy had been established, as it had been in America, the role of public opinion and of the press as its supporter changed significantly." Cooper won his war against the press in the sense that after years of prosecuting numerous suits for libel, the editors defamed him less frequently.[77]

He said that he feared that majority rule would bring ultimate disorder and injustice. In a letter to a friend, Cooper wrote regarding the failing security of the landed gentry: "There is a growing and most dangerous disposition in the people to take from those who have, and to give to those who have not; and this without any other motive than that basest of all human passions – envy. How far this downward tendency will go, I do not pretend to say; but I think it quite clear that, unless arrested, it must lead to revolution and bloodshed. ... Another such half-century will, in my judgment, bring the whole country under the bayonet." It is unlikely that Cooper herein was predicting the crisis of the Civil War. His fear was the blossoming of a crisis among the social classes for which he foresaw no proper blending or amalgamation. "The very existence of government at all, infers inequality. The citizen who is preferred to office becomes the superior to those who are not, so long as he is the repository of power, and the child inherits the wealth of the parent as a controlling law of society."[78]

In *The American Democrat* (1838), Cooper originally intended to produce a textbook on the American republican form of democracy. The work analyzed the social forces that shape and can ultimately corrupt such a system. He wrote: "The people ... which blindly yields its interests to the designs of those who rule through the instrumentality of newspapers, have only exchanged one form of despotism for another." Most newspapers in the early 19th century cost just pennies and were distributed through subscriptions that cost about four dollars a year. News items were often gleaned from foreign or distant rivals and reprinted, the only original work being the thoughts of the editor and a sheet of local advertisers. James Gordon Bennett of the *New York Herald* added a new dimension to penny press newspapers in 1835 through the introduction of paid observers – so-called "special correspondents" who made personal interviews to provide stories with details and a sense of authenticity. Newspapers were often read aloud to groups of concerned citizens engendering conversation and debate, and helping to solidify the opinion of the local community.[79]

The importance of the printed word in 19th-century America cannot be overestimated. Literacy was quite high among native-born Americans. In 1830, Alexis de Tocqueville reported that he did not find a man in Connecticut who could not read. In the

South at least 70 percent of the white male population could read, and in the North the ability to read may have run as high as 90 percent for both men and women. Middle and Upper class women were voracious readers especially of novels, and estimates of literacy based on the signing of legal documents fail to regard the fact that women were also the main writers of personal rather than business letters, the former unlikely to survive as historic documents. Books were read, reread, and loaned among friends and acquaintances. Many women and men turned to instructive reading, spending time with books on history, geography, painting, foreign languages, surveying, and needlework. A number of books were available on etiquette, manners, and propriety, the rearing of children, husbandry, and oratory. There was a renewed interest in the Bible and religion. In a largely Protestant society, Bible reading was an essential religious obligation. The layman's ability to read and interpret the Bible – not just recite it – advanced the ability to read other printed materials. Indeed, for the middle class, familiarity with scripture and the "right" literature became a mark of class distinction, producing a common experience, language, and values among the better sort.

The first book by Frances Trollope, *Domestic Manners of the Americans* (1832) has been her best known, but she also published novels with strong social themes, an anti-slavery novel a generation earlier than Harriet Beecher Stowe, a novel that described the evils of industrial factories, and two anti-Catholic novels. She disparaged American society as of a lower class than that of England and gave a generally unfavorable and partisan judgment of America as "commonplace." She was appalled by America's egalitarian middle-class and by the influence of religious evangelicalism that was emerging during the Second Great Awakening. In later years, Trollope continued to write novels and books on miscellaneous subjects, writing in all over 100 volumes. She derived no benefit from the transatlantic circulation of her *Domestic Manners of the Americans*, as it was not protected by copyright, and thousands of Americans were reading it. Of her short residence in America, Trollope wrote:

> I very seldom during my whole stay in the country heard a sentence elegantly turned, and correctly pronounced from the lips of an American. There is always something either in the expression or the accent that jars the feelings and shocks the taste. I will not pretend to decide whether man is better or worse off for requiring refinement in the manners and customs of the society that surrounds him, and for being incapable of enjoyment without them; but in America that polish which removes the coarser and rougher parts of our nature is unknown and undreamed of. There is much substantial comfort, and some display in the larger cities; in many of the more obvious features they are as Paris or as London, being all large assemblies of active and intelligent human beings — but yet they are wonderfully unlike in nearly all their moral features.
>
> Now God forbid that any reasonable American, (of whom there are so many millions), should ever come to ask me what I mean; I should find it very difficult, nay, perhaps, utterly impossible, to explain myself; but, on the other hand, no European who has visited the Union, will find the least difficulty in understanding me. I am in no way competent to judge of the political institutions of America; and if I should occasionally make an observation on their effects, as they meet my superficial glance, they will be made in the

spirit, and with the feeling of a woman, who is apt to tell what her first impressions may be, but unapt to reason back from effects to their causes. Such observations, if they be unworthy of much attention, are also obnoxious to little reproof: but there are points of national peculiarity of which women may judge as ably as men — all that constitutes the external of society may be fairly trusted to us. ...

I will not draw any comparisons between a good dinner party in the two countries; I have heard American gentlemen say, that they could perceive no difference between them; but in speaking of general manners, I may observe, that it is rarely they dine in society, except in taverns and boarding houses. Then they eat with the greatest possible rapidity, and in total silence; I have heard it said by American ladies, that the hours of greatest enjoyment to the gentlemen were those in which a glass of gin cocktail, or egging, receives its highest relish from the absence of all restraint whatever; and when there were no ladies to trouble them. ... I thought of mine host [in] Washington afterwards, when reading Scott's "Anne of Geierstein" [1829]; he, in truth, strongly resembled the inn keeper therein immortalized, who made his guests eat, drink, and sleep, just where, when, and how he pleased. ...

In truth, there are many reasons, which render a very general diffusion of literature impossible in America. I can scarcely class the universal reading of newspapers as an exception to this remark; if I could, my statement would be exactly the reverse, and I should say that America beat the world in letters. The fact is, that throughout all ranks of society, from the successful merchant, which is the highest, to the domestic serving man, which is the lowest, they are all too actively employed to read, except at such broken moments as may suffice for a peep at a newspaper. It is for this reason, I presume, that every American newspaper is more or less a magazine, wherein the merchant may scan while he holds out his hand for an invoice.[80]

During his visit to America in 1842, English author Charles Dickens found Americans – including so-called shop and mill girls – omnivorous readers of newspapers, novels, and literary magazines. "Nearly all the young ladies subscribe to circulating libraries," he wrote, "and it was their habit, after reading their copies, to send them by mail or stage-coach to their widely scattered homes, where they were read all over a village or a neighborhood; and thus was current literature introduced into lonely places." The mill girls seem to have shared a passion for self-improvement. They attended evening school, pooled their coins to engage music and language teachers, attended lyceum lectures, and were reputed to be avid readers. Harriet Hanson Robinson claimed that "the circulating libraries, that were soon opened drew them [the mill girls] and kept them there, when no other inducement would have been sufficient." She wrote of a "farmer's daughter from the 'State of Maine' who had come to Lowell [Mills] for the express purpose of getting books ... that she could not find in her native place." Young Lucy Larcom recalled, "The printed regulations forbade us to bring books into the mill, so I made my window-seat into a small library of poetry, pasting its side all over with newspaper clippings."[81]

These types of reading informed the cultural, social, and political landscapes of America in ways more powerful than modern observers today might think. Hidden herein

– disguised, if you will – was a good deal of propaganda and demagoguery. "I yet hope to hear," noted Dickens, "of there being some other national amusement in the United States, besides newspaper politics. ... I do know that I have never observed the columns of the newspapers to groan so heavily under a pressure of orations ... having little or nothing to do with the matter in hand." The American public then, like now, was highly polarized. Newspapers and magazine editors who attempted to walk a fine line of moderation on any topic of national concern quickly found themselves without readers.[82]

Competition and Consequence

After many years of research, in 1839, Cooper published his monumental *History of the Navy of the United States*, in two thick volumes that were reprinted many times. At the same time, a demand for distinctively American forms of writing had arisen within the literary circles of the young nation – a demand that Cooper had sought to fill with his fiction. The naval history had somewhat taken him away from his production of novels, yet there is no year between 1820 and 1851 in which Cooper did not publish at least one work. Nonetheless, *The Last of the Mohicans*, written in his first years as a professional author (1826), was arguably his best work. Yet not one of cooper's books appears on several lists of "best novels" today, nor do many of Scott's works. Not every writer can be Charles Dickens, James Joyce or Jane Austen churning out blockbuster after blockbuster; nor were all these literary works spectacular. Such criticism would have deprived the world of John Milton, the Bronte sisters, Harriet Beecher Stowe, Lew Wallace, or Margaret Mitchell.

Like the works of Scott, Austen, or Dickens, the tales of Cooper were steady sellers, but not best sellers in the modern sense like Mitchell's one off wonder, *Gone With the Wind*, General Wallace's durable *Ben Hur,* or Stowe's historically significant *Uncle Tom's Cabin*. Each of these had been said in their day to out-sell all others save the *Bible*, but they were followed by nothing significant. The five *Leatherstocking Tales*, though they stay in print and are still read by a substantial audience are quite unlike what are normally considered Classics. *The Last of the Mohicans*, in particular, has been translated to television, cinema, and other media quite as often as the works of other great writers and has become iconic, in its own way, of wilderness America without reliance on the other four parts of the Leatherstocking series.

The first true historical novels in English were written by women in Britain: Maria Edgeworth's *Castle Rackrent* (1800), Ann Radcliff's *Gaston de Blondeville* (written 1802), and Jane Porter's novel *Thaddeus of Warsaw* (1803), which went through at least 84 editions. Each of these predated Scott's history novels by at least a decade, and many of Cooper's works by two. Besides Scott's ground breaking Waverly series and other historic novels, the better-known adventure titles became available during the latter part of the century, many translated to English. The premier titles might fill the bookshelf of the historic fiction enthusiast: *The Last Days of Pompeii* (Bulwer-Lytton, 1834), *The Three Musketeers* and *The Count of Monte Cristo* (Dumas, 1844), *A Tale of Two Cities* (Dickens, 1859), *Lorna Doone* (Blackmore, 1869), *Michael Strogoff* (Verne, 1876), and the present author's own favorites as a boy, *Treasure Island*, *Kidnapped, The Black Arrow,* and *The Master of Ballantrae* (Stevenson, 1883, 1886, 1888, 1889). Many among these titles have been converted to screen and teleplays, some more than once.

It may be noted by the discerning reader that with the exception of Edgar Allan Poe and Washington Irving, Cooper's works went virtually unchallenged by other American authors before the second quarter of the 19th century. Even in Europe, only the historical fiction of Victor Hugo and Honoré de Balzac were contemporary with his frontier novels. Indeed, Cooper had come from flagging family affluence to personal reputation as an author in America, but he made most of his money in the international market partly because he had cornered the literary market in frontier stories. During Cooper's early period as a writer, English texts, less expensive and more fashionable, had almost closed the literary market to American authors.

Poe had enlisted in the Army in 1827 under an assumed name, and it was at this time his publishing career began, with an anonymous collection of poems, *Tamerlane and Other Poems*. The American reading public during this period seemed more interested in fiction than poetry, however. Poe switched his focus to prose thereafter and spent the next several years working for literary journals and periodicals, becoming known for his own style of literary criticism. His work forced him to move among several cities, including Baltimore, Philadelphia, and New York City. In 1835, he married Virginia Clemm, his 13-year-old cousin, and took up residence in the Bronx. The small wooden farmhouse, built by the Valentine family for its farm workers about 1812, once commanded an unobstructed view over the rolling Bronx hills to the shores of Long Island Sound. Poe often made allusions to the Fordham section of the Bronx in his works, especially in "The Bells," which are said to be the bells of nearby Fordham University (a Catholic institution set up by Bishop John Hughes) where he was given the freedom of the library. Poe was not a Catholic, but he enjoyed the company of the Fordham students who liked smoking, drinking, and playing cards. The village of Fordham was the first stop established for the Harlem Line of the NY Central Railroad, and it was quite out in the country. He often walked among the glades and ravines that today make up Bronx Botanical Park, and he is known to have paced back and forth along the nearby Highbridge over the Harlem River from Manhattan to the Bronx designed by John B. Jervis, America's leading consulting engineer of the Antebellum Era, who had begun his career as a laborer on the Erie Canal.

The Narrative of Arthur Gordon Pym of Nantucket (1838) is Poe's only complete novel. A few serialized installments were published in the *Southern Literary Messenger*, of which he was editor, but never completed. Contemporary reviews were generally unfavorable because the book was too gruesome in its details. The historical novel had branched off into various forms, such as love stories, detective stories, westerns, and gothic tales. Poe became especially good at the gothic and detective genres. He first Americanized the detective story in the 1840s with his tales in "The Murders in the Rue Morgue" (1840), "The Mystery of Marie Roget" (1842–1843, based on the actual murder in New York), and "The Purloined Letter" (1845). Ironically, although Poe is given credit for inventing the "detective" novel, in his first work of this genre he does not use the word *detective*. Prior to the general reorganization of the police forces of Britain, France, and the United States in the 1840s from agencies for spying on the population to crime fighters, it was nearly impossible to portray detection exploits to readers as exciting adventures. Poe was among the first well-known Americans to try to live by writing alone, and he failed to do so. He was found in great distress and dying in the streets of Baltimore in 1849. He was best known for his poem *The Raven* (1845).

Prior to Cooper, only Washington Irving among Americans had made inroads into the international market, and he tried to professionalize the writing of fiction. Concerned for his health, Irving's family financed an extended tour of Europe from 1804 to 1806; but the young man bypassed most of the usual sites and locations, and in their stead honed his social skills among European publishing and writing circles. He would later become one of Europe's most desirable dinner guests. In late 1809, while mourning the death of his teenaged fiancée, Irving completed his first major book, *Diedrich Knickerbocker's History of New York* (1809), a satire on the self-importance imputed to local history and contemporary politics. Never inappropriate or crude, Irving lampooned New York culture and politics in a manner acceptable to the literate classes of society. Irving commented on the history of the Dutch occupation, critiqued Jeffersonian democracy with a Federalist bent, and mocked literary history. The work was called "the first great book of comic literature written by an American." It was a huge success, but he did not write any more creative literature for the next six years.

Forced to turn to his writing to make a living, Irving went to work thereafter on what would become his most famous book, *The Sketchbook of Geoffrey Crayon* (1819-20) containing "Rip Van Winkle" and in later editions "The Legend of Sleepy Hollow." He then became a diplomatic attaché in Spain, where he researched his *History of the Life and Voyages of Christopher Columbus*, published in 1832, which was more scholarly than his other works. He published two more works, *A Chronicle of the Conquest of Granada* and *The Alhambra* while in Europe, before finally returning to New York in 1832 after 17 years abroad. He soon began to travel again, going on an adventure to the Western frontier in search of more settings for his stories. This trip resulted in three works, *A Tour on the Prairies*, *Astoria*, and *The Adventures of Captain Bonneville, U.S.A.*, published between 1835 and 1837.

A 19th century loophole in the US copyright law allowed American publishers to reprint foreign books almost at will. The intellectual property of foreign writers was up for grabs, and works by American authors were avoided as unsophisticated and less profitable. Dickens, Scott, and other popular British writers lost income while American publishers profited and American authors starved. Irving had argued with little success for stronger laws to protect professional writers from copyright infringement. He died in New York in 1859. The International Copyright Association was not formed until 1868, with William Cullen Bryant as president. Not until 1890 did authors, publishers, and printers' unions join together to support an international copyright bill. Its legislative goals were attained in 1891.

A significant number of "original" novels from the Victorian era actually appeared in either monthly or weekly installments in magazines or newspapers. Production in book form soon followed a successful run of episodes, but serialization was one of the main reasons that 19th-century novels were so long. The authors kept the story going as long as it was successful. Reading aloud to an intimate group became an activity with many of the characteristics of theater with a single reader providing entertainment to the listeners and a unique interpretation to the text. The wildly popular *Pickwick Papers* of Charles Dickens, first published in 1836, is considered to have established the viability of the serialized format, but many other works had appeared through this medium. Among the more significant American works released in serial format was *Uncle Tom's Cabin* by

Harriet Beecher Stowe, which was published over a 40-week period in 1851, the year of Cooper's death.

Nonetheless, Cooper was reportedly the highest-paid contributor to *Graham's Magazine*, receiving $1,600 in 1846 for the serial "The Islets of the Gulf, or Rose-Budd," later published in book form as *Jack Tier, or The Florida Reefs*. Cooper wrote this pseudo-erotic serial of naval life set in the Gulf as the Mexican War progressed. Cooper received another $1,000 for a series of biographies on distinguished naval commanders.

A stipend of $1,600 was no mean remuneration for a mere "scribbler." The average family income in the United States was a remarkably low $400 in period money ($11,000 in 2015 money). Laborers generally worked for less than might be thought – "a dollar a day and found" – and the overwhelming majority of families had little income in the form of hard cash. Most families outside the urban centers produced their own food and fuel at little cost other than their own labor. Shelter, fuel, and food could be had with the use of an ax, a hoe, and a musket. Little cash was needed when a well-aimed musket ball could bring down a month's meat. On the other hand, city life was becoming increasingly synthetic and regimented. The urban middle class found itself raised to a social level undreamed of in the previous century, but entry into the upper classes in America required both real money and the acceptance of those already considered the social elite. Many families were barred, therefore, from further upward mobility, and the middle class consequently expanded. On the other hand, a family with an average annual income of only $2,500 in period dollars could afford to hire a cook, a housemaid, and a nurse for the children. Doctors, lawyers, and upper-level civil servants – considered the "middle of the middle class" – made between $1500 and $2500 annually depending on whether they practiced in rural or urban areas of the country, respectively.[83]

During 1843-1844, Cooper reviewed in a serial the court martial of Commander Alexander Slidell Mackenzie who, while at sea in 1842, had hanged three crewmembers of the US training brig *Somers* for mutiny. One of the hanged men was the nineteen-year-old son of Secretary of State John C. Spencer. Mackenzie's handling of the *Somers* Affair, including its lack of a lawful court martial, was controversial. Spencer, along with two other sailors, was planning to seize the ship and then kill any among the trainees who opposed them before turning pirate. The incident inspired the novel *Billy Budd* by American author Herman Melville. The *Somers* affair also helped to advance the founding of the US Naval Academy. The *Somers* was serving as an experimental training ship as there was no naval academy at the time and as such included several teenaged midshipmen in her crew.

Mackenzie, a naval veteran of 27 years at sea, was tried for murder as well as eight other charges and fully exonerated. Mackenzie was himself an accomplished author and naval historian. His first work, *A Year in Spain, by a Young American* (1829), made him well known in America as well as in England. Other works followed: *Popular Essays on Naval Subjects* (1833), *The American in England* (1835), *Spain Revisited* (1836), *Life of John Paul Jones* (1841), *Life of Commodore Oliver H. Perry* (1841), and *Life of Commodore Stephen Decatur* (1846). Mackenzie's role in the *Somers* affair and his interpretations of recent naval history, which differed somewhat from those expressed in Cooper's naval history of 1839, made Mackenzie the subject of spirited attacks from the author.

Another American, Richard Henry Dana with *Two Years Before the Mast*, first published in 1840, won the biggest audience for a sailor's account of a voyage in this period. Dana sailed to California in the brig *Pilgrim*, and then wrote a book about the experience based on his shipboard journal. W. Clark Russell, author of *The Wreck of the Grosvenor* (1877), *The Frozen Pirate* (1877), and dozens of other sea-stories, called Dana's work the greatest sea-book ever written, and made positive comparisons with the novels of Daniel Defoe (three concerning *Robinson Crusoe* in 1719 and 1720 and the lesser known *The Life, Adventures and Piracies of the Famous Captain Singleton* of 1720). In 1841, Dana published *The Seaman's Friend*, which became a standard reference on the legal rights and responsibilities of sailors. A Harvard trained lawyer, Dana defended many common seamen in court.

VI. Feminine Victoriana

Cooper's female characters run the gamut of 19th century personalities, yet he treats each as requiring the protection of a male. It should be remembered that much of Cooper's work predated the formalized misogynism of Victoriana (1837-1901). Misogyny, a central part of 19th century sexist prejudice and ideology, has been an important basis for the oppression of females in male-dominated societies throughout history. Cooper did not actively seek to diminish women, but he sought to maintain a structured society tied to tradition and continuity rather than to progress and change – a romanticized version of the old aristocratic order as it was before the American Revolution – well mannered, chivalrous to women and children, and protective of all that was still fundamentally good in America. To paraphrase the immensely popular Sir Walter Scott, the ladies of the lower classes retained enough "insolence" to tell the aristocrats that any breach of proper formality between them was dishonorable to both. In other words, a female *will* act like a lady so that a male *can* act like a gentleman.[84]

In Cooper's day and at all levels of proper society, individual liberty, manliness, and respect for authority and position were held in such high esteem that one put his life and personal honor on the line to protect them. This often took the form of an overly aggressive attitude toward dueling, which Cooper, even with his combative personality, seems to have avoided. The practice was much more popular in the west and south than in the east, but it was not unheard of. Lyman Beecher, one of the most influential ministers of the period, gained popular recognition in 1806, after giving a sermon concerning the infamous duel between Alexander Hamilton and Aaron Burr in New Jersey. The young preacher had initially been frustrated: "My preaching seems not to move," he complained. "I speak against a rock." But when he preached "The Remedy for Dueling," on the occasion of the Burr-Hamilton duel, the Anti-Dueling Association of New York took note and published a popular reprinted copy (1809). Beecher's sermon asked how anyone could vote for a murderer (i.e. Burr). He first delivered the sermon at a few Long Island churches during 1805 and at a presbytery meeting in 1806, and then published it. To counter these sorts of unchristian behaviors, Beecher advocated a ballot-box solution in which Christians would sanctify the electoral process "by withholding your suffrages from every man whose hands are stained with blood, and by intrusting to men of fair character and moral principle the making and execution of your laws." The days of those who had sought to make church and state mutually supporting, had passed. The United States Constitution was a secular document that prohibited religious tests for office and direct state support of religious institutions. Beecher recognized that only if those who adhered to traditional Christian principles continued to populate America, would it remain a moral nation.[85]

On the softer side of personal honor, however, the social elite voluntarily assumed the role of benefactor and knight errant to all other levels of society. Like cavaliers on a quest, men felt obliged to counsel and defend not only their own families, but also all females and minor children placed under their protection. This often put females, especially young women of good birth and moderate fortunes, under the sometimes-unreasonable control of fathers, grandfathers, uncles, or brothers. If they married, the power of domination passed to a husband. Ironically, widowhood often freed women of the power of men, but only in the absence of an adult son and heir. At times, a particularly combative brother might involve himself in the affairs not only of his sister, but also of her close female companions with or without their permission. A boisterous or selfish brother might try to dominate a weaker or more dependent girl, but "generally the latter exerted a softening, sweetening charm. The brother animated and heartened, the sister mollified, tamed, refined." Sisters were like the polished cornerstones of a temple, brothers the rough-hewn foundations. The inferior position of sisters among siblings implied an obligation that was placed upon brothers to defend their honor and offer them support in times of need. This obligation was often extended to brotherless female cousins.[86]

In *Wyandotte* (1843), Cooper's characters Beulah and Maud Willoughby are considered sisters, one adopted. "As for Beulah and Maud … no place can be safer than under their father's eyes," notes the author. "The first had a staid, and yet a cheerful look; but her cheeks were blooming, her eyes bright, and her smile sweet. Maud, the adopted one, however, had already the sunny countenance of an angel, with quite as much of the appearance of health as her sister; her face had more finesse, her looks more intelligence, her playfulness more feeling, her smile more tenderness, at times; at others, more meaning. It is scarcely necessary to say that both had that delicacy of outline, which seems almost inseparable from the female form in this country," wrote Cooper. Beulah was a great favorite with their father. Maud being "only his darling." He listened always to whatever his natural daughter said with indulgence and respect. He often told the chaplain that his daughter Beulah had "the true feelings of her sex, possessing a sort of instinct for whatever was right and becoming, in a woman." [87]

These attitudes were very old ones, but they had been formalized during the complicated rise of Princess Victoria (1819-1901) to the throne of Britain. Initially an unlikely heir to the throne, she inherited the crown in 1837 at the age of 18, after her father Edward's three elder brothers had all died, leaving no legitimate, surviving children. King George III was in seclusion, bowed down with an incurable disease; and of all his large family, fifteen sons and daughters, many of whom were still living, not one had a successor to come after him or her as a legitimate heir to the crown. For twenty years the sole hope of the royal house had been the Princess Charlotte who died childless in 1817. At birth, Victoria was virtually buried in the line of succession behind her father, three uncles, and two cousins, who died in infancy. When she was only a few months old, Victoria's father died, closely followed by his father, poor old King George III. His surviving sons in the order of their birth followed this monarch: George IV and William IV, his second son Frederick having died in 1827. Since 1714, Britain had shared a monarchy with Hanover in Germany, but under Salic law women were excluded from the Hanoverian succession. This was not the case in Britain. Elizabeth and Mary before her had been Queen in their own right. While Victoria inherited all the British dominions, Hanover passed instead to her father's younger brother, fifth son and eighth child of George III, her unpopular uncle the Duke of Cumberland who became King Ernest Augustus I of Hanover.

When it became apparent that Victoria would be queen, William Lamb, 2nd Lord Melbourne was put in charge of the education of the female heir to the throne in England. He decided what books she should or should not read, and what plays she might or might not attend. He determined the extent and style of her wardrobe, although he did not choose it. Melbourne, who was prime minister when Victoria came to the throne and a political mentor to the young queen, was forty years her senior. The Duchess her mother avoided the court because she was scandalized by the presence of King William's bastard children, and perhaps prompted the emergence of Victorian morality by insisting that her daughter avoid any appearance of sexual impropriety. Victoria shared a bedroom with her mother every night, studied with private tutors, and spent her play-hours with her dolls and her pet dog. The product in 1837 of Lord Melbourne's censorship and her mother's attempt to control her was Queen Victoria, whose name became synonymous with prudery and the repression of women. Yet the girl herself was a rebellious romantic of sorts, as will be seen. Upon ascending to the throne, her mother was consigned to a remote apartment in Buckingham Palace, and Victoria often refused to meet her.

Melbourne was the husband of the notorious Lady Caroline Lamb who had a brief but open affair with the author Byron in 1812, a half dozen years before the birth of Victoria. Byron was then 24 and Caroline 26. This circumstance is thought to have affected a reactionary attitude in later years within Melbourne toward the proper role of women in society, which he transmitted to the future queen, and she to the broader culture.

Matters had come to a head at Lady Heathcote's ball in 1813, when Byron publicly spurned Lady Caroline, who responded by breaking a wine glass and trying to slash her wrists. She did not seriously injure herself, but polite society was scandalized, and her mental stability was called into question. She described Byron as "mad, bad, and dangerous to know." Three years later, her cousin Harriet, Lady Granville remained incredulous at Caroline's continued unrepentant behavior. Ultimately, it was Lady Caroline who prevailed on her husband to agree to a formal separation in 1825. Lady Caroline's obsession with Byron would define much of her later life as an author, as well as influencing both her and Byron's works. Lady Caroline Lamb's most famous work is *Glenarvon*, a Gothic novel that was released in 1816 just weeks after Byron's departure from England. Its rakish main character, Lord Ruthven, is an unflattering depiction of her ex-lover. She published three additional novels during her lifetime: *Graham Hamilton* (1822), *Ada Reis* (1823), and *Penruddock* (1823). She died in 1828.

In 1840, Victoria married her cousin Albert of Saxe-Coburg and Gotha, who became an important political adviser as well as the Queen's companion, replacing Lord Melbourne as the dominant, influential figure in the first half of her life. Victoria's mother was evicted from the palace. According to her diary, she enjoyed Albert's company from the beginning: "His excessive love & affection gave me feelings of heavenly love & happiness I never could have *hoped* to have felt before! He clasped me in his arms, & we kissed each other again & again! His beauty, his sweetness & gentleness – really how can I ever be thankful enough to have such a *Husband*!" Their nine children married into royal and noble families across the continent, tying them together and earning her the nickname "the grandmother of Europe." In 1861, Victoria's mother died, with Victoria at her side. This was followed by the death of Albert in the same year. The Queen was devastated and went into a prolonged seclusion, and the governance of the empire for the next 40 years generally fell to its Prime Ministers.[88]

Cooper's insistence on referring to women and girls collectively as "females" seems like the common practice at the time, and it should be remembered that women were the main consumers of novels. Nonetheless, his usage drew criticism, but, if from his female readers, it was much muted. James Russell Lowell, in his "A Fable for Critics" (1849), called attention to Cooper's undemocratic class-consciousness and to the limitations of his female characters: "The women he draws from one model don't vary, all sappy as maples and flat as a prairie." William Dean Howells in 1901, the year of Victoria's death, wrote, "Cooper's women lack variety and life and are utterly characterless and insipid." The prominent American editor continued, "The heroines of Cooper did not exist even in the imagination of his readers. There were certain figures in his pages, always introduced as females, and of such extremely conventional and ladylike deportment in all circumstances that you wished to kill them!" However, of Cooper's thirty-two novels, twenty-four have settings at least thirty years prior to their composition. The gender conventions ruling in those times were as stylized and out of fashion in the mid-19th century as a minuet, and it was the system that had been in effect fifty years hence that Cooper utilized in his fiction.[89]

Many of Cooper's usages with respect to women in his novels would rile the hackles of gender equality proponents today. *The Ways of the Hour* (1850) remains one of the best examples of Cooper's attitude towards the role of the female in American society. Of particular importance, in light of the typical theme found in Jane Austen and other "manners" novelists, is the ambivalent attitude Cooper displays toward the novel's heroine, Mary Monson, a strong and fiercely independent woman – the type of woman that Cooper felt would destroy the structure of the American family. Although he approves of her aristocratic taste and manner, he thoroughly condemns her "independent" nature, which causes her to leave her husband and demand control of her property and fortune. The heart of Cooper's criticism in *The Ways of the Hour* was the "Married Women's Property Act of New York State" (1849), which assured the property rights of women and effectively removed their money and estate from the sole control of a husband.[90]

In each of his novels, Cooper uses gender roles and social class to express his views of the ideal American society. The gender roles Cooper establishes are clearly reflective of the Cult of Domesticity that ruled antebellum America. Female characters are only allowed to wield power in enclosed spaces like the home, or in life or death situations. At one point in *The Last of the Mohicans*, Cooper found his two heroines Alice and Cora "on the threshold of the low edifice … surrounded by a clamorous and weeping assemblage of their own sex, that had gathered about the place, with a sort of instinctive consciousness that it was the point most likely to be protected. Though the cheeks of Cora were pale and her countenance anxious, she had lost none of her firmness; but the eyes of Alice were inflamed, and betrayed how long and bitterly she had wept." Cora Munro, the dark-haired daughter of Colonel Munro, is serious, intelligent, and calm in the face of danger. "Cora set the example of compliance, with a steadiness that taught the more timid Alice the necessity of obedience." Her mother, whom Munro married in the West Indies, was a mulatto or mixed-race woman, described as "descended remotely" from servants. Cooper writes: "Major Heyward, you are yourself born at the south, where these unfortunate beings are considered of a race inferior to your own." When captured, Cora is the only one who has the presence of mind to remember to leave a trail. She also defies Magua and resists his demands. Cora is at the heart of the love triangle between Uncas, who loves her and whom she admires, and Magua, who wants her as his wife, but whom she despises. Cora's blonde half-sister Alice is cheerful, playful, charming, and easily distracted. She is the daughter of Alice Graham, Munro's second wife. She ultimately marries Heyward. They are the only characters in the novel whose story ends happily in a romantic sense, yet in several screenplays both die.[91]

In *The Pilot*, with its pair of girlish cousins, Cecilia can't really be described as melancholy, but she is much more serious-minded, and more proper than Kate, who is active to the point of audacity. The latter is inventive of all sorts of schemes and dedicated to the management of her own affairs and to foiling the plots of any deceivers or oppressors. Mabel Dunham in *The Pathfinder* admits to the dominant social understanding: " 'I had better rely on my youth and feebleness,' said the girl, smiling, while her color heightened under her feelings. 'Among Christian men, a woman's best guard is her claim to their protection.'"[92]

Cooper, like a few authors including Shakespeare, was intrigued by the idea of women disguising themselves as men, especially young women posing as young men or boys. Kate Plowden in *The Pilot* was the first character in Cooper's sea fiction to impersonate a male. In *The Red Rover*, the cabin "boy" turns out to be a girl in disguise. This plot device is carried to its most implausible extreme in *Jack Tier*, when the wife of the ship's captain dresses up as a seaman and falls in love with a common sailor. We are told that she maintained her successful deception for twenty years! When commenting on this work, a modern critic described the novel as "an obscure work not always found in library stacks [that] remains largely unread, but it too deserves attention." This form of gender impersonation was not as farfetched as one might think. In an era when "clothing defined the man," gender roles and gender specific clothing went together in the minds of the beholder. Fashionable dress, hairstyle, and accoutrements were equally indicative of social groups and self-identification.[93]

Just forty-four days after the first American publication of *Red Rover* in 1828, the first theatrical adaptation was performed in the Chestnut Street Theatre in Philadelphia. A second adaptation of the novel was performed in the Park Theater, New York. The *North American Review* generally praised *Red Rover*. The reviewer, also comparing the text and style to that of Sir Walter Scott, commented, "Cooper has, in this instance, done more and better things for his name, than upon any former occasion." The reviewer was very critical of the use of the Indian native in his previous wilderness novels and was pleased that Cooper had returned to "his own element" of the sea from the "misuse" of the Indian which he was prone to in other novels.[94]

A Genuine Antebellum Personality

Cooper, of course, lived his entire adult life during a burst of historical activity. It is important, therefore, to put Cooper into a historical context. Cooper wrote *The Last of the Mohicans* in 1826, the same year in which Jefferson and John Adams died, and just 50 years after the signing of the Declaration of Independence. While one event had little to do with the other, the timing suggests just how limited US history was when he wrote. He was born simultaneously with the ratification of the Constitution and the choice of Washington as America's first President, and he died a decade before the Civil War. Cooper was a genuine antebellum personality.

As the century began, Central Park and the Brooklyn Bridge had not yet been considered; the Erie Canal had not been started; Volta had not invented the electric battery, Fulton the steamboat, nor Morse the electric telegraph. When Cooper wrote, America was not yet at war with the tribes of the plains, had not challenged the nations of the Southwest, and had not subdued the Seminole of Florida. Even with the passage of decades, Texas remained a republic, California remained Spanish, and Oregon remained a dream when Cooper penned the last of his five tales. Until 1846, the turmoil concerning Oregon gave rise to slogans such as "Fifty-four Forty or Fight!"

The white and Native residents of British Canada remained a strategic threat to the region and to the United States as they did through much of the 19th century. Westward expansion of both British North America and the United States saw an uncertain national boundary that was not extended west along the 49th parallel from the Lake of the Woods to the Rocky Mountains until the Treaty of 1818. The British suppressed revolts by French Métis in favor of American-style democracy in Ontario and Quebec in 1837, and Fenian raids by immigrant Irish-Americans took place across the nearby US-Canada border with many of the leaders fleeing as refugees to the United States. When Cooper died in 1851, few people had heard of an obscure congressman from Illinois called Abraham Lincoln.

William Mather was a friend of Samuel F.B. Morse (inventor of the electric telegraph) who was also a close associate of Cooper from New York. At one time Morse considered proposing to Cooper's daughter. Mather was a physician who never practiced medicine. He took his degree of Doctor of Medicine from Fairfield Medical College in Herkimer County, New York, in 1826, but devoted his career to chemistry rather than to medicine. He took some chemicals and visited Cooperstown in 1844 as an itinerant lecturer. He left a short, penciled reminiscence of the author:

> After giving my introductory lecture and when I was well started in my course, I was surprised to receive from Mr. Cooper an invitation to dine with him on a certain day. ... Of course I was punctual in accepting of his invitation. ... I do not recollect in particular about the pen ink and paper which he used and which occupied the table in the room. ... As far as I recollect his family consisted besides himself of four unmarried daughters ... highly educated and from appearances were accomplished young ladies. ... His father, Judge Cooper, was a great land holder and a pioneer settler in that portion of the state after whom I think the place was named. If the son James Fennimore was not a pioneer settler, he was at least a pioneer author at an early period when very few in this country had attempted to write a book or at least very few books written by American authors were read and our brethren across the Atlantic would ask the question: "Who reads an American book?" I have recently noticed an article in the *Century Magazine* in regard to Mr. Cooper as an author in which he is represented as one of the earliest if not first who produced readable books, which every body wishes to read and which have been translated and read in other languages than the English.[95]

Illustrations and Allusions

In his introduction to *The Last of the Mohicans*, Cooper proclaimed that he believed that his scenes needed no further illustration, and most of the information necessary to understand its allusions, "were rendered sufficiently obvious to the reader in the text itself." Modern printing and illustration were in their infancy – the former much advanced over the latter. Cooper was a master narrator. Take for example, the brilliant action of *The Last of the Mohicans* (1826), the overall excellence of *The Pioneers* (1823), the storm episode in the *Pathfinder* (1840), or the more general depictions of court days and the mustering of the militia. The narrator follows the actions of several characters at once, especially during combat scenes. He describes characters objectively but periodically makes reference to his own writing within the text. The author's perspective, which is heard in the voice of the narrator, is also complex. Many conflicting concepts are embodied in the long passages of description on which Cooper relied to flesh out his theme. He also produced some of the earliest and most effective landscape descriptions up to his time. Donald A. Ringe (University of Kentucky) has noted, "Our nineteenth-century ancestors were … better able to read pictures, both verbal and graphic, than we are, and contemporary writers appealed directly to their visual sense. ... To read a verbal picture in one of the novels is not an easy task, for Cooper was adept at adjusting his descriptions to suit his artistic purposes."[96]

The main processes used for reproduction of illustrations during the 16th and 17th centuries were engraving and etching on wood and metal. Engraving was a historically important method of producing images on paper in artistic printmaking, in mapmaking, and also for commercial reproductions and illustrations for books and magazines. Drawing on wood had wide implications. It demonstrated, first of all, the artistic excellence that could be achieved using the techniques of cutting and hatching across the grain. Intaglio, a family of printing and printmaking techniques in which the image is incised (etched) into a surface that holds the ink, normally utilized soft copper or zinc plates. Intaglio emerged well after the woodcut print. At the end of the 18th century, commercial lithography was introduced. This allowed even better illustrations to be reproduced. A flat print plate was used, enabling much longer and more detailed print runs than the older physical methods of printing. The pages printed by this method could be hand-colored in watercolors and stitched into the volume. At the beginning of the 19th century, illustrations increased the sales of previously published fiction. In 1836, the publication of Charles Dickens's *The Pickwick Papers* in an illustrated serialized format revolutionized the publication of new fiction. The popularity of illustrated fiction began to decline in the late 19th century, as illustrations lost their novelty and no longer guaranteed that a marginal novel would sell well.

VII. Who Was Natty Bumppo?

Natty Bumppo is something of an enigma. Although the child of white parents, Bumppo supposedly grew up among the Delaware Indians and was educated by Moravian Christians becoming a near-fearless warrior skilled in many weapons, one of which was the long rifle. How this happened among the pacifist Moravians is somewhat puzzling. The Moravians were better known for their music and hymnody than for their martial skills. Yet, they were also known for their excellent relations with the Native tribes of Eastern Pennsylvania. Nonetheless, Cooper's hero emerges full-grown from the pages of *The Deerslayer* with little further history. He was the lifelong friend of Chingachgook, a chief and son of a chief of the near defunct Mohicans, and his son Uncas. In Cooper's universe the two races, Native and white, do not understand each other's ways, even though they make many alliances with each other according to what they believe is in their best interest. In the course of the series, Natty Bumppo allies himself with various European pioneers, Anglo-American settlers, and military types as well as with his Mohican brothers.

Deerslayer unremarkable at first glance, only slowly shows his quality to those who consider him carefully; his appearance and his reality are at odds. "His face," wrote Cooper, "had little to recommend it except youth." Richard Morton of McMaster University notes: "Read in the biographical order, the Leatherstocking tales are seen to fall into the broad, quintessential American genre of the pilgrimage – the life-long quest, in effect the Puritan conversion narrative. The five novels tell the story of Deerslayer's conversion from a callow youth into the wise, pious old hunter of *The Prairie* – from the traumatic excitement of the Glimmerglass, through the reverses of *The Pathfinder* and the self-hatred of *The Pioneers*, to the apotheosis, the mythical transfiguration in the West." The young Bumppo might be seen as the embodiment of a nascent American republic, founded on innate strength and moral character but unsure of its way forward. [97]

Although the young Washington, the trail breaking Daniel Boone, and the deadly rifleman Tim Murphy have been posited as the basis for the character, Cooper did not base his creation of Natty Bumppo on a single person known to him, apparently drawing upon various individuals recalled from his youth in Cooperstown. One of these was Nathaniel Shipman who served as a scout and guide in the last two French and Indian wars. Judge Cooper, James Fenimore's father, had spoken about an aged white man, who in company with a Mohican Indian lived in a hut or cave near Otsego Lake. Judge Cooper constantly referred to the eccentric habits of the old hunter, and made his quaint sayings the subject of his daily conversations with his friends and acquaintances. It is evident from James Fenimore Cooper's "Chronicles of Cooperstown" published in 1838 that he had some person named Shipman in mind when he created the character of Leatherstocking, as he writes therein of "Shipman the Leatherstocking of the region." In the final analysis and in the absence of any definitive declaration by the author, the reader must depend largely if not entirely upon circumstances to guide them in this matter.[98]

Natty Bumppo is about as strange and unromantic a name as can be found for a hero. Nathaniel for "Natty," the surname Bumppo often evokes the "bump on a log" image for readers when first encountered. In fact, the name can be off-putting. There is no evidence that Cooper suffered any later discomfort with the name or why he chose it. Before his appearance in *The Deerslayer*, Bumppo went by the aliases of "Straight-Tongue," "The

Pigeon," and the "Lap-Ear." The character himself notes that "a name, implying knowledge, understanding and hence control, is a disturbing sign of human power." Like Dickens, Scott, and others among his contemporaries, Cooper provided each of his stories with a large number of auxiliary characters, averaging more than forty per novel. Many of these characters have one or more aliases, nicknames, or sobriquets. Chingachgook, for instance, is called both the Great Serpent and Indian John in various circumstances.[99]

However, in the preface to an 1876 edition of her father's works, Susan Fenimore Cooper felt compelled to explain how Bumppo changed his name: "After joining a hunting-party of the Delawares, among the mountains which overhang the Susquehanna, he returned laden with choice venison, and at a great feast solemnly received the name of the Deerslayer, in a speech by the father of Chingachgook." Among the native tribes, the giving of a name ended the period of early infancy. A new name was given when the child reached a new stage in life, as in attaining adolescence. The important activities of the culture were centered around the male. The boys were generally given names of the most powerful beings, while the girls were given protective names. These were often the names of long dead relations. Hence, the father of Chingachgook was Uncas, and the son of Chingachgook was also Uncas. Cooper got these names from John Heckewelder's book *History, Manners, and Customs of the Indian Nations who once inhabited Pennsylvania and the Neighboring States* (1818), which cited a Lenape word as "*chingachgook*" meaning "a large snake." Chingachgook is also known as "*le gros serpent*" in French. Cooper borrowed the name Uncas from the son of the Mohegan sachem *Owaneco* who was a 17th century leader among the Pequot of New England. The name was not common among the Mohicans.

Yet like his name, Bumppo's character brings out the notion that little is as it appears. A new name may provide a new kind of truth. Bumppo, the natural man unencumbered with the pains and pettiness of civilization, has a number of more romantic titles and descriptive nicknames in the books: the Deerslayer, the Pathfinder, Hawkeye, and "Leatherstocking," the last being his name among the English settlers. He is also called "La Longue Carabine" (the long rifle), and "Le Cerf Agile," (the agile deer) in French in the novels. So entrenched in American culture are some of these names that they have been adopted for use by business, the military, television, and geographers.

Though Natty's experiences and actions comprise the core of Cooper's five-part narrative, details concerning his origin are speculative and the genesis of his obvious symbolism is noticeably lacking. Throughout the series, Cooper's hero is associated with the vanishing wilderness as an idealized figure, without wife or child, and hauntingly loyal to a doomed way of life. Cooper, having grown up as a child of the frontier on Otsego Lake (the Glimmerglass that he thought the head waters of the Susquehanna), may have been channeling his own deep-seated frustrations with urbanization and the infant deaths of his daughter Elizabeth in 1813 and his son Fenimore in 1821. Although he had five adult daughters, his only surviving son Paul would not be born until 1824.

In his *Studies in Classic American Literature* (London, 1923), D.H. Lawrence noted that many of Cooper's other characters, described as heroes, are "always being so tightly pinned down by social restrictions as to be deprived of liberty. On the other hand, the hero of the Leatherstocking series was always free."[100] Deerslayer may be free, but he cannot be happy living away from the woods. He is liberated, but not a libertarian or a libertine. He is an outsider to the civilized world always looking for and feeling something sacred in the border regions and early settlements that he shares with his constant companions. *The Pathfinder* is the only book in the series to show Natty Bumppo in love, and the first of Cooper's books that made important imaginative use of the Great Lakes.[101]

Natty Bumppo (a.k.a. Hawkeye) and Chingachgook as depicted in
The Last of the Mohicans **by illustrator F.O.C. Darley.**

VIII. Cooper, the Moralist

Fictional characters possessed a remarkable ability to influence nineteenth-century readers. Uncle Tom, Topsy, Ivanhoe, Hawkeye, Hester Prynne, and Ebenezer Scrooge were deeply familiar characters to a society that read as much as nineteenth-century Americans did. These characters often seemed to become nearly as real and as influential to the reader as actual friends and relations. Authors, therefore, had to take great care to properly portray their characters: heroes as moral, villains as immoral, and subsidiary characters as ambiguous, confused, or deluded.

Cooper's narrative strategy is typical of antebellum novels written specifically to instruct young men. Those who make good and moral decisions become the heroes; those who make bad decisions have evil things happen to them, or to others because of them. Cooper always attempted to show his readers why they should want to imitate the hero. David Gamut of the *Last of the Mohicans* was the master of psalmody. His words, in his own language, "seem pregnant with some hidden meaning, though nothing present assisted him in discovering the object of their allusion. ... Hither the faithful singing-master had now brought himself, together with all his sorrows, his apprehensions, and his meek dependence on the protection of Providence. ... However implicit the faith of David was in the performance of ancient miracles, he eschewed the belief of any direct supernatural agency in the management of modern morality. In other words, while he had implicit faith in the ability of Balaam's ass to speak, he was somewhat skeptical ... in his air and manner that betrayed ... the utter confusion of the state of his mind."[102]

Cooper's adoption of the "Scottish Common Sense" philosophy facilitated his abandonment, in the later novels, of political for familial and religious solutions to national moral dilemmas. Scottish Common Sense philosophy was influential and evident in the works of Thomas Jefferson and turn of the century American politics. Cooper worked quickly towards these positions in his first few novels but wavered in his commitment to them as the decades advanced. Cooper summed up his complaints about the behavior of his countrymen, their provincialism and their lack of independence, in his satire *Home as Found*. When he imagines the possibility of a moral individual becoming a leader, the author hopes those around him can bypass the limitations of mere institutions and still function as a moral society. Cooper was not unique in emphasizing this moral facet of authorship, but he often did not receive credit for his efforts in this regard. In order to better understand the dilemma that faced Cooper, it is important to have some knowledge of the extremes, some might say the excesses, to which authors of the period had arrived.[103]

Scott once defined the romance as a narrative concerning "marvelous and uncommon incidents," whereas the novel accommodated "the ordinary train of human events and the modern state of society." Under these protocols many romances could be class as novels, and vice-versa. Cooper was obviously in the latter category. His *Leatherstocking Tales* are largely devoid of supernatural elements. His villains are driven by human impulses; his situations by genuine events; and many of his dangers are natural ones: storms, rapids, waterfalls, and, of course, other humans. Given these differences, what happened in the 19th century could best be described, not as the rise of the novel, but the rise of realism in fiction. In this regard Mark Twain noted in *Life on the Mississippi* (1883): "A curious exemplification of the power of a single book for good or harm is shown in the effects wrought by 'Don Quixote' and those wrought by 'Ivanhoe.' The first swept the world's admiration for the medieval chivalry-silliness out of existence; and the other restored it. … The good work done by Cervantes is pretty nearly a dead letter, so effectually has Scott's pernicious work undermined it."[104]

The authors of this new type of fiction were often accused of exploiting the medium to thrill, arouse, or horrify their audiences. Mark Twain continued:

> Sir Walter Scott with his enchantments, and by his single might checks this wave of progress, and even turns it back; sets the world in love with dreams and phantoms; with decayed and swinish forms of religion; with decayed and degraded systems of government; with the sillinesses and emptinesses, sham grandeurs, sham gauds, and sham chivalries of a brainless and worthless long-vanished society. He did measureless harm; more real and lasting harm, perhaps, than any other individual that ever wrote. … Scott is probably responsible for the Capitol building; for it is not conceivable that this little sham castle would ever have been built if he had not run the people mad, a couple of generations ago, with his medieval romances. The South has not yet recovered from the debilitating influence of his books.[105]

Jane Austen and Percy Shelley are generally accepted as having set the opposing moral limits for the English novels of the first decade of the 19th century. Austen's *Northanger Abbey*, the first of many novels concerning "proper manners" was completed in 1803 but not released for many years (1818). She had previously made a start with *Sense and Sensibility* (1811) and *Pride and Prejudice* (1813), and considered *Northanger Abbey* a satire on the popular Gothic novel. Austen had no public reputation as a writer during her short lifetime, as all her novels were published anonymously. Her realism and social commentary as well as her acclaimed plots gained her historical importance among scholars and critics as the "softer side" of contemporary literature.

Austen turned the conventions of the eighteenth-century novel on their heads by making her heroine in *Northanger Abbey* a plain girl from a middle-class family, by allowing her heroine to fall in love with the hero before he has given a serious thought to her, and by exposing the heroine's romantic fears and supernatural curiosities as groundless. The heroine of Austen's work, named Catherine, is inspired to visit an estate, Northanger Abbey, and from her reading of Ann Radcliffe's Gothic novel *The Mysteries of Udolpho*, Catherine expects the place to be dark, ancient, and full of Gothic horrors and fantastical mystery. Austen explained her use of another author's work within her own, "If the heroine of one novel be not patronized by the heroine of another, from whom can she expect protection and regard?" It turns out that Northanger Abbey is pleasant and decidedly not the Gothic of horror mongering authors. Realizing how foolish she has been, Catherine comes to believe that, though novels may be delightful, their content does not relate to everyday life.[106]

In contrast to other novels by Austen, the heroine of *Emma* (1815) seems immune to romantic attraction. This was a great departure from Austen's other works, in which the quest for marriage and financial security for the heroine were often important themes in the stories. Early reviews of *Emma* were generally favourable, but there was some criticism about the lack of structure. Maria Edgeworth, a prolific writer from Ireland, thought it "thin as water." Nonetheless, Austen showed therein that the possibilities of the novel were practically unlimited. The tragedy and horror of contrived situations were not needed, and the most ordinary of transactions, the most everyday of characters, could be developed into an infinite series of interactions with which novelists could amuse themselves and their readers.[107]

The Gothic genre had originated in England in the second half of the 18th century and had much success in the 19th. *The Castle of Otranto* (1764) by Horace Walpole is generally regarded as the first Gothic novel, initiating a literary genre that arguably gave an impetus to many other authors. Among these was Shelley's *Zastrozzi*, a Gothic novel that was published in 1810. While Walpole sought to restore the qualities of imagination and invention to contemporary fiction, Shelley's work contrasted negatively with the finery and deportment of Austen. *Zastrozzi* was described as "a short, but well-told tale of horror," a fiction that fed on terror. An 1810 reviewer wrote that the main character "Zastrozzi is one of the most savage and improbable demons that ever issued from a diseased brain. ... We know not when we have felt so much indignation as in the perusal of this execrable production. The author of it cannot be too severely reprobated. [Nothing] ... ought to save him from infamy, and his volume from the flames."[108]

The reception visited upon Shelley's work was affected by the author's unconventional lifestyle and uncompromising atheism, which made him a much-denigrated figure during his lifetime. He was ultimately displaced as an author of gothic horror by his young wife Mary Wollstonecraft Shelley and her *Frankenstien* (1818). Many readers could not accept that a young woman could write such a shockingly repellent tale. Shelley had abandoned his pregnant wife, Harriet, to run away with Mary, who was just 16 at the time. Mary also was pregnant when the couple married in late 1816 after the suicide of Percy Shelley's first wife. The body of Shelley's estranged wife Harriet had been found in an advanced state of pregnancy, drowned in the Serpentine in Hyde Park, London just three weeks before his marriage to Mary. The better classes of society were appalled at such goings-on.

The spectacular evolution of the British novel briefly faltered under the extremes of reactionary criticism, especially with the early death of Austen in 1817, only to be revitalized by social reform novelists such as Edward Bulwer-Lytton and Charles Dickens. Specific examples of the social problems that were addressed in such works, include poverty, conditions in factories and mines, the plight of child labor, violence against women, rising criminality, and epidemics because of over-crowding, and poor sanitation in cities. Yet the two men were critically different.

In 1832, Dickens worked as a political journalist, reporting on the Parliamentary debates in the House of Commons, and he traveled across Britain to cover election campaigns for the *Morning Chronicle*. His journalism, in the form of sketches in periodicals, formed his first collection of pieces published in 1836 as *Sketches by Boz*. Dickens' literary success began with the 1836 serialization of *The Pickwick Papers*. Within a few years he had become an international literary celebrity, famous for his humor, satire, and keen observation of character and society. Dickens once styled himself "The Fielding of the 19th Century," and he was able to reach through the cheap serialization of his novels a massive audience far beyond that which avidly read Bulwer-Lytton's metaphysical thrillers. Masses among the illiterate poor pooled their pennies to have each new monthly episode read to them, opening up and inspiring a new class of admirers. Dickens' second novel, *Oliver Twist* (1839), shocked readers with its images of poverty and crime. He made rapid progress both professionally and socially. He began a friendship with William Ainsworth, the author of the highwayman novel *Rookwood*

(1834), whose bachelor flat in Harrow Road had become the meeting place for a set of writers that included Bulwer-Lytton.

Dickens made a much-touted visit to America in 1842. He found Americans omnivorous readers of newspapers, novels, and literary magazines. Feted at fancy dress balls and formal dinners, Dickens toured American prisons, hospitals, mental institutions, orphanages, and the model textile mills that had recently opened in Lowell, Massachusetts. Crowds of admirers everywhere greeted him, but he found much of America disappointing in its lack of social progress. Dickens was aghast at many of the conditions he found in America: hideous tenements, loathsome prisons, and squalid taverns – a foul growth upon America's utilitarian society. He was particularly critical of the American press and the sanitary conditions of American cities. He wrote merciless parodies of American manners including several focused on the informality of rural conversations and the practice of spitting in public. He expressed a strong aversion for American politicians. Dickens also toured the West, or what was then considered the West. He disliked Cleveland, Ohio and reported that the Indians, who were so highly esteemed by the authors of romantic literature (i.e. Cooper), were actually wretched creatures. Moreover, he could not forgive the continued existence of slavery, and the final chapters of his *American Notes* were devoted to a criticism of the practice.

In the same vane, British author Rudyard Kipling wrote of "newspaper wars waged in godless Chicago" and described the city tenements there when he visited. Over 10 percent of the total population counted in the 1850 US Census resided in multifamily dwellings that were counted as single units in the sample. This high frequency of group living, when compared to the eighteenth century, demonstrates the increased use of tenements, boarding houses, hotels, and other large institutional domiciles in urban areas with which American society was simply not ready to deal. "I went out into the streets, which are long and flat and without end," wrote Kipling. "I looked down interminable vistas flanked with nine, ten, fifteen-storied houses, and crowded with men and women, and the show impressed me with great horror. Except in London ... I had never seen so many white people together, and never such a collection of miserables ... to huddle men together in fifteen layers, one atop of the other. ... Having seen it, I urgently desire never to see it again. ... They told me to go to the Palmer House, which is overmuch gilded and mirrored, and there I found a huge hall of tessellated marble crammed with people talking about money, and spitting about everywhere. Other barbarians charged in and out of this inferno with letters and telegrams in their hands, and yet others shouted at each other. ... The cabman said that these things were the proof of progress, and by that I knew he had been reading his newspaper, as every intelligent American should. The papers tell their clientele in language fitted to their comprehension that the snarling together of telegraph-wires, the heaving up of houses, and the making of money is progress. ... The thing you call your newspaper ought to have been sacked by the mob, and the managing proprietor hanged."[109]

In 1820, Bulwer-Lytton received acknowledgement as an author from Sir Walter Scott. This praise was a great catalyst to his career. Between 1827 and 1835, with his household expenditures amounting to approximately £3000 per year due to the extravagant lifestyle of his wife, Bulwer-Lytton became a prolific writer. During these years, he wrote thirteen novels, two long poems, four plays, a social history of England, a three-volume history of Athens, and other tales.

In 1828, Bulwer-Lytton's *Pelham* brought him public acclaim and established his reputation as a wit and dandy. It also demonstrated the power of the novel to affect society. A so-called "Silver Fork" novel of manners and fashionable life, herein the hero's mother, Lady Frances, helps to set a new fashion in men's evening wear, for in the novel she favors Black as opposed to the then-popular Blue. The book changed men's fashion as the upper classes quickly adopted the habit of using only black evening wear. Conversely, the range of fabrics and colors widened for women, but lighter colors were considered most suitable for young ladies. In a similar manner, Bulwer-Lytton's works were copiously illustrated with male characters in frock coats and full-length trousers.

Prince Albert, consort to Queen Victoria, is usually credited with popularizing both trousers and the frock coat. Admiration for the Prince among the educated middle-classes was expressed in a fascination with all things German. Albert was viewed as young and dynamic, and so was the culture of his home country. During the Victorian era, the frock coat rapidly became universally worn in Britain, Europe, and America as standard formal business dress, or for formal daytime events. It was also said with lesser authority that Albert, when dancing with ladies of the court, wearing the fashionable tight trousers of the day, would occasionally be embarrassed by the apparent rising of his private parts, which report may have added to the popularity of trousers. The trousers were cut with a straight leg and high waist, a plain finished hem and no pressed crease.

Bulwer-Lytton's historically based psychological crime thriller *Eugene Aram* (1832) raised a storm of protest because he made a murderer (a self-educated scholar) his hero. This seemingly violated the unwritten authors' obligation to pose a moral solution to their novels. Yet Bulwer-Lytton reached the height of his popularity with the publication of *Godolphin* (1833), a satirical insight into the day-to-day lives of the early 19th century British elite, his first book to embody an occult theme. He thought the supernatural indispensable to the success of the romantic novel. This work was followed by a series of novels with historic settings: *The Last Days of Pompeii* (1834), *Rienzi, Last of the Roman Tribunes* (1835), and *Harold, the Last of the Saxons* (1848).

Under the influence of Dickens, Bulwer-Lytton became very much involved in serial publications during the second half of his writing career. Of his eight novels produced between 1848 and 1874, six were published serially. In 1861, Bulwer-Lytton had composed the novel *A Strange Story* from a dream, and made arrangements with Dickens for the anonymous publication of the piece. They agreed upon £1500 (pounds) for the initial British serial rights, £300 for the American serial rights, and £1200 for the book publication. In addition to his writing, Bulwer-Lytton had a successful political career, serving twice in Parliament.

German composer Richard Wagner wrote the opera *Rienzi, Last of the Roman Tribunes* in five acts, with the libretto written by the composer after Bulwer-Lytton's novel of the same name. The title is commonly shortened to *Rienzi*. Written between 1838 and 1840, it was first performed in 1842, and was the composer's first success. General Phil Sheridan also had a horse that he named Rienzi. The horse was ridden by him in nearly every engagement in which he participated during the Civil War, including the important occasion of his ride from Winchester to Cedar Creek, Virginia, 19 October 1864, immortalized by Thomas Buchanan Read in his poem entitled, "Sheridan's Ride." Both the book and opera are based on the real life of Cola di Rienzi (1313–1354), a populist leader who attempted to unify Italy. These factoids give weight to the idea that historic themes were gaining popularity in the first half of the century. There are many stanzas, but the last honors the most honorable of all horses, Rienzi, who is now stuffed and on view at the Smithsonian Museum of Natural History.

> *Be it said, in letters both bold and bright:*
> *Here is the steed that saved the day*
> *By carrying Sheridan into the fight,*
> *From Winchester--twenty miles away!*

Ruined by reading

So great was the popularity of the novel that it drew criticism as a literary form. The Reverend Joel Hawes, a 19th century moralist, advised young men to avoid novels, suggesting that a young person's character could be "ruined by reading a single ill-advised volume." This, of course, was blatant hyperbole, but Hawes confessed that one book, "wisely selected and properly studied" could "do more to improve the mind, and enrich the understanding, than skimming over the surface of an entire library." [110]

A guide to propriety for mothers written by Lydia Child also decried "the profligate and strongly exciting works" found in the public libraries. "The necessity of fierce excitement in reading is a sort of intellectual intemperance" producing, in the estimation of the guide's author, "weakness and delirium" in women and young girls. Novels and romantic works were all identified as having "an unhealthy influence upon the soul" that should be avoided. [111]

In sharp contrast to librarians today, who generally rail against any form of censorship, library associations in the 19th century commonly regarded censorship as an obligation. As late as 1856, the Code of Public Instruction for the State of New York recognized the "necessity" of excluding from all libraries "novels, romances and other fictitious creations of the imagination, including a large proportion of the lighter literature of the day." The code also expressed an "obvious" disgust for works dealing with "pirates, banditti and desperadoes of every description." Unfortunately, for those who wished to ban the novel as a literary form, these were the very characteristics that made novels and novelists popular. [112]

Of these, the most familiar name is probably that of Lord Byron, who with Shakespeare, Scott, and Dickens, was among the most famous of British authors known to those outside of Britain. Few Americans read Byron today, but he typified the Romantic Movement in literature at the time; and politically, he was a "genuine and burning liberal." His advanced political views and notorious sensuality made him suspect. A historical verse-romance like *Mazeppa* was a transitional work in Byron's overall folio of output, and it might serve as an example. Its date of composition (1818) place it between the earlier tales such as *The Prisoner of Chillon* (1817), which chronicles the imprisonment of a monk and a martyr to the cause of liberty, and Byron's later satirical *Don Juan* (1821), which showcased the fictional libertine, rake, and womanizer as a hero. [113]

Byron's poem *Mazeppa* was also historical in nature as it opened with a scene of the protagonist Mazeppa and the Swedish King Charles XII, together with their armies, retreating from the Battle of Poltava (1709), where they were defeated by the Russians — which circumstance was quite true. The punishment of the hero for a sexual transgression — being tied naked to a wild horse set loose upon the steppes — was highly fantastic.

Yet the colorful legend circulated many decades before Byron addressed it. There are historical sources, moreover, which verify that a Ukrainian, Ivan Mazeppa served in the Polish Court seeking to create an uprising in Ukraine against the tsar. Currier and Ives published an illustrated edition of the poem in 1846, and Francis Parkman referenced it in his memoir *The Oregon Trail* in 1849.

Byron's scoundrel hero, Mazeppa (1846) LOC

Edna Kenton is known best for her work editing the *Jesuit Relations and Allied Documents*, but she also wrote a history of her famous frontiersman ancestor Simon Kenton (1930). Herein she recorded a circumstance quite similar to that reported in Byron's poem *Mazeppa*. Except for her sterling academic credentials, the story that she reports seems imaginative and implausible at best. Yet it is reported as fact in many histories of the frontier. Captured by the Shawnee Indians in 1778:

They got him [Simon Kenton] astraddle the horse, facing backwards. They bound his ankles beneath the belly of the black and then placed a loop over Simon's head and drew it snug around his neck. The other end of this line was tied around the horse's neck. The Shawnees mounted their own horses and led the black into a small clear area and here Bo-nah jerked away the blanket blinding the animal and whipped it smartly on the rump. Instantly the horse screamed in panic and began to buck and spin, doing all it could to dislodge its rider. It smashed against trees, scraping the hide off Simon's legs, and galloped under low branches, which slammed into his back or head with numbing blows. It tore through areas thick with brush and thorns and his body was raked and grooved in a hundred places while the Shawnees shouted and laughed. But somehow the frontiersman stayed on. If he were thrown off he would surely be strangled or his neck broken, and so he locked his legs as tightly as he could around the animal and managed to catch some of the mane hair in his bound hands behind him. He leaned forward and bowed his head as low as the throat halter would allow and closed his eyes tightly so that he would not be blinded. There he clung for what seemed an eternity, while the world turned into a swirling, slashing, pounding hell. Finally, utterly exhausted, the wild black stood spraddle-legged, its head low and its sides heaving.[114]

Camden Pelham wrote *The Chronicles of Crime* (1841), a series of memoirs and anecdotes about British criminals "from the earliest period." H. K. Browne, who went by the pseudonym "Phiz," the famous artist who illustrated Dickens' works, illustrated these also. A review of Pelham's work in *The American Journal of Psychology* noted: "The author thinks that the representation of guilt with its painful consequences is one of the best means of warning the young against the danger of temptation. To carry out this purpose, care has been taken to omit matter unfit for general reading. ... The benefit of reading details of this nature seems doubtful in the case of the young. The less the young read about or witness of cruelty, the better."[115]

The historically set novels of Irish American author Edward Maturin were particularly steeped in the romantic. His first book contained the interconnected stories of *Sejanus and Other Roman Tales* (1839) and was dedicated to Washington Irving. They included *Montezuma, the Last of the Aztecs* (1845), a brilliant, if overly impassioned, history; *Benjamin, the Jew of Granada* (1847), set in fifteenth-century Moslem Spain; and *Eva, or the Isles of Life and Death* (1848), a romance of twelfth-century England. One of his more fiery books was *Bianca* (1852), a story of a passionate love between a woman from Italy and a man from Ireland.[116]

If Horace Walpole was the father of the Gothic novel, then Ann Radcliffe was certainly its mother. The publication of her novel *A Sicilian Romance* in 1790 marks the real beginning of the full-fledged Gothic novel. Very few Gothic novels were published before then, but a flood of them appeared afterwards. Sir Walter Scott in 1824 recalled that when *A Sicilian Romance* appeared, it attracted an extraordinary degree of the attention of the public, and it was on the basis of its poetic imagery and scenery that Scott awarded Radcliffe the title of the first poetess of romantic fiction.

Ann Radcliffe's novels, many written in the late 1790s, were primarily "time-fillers for literarily inclined young women who had no children and did not care for society." Although she died in 1823, Radcliffe was the main source of "horror stories with a twist" for readers throughout the 19th century. The significance of her "horror-mongering" on later romantic literature cannot be overestimated. Her last novel, released in 1826, was *Gaston de Blondeville*. Actually written in 1802, this work preceded Sir Walter Scott's first historical novels and attempted for the first time to paint an authentic historical picture.[117]

Almost totally forgotten today, Matthew G. Lewis was a follower of Radcliffe whose writings "ran heavily to the florid romantic." He often disclosed the details of gruesome scenes, earning him the title of a horror-gothic novelist. His first novel, *Ambrosio, the Monk*, was universally read and widely condemned in Britain and America. Lewis was charged with being immoral and irreligious when it was discovered that he was recommending that certain passages from the Bible be kept from the young. His work was considered "vicious" and "terrible." Often referred to as the "immoral monk Lewis," he produced two romantic novels—*The Bravo of Venice* and *Feudal Tyrants*—as well as

Tales of Terror and *Romantic Tales*, which were based on German and Spanish legends; and in collaboration with Walter Scott, a collection of ballads, *Tales of Wonder*. His work is generally neglected today, but he had tremendous influence on the writers of his day.[118]

It is well known that Cooper exhibited a Deist form of morality and not the atheism of other authors among his contemporaries. The child of fallen away Quakers, he refused formal church membership in the Episcopalian sect until his own death was clearly imminent, and even then, he did so as a concession to the feelings of his wife and daughters. Church membership was a status taken quite seriously in the 19th century, yet only one person in 15 claimed official church membership at the time. In his time, any disdain of organized religion or Christianity was misrepresented as disrespectful, or even as a denial of the existence of God. He candidly doubted the claims of some among his contemporaries to know just what God had in mind on any given point, and in 1831, he wrote that any God who was so knowable as to be grasped by the mind of just any believer was "not elevated one whit above the level of humanity." He disparaged the rising Evangelical movement of his day as a "parade of morals" made as a show by humans to gain ascendancy over the lives of other humans. Cooper wrote: "I've heard it said that there are men who read in books to convince themselves there is a God ... but never could raise within me the solemn feelings and true affection that I feel when alone with God in the forest."[119]

Nonetheless, the frontier novels of Cooper avoided many of the possible moral pitfalls that entangled other authors, and they also helped to establish a picture of colonial settlement and Anglo-Native religious relationships for most students of the period. In *The Prairie* (1827), Cooper had satirized the frailty of conversion, especially in the attempt to bring Duncan Uncas Middleton to "the truth faith," that is to turn him from a Protestant into a Catholic. One of his most deeply spiritual books, *The Crater* (1847), is also one in which he takes aim at what he elsewhere called "religion by sects." The wild noise of the various Evangelical sects out stumping for God in the region surrounding the route of the Erie Canal also struck Cooper as *prima facie* evidence of social and spiritual conceit. "What Cooper lacked, then, was not a spiritual sense but any patience with self-proclaimed insiders on God's privy council," noted Barbara Mann of the University of Toledo. "It was dogma and institutionalized religion he loathed, seeing both as cynical power-grabs. Thus, however prissy critics like Francis Parkman might have caviled, disparaging him as crude and lewd, Cooper was exquisitely sensitive to the spiritual impetus."[120]

In *Savagism and Civilization* (1953), one of the earliest explorations of the ideological representation of Native Americans in Western thought and in American literature, Roy Pearce stated, "Cooper was interested in the Indian not for his own sake but for the sake of his relationship to the civilized men who were destroying him." The leatherstocking frontier was what Cooper called the "forlorn hope" in the march of civilization through the country:

> Histories of combats with beasts of prey, and of massacres by roving and lawless Indians, were the moving legends of the border. Thrones might be subverted, and kingdoms lost and won, in distant Europe, and less should be said of the events, by those who dwelt in these woods, than of one scene of peculiar and striking forest incident that called for the exercise of the stout courage and the keen intelligence of a settler.[121]

According to Emanuel Spenser, a historian writing in 1890, a chapter of romantic interest might chronicle the adventures and disappointments of any family who journeyed across the Atlantic to find a place where every man might become a great land-owner – a virtual paradise, with "climate healthy and delightful, scarcely such a thing as frost in winter, magnificent forests of a tree from which sugar flows, and a shrub which yields candles; venison in abundance, without foxes, wolves, lions, or tigers; the openings in the forest made passable for pack-horses, the discovery of salt springs, and the boiling down of the water to make salt; no taxes to pay; no military enrollments; no quarters to find for soldiers; a river abounding in fish of enormous size; and the land only five shillings per acre!" Log cabins were erected with comparative ease, and "dainty hands were not slow to give them touches of color." An honest title deed to any given number of acres of rich land was a powerful incentive to its clearing and cultivation, which few ambitious young men could resist. The families who planted their crude homes in this new country represented "its best blood, its industry, and its thrift, together with the heroism of all the ages." Yet Cooper emphasized manners and scenes in most of his novels characteristic of Americans and an America that generally did not exist when the Anglo-colonial frontier was actually being settled. [122]

Transition

A well-defined technique for novel writing was to combine fiction and history in such circumstances that ordinary individuals were placed into situations of historical stress. The author then worked his characters around and beyond a known historical outcome like the British defeat on the Monongahela in 1755. Thereby the reader was educated concerning virtuous behaviors and the historical causes and conditions of individual actions and reactions. It was inevitable that the Indian, who played such a pivotal role in the colonial period, make an appearance in popular literature. Native Americans had made literary appearances previously, especially in the late 18th century.

In 1793, Indians were the central figures in a curious tale done in the manner of a captivity narrative written in the form of a letter to Miss Susan Ten Eyck, *The History of Maria Kittle* by author Anna Eliza Bleeker. The period selected, as was commonly the case, was the French and Indian War. In Bleeker's tale, bloodthirsty savages butcher an entire frontier family save one woman, who is spared by an old Indian whom she had previously befriended, and who cares for her as she is carried off to Canada. This novel, which is insignificant as literature, took the popular Indian captivity story in a new direction, and it was possibly the first American fictional account focusing on Native Americans.

Charles B. Brown an American novelist, historian, and newspaper editor of the Early National Period is generally regarded as the most important American novelist before James Fenimore Cooper. Although Brown was not the first American novelist, the breadth and complexity of his work as a writer makes him a significant figure of the 1790s and first decade of the 19th century. He deliberately included American scenes and Native Americans in his stories. This was especially true of *Edgar Huntly, Or, Memoirs of a Sleepwalker* (1799). Indians have killed the immediate family of the title character when he was younger, and he currently lives with his uncle and two sisters on a farm outside of Philadelphia formerly the domain of the Delaware who have been driven away by the encroaching whites.

Edgar Huntley, an undiagnosed sleepwalker, is betrothed to Mary Waldegrave. The psychological addition of sleepwalking adds to the gothic nature of the story. The plot begins with an attempt to find the murderer of his friend and future brother-in-law, moves to the primeval forests of Pennsylvania, and ends in a darkened cavern. At the end of the novel the reader learns that it was an Indian that committed the murder. A Lenni Lenape has murdered Waldegrave, perhaps one that Huntly himself has killed in the course of the story, and he no longer has troubles with sleepwalking.

Brown's novels are often characterized simply as *gothic fiction*, because he modeled his work on the Gothic romances of writers such as Ann Radcliffe. Brown creates the Gothic feel in his historic fiction in order to create suspense. He does this through the use of scenery and setting, mysterious characters, hidden caverns, and so forth. Against a background of Indian depredations, there are travels through impenetrable forests, valleys, and crevices, attacks by "panthers," and a confrontation with a vengeful old Indian queen. Each of these was though to be typical of the American wilderness and far removed from the Old World of Europe.

Brown introduces the "Old Hag Deb" as the antagonist queen. It is she who is actually responsible for ordering all the murders. She has succeeded to the possession of the region and its governance has fallen to her under Indian law. Her abode is a hut guarded by three vicious dogs, and she demands the necessities of life from her neighbors as her due. The outbreak of atrocities seems to have been brought about by white refusal to recognize her authority. Nothing could be clearer than Brown's identification with Huntly's attitudes toward Indians. Brown reinforces the colonial concept of the Indian as a murderous savage whose every action, if not closely circumscribed, leads to inevitable tragedy. The Indian inspires amazement and wonder in the reader that is not without a romantic aspect and a sense of terror.[123]

Such as circumstance was not without a foundation in history. It is certain that among the Shawnee there were female chiefs, both for war and for peace. These were almost always related to the principle chiefs of the band or village, usually either their mother or sister. The female chiefs, or clan mothers, had the general responsibility of superintending the female affairs of the village. These duties of office were usually slight, but the office of *peace woman* was employed to prevent the unnecessary effusion of blood. Through this method, the women of the village might make entreaties to the war chief if the wider community did not countenance some military undertaking. The peace woman would go to the war chief and, sitting before him, would set forth the cares and anxieties felt by the women of the tribe. This usually took the form of appeals that he spare the innocent and unoffending against whom his hand was raised.

Among the Algonquian peoples of Pennsylvania was a woman known as Madame Montour. Born in Canada about 1667, her father was a French trader named Pierre Couc. In 1709, she became an interpreter for Governor Robert Hunter in New York where she met and married an Oneida chief. Her husband was killed in 1729 during a raid against another tribe in the Southeast. Madame Montour lived near Shamokin with her niece French Margaret and her son, Andrew (André). This clan mother was described as a distinguished woman with an engaging personality. Her son, known as Andrew Montour, performed a number of diplomatic errands for both the Pennsylvania and New York colonies, and he held a commission in Virginia as one of William Johnson's native captains. A Seneca warrior killed him in 1772.

Queen Esther was reported to be the daughter of French Margaret, along with her sisters Mary (Molly) and Catherine (Kate), each of whom were influential in her own right. Esther lived in a settlement near Tioga Point known as Queen Esther's Town. Of course, the designation as queen in reference to this clan mother was merely a British sobriquet. History assigns Esther the dark role of executioner of white women and children taken during the Wyoming Valley raid of the Revolutionary War.

The older sister of Joseph Brant, Mary (Molly) Brant was one of the most influential Native American women during the 18th century. Known in Iroquoian as Konwatsitsiaienni, Molly Brant married Sir William Johnson, by Mohawk rites, some time during the 1760s. As the sister of a Mohawk leader and the wife of a powerful and influential British trader, agent, and Baronet, she enjoyed a higher status than most Indian matrons. Even after the death of Sir William in 1774, Molly wielded immense power and authority within the traditional matriarchal structure of Iroquois government as a diplomat and stateswoman at the head of a society of Six Nations matrons. Whenever Iroquois loyalty to the Crown wavered, she was able to convince most of the Confederacy, and the Mohawks in particular, to continue their support of the British. Molly Brant has been described as a woman of high intelligence and remarkable ability who was at ease in two cultures. She personified the dignity and influence accorded to respected matrons among the Iroquois people.

A period drawing of Algonquian women and their typical cool weather dress made from tanned animal hides. Note the knee-high footwear (or leggings), the decorations and fringe, and the cradleboard on the woman's back on the right.

IX. The Background of Wilderness Warfare

Fiction as History

James Fenimore Cooper was a novelist, a writer of fiction. But his themes were founded on a genuine history, and his writing was so compelling as to take on the vale of history itself. Many of his characters, especially in *The Last of the Mohicans*, were based on real people, but for many readers his fictional characters have taken on the mantle of reality. This was partly because Cooper so expertly wove his fictional characters into genuine circumstances. This chapter deals briefly with the genuine history of wilderness warfare in the period about which he wrote in order to provide context to Cooper's novels.

Fort William Henry was on the southernmost shore of Lake George. It was the site of two important campaigns in the French and Indian War. Sir William Johnson erected it in 1755 after a signal colonial victory over the French regulars under Baron Dieskau, and Cooper immortalized its destruction less than two years later by the Marquis de Montcalm in 1757 in *The Last of the Mohicans*. Other than Fort Carillon at Ticonderoga, William Henry was possibly the most strategic, yet shortest-lived of the military posts on the New York frontier. This single location on the shores of Lake George was to be among the most dramatic scenes in Cooper's novels.

The French and Indian War in America (1754–1763) began with a skirmish in the Ohio country—actually western Pennsylvania—between French colonial troops and Virginia provincial troops commanded by a young provincial officer named George Washington. This war, named largely for the widespread participation of the native nations of the Northeast woodlands on the side of France, was the pivotal conflict in deciding the political fate of North America. Although Frenchmen and Indians fought side-by-side in the metaphorical sense, the Indians considered their war a twin set of parallel conflicts — one against the British, which they fought at the behest of the French, and the other against the Iroquois, which they fought to avenge very old wrongs.

The year 1608 seemingly set off the settlement of North America. A person wagering in 1608 on which European kingdom would ultimately gain North America might with reason choose Spain. That kingdom controlled wealthy colonies not only in South and Central America but also numerous islands in the Caribbean and much of the North American southwest. A Spanish courtier wrote, however: "What need have we of what is found everywhere in Europe? It is toward the south, not toward the frozen north, that those who seek their fortune should bend their way; for everything at the equator is rich." Spain seemingly abandoned the northeastern woodlands to its European rivals, chiefly Holland, England, and France, to do with as they pleased. Yet as the seventeenth century opened none of these had established a colony in the New World, and Spain was still busily exploiting its claims in Latin America, the West Indies, and Florida.[124]

Within a few decades Spain's Bourbon cousins in France gained some sugar islands, and much of the far north. The Dutch had a significant colony at New York (New Netherlands), and the English were isolated in a few starving villages scattered along the Atlantic seaboard. The English were seemingly busy consolidating their own kingdom (England and Wales with Scotland,). There would be three attempts in 1606, 1667, and 1689 to unite the countries by Acts of Parliament, but it was not until the early 18th century that the political establishments came to support the idea of Great Britain. The two countries had shared a monarch since the Union of the Crowns in 1603, when King James VI of Scotland inherited the English throne from his cousin, Queen Elizabeth I, as James I. The Act of Union would not be accomplished until 1707. Ireland was not included in the union until 1801.

It can be said with some authority that the French and the Iroquois were in turmoil almost without interruption throughout the 17th and 18th centuries. The French formed a long-standing enmity with the Iroquois in 1609 when Samuel de Champlain, in the company of friendly Montagnais and other Algonquians, met a large party of Mohawk at Crown Point on the southern shore of the lake that would bear his name. The Indians and their traditional enemies engaged in a series of long-range insults and lined up for a battle that probably would have resulted in a few minimal casualties, but the French intervened with their muskets causing the death of several important Iroquois warriors thereby changing forever the face of Indian warfare in the Northeast.

The Dutch were probably the first to introduce firearms to the Indians during their brief regime, in this case to the Mohawk who lived nearest to the Dutch post at Fort Orange (Albany). Yet the French were the first to acquire an unsavory reputation among other Europeans for supplying firearms to the Indians specifically for use against whites. The French responded by condemning the English traders for the same practice, and the English blamed the Dutch, who in turn looked again to the French. While dealing in firearms with the Indians was initially made a capital offense in New Netherlands, of 700 Mohawk warriors appearing for a council at Trois Riviers in 1641, the Jesuit Father Barthelemy Vimont reported that almost 400 had firearms acquired from the Dutch. Evidence suggests that more than 30,000 beaver pelts were traded to the Dutch for muskets, powder, and ball during this period.

In 1664, the English drove the Dutch from New Netherlands, and in 1667 assumed its governance. By 1676, almost all the tribes of New England had converted to firearms, and many of the western tribes were armed with gunpowder weapons to a lesser extent, which reflected their distance from the source of supply. The native war practices in terms of tactics, prisoners, and personal behavior on the field of battle changed little even with the introduction of firearms. Nonetheless, martial strategy among the tribes shifted from the use of petty skirmishes to the waging of major battles, and from a generally defensive to an offensive posture. As late as 1669, the Algonquian-speaking tribes of New England had launched a multi-tribal, full-scale attack on Iroquoia (known as the Ouragie War for one of its prominent leaders), and they were delivered a heavy defeat at the hands of the Mohawk who rallied to the defense. Thereafter, many New England tribes left the Berkshires and White Mountains region and migrated to the St. Lawrence River valley where the French welcomed them with food, clothing, trade goods, and firearms. This left the Mohawk the dominant force in much of Central New York from the headwaters of the Delaware to the Connecticut River.

The French claimed a great swath of the North American heartland as their own based on Royal Charters and the early exploration of the region by Jesuit missionaries and others. Their claims held great weight as being legitimate under European law. The French interest in Canada focused foremost on the fishing off the Grand Banks of Newfoundland. However, at the beginning of 17th century, France became more interested in fur from the interior of North America. The fur trading post of Tadoussac was founded in 1600, eight years before any successful English or Dutch settlement. Four years later, Champlain made his first trip to Canada in a trade mission for fur. French fur traders established the first permanent French colony in North America at Port Royal in Nova Scotia in that year. In 1608, Champlain founded a fur post that became the city of Quebec. This was in the same year as the founding of Jamestown in English Virginia. Champlain forged alliances between France and the Huron and Ottawa against their traditional enemies, the Iroquois, and then he and others continued to explore North America. The Canadian city of Trois Rivières was founded in 1634. In 1642, Montreal was established as a fort for protection against Iroquois attacks. These with Quebec remained the main centers of French population in the north.

Following the capitulation of Quebec to Sir David Kirke during the Thirty Years War (1618-1648), the British briefly occupied the city of Quebec and the colony of Canada from 1629 to 1632. Accompanied by his brothers Lewis, Thomas, John, and Jarvis, Kirke had set off in three ships to establish English trade in the St. Lawrence Valley for a group of private investors chartered by the Crown as a means of extending English influence in exploration and colonial development. Sir David became governor of Newfoundland and collector of a toll levied on all boats fishing in Newfoundland waters. The initial seizure of Quebec was coincidental with the establishment of Massachusetts Bay Colony by royal charter. Following the Treaty of Saint-Germain-en-Laye, France again took possession of the colony of Quebec in 1632 and was compensated for its losses. Hence the English had recognized French occupation of the region in writing, and reaffirmed French sovereignty in Canada in the Treaty of Ryswick of 1697. In 1713 in the Treaty of Utrecht, however, France ceded to Great Britain its claims to Newfoundland and to the Hudson's Bay Company territories in the so-called Rupert's Land named after Prince Rupert of the Rhine, a nephew of Charles I and the first Governor of the Hudson's Bay Company. It also included parts of the states of Minnesota, North Dakota, Montana and South Dakota. France agreed to restore the entire drainage basin of Hudson Bay to Britain and to compensate the Hudson's Bay Company for losses suffered during the war. They also ceded the Acadian colony of Nova Scotia. These cessions weakened their case and were not settled until the Peace of Paris in 1763.

Father Jacques Marquette (standing), Louis Jolliet, and their companions descending the Mississippi River in 1673. Hand colored wood engraving of the 19th century.

Many of the French claims to North America were based on the explorations of Jesuit missionaries. The Doctrine of Discovery was a key premise for non-Indigenous governments to legitimacy and sovereignty over Indigenous lands and territories. European monarchies treated indigenous land as unoccupied, as long as Christians were not present. Between 1642 and 1649, the Indians killed eight French Jesuit missionaries. Many natives considered the missionaries to be malevolent shamans who brought death and disease wherever they traveled because their arrival had coincided with epidemics after 1634 of smallpox and other infectious diseases of Europe, to which aboriginal peoples had no immunity. The first of these was Rene Goupil, a Jesuit brother who was captured and killed by the Iroquois. The best known of these victims was Isaac Jogues who suffered capture twice. Jogues, in the company of Goupil and several Huron Christians, was captured by a war party of Mohawk who took their captives to their village of Ossernenon (now Auriesville, New York) on the Mohawk River, about forty miles west of Albany. They were ritually tortured and Jogues lost two fingers on his right hand. Jogues survived this event and lived as a slave among the Mohawk for some time. Dutch traders from Fort Orange, who were Protestants, ransomed him and gave him money for passage down the Hudson River to New Amsterdam. Jogues was thereby the first Catholic priest to visit Manhattan Island. He took ship to France but in the spring of 1646, Jogues was sent back to the Mohawk country along with Jean de Lalande to act as ambassador among them. Some among the Mohawk regarded Jogues and other missionaries as evil practitioners of magic and killed the men throwing their bodies into the Mohawk River. Today, in Auriesville, New York, the Shrine of the North American Martyrs is dedicated to the Jesuits who sacrificed their lives and remain the only canonized martyrs of the United States. At Fordham University in the Bronx, a freshman dormitory — called Martyrs' Court — has three sections, which are named for John Lalande, René Goupil, and Isaac Jogues.[125]

In 1656 during a time of relative peace, Sainte Marie de Ganentaa was the first of several new missions to be established, located among the Onondagas under Father Simon Le Moyne. Within thirteen years, the Jesuits had missions among all five Iroquois nations, in part imposed by French attacks against the native villages in present-day Central New York. Relations between the French and the Iroquois were tense, however, and the missions were all abandoned by 1708. That year party of drunken Indians burned the chapel and rectory at Onondaga.

The blackrobed Jesuits seemingly harbored a quiet distaste for cooperation with the secular French authorities. They openly challenged the ministers of the civil government with remarkable success especially with respect to trading liquor to the Indians. Finally an Intendant of justice, police, and finances was appointed to act as a business manager for the King. The Intendant had powers that could be exercised without consulting the governor, and he was positioned as a barrier between the civil government and the Bishop of Quebec so that the church could no longer interfere in purely civil matters. By 1667, the Jesuits had established a station among the Algonquians and Huron near present-day Green Bay, Wisconsin, and a large Jesuit establishment was based at Kaskaskia in Illinois country. In 1673, Jesuit Father Jacques Marquette and French-Canadien explorer Louis Jolliet undertook the journey and explored the Mississippi River as far south as the mouth of the Arkansas River. Many colonial officials in French

America discreetly questioned the motives of the Roman Catholic clergy, suggesting that the Jesuits in particular considered New France their own private domain.

At the end of the 17th century, René-Robert Cavalier, Sieur de La Salle established a network of forts going from the Gulf of Mexico to the Great Lakes and the Saint Lawrence River. With approval from Paris, Antoine de Lamothe Cadillac set out in 1701 to build a fort and trading post on the river between Lake Erie and Lake Huron. The purpose was to control the traffic on the river, secure the rich trade in furs in the Great Lakes region for France. He chose a site on a bluff overlooking the strait between Lake Erie and Lake Saint Clair, where he and his men spent some weeks building Fort Ponchartrain du Detroit (which means the strait).

The French, therefore, had a long history of possession in the heartland of North America, but they commanded this vast region from only two substantial colonial centers—one in Canada (Quebec) and one in Louisiana. In theory, Louisiana was subordinate to Canada. Mobile served as French Louisiana's first capital. The southern seat of government moved to Biloxi in 1720, and then to New Orleans in 1722. The foundation of the Franco-Indian alliance relied on a metaphorical relationship of the governor/father (Onontio) in Quebec and all his "native children." However, the familial model so common among Native Americans implied both subservience and obligations. In a report to his superiors, one French official noted, "You know ... that all the [Indian] nations of Canada regard the governor as their father, which in consequence, following their reasoning, he ought at all times to give them what they need to feed themselves, clothe themselves, and to hunt." The French relieved the factionalism of village politics somewhat by recognizing a number of Alliance Chiefs who might represent their people outside the confines of the village "no matter what political or social position he held within his own society." These men mediated disputes among the allies and might act as a strategic counsel during military campaigns against outsiders.[126]

"Conference Between the French and Indian Leaders Around a Ceremonial Fire" by
Emile Louis Vernier (1829-1887)

British colonial governors attempted to replicate the relationship the French had with the Algonquian nations, but few were successful. The fault may reside in the fact that there were so many British governors, each pursuing policies for his individual colony that were sometimes at cross-purposes with his neighbors. The threat of warfare jeopardized this borderland balance. This was particularly true of New York, Pennsylvania, and Virginia, which colonies could not even agree on the limits of their own boundaries. Such details created for the Indian nations a complicated world requiring precarious diplomacy, careful management, and constant compromise with a great number of British "chiefs" who spoke with many voices, unlike the all-powerful and single-minded Onontio (French governor) in Quebec. The success of William Johnson in bringing the Iroquois into an alliance with the British may reside in his insistence that only he speak as the agent of the government to the Indians—a point he argued vociferously with Conrad Weiser, George Croghan, James Adair, John Lydius, and other agents on more than one occasion.

As an Anglo-Irish Catholic immigrant, William Johnson had limited opportunities for advancement in the British Empire other than by using his instinctive and intuitive understanding of the Indians. Johnson moved to the Province of New York to manage an estate purchased by his uncle, Admiral Peter Warren, which was located in the Mohawk.

The French and Indian War was the most extensive of the colonial wars between Britain and France. It began as a dispute over the ownership of the Ohio Country, a fertile and well-watered region with somewhat nebulous borders. Many of the battles fought by Virginia to evict France from its territory were actually fought in Pennsylvania or Kentucky, which was considered a western county of Virginia for some time. Even coastal Connecticut claimed land in the Wyoming Valley of present-day Pennsylvania and in the Ohio Country based on its early royal charter, which had granted it land along lines of latitude all the way to the so-called western ocean. By the 1780s, seven of the thirteen original colonies had enunciated claims to areas in the west. These so-called "landed states" had a great potential advantage over the six "landless states." It was assumed that the future sale of western lands would enrich the landed states and allow them to operate without any form of internal taxation. The landless states feared that they would lose residents thereby and dwindle into insignificance.

Both Connecticut and Massachusetts claimed lands in the Old Northwest although other colonies lay between them. Connecticut put forth a claim to a swath of land from its western boundary to the Mississippi River. Its claim to a portion of Pennsylvania was asserted only half-heartedly because of the strength of a more recent charter held by that colony, but troops raised there in the Revolution were identified as from Connecticut. Virginians felt confident that they had the best claim to lands in the west among all the colonies. The old dominion asserted its right to a huge tract that fanned out to the Mississippi to the west and the Great Lakes to the north, which encompassed the expanses of the Old Northwest (the Ohio Country) based on grants limited by the watershed of several western rivers. Connecticut's claim to an area known as the Western Reserve was maintained until 1795, when it was purchased by the Connecticut Land Company.

The territory between the Connecticut River and Lake Champlain was likewise also claimed by both New Hampshire and New York, whose claims extended eastward to the Connecticut River. Since the Massachusetts boundary extended to a point 20 miles east of the Hudson River, New Hampshire assumed the area west of the Connecticut also belonged to New Hampshire. New York based its claim on the letters Patent, which granted Prince James, Duke of York, brother of King Charles II, all of the lands west of the Connecticut River to Delaware Bay. New York appealed to the Board of Trade, requesting a confirmation of their original grant, which finally resolved the border dispute between New York and New Hampshire in favor of New York in 1764. This infuriated residents of the area, including Ethan Allen and his Green Mountain Boys, ultimately leading to the establishment of the self-declared Vermont Republic and a general rebellion against the New York government. Following the Revolution in 1790, New York consented to the admission of Vermont into the Union, ceded control of the New Hampshire Grants to Vermont and stated the New York-Vermont boundary should be the western edge of the New Hampshire Grants and the mid-channel of Lake Champlain. Vermont's border with New Hampshire was the western bank of the Connecticut River.

Necessity

Warfare brought the borderlands into existence, but it also undid them. Once its strength, French reliance on Indian allies became a liability. The thin reach of France in North America made its hinterland the weak point of empire, and it was in the borderlands that the British chose to strike their decisive blows. A series of colonial wars between the French and English shattered the balance of forces in the forests and transformed the Great Lakes borderlands into a boundary between emerging nation-states. At the end of the process with the Seven Years' War (1756-1763), the Indians had lost their autonomy and the French their land.[127]

George Washington started the French and Indian War, and it quickly spread around the world as the Seven Years War. The French had launched a program of fort building in the Ohio country in 1754. Governor Robert Dinwiddie of Virginia was very concerned when he learned that the French were building forts on the Allegheny River and Lake Erie, and he sent Major Washington with a strongly worded message of protest to the French commander in the region. The overland journey of Washington to the French post at Fort le Boeuf was more than 500 miles, and it was very difficult. Here Washington presented Dinwiddie's message to the commandant who promised to forward it to his superiors for their consideration. So much for the niceties of diplomacy!

This brief exchange was followed by the arduous return of Washington and his guide Christopher Gist to Williamsburg. After delivering his message to the French, Washington's Indian guide turned on them and attempted to murder them. Overcoming the Indian guide, Washington decided to let him go – but then proceeded as quickly as possible in case the guide returned with additional hostile Indians. Eventually, Washington and Gist had to abandon their horses and walk, as the snow was too deep for the animals. Reaching the Allegheny River, they built a raft to attempt to cross it. While doing so, however, Washington was knocked overboard by the ice-strewn river. To dry out, Washington and Gist sought refuse on an island in the middle of the river where they spent the night in wet clothes without being able to maintain a fire. Luckily, in the morning they awoke to discover that the river was totally frozen over with ice, allowing Washington and Gist to walk to the shore. Afterwards, Washington proceeded as quickly as possible all the way back to Williamsburg to report the French response to Virginia Governor Dinwiddie.

1753 - Washington Crossing the Allegheny by Carl Rakeman

When the House of Burgesses met in February, Dinwiddie immediately informed it of the French threat. Dinwiddie concluded by telling those in the Assembly that the "Season for entering upon Action" was at hand. The burgesses proved less cooperative than Dinwiddie had hoped. An inadequate grant of £10,000 for protecting the frontier was passed, but it was filled with restrictions as to how the money could be spent. The words of Governor Dinwiddie and the actions of the French and Indians echoed through the pages of America's newspapers in 1754. The news of the war continued unabated in America's press until the French officially relinquished their claims to the Ohio and Canada in 1763. The newspapers not only covered the war effort, but they also promoted a unity of consciousness for colonists along the Atlantic seaboard.[128]

Dinwiddie wrote in a private letter to James De Lancey (Susan Cooper's grandfather) in New York that he fully realized the futility of raising enough Virginia militia for the campaign and decided to use the funds to enlist a provincial force of six companies composed of 50 men each. He asked De Lancey to encourage New York to support the campaign. To encourage enlistments, the governor issued a proclamation promising that a grant of 200,000 acres on the east side of the Ohio would be distributed among those who volunteered for service in the army. (Washington would be placed in charge of distributing this grant after the war.) Both New York and South Carolina were to send independent companies of provincial troops, and it was hoped that others might be added from the other colonies.[129]

Washington actively campaigned for the command of this force. Even before the receipt of his commission as lieutenant colonel, he had established headquarters at Alexandria and was actively engaged in recruiting and preparing for the campaign. Contemplating the significance of the expedition, he began a diary of his activities. The diary was among the papers, which he abandoned at the surrender of Fort Necessity. Retrieved by the French, it became part of a pamphlet published in Paris in 1756. In addition to the diary, which appeared as document No. VIII in the first part of the pamphlet, numerous other letters and journals were included with editorial notes justifying French activities in the Ohio Valley. In 1757, a copy of the pamphlet was captured on board a French ship taken as a prize, and was translated and published by Hugh Gaine in New York under the title *A Memorial Containing a Summary View of Facts with Their Authorities, in Answer to the Observations Sent by the English Ministry to the Courts of Europe*. This translation was thereafter referred to as a Memoir. Two additional printings, one by J. Parker in New York and one by James Chattin in Philadelphia, appeared also in 1757. Two English editions were also published. As the original of the diary has not been found, the accuracy of the version published in the Memoir must remain questionable. The authenticity of at least one of the documents in the Memoir was disputed in England in 1756 before an English translation appeared in print. Aside from variations in spelling of places and proper names, it seems that the French translator closely followed the original diary.[130]

Shortly after his return to Williamsburg in January 1754, Washington had written a detailed account of his journey to the Ohio Valley and a description of all that he had seen. This was a separate piece from the diary. This account, entitled *The Journal of Major George Washington*, was so well received by Governor Dinwiddie that he had had it published in March in both Williamsburg and in London. The string bound pamphlet cost one shilling. *The Journal of Major George Washington* included not only Washington's careful account of his experiences in the Ohio country, but also Dinwiddie's letter to the French and the French reply. The story of Washington's journey, published as quickly as the ink could dry, had made him an overnight sensation in the colony. Like an adventure novel, the narrative contained a wilderness trek, an icy river crossing, and a heroic survival:

> Getting off the Island on the Ice in the Morning ... we went to Mr. Frazier's [an Indian Trader, at the Mouth of Turtle rock, on the Monongahela]. We met here with 20 Warriors, who were going to the Southward to War, but coming to a Place ... where they found 7 People killed and scalped, all but one woman with very light Hair, they turned about and ran back, for Fear the Inhabitants should rise and take them as the Authors of the Murder: They report that the People were lying about the House, and some of them much torn and eaten by Hogs; by the Marks that were left, they say they were French Indians of the Ottawa Nation, Etc. that did it.[131]

The Journal of Major George Washington is of considerable historical significance. The journal provides a first-hand glimpse of frontier diplomacy, the beginnings of the French and Indian War, as well as early indications of Washington's physical vigor and leadership ability. The first British edition was printed by Thomas Jefferys, an engraver from England's Board of Trade, and appeared in June 1754 with a map that was not included in the Williamsburg printing. The 1754 journal not only appeared in monograph form but was published in several newspapers. Washington later commented: "It was an extraordinary circumstance that so young and inexperienced a person be employed on a negotiation with which the subjects of the greatest importance were involved." With his first publication, Washington became known both throughout the colonies and in prominent circles in England.[132]

Thus Washington became one of America's first frontier heroes, and his narrative one of its first best sellers. It was not surprising therefore, that Dinwiddie placed Washington in charge of expelling the French from the Ohio country later that year. Dinwiddie gave Washington a regiment of 400 Virginians and attached them to two independent companies of regular troops and a few allied Indians to serve as guides and scouts.

Meanwhile, the French governor sent his own aide, Captain Pierre de Contrecouer, with a force of 1,100 men to reinforce the western forts and to build a new post at present-day Pittsburgh to be called Fort Duquesne. Contrecouer, was advised by friendly Indians that most of Washington's force was camped in the Great Meadows east of the Monongahela. The French commander then chose Ensign Coulon de Jumonville de Villiers to lead a small group of soldiers to meet Washington en route and require him to leave the dominions of France. If he refused, Contrecouer promised to bring his entire force down upon them. That these two young men, de Jumonville and Washington, would meet in the wilderness of North America was fated to set almost all the kingdoms of Europe to war. Battles on land and sea would be fought in Europe, the Caribbean, and in the subcontinent of India.

The night of 27 May 1754 was a rainy one, and de Jumonville and his small detachment had taken the opportunity offered by an overhanging cliff to spend the night out of the rain. Meanwhile, Washington, with a small group of soldiers and friendly Seneca Indians under the war leader Monakaduto, had gone forward from the Great Meadows to attempt an observation of Contrecouer's camp at the forks. They accidentally found de Jumonville's party huddled around a warming fire. Washington placed his men around the campsite in a semicircle, and caught the French party totally unawares against the cliffside. No one acknowledged firing the first shot, but a brief fight ensued during which the French party suffered 8 dead and 21 captured. Two Frenchman escaped in the dark. At this point, Monakaduto grabbed de Jumonville, who had surrendered, and murdered him with a single blow of his hatchet to his skull. The British soldiers quietly watched as the Seneca scalped the dead. Although the Seneca were considered allies as part of the Iroquois Confederacy, they often appear as the instigators of diplomatic and other troubles for the British in the historic record.

Washington selected a group of 40 men and Indians to fight a French contingent the Seneca scouts had discovered. Illustration by Frederick Coffay Yohn.

Washington then retreated to the Great Meadows and immediately began fortifying the camp. A rough stockade was erected to house the sick and wounded, and the resulting structure was named Fort Necessity. Contrecouer, having learned of the murder of de Jumonville, immediately sent word to the young man's brother, Captain Coulon de Villiers, to assemble a force of 1,400 French troops and Indian allies to attack Washington's poorly constructed post. On July 4, the French attacked. The British were forced to keep under cover as the French and Indians peppered their positions with musket shot and arrows from two nearby hills. The colonial position, initially occupied by a British detachment under Captain William Trent, was hardly a well-chosen one. Trent had begun the fort; but for some unexplained reason had gone back to Wills Creek leaving an Ensign with forty men at work upon it. By nightfall, 30 of Washington's men were dead, and 70 were wounded. With one quarter of his force as casualties and the situation becoming worse by the moment, Washington chose to accept an offer to surrender.

The terms were very generous. Washington could retire with drums beating and flags flying, but he was required to sign a statement to the effect that he had "killed" de Jumonville. Jacob van Braam, Washington's Dutch interpreter, translated the articles of surrender, which were in French, for Washington. Why this should be necessary is unclear. Washington spoke French. In any case, the section assigning responsibility for the death of de Jumonville actually read, "l'assassinat du Sieur de Jumonville," an assassination! This was clearly untrue, and there is no evidence that Washington had personally killed anyone. The British colonials returned to Virginia unmolested.

Preparations

The French used the time between the surrender of Major Washington and the declaration of war in Europe to fill Quebec with reinforcements and marshal their Indian allies. The French forts in the Ohio country and Fort Duquesne were completed and garrisoned. Finally, a new and highly experienced officer was given command of all the French forces in North America. This was Baron Ludwig August Dieskau, a professional soldier of European birth who had learned his trade in the wars on the continent of Europe. It was he that Louis Joseph Marquis de Montcalm would come to replace.

Traders had led the French advance into the Great Lakes hinterland, followed by missionaries and those free spirits who wished to escape the tyranny of civilization. From a base in the St. Lawrence, French traders fanned out into the interior, adopting aboriginal technologies for communication and transportation, and forming personal relationships with both native men and women. French penetration and the advantages given to Indian groups north of the Great Lakes brought French Indian allies into conflict with the Iroquois to the south, who themselves were engaged in analogous trade relations first with the Dutch and later with the English through the Hudson – Mohawk River waterway. British encroachment and French defensiveness presented Indians in between with both possibilities and perils. Many Indians favored English goods and drove harder and more expensive bargains with their French allies. Nor were the military bonds quite as solid as the French thought.[133]

It was not considered prudent to attempt to wage war in the wilderness without the support of Indian allies. Jolicoeur Charles Bonin, a soldier of the French and Indian War period, has left a vivid journal of his time in the northeast woodlands. As a private soldier who fought beside the Indians at the Monongahela against the British under Edward Braddock, his observations of the French allied Indians of the 1755–1763 period are invaluable due to their perspective. He wrote, "The character of these people is a mixture of simplicity and trickery, nobility and meanness, vanity and politeness, good nature and treachery, valor and cowardice, humanity and barbarity." Published many years after the fact, Bonin's journals include several additions to his observations credited only to J.C.B., who most historians believe to be the same Jolicoeur Charles Bonin. [134]

According to their diaries and journals, English colonials seem to have been easily convinced of their inability to withstand a determined Indian attack, and they were often more willing to surrender to groups of assailants led by French officers than to those composed of only native warriors. However, the French, often outnumbered by their Indian allies and in all practicality unable to check their vengeance for the losses accumulated in the assault, sometimes allowed the terms of a surrender to be "shamefully violated." Instead of finding the promised protection of the French, the survivors were often "abandoned to the fury of the Indians." At Casco Bay in King William's War, for instance, the defenders held out for four days before surrendering to the French officers in charge. Following the capitulation, the French simply stood by while the Indians killed more than 100 English of all ages from among the captives.[135]

Mixed race individuals among the French were very influential in bringing the tribes to aid them. Men such as Charles Langlade and the Joncaire brothers maintained their status as clan members as they moved among the Native Americans speaking at their councils and leading their war parties. This feature of clan-based Indian society figured prominently among the coureurs de bois, woodsmen, bush lopers, and fur traders who married native women and had children with them. All of their progeny were considered full clan members because questions of legitimacy flowed through the females. Among the Europeans, they were often looked down upon as mere "half-breeds" who were useful in dealing with the Indians but unsuited for proper society.

Samuel Champlain, while serving as governor of New France in the 17th century, reportedly proposed a policy of intermarriage between young Frenchmen and the daughters of the Algonquians. The Indian nations, deprived of their young men through disease and intertribal warfare, were eager to have their widows and daughters married off to Frenchmen who could guarantee their supply of European goods and weapons. There was an amazing lack of French women and girls among the population, which may explain why so many Frenchmen took Native American wives. The Crown earnestly attempted to resolve this inequity by finding peasant girls of good character in France to serve as wives for the colonists. These young women were called the King's Daughters, or *Filles du Roi*. Moreover, the French Crown was suspicious of sending its citizens to the New World and hoped that intermarriage with the indigenous population would produce a corps of on-the-spot Frenchmen to populate its colony. Indian wives taught their European husbands, and later their mixed race children, the ways of the forests, and the Frenchmen advanced a paternalistic relationship between themselves and their newfound kinship groups. Many of the European fathers of mixed-race children provided for their European-style education and supported them as they would have if they had been wholly French.

Sexual relations between native women and Frenchmen created a great deal of unease among the Jesuits and the officials of government, but the priests considered marriage between the parties only a partial solution. They considered all mixed race offspring of unmarried couples *metis batards,* even if they were married according to Indian rites. Those that were married under the auspices of the Church were considered *metis legitimes.* The Jesuits noted that the *metis batards* invariably followed the Indian way of life and were loyal to their mother's tribe, while the *metis legitimes* became French in their outlook, culture, and loyalty. "Metis batards may have become Indian, and metis legitimes French, but both, nonetheless, represented significant ties between the two peoples. ... Priests and officials in France feared betrayal and corruption, but local commanders realized that such connections could be useful."[136]

The social identity of mixed-race children among the Indians was strongly determined by the tribe's kinship system. Among the matrilineal tribes, the mixed-race children generally were accepted and identified as Indian, as they gained their social status from their mother's clans and tribes. By contrast, the child of a white woman and Indian man was often considered "white." Such mixed-race children and their mothers would be protected, but the children could belong to the tribe as members only if formally adopted. Children, whether of a white or native mother, seem to have been invariably adopted with little difficulty. Ultimately, a number of mixed race persons from the Northeast woodlands would form a separate people, the Métis, who mediated between the French and the Algonquians in the 18th century and who would challenge the British government of Canada in the 19th century.

Charles Langlade was a Great Lakes fur trader and war chief who was important to the French in protecting their territory. His mother was Ottawa and his father a French Canadien. Leading French and Indian forces, in 1752 he destroyed Pickawillany, a Miami village and British trading post in present-day Ohio. Pennsylvania blacksmith and Indian trader John Fraser had set up shop on this site, supplying Indians in the region with trade goods and repairing their guns and other metal wares. His business was an example of the western expansion of Pennsylvania's fur trade that prompted the French to fortify the Ohio Country. The French wanted to punish the Miami chief Old Briton (Unemakemi or La Demoiselle) for rejecting the French alliance and dealing with the British traders. The raid resulted in the deaths of Old Briton and at least one English trader. Although Fraser was fortunately absent at the time of the attack, two other of his traders and all his goods were captured. In 1755, Langlade led a group of Ottawa and Ojibwa in the defense of Fort Duquesne and is generally credited with being the architect of the British debacle on the Monongahela. He also took part in the siege of Fort William Henry, and later he led a group of Ottawa warriors at the Battle of the Plains of Abraham in the defense of Quebec in 1759.

Daniel and Chabert Joncaire were the sons of Chabert Joncaire, a French trader adopted into the Seneca nation, and his native wife. Through his intercession with his Indian relations, in 1720 the elder Joncaire built a trading post near the present site of Fort Niagara were the Niagara River empties into Lake Ontario. Using both the influence of their father and the kinship ties of their mother, Daniel and Chabert (the sons) became greatly successful in persuading the Seneca to remain neutral to British overtures and in attracting the Algonquian and Huron of the west to the French. Captain Chabert Joncaire finished building Fort Machault in April 1754. It was named in honor of the prominent

French Minister of the Marine at the time of its construction. It was also known as "Venango," the name of the nearby Delaware Indian village. In 1763, during Pontiac's Rebellion, Venango, now a British fort was captured by Seneca/Mingo warriors led by Guyasuta (a.k.a. Kiashuta). The 12 to 15 soldiers of the fort were killed outright, except for the commander, Lieutenant Francis Gordon, who was forced to write a letter detailing the Indians' grievances against the British. He was then slowly tortured and roasted to death at the stake, and the fort was burnt to the ground.

In their intertribal diplomacy, the Joncaire's attempted to replicate the powerful influence of William Johnson among the Mohawk. During the 1750s, both Joncaire brothers, Daniel and Chabert, moved throughout the Indian nations doing everything in their power to convince the Seneca to reopen their long standing enmity with the Catawba tribes of South Carolina or Cherokee of Georgia in order to keep the English frontier settlements in turmoil with war parties going back and forth on the Warrior's Path, a trail used for 5,000 years by Native Americans. The Warrior's Path followed the Shenandoah River valley through the backcountry of the English settlements to the southern colonies. Every year parties of Iroquois from New York descended the Warrior's Path to the south to attack their traditional enemies. Under these circumstances unfortunate accidents with whites, who they might contact en route, were bound to occur, and the Joncaire's hoped that the situation might swiftly degenerate into an English–Iroquois war.

This strategy was not without precedent. In the 17th century, Doeg natives had begun a war with Virginia by simply killing a few hogs that the settlers had loosed into the margins of the forests to feed on acorns and roots. In the summer of 1675, the local militia from Virginia crossed into Maryland and slaughtered almost two-dozen innocent Doeg and Susquehannock Indians in a feud over the missing hogs. The Indians retaliated, and the whites demanded further retribution. Back and forth along the frontier, raid and counter-raid followed. In spring 1676, thirty-six whites living on the Rappahannock River were killed during a series of Indian attacks. Virginia settlers, terrified by the renewed hostilities, found themselves clustered for defense in their backwoods settlements. As a consequence the local companies lashed out in unauthorized raids at any Indians they could find. This action was successful in suppressing the Indian attacks, but it caused a crisis in the colonial government between the governor, William Berkeley and his council in Virginia led by Nathaniel Bacon known today as Bacon's Rebellion.

Nathaniel Bacon was only twenty-six, but he maintained a successful plantation on the James River and had enough wealth and influence to sit on the council of the elderly royal governor, William Berkeley. It is certain that Bacon was neither a hotheaded youth nor a romantic cavalier defending the oppressed. His motives for defying the royal governor at this time are unclear, and his early death prevented him from leaving a detailed written account.

Bacon's Rebellion (1676) took place exactly 100 years before the adoption of the Declaration of Independence, a circumstance not lost on the Patriots of 1776. Nathaniel Bacon's forces were "a little reminiscent of European mercenary armies of the sixteenth and seventeenth centuries ... where the government lost control of the war while trying to wage it more effectively." Royal troops were sent to the Virginia colony, and thereafter the upheaval slowly died down. The royal authorities duly noted Bacon's Rebellion at the time, and it may have accelerated and justified the transformation of the Virginia Company's settlements into a royal province. Ultimately Governor Berkeley had forts built and a few dozen mounted soldiers were hired to range, or patrol, between them—the first rangers in American history.[137]

Meanwhile, the Iroquois Council had declared the Joncaire brothers double-tongued and not to be trusted, and the backcountry conflicts they had hoped for were largely avoided. Daniel Chabert, reporting to the French authorities in 1751, wrote:

> Though we seem to be holding our own, or even gaining, in the immediate Iroquois country, such is not the case on the Ohio. Because of pressure we have brought to bear, the Delawares have now moved away from our immediate reach and deep into the Ohio country, close to their brother tribes, the Shawnee and Miami. Almost all of the Ohio Indians are showing strong affection for the

English who sell them goods at low rates, make ample gifts and give them gunpowder for just asking.[138]

The Indians were largely dependent on Europeans for powder and ball as well as for repairs to metal items. Trade muskets, while widely available, were not as fine as those of the colonists or the regulars. The performance of early muskets was effective for the styles of European warfare at the time, whereby soldiers tended to stand in long, stationary lines and fire at the opposing forces. Precise aiming and accuracy were not necessary to hit an opponent, but even this was often a matter of happenstance. The rifle, on the other hand, was originally a sharpshooter's weapon used for targets of opportunity and deliberately aimed fire. These weapons used a set of spiral grooves in the barrel to give a stabilizing spin to the ball, and first gained notoriety through their use by American frontiersmen. There is no evidence of rifles being distributed among the tribes.

Most Indian warriors favored their traditional weapons as more dependable. Noted military historian John K. Mahon (University of Florida) has pointed out that the Indians "never really mastered the white man's weapon." The musket and rifle could be deadly from ambush or from behind fortifications, but the tomahawk and knife – one in each hand – were equally effective for infighting. The further west that one traveled, the less likely was it to encounter Native Americans with firearms. Even when possessed of firearms the Indians often found themselves with unserviceable weapons for lack of powder or repairs. Those Frenchmen charged with the development and expansion of trade with the native population generally understood this dependence on Europeans for repairs and used it as a means of binding the Indians to them. English traders, on the other hand, understood their role as providers of powder and shot but seem to have avoided dealing in repairs, choosing instead to supply an entirely new weapon to their customers, albeit at an exaggerated cost in terms of furs to the individual Indian.[139]

The military of New France consisted of a mix of regular soldiers of the French Army, French Navy and Canadien volunteer militia units. In 1664, the French finance minister Jean-Baptiste Colbert ordered the Carignan-Salières regiment of 400 men to reinforce the existing 100-man force in New France. This reinforcement was motivated largely by mercantile ambitions concerning the government monopoly in furs. Its purpose was to control the population and police the Indians. Montreal was in a constant state of alarm as the Mohawks periodically blockaded the Ottawa River in their own attempt to monopolize the fur trade from the supply side. Small bands of Mohawk, breaking off from their watch of the river, would terrorize the French *habitants* by destroying their livestock and menacing solitary farmers. The Mohawk were considered the most steadfast of British Indian allies, but they were not above taking bribes from the French in the pursuit of their own tribal initiatives and personal ambitions.

Hand-colored engraving by L.F. Labrousse in *Costumes de different pays* (1787). Jacques Grasset de Saint-Sauveur, a resident of Montreal until 1764, designed the engravings and wrote the text. Note that the musket is slung in an auxiliary position.

In 1669 Louis XIV ordered that all men in New France between the ages of 16 and 60 do mandatory military service so that every parish would have its own militia. The Canadien militia companies borrowed many of their tactics and woodland skills from the Indians, and they excelled in skirmishing in the woods. They usually served alongside the more numerous Native Americans that were loyal to the French and the Compagnies Franches de la Marine.

The European population of French Canada was very small, however, and the government was reticent to develop an extensive armed militia. The thirteen English colonies had, by the time of the French and Indian War (1754), accumulated a population estimated at 1.3 million persons, black and white. This was an overwhelming advantage over New France, where the population never exceeded 80,000, but the French were massed along a densely populated stretch of the St. Lawrence River that was perhaps just eighty miles long. The majority of the English population clung to the coastal settlements and cities spread over 1000 miles, leaving the frontier regions sparsely populated by comparison.

The Compagnies Franches de la Marine were instituted in the 17th century and sent to the French colonies in India, the West Indies, and North America. The independent companies (compagnies franches) chosen for colonial duty were formed into a distinct establishment of regular colonial troops. The men generally volunteered for long-term service, and most retired in Canada at the end of their military career where they found wives among the natives. As they were raised, supplied, and administered by the Ministry of the Marine in France, they were known as the Compagnies Franches de la Marine. These men were not sailors; rather they should be considered land forces paid through the naval accounts, as were all French colonial expenses. These units ultimately numbered more than 32 companies including artillery, but they were scattered in forts and outposts over a vast territory stretching from Acadia to the Great Lakes and Louisiana. It has been pointed out that the training of the soldiers of La Marine was better than that of the common English militia, and their officers had far more freedom of action than their counterparts in the regular army in responding to unrest on the frontiers. The compagnies franches were raised as a shield against the Iroquois, but they took part in almost every engagement against the enemy in North America from 1684 to 1760.

In 1668, the fur trade entered a new phase. Two French citizens, Pierre-Esprit Radisson and Médard des Groseilliers, had traded with great success west of Lake Superior in 1659-60, but upon their return to Canada, the authorities seized most of their furs as being taken outside the government monopoly. Their treatment in Canada caused the pair to go to New England where they ultimately formed the Hudson's Bay Company. The initial French government monopoly in furs was thereby broken and transferred to what was called the Compagnie des Habitants. Thereafter, the fur trade was opened to any settler who wished to pursue it.

Radisson was a prodigious writer. Unfortunately, he was also considered an equally prodigious liar, rogue, and fabricator of tall tales by many of his contemporaries. Nonetheless, some of his more extraordinary experiences have found verification through a careful reading of the *Jesuit Relations*. The reports of Radisson's early life among the Indians fill no fewer than six volumes titled *Voyages*. Five of these were published in English and the last was published in Radisson's native French. In the first of these volumes, Radisson described his time as a captive among the Mohawk, his adoption into the tribe, his Indian foster family, his part as a member of a small war party, and his return to white society by way of Albany. This volume covers the important years of 1652 and 1653 when the Iroquois, and the Mohawk in particular, were at the height of their power among other nations in the northeast woodlands.

It would be an error to think that the habitants of Canada enjoyed any freedom of action in their lives. Young men were required to follow strict regulations forcing them to marry, to settle on the land, and to develop farmsteads. Habitants were required to clear two acres of land (two square arpents) each year to maintain their *censive* (land grant). Once the habitant became a *censitaire*, or landholder, he was responsible for paying a rent as well as fishing and milling fees in cash to the *seigneur* who actually owned his land. Abandoning their land in order to traffic in furs without a license could bring stiff penalties, deportation, or even death. The Ministry of Marine chose to rely on professional troops to police New France and only raised the habitants of Canada (militia) in the most severe emergencies.[140]

In 1746, four battalions of regular French troops were sent to Canada. These troops were called Troupes de Terre. In 1755, attesting to the military buildup required by the Seven Years' War, four additional battalions arrived with Baron Dieskau, and two more battalions came to America with Montcalm in 1756. Four battalions arrived in 1757 and 1758. The Troupes de Terre were almost always composed of understrength European units, and they were reinforced by companies of French militia and Indian allies. They included men from a number of veteran regiments: La Rein, Bourgogne, Languedoc, Guienne, Artois, Royal Roussillon, La Sarre, Bearn, Berry, Cambis, and Volontaires Etrangers. The unit integrity of these regiments was almost always respected during campaigns, so that, for instance, only La Reine and Languedoc were present at the Battle of Lake George in 1755, and only Guienne, Bearn, and La Sarre were at the siege of Fort Oswego in 1756.

"Our councils were darkened wisdom"

The British plan for the conflict in North America would require the cooperation of the provincials and the Crown to a degree never before experienced, but the British regulars viewed the colonial volunteers as undisciplined, untrained, seditious, or worse. Two under-strength regiments of British regulars from Ireland (44th and 48th) were immediately transferred to Virginia. These were the first regular British troops ever sent to the Atlantic colonies, and they were meant to ensure discipline and order among the unprofessional militia. Other regulars had served in Atlantic Canada and the Caribbean, but none previously on the frontiers. The two regiments were each 500 strong, having been recruited to that figure by drafts from other regiments serving in Ireland, and were ordered to be brought up to 700 effectives by provincial enlistment. A total of six thousand regulars were promised, and the colonials were asked to supply 10,000 provincials. Finally, Major General Edward Braddock was made commander of all military affairs in North America so that the colonials might come to learn how a war should be fought.

The fact is that the colonial militia had successfully waged several wars on the frontiers. There was one undeniable unifying characteristic of all colonial forces. Whether set against natives or Europeans, the respective colonial governments attempted to enforce unequivocal recognition of their own sovereignty by using the forces that they had at hand. "Border warfare was the only school in which the yeomanry had been trained up, and as soon as the exigency was over they returned to their farms or workshops." This is a repetitive phenomenon in the development of frontier communities. Initial fear supports community action and substantive defenses. Growing familiarity with the surroundings becomes expansion and personal complacency, which ends in unexpected tragedy, panic, and renewed calls for community action and defense. A more consistent or formal military presence among the settlers was envisioned, but the deployment of professional soldiers was thought to threaten individual liberties as it had in Ireland and Scotland. Moreover, the colonies had answered every call for volunteers responsibly. One in seven had died in the service of the King in three previous wars, many through the irresponsible actions of British officers. Not until the final struggle for control of the continent did armies from Europe join the fray.[141]

The colonists constantly resorted to the same expedient when faced with an Indian war. They raised a large force of inexperienced and only moderately trained men from among their militia, and placed them under the command of untested leaders or provincial officers. They then tried to prosecute a plan of attack requiring precision, secrecy, and flawless execution against targets that were sometimes hundreds of miles away in the geographical vastness of a primeval wilderness. Moreover, most of the colonials were uninterested in how these operations might affect the outcome of a larger American or imperial conflict, and only viewed them as a defensive response to their local emergencies. Historian John Ferling has noted, "Disunity among the colonies was a formidable obstacle to military success, as was Britain's habitual lack of interest in the American theater." Not until several decades had passed did the English realize that their frontiers could best be secured by destroying the French presence in Canada.[142]

These attitudes, a relic of several decades of Anglo-colonial and British dispute, were clearly reflected in Cooper's novels, especially *The Last of the Mohicans*. Cooper wrote in the first pages of his masterwork:

> The imbecility of her military leaders abroad, and the fatal want of energy in her councils at home, had lowered the character of Great Britain from the proud elevation on which it had been placed by the talents and enterprise of her former warriors and statesmen. No longer dreaded by her enemies, her servants were fast losing the confidence of self-respect. In this mortifying abasement, the colonists, though innocent of her imbecility, and too humble to be the agents of her blunders, were but the natural participators. They had recently seen a chosen army from that country, which, reverencing as a mother, they had blindly believed invincible — an army led by a chief [Braddock] who had been selected from a crowd of trained warriors, for his rare military endowments, disgracefully routed by a handful of French and Indians, and only saved from annihilation by the coolness and spirit of a Virginian boy [Washington].[143]

Two years later, General John Forbes would draw on his own European experience and a staff analysis of Braddock's ultimate defeat to draw up a highly successful plan of operations against the Indians. Forbes's plan called for the use of his own Indian allies to reconnoiter the line of march; American frontiersmen to screen the column; disciplined bayonet charges to disperse ambushes; and a well-guarded line of depots and supplies to eliminate long wagon trains. British commanders with whom Forbes had served in 1746 and 1747 in Scotland and in continental Europe had employed tactics much like these.

Cooper is not out to demonize the British or those who were loyal to them in his novels. His wife, Susan De Lancey had devoted Tory ancestors, and Cooper may have attempted to walk a fine line between revolutionary and loyalist for the sake of his wedded bliss. Yet Cooper is clearly a committed democrat picturing Hawkeye as the virtuous backwoodsman in opposition to the hierarchical British regulars.[144]

Chief among these was General Edward Braddock who arrived in America in February 1755. By April, he had called upon several colonial governors to meet at Charleton House in Alexandria, Virginia to develop a strategy for the forthcoming campaign: Shirley of Massachusetts; Dinwiddie, Virginia; Dobbs, North Carolina; Morris, Pennsylvania; Sharpe, Maryland; and Delancey, New York at Alexandria Also in attendance was William Johnson, who had been given supervision of British Indian policy as Superintendent of Indian Affairs. The Alexandria meeting was historic, and it laid down four simultaneous operations. The first proposal was for an expedition to secure the forks of the Ohio River and destroy Fort Duquesne. This operation was to be under the command of Braddock who would take the bulk of the regulars with him as well as provincials from Virginia, Maryland, and North Carolina to act as scouts, baggage guards, and road builders.

The second was for the removal of all the French in Nova Scotia and the reduction of Fort Beauséjour in Acadia. This was the responsibility of the royal governor of Nova Scotia, Charles Lawrence, who would be aided by British Colonel Robert Monckton, 270 redcoats, and 2,000 colonial volunteers from Massachusetts. Governor William Shirley of Massachusetts would campaign along the New York shore of Lake Ontario reinforcing

Fort Oswego and attacking French Niagara. And finally, William Johnson would attempt to secure the Lake George – Lake Champlain channel.

The Campaigns of 1755

The difficulties faced by Braddock were increased by the choice of the Virginian route into the wilderness in preference to the easier course, which could have been taken from Philadelphia. The base, Fort Cumberland, at the foot of the Blue Ridge, was not readily accessible. Nevertheless, preparations were pushed forward and the troops were safely concentrated at the Fort in two columns. One had marched by way of Frederick in Maryland and the other in part along the Winchester road, south of the Potomac. A fortified camp was created at Little Meadows. In mid-June the little army, made up of two small brigades, started upon its tragic march miles over the Alleghany Mountains and several lesser ridges, clad with primeval forest and swarming with hostiles, to Fort Duquesne. The hardships of the march and constant use of salt provisions caused a great deal of sickness among the regulars. Sir Peter Halkett led the way with the first brigade, consisting of the 44th (700 effectives), with 280 New York, Virginia and Maryland colonials and 50 carpenters, 980 in all. The second brigade was under Col. Dunbar and was made up of the 48th (650 strong), some 800 colonials from the Carolinas and Virginia and 85 carpenters, the personnel of the whole force being about 2,000. The pace being too slow for the General, the weaker men, to the number of 600, under Dunbar were ordered to proceed at a more leisurely pace. Then with 1,200 regulars and 200 provincials the march was pressed on. In 1902, historian Arthur G. Bradley drew a graphic picture of the discomforts of the march:

> A strange enough sight in those wild woods must have been the long train of jolting wagons, dragged by ill-conditioned horses, growing daily weaker; the clumsy tumbrels and artillery and ammunition carts jolting and crashing over the rough-made track; the strings of heavily laden pack-horses, stung by deerflies and goaded by drivers' whips, sliding and slipping over limestone slabs, and floundering amid stumps and roots; the droves of stunted cattle shambling unwillingly along the unfenced track; the fresh-faced soldiery, in tight scarlet uniforms, pigtails and pipe clay, mitre hats and white-gaitered legs, sweltering in the fierce, unwonted heat of an American midsummer sun."[145]

Putting the details of Braddock's defeat on the Monongahela aside for the moment, the other three prongs of the British offensive of 1755 should first be better explained in order to put the disaster in perspective both historically and with respect to its significance as a fictional setting. This is especially true since many of the following circumstances were taking place simultaneous with Braddock's Campaign, yet in isolation from it due to the vast distances and poor means of communications involved. The chronology is also disruptive to the narrative: the capture Fort Beauséjour in Acadia taking place 18 June 1755, the battle at the Monongahela 8 July 1755, that at Lake George 8 September 1755, and the fall of Oswego on 10 August of the following summer. The reader's patience will be rewarded in Chapter XI.

Acadian militias heavily supported by local Indians had deployed an effective resistance for over 75 years through six wars with the English. During Queen Anne's War, the members of the Wabanaki Confederacy from Acadia raided Protestant settlements along the Acadia / New England border in present-day Maine in the Northeast Coast Campaign (1703). Micmac natives and Acadians resisted the New England retaliatory raids at Grand-Pré, Piziquid, and Chignecto in 1704. Despite a British conquest in 1710, Nova Scotia and Acadia remained primarily occupied by Catholic Acadians and Micmac. During the next conflict known as Father Rale's War (1722–1725), some Acadians, the Wabanaki Confederacy, and the French priests participated again in defending Acadia at its border against New England. France launched a major expedition to recover Acadia in 1746. Beset by storms, disease, and finally the death of its commander, the French expedition returned to France in tatters without reaching its objective.

An aerial view of the remains of Fort Beauséjour (Cumberland).

Governor Lawrence had easily captured Fort Beauséjour (renamed Fort Cumberland) in 1755, and had then embarked on what has since become known as the "Great Expulsion," the forcible removal of more than 12,000 Acadians from Nova Scotia. Although they had steadfastly refused to take a loyalty oath to Britain, the presence of Acadian irregulars helping in the defense of the French fort constituted a "violation" of Acadian neutrality agreed to at the end of the previous war. The thought of getting rid of the Acadians was first expressed not long after the capture of Port Royal in 1710 and one that was expressed numerous times as the 18th century wore on. In his expulsion order of 11 August 1755, Lawrence wrote: "Clear the whole country of bad subjects ... and disperse them among ... the colonies upon the continent of America. ... Collect them up by any means. ... Send them off to Philadelphia, New York, Connecticut and to Boston." Thus an entire people were yanked off their lands like so many weeds to be herded and prodded onto wooden sailing vessels. Thousands of Acadians died in the expulsions, mainly from disease, exposure, and drowning when several transport ships carrying the displaced Acadians were lost at sea. Throughout the expulsion, French Acadians allied themselves with the Wabanaki Confederacy (Micmac, Maliseet, Passamaquoddy, Abenaki, and Penobscot) who continued a guerrilla war against the British, which had been in effect since 1744. "They will be treated as Rebels," wrote Lawrence, "their Estates and Families undergo immediate Military Execution, and their persons if apprehended shall suffer the utmost Rigor of the Law, and every severity that I can inflict." [146]

The Micmac (Mi'kmaq) militia had deployed an effective resistance against the English for over 75 years before treaties were created and the Burial of the Hatchet Ceremony took place in 1761. The first documented warfare between the Micmac and the British was during the First Abenaki War (an offshoot of King Philip's War in Maine / Acadia). In the 17th century, the French had converted the Micmac to Catholicism, in wholesale lots, and proceeded to control them through the missionaries who lived among them. These Jesuits were influential among the Micmac. Father Sabastien Rale spent more of his life among the Algonquian-speaking Abenaki nation than he did in European society. The French also made a point of gathering their Indian friends together once a year giving them gifts of powder, lead, flints, and axes. A contemporary observer, Marc Lescarbot, in his history, deals with the tools and weapons of the Micmac. As he explains, the bows and arrows were "strong without fineness." Eagle feathers were used for the arrows. Originally, bone was used for their arrowheads, but the natives quickly converted to using iron. Their maces, or clubs, were made out of hard wood. They used animal gut for bowstrings. Micmac militias were composed of superior warriors who worked independently as well as in coordination with the Wabanaki Confederacy, French, and Acadian forces throughout the colonial period to defend their homeland. In present-day Maine, the Micmac and the Maliseet raided numerous New England villages through 1755-1758. Interestingly, Lescarbot's history put the Jesuits into a less than favorable light at a time when the religious and civil governance of New France was in turmoil. [147]

The successful expulsion of the Acadians would become the subject of *Evangeline*, an epic poem by the American poet Henry Wadsworth Longfellow, written in English and published in 1847. Longfellow relied heavily on Thomas C. Haliburton's *An Historical and Statistical Account of Nova Scotia* (1829) and other books for background information. A reviewer for *The Metropolitan Magazine* said, "No one with any pretensions to poetic feeling can read its delicious portraiture of rustic scenery and of a mode of life long since defunct, without the most intense delight."[148]

The Governor of Massachusetts, William Shirley would lead a third expedition to reinforce the important British post at Fort Oswego on Lake Ontario before undertaking the reduction of the French post at Niagara. Oswego was important because it largely neutralized the French presence on the lake at both Fort Niagara and Fort Frontenac (Kingston). For many years, Niagara was of less value to the French as a gateway to the Western Lakes than as part of a road, difficult, but practicable, to the Ohio country. It must be borne in mind that when the French spoke of the Ohio, they meant also the southwestern reaches of the Allegheny Plateau; so that Le Boeuf Creek, down which they voyaged within Pennsylvania, and the Conewango, fed by Chautauqua Lake in New York, brought the Ohio within a very few miles of Lake Erie. Lakes Erie and Ontario, styled the Lower Lakes, were part of the highway by which France had gained the interior of the continent.[149]

The successful first Siege of Louisbourg on Île Royale, now Cape Breton Island in the previous war in 1745, which Shirley had a major role in organizing, was one of the high points of his administration. In 1748 and much to the consternation of the Anglo-Americans who had secured it, the British had returned the fortress to the French for the single city of Madras in India. Massachusetts' troops had taken the lead in capturing the troublesome French citadel, which had supplied and directed raids by their Native allies (Micmac, Abenaki, Maliseet, Penobscot, Passamaquoddy) on the New England frontier. When news broke of the return of the fortress, the distressed population of Boston rebelled. Onrushing Bostonians surged through the streets, the crowd swollen to more than a thousand—all for possession of a city thousands of miles away in India. Parliament voted, thereafter, to ransom Louisbourg from the colonies. The sum coming to Massachusetts was in excess of £138 thousand pounds sterling in copper and silver coins, which they then demanded as payments for taxes and fees. This sum in coin, calculated at the ruling exchange rate, very nearly canceled the outstanding paper debt of the colony. There can be no doubt that the bitterness engendered by this circumstance was one cause of the Revolution.[150]

Shirley considered himself a great strategist, but many of his other plans failed to materialize. When rumors reached Boston in 1754 of French military activity on the Massachusetts northern frontier (now Maine), Shirley was quick to organize an expedition to the Kennebec River to bolster the area's defenses. Funds were appropriated, taxes increased, troops raised, and deployments begun. The rumors proved false. He also revived the idea of an expedition against Fort St. Frédéric at Crown Point, although he limited his objectives to the establishment of a fort at the southern end of Lake George. This also had failed to happen, but it was the genesis of Johnson's present campaign.

As one of his first official acts of the new war, Shirley made a proclamation offering bounties of £20 to £50 (pounds) in colonial money for the capture or the scalps of the Indians allied to the French, but he did little of lasting value. It was quickly commented that the scalp of any Indian, enemy or friend, might be brought forth in order to claim the bounty. Nonetheless, it is hardly correct to blame the British for establishing the practice. The taking of a scalp or hairlock as a trophy or proof of having killed an enemy in warfare was an ancient Native American custom. Colonials expressed a great fear of scalping. William Dunbar a British Regular officer noted: "Our men unaccustomed to that way of fighting, were quite confounded and ... were seized with ... panic." Another British officer noted: "The men from what stories they had heard of the Indians in regard to their scalping ... were so panic struck that their officers had little or no command over them."[151]

Scalp-taking was considered part of the broader cultural practice of the taking and display of human body parts as trophies, and may have developed as an alternative to the taking of human heads, for scalps were easier to take, transport, and preserve for subsequent display. Scalping developed independently in various cultures in both the Old and New Worlds. As recently as 1746, the British had taken the heads of Scottish rebels and mounted them on stakes above the gates of several cities. Certain tribes of Native Americans practiced scalping, in some instances up until the end of the 19th century. The *Jesuit Relations* states with regard to an Iroquois attack on Hurons and French near Montreal in 1642, "Three of these they beat to death, scalping them, and carrying away their hair, and taking the two others captive." In 1697, on the northern frontier of

Massachusetts, captive settler Hannah Dustin murdered ten of her Abenaki abductors during a nighttime escape. She presented the ten scalps to the Massachusetts General Assembly, and was rewarded with bounties for two men, two women, and six children.[152]

In the American Revolution in 1782, Benjamin Franklin perpetrated a hoax concerning scalps in the British press for propaganda purposes. The Indian atrocity article appeared to be a legitimate letter from an American militia officer, Captain Samuel Gerrish, to his commanding officer describing a captured letter and packages, which had been intended for the British governor of Canada. Franklin went so far as to propagate a color scheme by which the scalps could be identified, a scheme that did not exist. The officer wrote that he had found among the packages, 8 large ones containing scalps taken by the Seneca Indians from the inhabitants of the frontiers of New York, New Jersey, Pennsylvania, and Virginia, and sent by them as a present to the governor of Canada, in order to be transmitted to the king in England.

Shirley also argued with the governors of New York and Connecticut concerning recruitment outside their colonies. This while his own son was recruiting for Massachusetts in New York. A frosty relationship he had with acting New York Governor James De Lancey continued with his replacement, Sir Charles Hardy, who forwarded unflattering reports concerning the disputes to his government friends in London. When Shirley and Johnson met in July 1755 before their respective expeditions set off, Shirley next sought to bypass the Indian agent and negotiate directly with the tribes for native recruits. Johnson reacted negatively to Shirley's clumsy Indian diplomacy, which threatened to harm the British relationship with the Six Nations. Johnson immediately requested that the Board of Trade clearly delineate his position. "Governor Shirley's interfering in the authorative and ill judged manner he has done, was injurious to the true system of Indian affairs, a violation of my commission and an arbitrary insult upon my character." The Board supported Johnson in his position, but this dispute created an irreparable rift between the two men.[153]

Finally at the Alexandria war council, a fourth colonial force was placed under the command of William Johnson who, with his Mohawks, was to attack the French post at Crown Point at the southern end of Lake Champlain. Tiyanoga, a Mohawk war leader known as *King Hendrick* among the English, was influential in marshalling the power of his tribe and specifically the Wolf Clan on the side of the British for the fourth and final campaign contemplated at Alexandria – Crown Point, but he did so through the force of his personality rather than through any innate political authority. Johnson considered Tiyanoga a friend. Moreover, the English had built Fort Hunter with an Anglican mission near his village in 1711. The Mohawk village, near Schenectady, became mostly Christianized in the Protestant faith early in the 18th century. This was unusual among the members of the Confederacy who generally maintained their traditional beliefs.

It is also noteworthy that the Iroquois, unlike their Huron cousins who quickly allied to their Algonquian neighbors, rarely fought a war with help from outside their own confederacy. There was a definite pecking order within the Confederacy, however. The Mohawk, Onondaga, and Seneca were addressed as "elder brothers" and the Oneida, Cayuga, and Tuscarora were addressed as "younger brothers." The war-like Mohawk and the Oneida often teamed up in any undertaking, and the Seneca and Cayuga would generally oppose them or acted independent of them. The Onondaga often played the roll of diplomatic neutral. If there was a weakness to this system, it was that all major decisions had to be unanimous. Debates, although heated, nearly always led to a unanimous decision, often that the minority might proceed in following its own will. The Nations stood together, and that made them strong.

The members of the Five Nations modeled their confederacy for some time on the traditional dwelling known as a *longhouse*. The Mohawk were the keepers of the eastern door; the Seneca that of the western door. These two were the most numerous and warlike of the confederated tribes. The Onondaga were the mediators and keepers of the great central fire, while the less numerous Cayuga and Oneida were the younger brothers who lived among them. The Tuscarora, fearing increased aggression by white Carolinians in the 18th century, removed to Iroquoia to ally themselves in a subsidiary role with the Five Nations (who became the Six Nation Confederacy about 1722). The Tuscarora seemingly formed a strong association with the Oneida with whom they allied in 1776 to support the patriots during the American Revolution. This split the confederacy into pro-British and pro-Patriot factions. These two groups had been Christianized largely through the efforts of Reverend Samuel Kirkland, a Congregational missionary and ardent patriot. Kirkland was able to win the help of the Oneida and Tuscarora for the patriots by appealing to them on religious grounds, suggesting that the Crown would force the Anglican religion upon them if the patriots lost.

The common arrangement of family cooking fires and smoke holes in the interior of a longhouse is seen in this illustration. The longhouse was a residence for a kinship group with individual families occupying the cubicles at the sides.

For the campaign against Crown Point, Johnson was given the rank of major general of provincial forces, a detachment of royal artillery under Chief Engineer Captain

William Eyre, and a boat ride up the Hudson to the limits of its navigation. Eyre came to Virginia with Major-General Edward Braddock early in 1755 as captain in the 44th regiment, but was immediately posted to the colony of New York. Nothing is known of the early life of William Eyre except that he had considerable military experience in Europe before coming to North America. In 1745, Eyre fought in Scotland with the government forces against the Jacobite uprising, and in 1747 he worked as an engineer defending Bergen op Zoom, Netherlands.

Eyre had begun the palisaded Fort Lyman (Edward), and then joined Johnson's main force in time to fortify the campsite at the head of Lake George. The fort at Edward was a three-bastioned, Vauban-style fort, surrounded by a dry moat that was 14 feet wide and 8 feet deep. Fort Edward is most notable for its association with Robert Rogers and his Rangers. Adjacent to the Fort, on an island situated at the great bend in the Hudson River, was the base camp of Rogers' Rangers during much of the French and Indian War. There was on this site, named Rogers Island, a hospital, a blockhouse, barracks, and Ranger huts. Eyre later designed and supervised the building of Fort William Henry. In March 1757, he successfully commanded its 500-man garrison against a force three times as large attacking under François-Pierre de Rigaud de Vaudreuil. His brother, Governor Pierre de Rigaud de Vaudreuil referred to Eyre as "an officer of consummate experience in the art of war."

The present village of Fort Edward, New York, was called "The Great Carrying Place" because it was the portage between the Hudson River and Lake Champlain. The first fortification to have been built in the location was Fort Nicholson garrisoned by 450 men under the command of Colonel Francis Nicholson in 1709, during the conflict known as "Queen Anne's War." John Henry Lydius, a Dutch fur trader, came to the site of Fort Nicholson to construct a trading post in 1731. Lydius may also have built a sawmill on Rogers Island. It is unknown whether the Lydius post was destroyed and reconstructed in 1745 when many French and Indian raids were being conducted on the Hudson River. The garrison in Fort Edward was enlarged after the "massacre" at Fort William Henry. Fort Edward was now the sole northern outpost for the British in New York.

After leaving a portion of his force to build Fort Edward near the landing on the Hudson River, Johnson had moved to the southern shore of the lake. Of the Lake George site, Johnson wrote, "I found it a near wilderness, not one foot cleared. I have made a good wagon road to it ... never was house or fort erected here before. We have cleared land enough to encamp 5000 men. The troops now under my command and the reinforcements on the way will amount near that number." Johnson initially had nearly 5000 colonials at his command, but Shirley shifted some of Johnson's men and resources to his own campaign at the last minute. The forts, Edward and William Henry when completed, would guard the portage between the waters of Lake George and the Hudson River to prevent any large-scale French invasion. [154]

During the year following the construction of Fort William Henry, the outpost served as the base of operations for English raiding parties, including those of Rogers' Rangers. It was also the rendezvous point for John Winslow's ill-fated expedition against the French. The first attack was launched against it in the winter 1757 by a French force of 1500 regulars and their Huron allies, led by Sieur de Rigaud de Vaudreuil. The French troops mistakenly built campfires that revealed their position to the British pickets and prevented a surprise attack on the garrison. When the French reached the fort, it was met by a withering fire from the garrison and driven off after they nearly succeeded in firing the fort by igniting the nearby outbuildings. A heavy snowfall helped to quench the flames and prevent the fort's complete destruction. Vaudreuil was forced to withdraw his troops and retire through deep snowdrifts back to Fort Carillon at Ticonderoga. During that turbulent year, the fort again repulsed the French military machine, which sent raiders to destroy the flotilla of boats that were being assembled to advance up the lake. A third attempt to eliminate the post was successfully led by the Marquis de Montcalm.

The Champlain-Richelieu Channel in Fiction and History

Formed by the St. Lawrence and Richelieu Rivers, Lake Champlain, Lake George, and the Hudson River, this historic "Warpath of the Nations" provided an avenue over which the French and British armies and their Indian allies moved in their military operations for the conquest of North America. Known today as the Richelieu-Champlain Channel, it was already an important pathway for the Iroquois, and it soon became one for French traders as well. In colonial times, Lake Champlain was used as a water passage (or, in winter, along the surface of the ice) between the Saint Lawrence and the Hudson valleys. Travelers found it easier to journey by boats and sledges on the lake rather than to go overland. Independent fur traders among the French and among the French-leaning tribes often made their way to Albany where they received better value for the furs than in Canada. The French regime built several forts along the length of the Richelieu River and on the shores of Lake Champlain in order to stem this trade and protect the approaches to their territory. The English would also fortify the passage from their end, making the region one of the most highly fortified on the continent.

A map of the region with an overlay of modern-day boundaries and cities shows the proximity of many of the places used in Cooper's books.

It should be noted that in June 1775, Richard Montgomery invaded Canada by this route capturing Fort St. Johns and then Montreal in November 1775. He then united with Benedict Arnold who had led an army up the more difficult course of the Kennebec River in an advance on Quebec City. On December 31, facing the year-end expiration of their troops' enlistments, Patriot forces advanced on Quebec under the cover of a blizzard. Montgomery led the attack on the city, but was killed during the battle. The British found his body and gave it an honorable burial. In this failed attack Arnold received his first leg wound in the service of the Revolution. Patriot Daniel Morgan assumed command and made progress against the defenders, but halted to wait for reinforcements. By the time the rest of Arnold's army finally arrived, the British had reorganized, forcing the Patriots to call off their attack.

In 1762, Montgomery had been promoted to captain in the British army and served on the shores of Lake Champlain, at Ticonderoga, and in the campaign against Havana. After that he resided in America awhile, but revisited England. In 1772, he sold his commission and bought an estate at Rhinebeck, on the Hudson. He married a daughter of Robert Livingston, was chosen a representative in the Colonial Assembly, and was a member of the Provincial Convention in 1775. His death was regarded as a great public calamity.

Arundel is the first in a Revolutionary War trilogy (1929-1933) by historian Kenneth Roberts, following the adventures of several fictitious residents of what later became the state of Maine, and particularly detailing Arnold's expedition, which was probably the most amazing feat of arms performed by any military force during the Revolutionary War. Unanticipated problems beset the expedition as soon as it left the last outposts in Maine. The portages up the Kennebec River proved grueling, and the boats frequently leaked spoiling food supplies and gunpowder. More than a third of the men turned back between the Kennebec and Chaudière rivers where the land proved a swampy tangle of lakes and streams.

Roberts' sources included several journals kept by officers in Arnold's little army including of Captains John Lamb, Henry Dearborn, John Topham, and Simon Thayer. These first-person accounts supply many of the day-to-day details that make the story compelling. *Rabble In Arms* is the second novel of the trilogy; the third volume of the trilogy, *The Lively Lady* concerns the war of 1812. In *Oliver Wiswell* (1940), Roberts portrayed the view of the Loyalists in the American Revolution. The hero of the story, Oliver Wiswell, is a very compelling and sympathetic character. The reader witnesses the brutality of rebel mobs as they tar and feather those whose beliefs differ from their own. The heroes of *Arundel* and *Rabble in Arms* are from Kennebunk (then called Arundel), while Langdon Towne, the chief character of Roberts' better known *Northwest Passage* (1937), is depicted as being from Kittery, Maine.

Northwest Passage was first published in serial form in the *Saturday Evening Post*. The story became a national sensation and was the second best-selling novel in the U.S. in 1937, behind only *Gone with the Wind*. Much of the novel follows the genuine exploits and character of Robert Rogers, the leader of Rogers' Rangers. Chosen as one of Rogers' aides, Towne sets out with a force of Rangers, Stockbridge Indians (Mohican) and Mohawk Indians, to ascend the channel and attack the French mission and Abenaki stronghold at St. Francis. Rogers and his men endured significant hardships to reach the village from the British base at Fort Crown Point, and even more hardship afterwards. As they were behind enemy lines and far from any support, all their options were relatively poor. They returned by way of the Connecticut River. The book later served as the basis for a 1940 movie starring Spencer Tracy and Robert Young and a disappointing 1958-59 TV series. Within both the book and the movie, the character of Rogers expresses a distrust of the Mohawks and a close dependence on the Mohicans.

Roberts was a Pulitzer Prize winner. He worked first as a journalist, becoming nationally known for his work with the *Saturday Evening Post* from 1919 to 1928, and then as a popular novelist. He was hampered in his writing by the absence of two court-martial transcripts: the trial of Lieutenant Stevens and the trial of Rogers himself, which was a key element in the book. The transcripts had been lost for over one hundred years, and several historians had claimed that Rogers' allies had suppressed the transcripts to cover up embarrassing details about Rogers. Roberts, however, believed that Rogers' enemies Gage and Johnson had destroyed the transcripts and that copies still might exist at the Colonial Office in England. To that end, he hired a full-time English researcher to hunt for the transcripts. After an extended search, when the novel was almost complete, copies of both transcripts favorable to Rogers were located.

Drums Along the Mohawk was a 1939 historical film based upon a 1936 novel of the same name by American author and Newbury Award winner, Walter D. Edmonds. A central feature of the plot is the Battle of Oriskany, a pivotal engagement during the American Revolution, in which the British from Canada attempted to occupy the Hudson Valley. The film portrays only Indians and Tories as antagonists; British soldiers are seldom referenced or seen. The fort besieged in the book has not been identified, but several local "forts" in New York experienced similar attacks. Among them were German Flatts, Old Stone Fort in Schoharie, Middle Fort in Middleburg, and Fort Schuyler (Stanwix) in Rome. The book is peopled with historical persons such as General Nicholas Herkimer, Adam Helmer, and William Caldwell. The film was nominated for two Academy Awards. The book was on the bestseller list for two years, second only to Margaret Mitchell's famous 1936 novel *Gone with the Wind* for part of that time. Edmond's *The Musket and the Cross: The Struggle of France and England for North America* (1968) is one of the best histories on the subject.

Lake Champlain has been called the Lake of the Iroquois, and *Petawabouque*, meaning alternating land and water because of the many islands within it. The Iroquois themselves called the large sheet of water the *Lake-Gate*, or, in their own speech, *Caniadeguarante*. The Lake George was called *Andiatarocte* or *Here-the-Lake-Valley-closes*, a name that was geographically correct.

X. The Battle of Lake George

William Johnson had been assigned the task of reducing the French fort at Crown Point. Given the tactical objective, the expedition was a failure, but strategically the effort was an immense success. Besides 200 Mohawk, Johnson had troops from several colonies: New York, Connecticut, Massachusetts, New Hampshire, and Rhode Island. The English had received information that Fort St. Frédéric at Crown Point was defended by only 800 Frenchmen and whatever Indians they could muster. The only British regulars with Johnson were the detachment of artillery from New York tasked with the upcoming siege and reduction of the French post, the remainder of the regulars being committed to accompany General Braddock or Governor Shirley. Departing Fort Lyman (re-named Fort Edward in 1756) with 1,500 men and 200 Mohawks in August 1755, Johnson moved north and reached Lac Saint Sacrement on the 28th. Johnson erected a temporary camp of brush and logs as a stepping-off position for the campaign. He named the lake George for the king and the fort William Henry in honor of a member of the royal family. More than a century after French Father Isaac Jogues had passed among its beautiful islands, in his bark canoe, an English army lay encamped on the southern shore of the lake the Jesuit had called Saint Sacrement.

Order of Battle: Provincial Regiments (2932 effectives)
1st Mass., Col. Timothy Ruggles, 450
2nd Mass., Col. Moses Titcomb (killed), 450
3rd Mass., Col. Ephraim Williams (killed), 450
1st Conn., Maj. Gen. Lyman, 450
2nd Conn., Lt. Col. Whiting, 450
Rhode Island, Lt. Col. Cole, 250
Three composite companies of CT / NY, Maj. Fitch, 200
Indians, 250

Order of Battle: French Forces at Lake George: 1500
La Reine Battalion, 100
Languedoc Battalion, 100
Comp. Marine & Canonniers-Bombardiers, 50
Militia, 650
Indians, 600

However, before reinforcements could arrive, the French confronted Johnson with troops under Jean Erdman, the Baron Dieskau who knew of Johnson's occupation of the Lake George shoreline from papers taken at the Monongahela. Leaving the majority of his 3,000 men in the St. Frédéric/Carillon area, he set out south with 250 regulars, 650 Canadians and 600 Indians. This was probably an error. Splitting your forces in the face of a superior or indeterminate enemy is not generally a good idea. Both commanders were seemingly unsure of the numbers or quality of the troops that they faced. Yet Johnson's forces were close enough to support one another, Dieskau's were not. After ordering the construction of a fort at the portage at Ticonderoga, Dieskau quietly moved the French army up Lake George to within striking distance of Johnson's camp. Dieskau first mounted an expedition to cut the supply lines of the attacking English forces.

Believing there was only a token force at Fort Lyman (Ft. Edward), Dieskau hoped to effectively end the threat by cutting off the invaders supplies.

Finally learning of the French approach on the morning of 8 September 1755, Johnson sent a large party of Massachusetts and Connecticut men and 100 Mohawks under Col. Ephraim Williams back along the wagon road toward Fort Edward as a precaution. This detachment, which was ambushed some miles from the lake, became known as the "Bloody Morning Scout." Hearing the gunfire only a short time after Williams' group had left, Johnson immediately dispatched Lt. Col. Edward Cole with some 300 men to assist him. Most of the New Englanders fled toward Johnson's camp, while about 100 of their comrades under Nathan Whiting and Seth Pomeroy and most of the surviving Mohawks covered their withdrawal with a fighting retreat. In the morning engagement, the colonials suffered their greatest losses. The American rearguard was able to inflict substantial casualties on their overconfident pursuers. Pomeroy noted that his men "killed great numbers of them; they were seen to drop like pigeons." One of those killed in this phase of the battle was Jacques Legardeur de Saint-Pierre, the highly respected commander of Dieskau's Canadien and Indian forces. His fall caused great dismay, particularly to the French Indians. The bodies of the dead were thrown into a nearby pond, called thereafter "Bloody Pond."[155]

Saint-Pierre had spent a number of years among the western Indians in present-day Wisconsin and Minnesota with his adventurer / trader father where he obtained an excellent knowledge of the Indian languages and the business conducted in the trading posts. In 1724, he began military service as a second ensign with the colonial regular troops. Because of his skills as an interpreter, his early active duty involved building loyalty and support among the Ojibwa, Cree, and Sioux to assist the French in future campaigns against other Indian tribes. From 1748–1750 he served at Fort Michilimackinac during which time he was promoted to captain. The whole period was spent negotiating a fragile peace between the warring Indian nations. Returning from the western forts in 1753, Saint-Pierre was assigned to the Ohio Country, where he was present for Washington's diplomatic mission and was in the party that defeated Washington at Fort Necessity. In 1755, he had led a large contingent of Canadien militia and Indians from Montreal against the Bloody Morning Scout and was immediately killed.

Meanwhile, Col. Joseph Blanchard, commander of Fort Edward, becoming aware of the battle in the distance, sent out 80 men from Nathaniel Folsom's company of the New Hampshire Provincial Regiment and 40 New York Provincials under Capt. McGinnis to investigate:

> Hearing the report of guns in the direction of the Lake, they pressed forward, and when within about two miles of it, fell in with the baggage of the French army protected by a guard, which they immediately attacked and dispersed. About four o'clock in the afternoon, some 300 of the French army appeared in sight. They had rallied, and retreating in tolerable order. Capt. Folsom posted his men among the trees, and as the enemy approached, they poured in upon them a well directed and galling fire. He continued the attack in this manner till prevented by darkness, killing many of the enemy, taking some of them prisoners, and finally driving them from the field. He then collected his own wounded, and

securing them with many of the enemy's packs, he brought his prisoners and booty safe into camp. The next day the rest of the baggage was brought in, thus securing the entire baggage and ammunition of the French army. In this brilliant affair, Folsom lost only six men, but McGinnis was mortally wounded, and died soon after. The loss of the French was very considerable.[156]

After recovering his wounded and taking several prisoners, Folsom returned to Fort Lyman. A second force was sent out the next day to recover the abandoned French baggage train. Lacking supplies and with their leader gone, the French retreated north.

Johnson's own account of the battle on the shore of Lake George in the form of a dispatch was reported in the colonial newspapers less than a week later:

> About half an hour after 11 the enemy appeared in sight, and marched along the road in a very regular order directly upon our center. They made a small halt about 150 yards from our breastwork, when the regular troops (whom we judged to be such by their bright and fixed bayonets) made the grand and center attack. The Canadiens and the Indians squatted and dispersed on our flank. The enemy's fire we received first from the regulars in platoons, but it did no great execution, being at too great a distance, and our men defended by the breastwork. Our artillery then began to play upon them ... [and] the engagement now became general on both sides. The French regulars kept their ground and order for some time with great resolution, but the warm and constant fire from our artillery and troops put them into disorder. ... About 4 o'clock, when our men and Indians jumped over the breastwork, pursued the enemy, slaughtered numbers and took several prisoners, amongst whom was Baron de Dieskau ... badly wounded in the leg and through both hips, and the surgeon fears for his life. [He died in a few days.][157]

William Johnson sparing Dieskau in a painting by Benjamin West (c. 1764)

The Canadien forces had wisely declined to join a frontal attack on a prepared position, having lost their leader in the first engagement. In an effort to shame his Canadien allies into attacking, Dieskau had formed his grenadiers into an attacking column and personally led them forward around noon. Charging into heavy musket fire and grape shot from Johnson's three cannon, Dieskau's attack had bogged down. Johnson's colonials had defeated a European Army amid the freshly cut stumps of a primeval forest. During the battle Johnson received a wound in the thigh that was very painful, but he won the day. Precise casualties for the Battle of Lake George are not known. Sources indicate that the Anglo-colonials suffered between 262 and 331 killed, wounded, and missing, while the French incurred between 228 and 600 casualties. The Colonial losses did not include Indian allies, but their dead included Colonel Williams, Colonel Titcomb, Major Ashley, Captains McGinnis (a.k.a. Maginnes and McGennis), Keyes, Porter, Ingersoll, and twelve other officers. The victory at the Battle of Lake George marked one the first victories for American provincial troops over the French regulars and their allies. An observer of the battle noted of the enemy Indians: "Their Flight was so hasty, that they dropt some of the Scalps of our Men, which we recovered." [158]

One week later Johnson was still planning to move against Crown Point, which was his strategic objective. However, the expedition was fated to stall on the shores of Lake George. Tiyanoga died fighting for the British at the battle, and many of the Indians, as was their practice, melted back into the forests in order to mourn the deaths among their number. It was thought foolish to proceed without their support. Moreover, word of the disaster that had befallen Braddock in Pennsylvania had just been received. The colonial governments seemed satisfied to end the campaigning year of 1755 with a victory in hand rather than risk success with another engagement. They garrisoned the fort with a mixture of provincials and regulars, and recalled Johnson.

Although the Battle of Lake George was hardly a decisive victory, the British needed a military hero in the face of so many setbacks, and Johnson became that man. William Johnson's stature had never been higher. A Bostonian wrote, "This is the first time Mr. Johnson or any of his men ever fought an enemy ... so that the ... militia of New England have all the glory of the most obstinate and long engagement." Never was an American victory so generously rewarded. A Boston newspaper reported that the respect shown to Johnson "was equal to what might have been paid to a Marlborough on his return with victory from Flanders." A group of citizens rode out from Albany to greet him on the road and ride in ceremony with him into the city. The ships at the wharf fired their cannon in salute. His Royal Majesty, George II, made Johnson a baronet for life, and Parliament voted Johnson £5,000. He was thereafter Sir William Johnson, the Mohawk Baronet.[159]

This period illustration is of the Mohawk war leader Tiyanoga, known to the English as King Hendrick. He wears a combination of native and European articles. The metal pipe tomahawk, metal gorget, ruffled shirt, and woolen blanket are all accommodations of native dress taken from the whites.

Not every Anglo-colonial was convinced of Johnson's status as a hero. In *Luke Gridley's Diary of 1757* (published in 1906), the author notes a conspiracy to denigrate the role of anyone other than Johnson in the victory. Among his officers, some of them afterward becoming notable even in death, were General Phineas Lyman; Colonels Ephraim Williams, Timothy Ruggles, and Moses Titcomb; Lieutenant-Colonels Nathan Whiting and Seth Pomeroy; Captains Philip Schuyler and Israel Putnam. Supposedly, General Lyman, commander of the Connecticut brigade, had taken command of the forces when Johnson had been wounded and repulsed the attack of the French and Indians. Lyman had led the advance up the Hudson and had begun the construction of Fort Lyman, afterward named Fort Edward. This claim contains, strangely enough, a connection to Cooper and *The Last of the Mohicans* through his wife, Susan De Lancey:

> A provincial governor, the energetic and sensible if tactless and over-confident Shirley, then held the field for a while, and the solitary success of nearly three years was achieved by Lyman's New-Englanders; it won a baronetcy and £5000 not for the victor, however, but for the late Admiral Warren's nephew, William Johnson, who despite the value of his Indian diplomacy, had shown neither military conduct nor courage. His jealousy of Shirley's interference began a feud which was taken up by his kinsmen, the powerful De Lanceys; and Shirley was deposed through their influence ... plus the inter-provincial grudge between New York and New England which wrought so much evil in the Revolution. An English colonel, Daniel Webb, for no historically assignable reason, was then sent over as a place-warmer for two Scotchmen: James Abercrombie, another court favorite, who in turn was to be *locum tenens* for John Campbell, Earl of Loudoun.[160]

Samuel Blodget, a civilian sutler who provisioned military forces, was present at the battle of Lake George in 1755 and afterwards prepared a crude drawing of the battle from his observations. Although he had little education, Blodget possessed a shrewd marketing sense. He persuaded Thomas Johnston, one of Boston's best engravers, to prepare the scene for publication, and Richard Draper, a Boston printer, edited the entrepreneur's semi-literate account for a general audience. Being from a person not part of the army and free to evaluate the battle from more than one perspective, Blodget's account rings with a greater authenticity than that of Johnson, who spent a good deal of the battle in his tent wounded. General Phineas Lyman, a Connecticut lawyer and Yale tutor, commanded the English with spirit and bravery during much of the battle. Johnson was later accused of suppressing Lyman's role in his dispatches in order to increase his own. Blodget noted, "I took Position at the Eminence where the Field-Piece was planted, from whence I could, with Advantage, view the Action, in all its Parts, from the Beginning to the End of it: Though I must confess, the thick Smoke, which arose from the Discharge of so many Guns on both Sides, rendered the Sight less clear than I could have wished."

The map (Plan of Battle) probably first appeared as an insert between the first two pages of the pamphlet, which Blodget was selling at his store in Boston by mid December—barely three months after the battle. The original Boston Plan and pamphlet seem to have quickly attracted the notice of Thomas Jefferys an enterprising map publisher of London, who reprinted them without delay, the Plan bearing the date 2 February 1756. "All of which is carefully and neatly struck off from a large Copper Plate." Nonetheless, Blodget's work was "virtually lost" among the papers of the Massachusetts Historical Society until the end of the 19th century when the Plan and a separate pamphlet and key to it were reunited (1909). The London issue of the Plan had several times been reproduced in historical works, mostly in a reduced and mutilated form, without any indication of its origin and without the key to the references that Blodget had provided. As to the Plan itself, Jefferys refers to it as "the only Piece that exhibits the American method of Bush Fighting." [161]

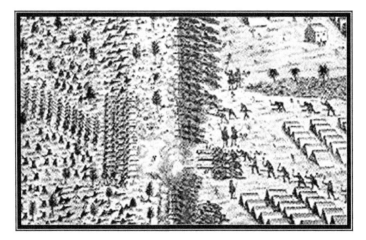

A detail from Blodget's map of the main field of the battle suggests that the French and colonials (right) fought in a regular order while the Indians were arranged as skirmishers.

Blodget notes that the "breastwork" mentioned by Johnson in his newspaper report was actually a tangled of horizontal trees. "All the rest was in its natural State of Wildness, covered with Pine Trees, and a thick undergrowth of Shrubs interrupted with Brakes, both Waist-high." Blodget further notes it "was nothing more than the Bodies of Trees laid singly on the Ground. They were hastily felled while our Men were retreating from the former Battle [the Scout], and not in Number sufficient to lie all of them contiguous to each other. The under-growth also was all cleared away about the Camp for which Reason, the Enemy were better defended than we were." Both the Canadiens and the Indians "became invisible" by squatting below the natural underbrush and reaps of branches and concealing themselves among the uncut trees of the forest. In particular, there was a long fallen tree and a rise in the ground "15 rods" (75-80 yards) in the colonial front and a swamp to their flank from which the enemy Indians did the colonials "great mischief," they enemy being covered until they rose to fire. It was from the swamp that the colonials received most of their wounds.[162]

A good part of Blodget's account regarded the Bloody Morning Scout. The enemy seemingly having chosen their ground carefully in a place on the new road cleared of trees and scrubs in which the colonials might find the cover:

> The Form in which the French and Indians appeared, being like that of a Hook; for so they had placed themselves, extending a curved Line from their Front on each Side of the Road, near half a Mile on the Right, and about one half that Space on the Left. They had Opportunity to do this, as they had received Intelligence from a Scout they had sent out, that a considerable Body of our Men was marching in order to oppose them. The Reason of their thus forming themselves was this — on the Left of the Road, all along the Line they had placed themselves in, they had the Advantage of being covered with a thick growth of Brush and Trees and such as is common to swampy Land as this was. On the Right, they were all along defended, as with a Breastwork, by a continued Eminence filled with Rocks, and Trees, and Shrubs as high as a Man's Breast. Our Men, while marching in the Road, were within 150 Yards of the Enemy, who lay invisible on either Side. They had posted themselves in the most advantageous Place there was between the Camp and the Fort for an Ambuscade. And considering this, together with their great Superiority in Numbers, being upwards of 2000, 'tis a wonder they had not entirely routed and destroyed this Detachment. Our Men must have behaved with the utmost Bravery, and Wisdom too, or they could not have made so honorable a Retreat, killing even more of the Enemy, than they lost themselves, as the French General owned, after he was taken. Tho, in this Fight, which began about two Miles and a half from the Camp, our loss, both of Officers and private men, was much greater than in the other Battle.[163]

Some 300 Indians of the French contingent seemingly went back to the field of "The Bloody Morning Scout," to scalp and plunder the dead. While resting with their scalps and pillage some seven miles from Glen Falls and two from Lake George, they were surprised by 200-300 New York and New Hampshire men under Captains McGinnis and Folsom, who had been sent from Fort Edward to the aid of General Johnson. A sharp fight resulted in the utter rout of the French contingent. Captain McGinnis, commanding the English, was mortally wounded.

The death of Col. Williams during the Bloody Morning Scout was widely mourned. Williams led a regiment of ten companies. Among those companies were Burke's Rangers and Roger's Rangers. Among his aides was William "Billy" Williams, who would be a signer of the Declaration of Independence from Connecticut. Col. Williams, whose body had remained untouched by the French-led Indians, was laid to rest beneath a pine tree close to the military road. He was just 40. The death of Col. Williams provided the funds for the establishment of Williams College. Ebenezer Fitch, first President of

Williams College, describe the colonel in a biographical sketch published in 1802. Fitch noted, "Williams' kind and obliging deportment, his generosity and condescension, greatly endeared him to his soldiers ... When at Fort-Massachusetts, he frequently entered into the pastimes of his soldiers, upon an equal footing with them, and permitted every decent freedom; and again, when the diversions were over, he, with ease and dignity, resumed the Captain." His body was disinterred in the early 20th century and moved to the chapel at Williams College. A stone etched with Williams' initials on it and the year of his death still stands at the original Lake George gravesite just across the street from a monument erected by Williams College alumni. The monument marks the site of the ambush. [164]

The William's family was very influential in western Massachusetts. In 1738, Ephraim William, Sr. (1691-1754), father of Col. Williams, settled with his family at the Indian mission in Stockbridge, Massachusetts, one of four white families invited to do so. These colonials hoped to serve as Christian exemplars for the families of Mohican Indians who had gathered nearby in the Housatonic Valley under the missionary John Sergeant (1710-1749). The Mohicans, in six main family groups, came from New York west over the Taconic Mountains to live along the river in Massachusetts and Connecticut in order to escape the ravages of the Mohawks. The Williams family quickly became involved in the Stockbridge mission. Sergeant, who had married Ephraim Sr.'s daughter Abigail, established an Indian boys boarding school, an educational and Christianizing venture, and Abigail (Williams) Sergeant was herself installed as headmistress of the Indian girls school before her first husband's untimely death. When Rev. Jonathan Edwards (1703-1758) was called from Northampton to fill the vacant ministry, hostilities between him and the William's family flared over theological issues and the management of the Indian schools and mission.

Meanwhile, Abigail had married Joseph Dwight. Upon the outbreak of King George's War (1744-1748), Dwight had taken command of a group of local Massachusetts militia as their colonel, and rose to the rank of brigadier general (1745) commanding the Massachusetts Artillery. During the French and Indian War in 1756, he commanded a brigade of militia in the Lake Champlain region.

Numerous family members had enlisted under Col. Ephraim William's command for the Lake George campaign: cousin Rev. Stephen as chaplain, brother Thomas as surgeon, half-brother Josiah as ensign, cousin Billy as quartermaster, Perez Marsh, a cousin-in-law, as surgeon's mate. This was not unusual. Volunteer regiments were in some measure bound by kinship ties with fathers, sons, brothers, and cousins all serving in the same unit.

The Death of Colonel Williams (1755) by Frederick Coffay Yohn

On 10 November 1755, Abigail Dwight, the sister of Col. Ephraim Williams, wrote of the Bloody Morning Scout to Abraham Booker. Her letter opens a door on the very personal fears and reactions of an individual caught in such an ambush, as well as the feelings of those who heard the reports at home:

> We of our mournful afflicted family have been plunged in such a depth of sorrow from the late sad catastrophe at Lake George that [we] could scarcely attend to anything but lamentation & weeping. My eldest Brother Col. Ephraim Williams was among the slain, as you have doubtless heard …
>
> [My other brother Josiah] was an Ensign in his regiment … He took a tree to stand his ground agreeable to the orders, discharged his gun at an Indian about 5 rods before him, which took his life. He fell & yelled. My brother squatted to recharge before he retreated & as he was throwing in his powder he received a shot (from one of the savages who had flanked him) into his right thigh. The ball came out at his left buttock, cut the string of his bladder in passing through his body. Immediately he saw from whence came the shot. The savage running toward him with his hatchet, he instantly started & ran about one-half a mile, life failing. Crept into a hole made by two trees blown up by the roots, lay in water until he was a little revived. Saw his blood so thick where he went in that he expected to be followed for his scalp.
>
> When the retreat had past him, as he was a little before, took courage & went out & as one & another was retreating without wounds, he sometimes got a little help by hanging to their shoulders. Sometimes when all left him, as was the case several times, he crawled along himself till at length was quite spent & forsaken by all his fleeing friends. Giving over hopes of deliverance, there came a young Mohawk in his retreat. Offered his back, took him up, & ran near a quarter of a mile with him into the camp. So marvelous a wonder was his escape from the jaws of [death].

Well now his life was almost gone, the enemy almost upon the camp. The battle come on & long it lasted. No care could be had for the wounded. But all things are ordered in wisdom. My second brother, Doctor Thomas Williams, being the Chief Surgeon of that regiment, took a most tender special care of him ... As Divine Providence would have it, by degrees he has mended & now got home in a horse litter & yesterday sat upright in his chair some minutes.

The world with half an eye must know nothing can be done [against the French] at this advanced season. & indeed upon the first plan, it was plain as the sun in the fairest day, as soon as Braddock was defeated, that the Crown Point army would have all Canada to fight & with your savages & regulars could make 25,000 men & would do it at any expense rather than have the finest key and door to their whole country cut off the hinges. & for us to desire it, the vast expense of money & what is infinitely better, blood in such wicked profusion, is not only sordid cruelty but the most ridiculous & unjustifiable murder of ourselves ...

We can hardly keep the army at Lake George with 6 days provisions ... Upon the whole it looks as if our councils were darkened wisdom, in a remarkable manner hid from those that should be wise. When there is a plan laid with a rational prospect that it can succeed against the French, we shall probably see a war declared. The whole country of Canada, in the several dispersions of it, attacked at once.[165]

To the European mind of the eighteenth century the concepts of wilderness and civilization were at opposite ends of a spectrum with a scale in between suggesting a thorough shading or blending of the two at the center, which was called "the frontier." The frontier was possibly best described in European terms as *ploughed* – a balance between man's needs and God's clockwork nature. "The frontier [was] the outer edge of the wave-the meeting-point between savagery and civilization." The greatest cities of Europe were small and unsophisticated by comparison with those of today; yet London or Paris were certainly well along toward a synthetic condition of life remote from the fields and pastures of the rural peasant. On this scale, the modest New World settlements of the eighteenth centuries, even those highly urbanized ones in Albany and Quebec, were nothing but outposts on a wilderness frontier.[166]

One of the problems with the frontier was that it constantly shifted. As settlers moved into the wilderness the frontier went with them. Moreover, the peace treaties of the 18th century utterly failed to fix the boundaries between the European signatories, and the natives generally failed to honor any boundary that was not established by force of arms. Forts on the frontiers were constructed of masonry, timber, earthworks, or a combination of these materials. The choice of a particular material was largely a matter of availability, with timber being the most commonly used material for new or temporary structures. The building of a fort better defined the frontier than a surveyor's line. Governor Hardy wrote to the Board of Trade in January 1756, emphasizing the importance of Johnson's victory and the new British forts on the New York frontier:

> The advantages resulting from these forts are very considerable. Fort Edward stands at the Great Carrying Place on Hudson's River near 50 miles above Albany, and is the common passage from Canada to Albany, whether they come by Lake George, the South Bay [of Lake Champlain], or Wood Creek.

Fort William Henry secures the passage by Lake George to Hudson's River, Schenectady, and the Mohawk's country ... By Fort William Henry ... we shall be masters of the waters that lead to Crown Point and may facilitate any enterprise on that place or further up Lake Champlain should such be thought advisable.[167]

Fort Carillon, known as Ticonderoga, was one of the most complete on the frontier in terms of the 18th century science of fortification. It was begun at the same time as Fort William Henry, but unlike the latter, it survived into the American Revolution.

The Marquis de Vauban (Sabastien La Prestre, 1633-1707) is generally credited with developing the distinctive shape of frontier forts and their outworks. Vauban's *First System of Fortification* centered on elaborate "star forts" and fortified redoubts and counterguards. Vauban relied heavily on simple geometry in the design of his fortifications, and he used the idea that the trajectory (path) of a bullet or cannonball was always in a straight line. Using these two principles, the plans for a fortification could be made using a drawing compass, a ruled straight edge, and a set of dividers. The actual structure could be taken from a paper layout or model and built at the intended site with simple surveying tools and nothing more than pick-axes and shovels.

The first step in designing a fortification was to draw a polygon around the area to be defended. Squares, pentagons, and hexagons were commonly used in Europe to defend whole cities, but most forts in North America were based on the square. Ideally these were equilateral figures, but engineers often changed the length of the sides to accommodate the natural defensive features of the ground. They also understood that the area enclosed by the polygon needed to be as small as possible due to the limited number of men available to defend the walls.

As an example, historians and archaeologists believe that the interior of Fort Pitt may have been as small as forty-five feet square, requiring the building of an adjacent defensible camp to house the increased number of soldiers in time of war. The entire garrison of the fort at Ticonderoga could not have played a game of regulation football on the fort's parade due to its small size.

Most forts built in North America had sides measuring between 25 and 100 yards. This may reflect the major purpose of the frontier outpost, which was one of resisting small raids and providing a home for the border patrols and rangers. It also suggests a greater dependence on the musket rather than the cannon, as a side was rarely made longer than the effective range of a musket shot. The increased reliance on the tactical use of the musket as a defensive weapon on the eighteenth-century frontier was probably brought about by the lack of effective artillery, which was difficult to haul through the wilderness. Most colonial outposts had no more than a few small cannons or swivel guns for use against personnel. By limiting the length of a side, the military engineer could defend adjacent structures without ever being out of range of either musketry or cannon fire.

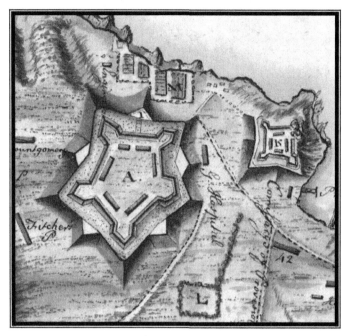

The plan of Fort Crown Point (A) built by the British in 1759 also indicated the old French post known as Fort St. Frédéric (K) which was completed in stone and destroyed when the French abandoned it. They British used it and a redoubt (L) as outworks. LOC

Once the length of one side of the fundamental polygonal shape had been determined, the "rampart" or the "curtain wall" of the fort was laid out between the points of the star. These points were known as "bastions." Continued planning around the figure formed a defensive work with a bastion at each angle, or corner, of the original polygon. Hexagonal works, therefore, had six bastions; pentagonal ones, five; and squares, four. The resulting figure was known as a "front of fortification."

An excavation commonly called the "ditch" or "moat" enhanced the front of fortification. The ditch was usually between fifteen and thirty feet deep. While widths varied, the material dug out of the ditch was often used to raise the bastions and ramparts. The outermost edge of the ditch ran parallel to the shoulders of the bastions, leaving large areas known as "killing grounds" between them. The main entrance to the fort, and one or more "sallie ports," were often directed through the ditch. The entryway to most North American forts in the eighteenth century was either through the ditch or over a narrow bridge that crossed the ditch. This bridge could sometimes be raised. Some forts had wet ditches, or ditches that could be suddenly flooded. Wet ditches better served the purpose of preventing undermining of the walls, but they were particularly unpopular in the colonies because of the health hazard associated with damp air and stagnant water. They also inhibited the defenders' ability to counterattack.

Notwithstanding minor differences, the bastion remained the basic unit of defense. Its shoulders and flanks, topped by a parapet, commanded an unobstructed field of fire in which there was no cover for attacking infantry. Two adjacent bastions had a geometrically correct field of crossfire everywhere between them. The tip of the bastion was called the "salient angle." A besieger standing directly before the salient was open to fire from either of the adjacent bastions and from the rampart above the curtain wall. In other words, the bastion could not be used as cover by the attacker. The access to the bastion from within the fort was small and elevated above the parade, but every bastion was open to fire from defenders at some other point within the fort, a factor common to all the plans for defensive structures on the frontier.

Bomb-proofs were often built into the base of the bastion for defense against incoming mortar and cannon fire. A water supply, powder room, storeroom, or hospital might be located deep within the bastion with access from within the fort. Behind the curtain walls, or beneath the ramparts, fortified rooms called "casemates" were erected. Barracks, storerooms, offices, and stables could be found herein. The casemates were accessed from the parade and often had firing loops or firing slits that faced outward toward the enemy's position. These often looked out into a great ditch, or dry moat, through which the enemy troops were forced to pass.

The Fort William Henry "Massacre"

Lake George was a mere sheet of pretty water, but it was effectively defended by four forts place some few miles from the end of the lake: two English (Edward on the Hudson and William Henry on the lake) and two French (Carillon at the La Chute portage and St. Frédéric at Crown Point). It was at William Henry that Cooper chose to place his most dramatic setting.

Writing only a decade after the War of 1812, Cooper simply could not write a novel in which Americans were viewed as British. Moreover, Cooper attributes a bristling independence and rather early dissatisfaction among the colonials with the British military in *The Last of the Mohicans*, which story takes place in 1757. Instead, he Americanized his novels contrasting, for instance, Hawkeye with Duncan Heyward – the wilderness fighter against the trained regular soldier.

Nor could he make the Iroquois his protagonists. These too had recently been in arms against America as British allies, so he chose the Mohicans, which nation had not occupied the region of his story for a century, but who had sacrificed themselves for the patriot cause in the revolution. In particular, the Iroquois were not called Mingo, nor was any of the Six Nations. The Mingo villages in the Ohio country (actually West Virginia) were increasingly composed of an amalgamation of renegade Seneca, Huron, Wyandot, Susquehannock, Shawnee, and Delaware migrants and refugees.

The Iroquois Confederacy did not invest Fort William Henry as allies of the French, but some mission Indians formerly of their nation from Canada may have been present. These Caughnawagas of St. Francis and La Prairie had separated from their Iroquois relatives more than a century hence. The Jesuits controlled all the missions to the Indians in New France, including one in Illinois (established in 1690), eighteen in the Georgian Bay area of Huronia, and three large conclaves in the St. Lawrence Valley in Abenaki territory. The Indians that attacked the fort, particularly the Huron and Ottawa, were mostly traditional enemies of the Iroquois Confederacy from the Great Lakes region having been recruited for the French campaign.

Cooper referenced the Huron more than 100 times as enemies of the British in his five tales – particularly in *The Deerslayer*. It was through the character Hawkeye, however, that Cooper most strongly condemned that nation. "'A Huron!' repeated the sturdy scout, once more shaking his head in open distrust; 'they are a thievish race, nor do I care by whom they are adopted; you can never make anything of them but skulks and vagabonds.'" The Huron of the historic period were so mixed by intermarriage with the Algonquians (with whom they had sought refuge during the dispersal) that they seem to have lost some of their cultural identity and social character as Iroquoians. Consequently all of the original Huron clan names have been lost in the dustbin of history, but they are thought to have paralleled those of the Seneca. The author also exposed his dislike for the Iroquois through Hawkeye: "To me every native, who speaks a foreign tongue, is accounted an enemy, though he may pretend to serve the king! If Webb wants faith and honesty in an Indian, let him bring out the tribes of the Delawares, and send these greedy and lying Mohawks and Oneidas, with their six nations of varlets, where in nature they belong, among the French!" [168]

In 1666, the French had decided to chastise the Mohawks. The first attempt misfired, but in 1667 under the Marquis de Tracy a force of 1,100 men descended into the Mohawk River valley burning one village after another. Near the confluence of the Mohawk River and Schoharie Creek (Fort Hunter, New York), was one of the principal population centers of the powerful Mohawk nation known as Teantontalogo, or the Lower Mohawk Castle. The Upper Mohawk Castle, at Canajoharie some thirty miles further inland, had a larger population. As the attack came late in the season the Mohawks lost much of their crops for the winter and faced starvation. They therefore joined with those tribes of the Iroquois Confederacy more inclined toward the French, and sued for peace. But they never forgave! Iroquois policies were rarely so straightforward as to include a simple unilateral surrender.

The natural ferocity and military discipline of the Mohawks had made them masters of the forests and had effectively eliminated the power of lesser tribes. The Mohawks held and strove to maintain a trading monopoly first with the Dutch and then with the English. They imposed onerous conditions upon the tribes who wished to trade with them, extending even to the nations of their own confederation. In an attempt to underscore their new position, Mohawk war parties passed down Lake Champlain to raid the French settlements in the St. Lawrence River valley and disrupt the northern fur trade. They attacked and destroyed the Montagnais village at Trois-Rivieres, and Mohawk war parties constantly filtered back and forth across the Lake Champlain and Connecticut River valleys from Agawam to Quebec. As a result, many of the Algonquian-speaking peoples of frontier New England were driven north to the French missions, and the natives who remained in the region went out of their way to avoid offending the Mohawks. Nonetheless, the Mohawks continued to harass the Mahican refugees in their villages in southwestern Vermont and western Massachusetts for many years. In the 18th century, the Mohawks were the most reliable of English allies.

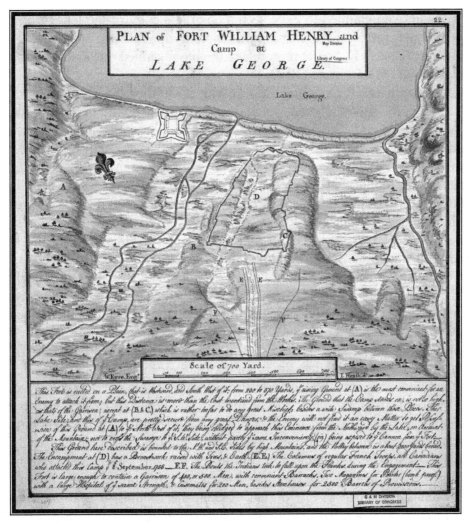

The French plan of attack against Fort William Henry clearly shows the outline of the fortified camp (D). The fort itself was an unassuming edifice made of wood. The camp had a breastwork made of tiers of earth. LOC

A few of the nations allied with the French at William Henry had traveled hundreds of miles to join Montcalm. Others like the ubiquitous Abenaki were from nearer to home. The Abenaki and other Christian Indians had been the bulwark of French-Indian power in the east, but they were now hanging aloof licking their wounds from attacks by colonial rangers and militia. Many western tribes—the Ottawa, Menominee, Winnebago, Mississauga, Fox, Sac, Illinois, Huron-Petun, Pottawatomie, and others—had to be drawn to New York from more than 1500 miles through the copious distribution of gifts and presents and the promise of plunder and captives. Some of these came in small war parties, and many were very young warriors, who lacked the discipline of veterans, intent upon gaining their reputations.

Among the British officers who Cooper used as villains in his story was the perfidious Major General Daniel Webb, commander of Fort Edward who refused in writing to support Lieutenant Colonel George Munro during the siege of Fort William Henry (1757). This infamous circumstance was set in history over the intervening years and made a part of American folklore by Cooper and numerous Hollywood film directors

(Clarence Brown, 1920; George B. Seitz, 1936; and Michael Mann, 1992). Historian Francis Parkman, who claimed to have seen a complete copy of the letter from Webb to Munro in Colonel Joseph Frye's *Journal*, reported the text in *Montcalm and Wolfe* (1881); and historian Ian K. Steele reproduced the bloodstained original in *Betrayal: Fort William Henry and the Massacre* (1990).[169]

Lt. Col. Munro was left to defend the fort with 2,300 men (only 1,600 of whom were fit for battle). Munro – outnumbered, outgunned, and charged with defending the families of his provincials – acceded to Montcalm's offer of an honorable surrender. Meanwhile, Webb laid quiet with 2000 troops just 17 miles distant, sending expresses to New England for additional help, which could not possibly arrive in time. It is not altogether certain that Webb could have relieved the siege of William Henry. He had some responsibility to maintain a sufficient force at Fort Edward, and a column of even 1000 men would not have displaced Montcalm's 7000. Nevertheless, Montcalm's looming victory was threatened by shortages of ammunition and supplies among the French. A fact concerning which, the British were oblivious. It was the refusal of Webb to attempt a relief that caused Montcalm to offer terms of surrender. The British could march out with the honors of war, and be escorted to Fort Edward by a detachment of French troops. The Indians shattered the gentlemanly cooperation between the British and the French.

According to historian Francis Parkman, the border population "regarded Indians with a mixture of detestation and horror. Their mysterious warfare of ambush and surprise, their midnight onslaughts, their butcheries, their burnings, and all their nameless atrocities, had been for years the theme of fireside stories; and the dread they excited was deepened by the distrust and dejection of the time." Scores of corpses had been found scalped among the ruins of tiny settlements and isolated farmsteads throughout the border regions, and an equal number of despondent and humbled captives had trudged north through the forests to be tormented and sold to the French. The Indians who had raided New England tended to take captives for ransom or adoption, not for murder! William Johnson, noted the practice in his journal: "When the Indians lose a man in action, & chance to take an enemy prisoner, he belongs to the family of the deceased, who take great care of him, & look on him in the same light as on the person lost & even leave him the same fortune." Captives were frequently exchanged for valuables, for pledges of peace, or for other prisoners. When the English marched out on the morning of August 10, they were terrified that the French could not control the Indians. Unfortunately, they were correct. [170]

The English passed a troubled night in Fort William Henry as the Indians pillaged the fortified camp. Illustration by Frederick Coffay Yohn.

When the column of dejected English at last began to move, Jonathan Carver, a provincial volunteer noted in his journal that "the Indians crowded upon them, impeded their march, snatched caps, coats, and weapons from men and officers, tomahawked those that resisted, and, seizing upon shrieking women and children, dragged them off or murdered them on the spot ... A frightful tumult ensued ... Montcalm ... and many other French officers, threw themselves among the Indians, and by promises and threats tried to allay their frenzy." Abenaki Christians from the mission of the Penobscot reportedly gave the signal for the butchery to begin. Munro, who is brutally killed in the novel, actually survived the massacre dying in Albany some months later. Joseph Frye was seized by a number of Indians, who, brandishing spears and tomahawks, threatened him with death and tore off his clothing, leaving nothing but breeches, shoes, and shirt. Captain Burke of Massachusetts was stripped, after a violent struggle, of all his clothes; then broke loose, gained the woods, and spent the night shivering in the thick grass of a marsh. He ultimately reached Fort Edward. Carver declared that, when the tumult was at its height, he saw officers of the French army walking about at a little distance and talking with seeming unconcern. Three or four Indians then seized him, brandished their tomahawks over his head, and tore off most of his clothes, while he vainly claimed protection from a French sentinel, who called him an English dog, and violently pushed him back among his tormentors. [171]

The massacre ended in fits and starts with as many as fifty English dead. To his credit, Montcalm succeeded in ransoming about 400 English in the course of the day, but the Indians decamped in a body toward Montreal with about 200 captives. The Indians had lost a fair number of warriors in the operation. The Ceremony of the Dead, or the condolence ritual, was widespread among the tribes. Condolence rituals cleansed those who were in despair of their grief and helped to refocus the attention of the living on the needs of the survivors. The replacement of dead family members with captives, or those adopted for the purpose, was not only an attempt to maintain the size of the tribe but was also a means of raising up a successor to fill an important position in clan life.

Cooper's books offered a great opportunity for some rather dramatic images. This print exhibits many of the prejudices and myths that Cooper's works reinforced; yet it is generally correct with respect to costume, weapons, and accoutrements. Illustration by F.O.C. Darley.

Following the massacre, Montcalm razed the fort and covered the charred remains with sand. The task occupied several days. The barracks were torn down, and the huge pine-logs of the rampart thrown into a heap. The dead bodies that filled the casemates were added to the mass, and fire was set to the whole. The mighty funeral pyre blazed all night. William Henry remained a ruin until 1953 when the present replica was erected on the site.[172]

Yale College president Timothy Dwight, in a history published in 1822, apparently coined the phrase "massacre at Fort William Henry," based on Carver's 1778 journal. Carver served in the Massachusetts militia. Cooper was clearly influenced by Dwight's history, but his attitudes toward frontier warfare were not without deeper roots in the colonial experience.

XI. A Fondness for Griping

The reader needs now to step back two years to an earlier military debacle leaving the shores of Lake George and traveling several hundred miles west to the Monongahela River. General Edward Braddock – a British regular initially considered America's savior in 1754 – exhibited contempt for wilderness warfare in his attitude towards both provincials and Indians. The colonials, for their part, thought the redcoats imperious and inept. These attitudes also come through in Cooper's fiction.

Braddock expected to seize Fort Duquesne easily, and then push on to capture a series of French forts, eventually reaching Lake Erie. Braddock set off into the wilderness building a road for his army ahead of him. The physical achievement of clearing this road exceeded any other road-building project undertaken in North America to that time. Braddock's route ran from the Potomac River in Maryland along Nemacolin's Path, an Indian route marked by frontiersmen Christopher Gist and Thomas Cresap and authorized by the land speculators of the Ohio Company of Virginia in 1752. Military roads were generally considered a benefit of woodlands campaigns especially for land speculators. General John Forbes, in 1758, cut a wagon road to Pittsburgh almost directly over the Allegheny Mountains, later known as Forbes Road, building a series of fortifications to serve as supply depots; and General John Burgoyne built his from Whitehall to Saratoga in 1777 to benefit Loyalist landowners among his commanders. These roads served to open the wilderness to settlement in the early years of the United States.

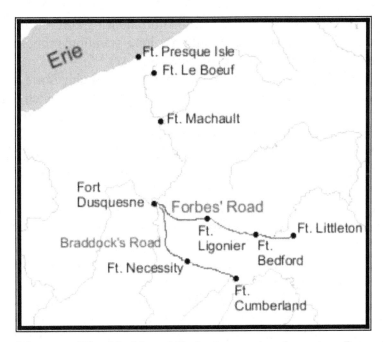

A map of the area of Braddock's and Forbes' campaigns in western Pennsylvania.

Braddock is noted at this time for his own ironic statement before his death at the hands of French allied Indians: "These savages may, indeed, be a formidable enemy to your raw American militia but upon the King's regular and disciplined troops, sir, it is impossible they should make any impression." Braddock mostly failed to recruit Native Americans from those tribes not yet allied with the French. He had eight Indian scouts forced upon him (Mingos) described as "Ohio Iroquois" or "Ohio Seneca." Evidence suggests that he was almost as contemptuous of his own ranger companies as he was of the Indians. Braddock's subsequent defeat and death at the Monongahela River in 1755 was the most significant event in British colonial history to that time. [173]

The defeat shocked the colonial public. "Our danger is also further increased by the melancholy defeat of General Braddock," wrote one colonial editor. "A whole army ... routed and several hundred cut off by inhuman brutes perhaps scare a tenth of their number." A Philadelphia newspaper printed, "In consequence of this shameful defeat the frontiers of several southwestern provinces lay exposed to the enemy and how much innocent blood may be inhumanly sacrificed to the cowardice of the British soldiers in that action ... We have the highest reason to fear the worst." General James Innes at Fort Cumberland at Wills Creek, Maryland, a vital link in the British communications to the west, wrote: "I have this minute received the melancholy account of the defeat of our troops, the General killed and numbers of our officers, the whole army taken; in short the account I have received is so bad that, please God, I intend to make a stand here. It's highly necessary to raise the militia everywhere to defend the frontiers." Only the reports of Johnson's victory at Lake George some weeks later allayed colonial fears somewhat.[174]

The colony of Pennsylvania, with a huge frontier left unguarded by decades of neglect fostered by pacifist Quaker control of the legislature, suddenly began a fort-building program after Braddock's defeat. The violence that militarists and pacifists alike dreaded took on the form of an unremitting terror of Indian attack. With armed colonists displaying the mutilated bodies of victims on the capital steps and frontier families huddling together in their homes in the face of imminent capture, torture, or death, the assembly finally gave in to Benjamin Franklin's long-standing proposal for an unpaid volunteer force in the form of the colony's first Militia Act.[175]

In December 1755, the colony voted to build four major forts in Northampton County. These were Forts Hamilton, Norris, Allen, and Franklin, which guarded the gaps in the Blue Ridge Mountains. The last was named for Benjamin Franklin, who was instrumental in moving the appropriations through the legislature. Fort Hamilton, located in modern-day Stroudsburg, was a simple palisaded house, with four half-bastions, 80 feet square, and garrisoned by 60 to 100 men and horses. The Pennsylvania colonial militia built it from plans supplied by Franklin.

The intensity of Pennsylvania's fort-building program was best characterized by Franklin's personal direction of the construction of Fort Allen (present-day Allentown). Repeated attacks on the Moravian missions on the frontier prompted Franklin to travel with 165 colonial soldiers to the proposed site of the fort in the dead of winter. Within just two days a passable stockade was completed. The fort had one bastion centered on each of two opposing walls and two half bastions at the opposite corners to cover the walls from insult. Three blockhouses were erected inside, and the fort contained its own water well. This may have been the best built of all the Pennsylvania provincial forts.

According to New Jersey Colonial Documents, on 27 November 1755, the Moravian settlement at Gnadenhutten in Pennsylvania was attacked, the residents killed, the dormitory, meetinghouse, and other buildings burned to ashes. Col. John Anderson and a contingent of 400 men from Newton, New Jersey started out to help the Pennsylvania settlers, but were told before they arrived not to bother. It was too late!

It was almost impossible to efficiently defend this frontier. "To block up the mouths of the rivers with forts, isolated from all support, was equally idle, as was proved by the utter failure of every such attempt. Herein lay the weakness of the English. They were compelled to receive the enemy at their own doors, and that disadvantage they labored under from first to last."[176]

The Colonial Documents of New Jersey contain a letter from Easton, Pennsylvania dated 15 December 1755. "The country all above this town, for fifty miles is mostly evacuated and ruined, excepting only the neighborhood of the DePue's five families [a garrison house at present-day Shawnee near the Delaware Water Gap], which stand their ground ... The Enemy made but few prisoners, murdering almost all that fell into their hands." It was against this backdrop that the Governor approved legislation to provide £10,000 pounds for the war effort and ordered that forts be built along the Delaware River to protect Sussex County, New Jersey residents from such attacks.

Many smaller outposts—optimistically called forts—were also built on the Pennsylvania side of the river. One of these was Fort Hyndshaw, a 70 foot square made of saplings driven into the ground around Lt. James Hyndshaw's home in the town of Shoemaker's, Pennsylvania (very close to present day Bushkill and inside the Tock's Island National Park). It had two lightly built bastions on opposite corners to protect the walls from attack by fire. Between eight and twenty-five militiamen were assigned to the fort in 1756, but were removed in 1757 to Fort Hamilton further south in the Delaware Valley. Several nearby garrison houses (Brinks at Bushkill, Capt. James Van Etten's home, Tishhock's, and Henry Cortracht's home) were somewhere in Upper Smithfield Township. All these posts were created to protect the local farmers as they worked their fields. Indians attacked Van Etten's home in 1756.

On 24 June 1756, Commissioner Young traveled to Fort Hyndshaw on "a good Plain Road from Depue's," but he noted that many of the structures along the way were "Deserted and the houses Chiefly Burnt." Franklin had issued the following order from Bethlehem to Capt. James Van Etten of the Smithfield militia:

> For the better Security of the Inhabitants of that District, you are to post your men as follows: Eight at your own house, Eight at Lieutenant Hyndshaw's, Six with a Sergeant at Tishhock's, and Six with another Sergeant at or near Henry Cortracht's, and you are to settle Signals, or Means of Suddenly alarming the Inhabitants, and convening your whole Strength with the Militia of your District, on any necessary Occasion ... Every Man is to be engaged for one month, and as the Province cannot at present furnish Arms or Blankets to your Company, you are to allow every Man enlisting and bringing his own Arms & Blanket, a Dollar for the Use thereof over and above his Pay ... You are to acquaint the Men, that if in their Ranging they meet with, or are at any Time attacked by the Enemy, and kill any of them, Forty Dollars will be allowed and paid by the Government for each Scalp of an Indian Enemy so killed, the same being produced with proper Attestations."[177]

Following Franklin's request, Van Etten had kept a daily journal, which gives a well-rounded account of his experience commanding Fort Hyndshaw. In his diary, Van Etten recorded the many activities he and his men carried out while stationed there. A majority of the entries include: reporting on the skirmishes with the Indians; having the soldiers collect and cut firewood; venturing outside of the fort walls for scouting expeditions;

guarding settlers as they harvested their crops; and working with the men as they practiced their marching exercises. Van Etten also discussed the weather and how his men assisted neighbors with their food stores and buried settlers and livestock killed by Indians. In one interesting journal entry, Van Etten reports that he traveled outside the fort to visit a blacksmith in order to commission an instrument for removing a bullet from his horse, which had been shot. Van Etten's journal ends abruptly on 21 July 1757, and it is believed that Fort Hyndshaw was abandoned around that time as well. Through the written accounts and records of Young and Van Etten, researchers are able to have a better understanding of the life of a soldier during this period in Pennsylvania's history.

Edward Marshall, who had taken part as a young man in the Walking Purchase of 1737 that had defrauded the Delaware of much of their land, thereafter lived on an island in the Delaware River near present-day Marshall's Creek, Pennsylvania. Because of his efforts, Marshall, who had run the last leg of the Purchase, was awarded the promised 500 acres of land, and ultimately, the village of Marshall's Creek was named in his honor. The Indians later took their revenge. In 1747, they ambushed and killed his son; and in 1756 a party of 16 Delaware attacked his home killing and scalping his wife and son and wounding his daughter. Marshall escaped the raid without injury.

They Promised Great Matters

Having patiently endured the previous diversion from the campaign of 1755, the reader should note that the defeat of Edward Braddock at the Monongahela was the most significant circumstance in poisoning the relations between Anglo-America and the British crown prior to 1764. The debate began soon after the Battle at the Monongahela and continues to this day on how Braddock, with professional soldiers, superior numbers, and artillery, could fail so miserably in an ambush engineered by mixed race coureurs de bois, French bush-lopers, and a few hundred enemy Indians. Some blamed Braddock, some blamed his officers, and some blamed the British regulars or the colonial governments. His aide de camp, George Washington, for his part, supported Braddock but found fault with the redcoats. None blamed the true-bred Anglo-colonial frontiersmen — hunters and trappers, rangers and scouts, and the like. They had survived the battle, and like their cousins on Lake George they had seemingly demonstrated the superiority of the colonial woodsman.

Several pages in William Makepeace Thackeray's novel *The Virginians* published in 1857, are devoted to Braddock's arrival in Virginia in 1755. Thackeray, an English novelist of the 19th century better known for his *Vanity Fair* (1847), is said to have talked to and interviewed Virginians one generation removed from the actual events of the time. Thackeray portrayed Braddock as enjoying a sympathetic relationship with Governor Dinwiddie and with Benjamin Franklin. Thackeray wrote: "Mr. Franklin, [looked] innocently at the stout chief, the exemplar of English elegance, who sat swagging from one side to the other of the carriage, his face as scarlet as his coat - swearing at every word; ignorant on every point off parade, except the merits of a bottle and the looks of a woman; not of high birth, yet absurdly proud of his no-ancestry; brave as a bull-dog; savage, lustful, prodigal, generous; gentle in soft moods; easy of love and laughter; dull of wit; utterly unread; believing his country the first in the world, and he as good a gentleman as any in it." Thackeray made a further unflattering description of "Braddock's heavy person and great boots, as he floundered through the Virginian woods, hunting, as they called it, with a pack of dogs gathered from various houses, with a pack of negroes barking as loud as the dogs, and actually shooting the deer when they came in sight of him." Thackeray ascribed the failure of the expedition to "the panic and surprise certainly, but more especially to the delays occasioned by the rapacity, selfishness, and unfair dealing of the people of the colonies towards the King's troops who were come to defend them." [178]

At the end of the Alexandria Conference, Braddock wrote to the representatives of the Crown in London: "Mr. Shirley with the other northern governors met me at this place last week [and] we settled a plan for operations ... [but] I have been greatly disappointed by the neglect and supineness of the assemblies of those provinces, with which I am concerned. They promised great matters and have done nothing whereby, instead of forwarding, they have obstructed the service."[179]

Braddock immediately faced a torrent of supply problems for his army of several thousand men. "One hundred fifty wagons, with 4 horses to each wagon, and 1500 saddle or pack-horses are wanted for the service of His Majesty's forces." Appraised of this problem, Franklin noted: "The General ... had sent thro' the back parts of Maryland and Virginia to collect wagons ... [which] only amounted to twenty-five, and not all of those were in serviceable condition. The General ... exclaimed against the ministers for ignorantly landing him in a country destitute of the means of conveying their stores, baggage, etc." Through tact and ingenuity Franklin was able to furnish the wagons and horses that Braddock needed from the farmsteads of Pennsylvania.[180]

Franklin described Braddock at the time: "This general was, I think, a brave man, and might probably have made a figure as a good officer in some European war. But he had too much self-confidence; too high an opinion of the validity of regular troops; and too mean a one of both Americans and Indians." Four of Braddock's horses were killed under him. On his fifth steed, he finally fell. The bullet went through his chest and hit one of his lungs. He died four days later and was buried in an unmarked grave in the roadway.[181]

As a volunteer aide-de-camp, Washington essentially served as an unpaid and unranked gentleman consultant, with little real authority. The five companies of colonial Virginians (Captains Stevens, Hogg, Waggoner, Cocke, and Perronee) had managed to fight effectively from the trees as a rear guard. It was not clear at the time, however, that the skirmish tactics that American colonials subsequently learned from frontier fighting, where men took cover and fired individually (Indian style), were the superior methods to be used in the American environment. There is little evidence in the fighting that previously took place under Washington in 1754 at Fort Necessity to suggest that the Virginia Regiments were particularly competent at Indian fighting. John Fraser of the Virginia Regiment, Braddock's Chief of Scouts tasked with protecting the column from the very ambush into which it fell, had been at Fort Necessity. The colonels of the Irish regiments (approximately 1350 men) filled out with Virginia recruits, Sir Peter Halkett and Robert Dunbar were hardly enthusiastic participants.

Nor is it entirely clear from the contemporary accounts which of the American companies were present on the main field at the battle as there was movement between the main army and Dunbar's rear party in the escorting of supplies. Moreover, the order of battle on the day of the fight has been reported differently among the sources. British sources suggest that the main body was arranged in two brigades:

> 1st Brigade commanded by Sir Peter Halkett: 44th, Rutherford's, Gates', Polson's, Perronee's and Waggoner's and Dagworthy's Maryland rangers.
> 2nd Brigade commanded by Colonel Robert Dunbar: 48th, Captain Demerie's South Carolina Detachment, Captain Dodd's, Captain Mercer's carpenters, Stevens', Hogg's and Cox's.

The regular officers' contempt for the provincial gentlemen was obvious throughout the operation. One British officer wrote that the American officers were totally ignorant of military skills. This was often displayed as a general neglect for protocol. The regular officers constantly refused to consult with their colonial counterparts when planning operations, and often kept the provincial troops out of combat assigning them to ditch-digging and other fatigue duties. It can be definitely said that Polson's and Perronee's companies (designated as pioneers and carpenters) were present at the head and tail of the column as part of the working parties under Sir John Saint Clair in order to carry out the work on the new road – one party blazing the path, while the other completed the bridges and grading. It is likely that Waggoner's and Stevens' companies were present.

In 1752, William Smith, John Morin Scott, and William Livingston founded a weekly journal, the *Independent Reflector*. The *Reflector* was New York's first serial non-newspaper publication and the only one being published in British North America at the time. It was used as a platform for challenging the powerful De Lancey faction, most notably over the founding of King's College as an Anglican institution. After the suspension of the *Reflector* in 1753, William Livingston edited "The Watch Tower" in the *New York Mercury* (1754-1755), which became the recognized organ of the Presbyterian faction. Livingston, Governor of New Jersey since 1776 led the New Jersey Delegation to the 1787 Constitutional Convention and was one of the signers of the Constitution. In *A Review of the Military Operations in North America* (1757), he noted of the Braddock defeat:

> Unapprehensive of the approach of an enemy, at once was the alarm given by a quick and heavy fire upon the vanguard under Lt. Col. Gage. Immediately the main body, in good order and high spirits, advanced to sustain them. Orders were then given to halt, and form into battalions. At this juncture the van falling back upon them in great confusion a general panic seized the whole body of the soldiery, and all attempts to rally them proved utterly ineffectual. ... So great was the consternation of the soldiers that it was impossible to stop their career—flying with the utmost precipitation three miles from the field of action; where only one hundred began to make a more orderly retreat. What was the strength of the enemy has hitherto remained to us uncertain. According to Indian accounts, they exceeded not 400, chiefly Indians; and whether any were slain is still to be doubted, for few were seen by our men, being covered by stumps and fallen trees. Great indeed was the destruction on our side. Numbers of officers sacrificed their lives through singular bravery. ... But ... however censurable the conduct of the soldiery may be thought, Mr. Braddock, too sanguine in his prospects, was generally blamed for neglecting to cultivate the friendship of the Indians, who offered their assistance, and who, it is certain, had a number of them preceded the army, would have seasonably discovered the enemy's ambuscade. The Virginian rangers also, instead of being made to serve as regulars in the ranks

with the English troops, should have been employed as out-scouts. But this step, so necessary to guard against surprise, was too unhappily omitted, the whole army, according to the representation above mentioned, following only three or four guides. When the routed party joined the second division, forty miles short of the place of action, the terror diffused itself through the whole army.[182]

One explanation of the defeat was based in the fact that sixty-three of the eighty-six officers involved in the action were casualties. Another explanation rests on the poor performance of the British regulars, who were said to have panicked and become hopelessly entangled with their fellows in the woods. Yet the only soldiers in Braddock's force who were likely to have had experience in Indian warfare were Captain Edward Bryce Dobson's North Carolina rangers and a company of Maryland Rangers commanded by Captain Eli Dagworthy.

Almost certainly there was a debilitating legacy among the officers of Braddock's command rooted in the Scottish Rebellion in late 1745. Braddock, himself of Scottish ancestry, may have taken part in the hectic marching through England in the attempt to catch the Jacobite army. Braddock was well known to the Duke of Cumberland, known as the "Butcher" for his persecution of the Scots rebels. Braddock and his adjutant Capt. Robert Orme treated the three senior officers of Scottish heritage (Halkett, Dunbar, and Saint Clair) with contempt. Orme had served with Braddock in the prestigious Coldstream Guards. Several of the Virginia officers may have been fugitives from the rebellion (Polson, Craik, Stevens, and Hogg). British officers openly accused Polson of being a Jacobite, and he demanded and received a court martial to clear his name. No outcome is recorded for the court martial. It may be assumed that it was favorable to Polson. Even if Polson was a rebel, it is hard to see how any evidence could be obtained to that effect in such a remote location. The majority of these farmer-militia were fierce Scotch-Irish Presbyterians who had been mistreated by the Royal government during the previous decades. Historian James Webb, U.S. Senator from Virginia, himself an offshoot of Scots-Irish frontier ancestors, has noted that the "values-based combativeness, insistent egalitarianism, and ... refusal to be dominated" were shared characteristics of these American frontiersmen.[183]

It is true that the British officers of the regular army only slowly learned to avoid ambushes in the wilderness by altering their campaigning routines, columns of march, ability to maneuver, and defenses against encirclement. Braddock's defeat in 1755 and that of Major James Grant's detachment at Fort Duquesne in 1758 would seem to confirm this statement. Yet the reputation of the British for massive ineptitude under frontier conditions was probably undeserved. Grant mishandled his forces by advancing in separate detachments, which were defeated in detail, and Braddock's men, rather than being poorly led, appear to have panicked and disobeyed their officers. Without exception, British regular officers seem to have been knowledgeable in the tactics of irregular warfare and the methods of combating them. They were thoroughly acquainted with the concepts of skirmishers, flankers, and advanced parties of scouts, which were included in their technical literature and training manuals. This is not to suggest that European warfare was being "revolutionized," but rather that certain aspects of warfare were increasingly affected by the activities of irregulars in all theaters of operations and had been addressed in terms of military training and tactics.

The opposite conclusion was somewhat promoted by the actions of inept British commanders who ordered a series of unsupported frontal assaults in impossible situations, such as in the British attack on Fort Carillon (Ticonderoga) in 1758 or the attack on the Beauport Lines at Quebec in 1759. In the provincial armies, however, there was relatively little struggle over the adoption of European-style methods of warfare with their straight lines of soldiers firing at one another across open fields. Colonial regiments paraded, marched, and practiced the evolutions of linear tactics in much the same manner as British regulars, although without their crisp precision. This leaves the reader with the unmistakable perception that much of what was said of the inability of the British regulars to wage war in the American wilderness was based in a colonial fondness for griping.

Unfortunately, William Shirley had become commander-in-chief of British forces upon the death of Braddock. The fortification on Lake Oswego where the Oswego River entered the lake had been further strengthened by Shirley and garrisoned with some 1600 troops, two-thirds British regulars and some colonials. Shirley also had Fort Ontario built on the other side of the river and a small outpost called Fort George on the same side of the river and then had return to Albany with parts of three Massachusetts regiments. Fort Oswego was the strongest of the three British forts and had the largest garrison. The log palisade forts established a British presence on the Great Lakes. They were located on an earlier fort site from the previous war.

French and Indian forces under Gaspard-Joseph de Léry overran Fort Bull at the Great Carrying Place east of Oneida Lake (near Rome, New York) in March 1756. Notified of a second French advance with 3,000 troops and Indians (1300 being regulars) in 200 vessels (mostly canoes) from Fort Frontenac, the British commander at Oswego, Col. James Mercer withdrew the soldiers from the smaller outposts on 10 August 1756 and prepared to make a stand at Fort Oswego. Given the dominant military theory of the day, which said that an attacker needed three times the number of the defenders to successfully prosecute a siege, Mercer should have been able to hold the post without additional aid. On the following day, however, Montcalm opened fire on the British position, using cannon taken earlier from Braddock's fleeing forces. The cannonade lasted from daybreak to six in the evening. The British commander was killed in the fighting and the disheartened garrison surrendered shortly thereafter.

The British surrendered about 1,700 people, including laborers, shipbuilders, women and children. When the fort was opened to the Canadien militia and Indians, they rushed in and began plundering the fort, opening the barrels of rum and getting drunk on the contents. Amid the confusion some of the British tried to escape, and were tomahawked and killed by drunken French or Indians. General Montcalm, shocked by the behavior, was eventually able to prevent further killings, although he claimed it would cost the French King eight or ten thousand livres in presents. The prisoners that were not massacred by the Indians arrived safe at Quebec in November. They were conveyed down the St. Lawrence in bateaux and Indian canoes, arriving at Quebec at the commencement of winter. In the spring of 1757, these English prisoners, or a portion of them, were sent to France and held in Le Havre until 1759 when they were exchanged.

Near the back of *Gentlemen's Magazine* (London, November, 1756) was the "Historical Chronicle" which had the latest news reports of the day, one bit noting: "We have seen our colonies in America abandoned in a manner to the ravages of the enemy.

They have either been unassisted from hence, or, what is worse, they have had only insufficient succors under improper & injudicious leaders who have fallen victims to their own inexperience & temerity."[184]

One of the captives, Benjamin F. Taylor had entered the Colonial Army in 1753. His grandson, Augustus Campenfeldt Taylor told the story of Fort Oswego as he heard it from Benjamin when he was an old man. Benjamin enlisted at aged 16 years. He was at Fort Orange, Albany for some time and afterwards actually engaged in war with the French and Indians on the northern frontier. Taken prisoner at Fort Oswego 1756, he remained a prisoner of war for four or five years. His grandson wrote:

> Their rendezvous was at Fort Orange, Albany, where they awaited supplies and orders. In 1755 the Colonial Governor planned a grand campaign against the French and Indians; one commanded by Gen. Braddock against Fort Duquesne; one commanded by Gen. Johnson against Crown Point; one commanded by Gen. Shirley against Fort Niagara. England was to furnish munitions of war and 6,000 men—the Colonies to raise 10,000 more. All of these campaigns were entire failures. Gen. Shirley with an army of near 2,000, including friendly Indians, advanced in 1755 to the northern Frontier, to Lake Ontario. He went up the Mohawk trail, then the only passable route to this northern lake, striking the lake near its mouth, to proceed hence by water to besiege Fort Niagara, situated near the head of the lake. 6,000 troops were to follow this advance guard. But in consequence of bickering between Colonial and English officers, they failed to make the connection. The advance guard reached the frontier and built two forts, or more properly called, stockades, both near the mouth of Lake Ontario, one on each side of the Oswego River, one called Ontario and the other Oswego. Owing to the desertion of their Indian allies, and severe sickness amongst the Colonial soldiers, the main object of the campaign was abandoned. Gen. Shirley left Col. Mercer in command, returning to Fort Orange, Albany. …
> In the spring of 1756, the French, seeing the deleterious and fatal mistakes of the English, profited by their failures. The Marquis de Montcalm had just been appointed Governor and General of all the French forces in Canada. He collected together at Fort Frontenac, now Kingston, a force of 5,000 men, mostly Indians, crossed Lake Ontario with 30 pieces of cannon, and besieged Fort Ontario. After a bloody fight Col. Mercer was forced to evacuate the place, retiring across the river to Fort Oswego. … Significant elements of the two Massachusetts regiments including Benjamin Taylor, which were under the overall command of Colonel James Mercer of Pepperell's Regiment, overwintered at Fort Oswego, and suffered significantly due to the shortage of supplies, especially food. Many men died during the winter from diseases such as scurvy, and there had been serious discussion of abandoning the position for want of supplies. While the garrison nominally approached 2,000 men in size, less than 1,200 men were fit for duty. … [Grandfather] returned to America about the year 1762. Sailed for Boston in a bark which was wrecked off the harbor; reached New York by a coaster; by sail to Peekskill; foots it out to Yorktown, where he was born.[185]

Montcalm rewarded his Indian allies by allowing them much of the victory spoils and hoped to placate other local natives by destroying the forts. The French took away some

1700 prisoners, 121 cannon and destroyed what they couldn't take with them. This decisive defeat caused some among the Oneida and Seneca to switch to the French side or undertake a cautious neutrality. The French victory at Oswego "wrought marvels among the Indians, inspired the faithful, confirmed the wavering, and daunted the ill-disposed. The whole west was astir, ready to pour itself again in blood and fire against the English border."[186]

In a council with his commanders in September, Shirley decided to proceed with plans to reduce Fort Niagara, but one week later he suddenly and without explanation reversed the decision. He seemed overwhelmed, distracted, and indecisive. Shirley returned to Albany, claiming a preoccupation with the need to manage the entire British war effort on the continent. Lord John Campbell, Earl of Loudoun (a.k.a. Loudon) arrived in America in the summer of 1756 to replace Braddock as military commander. He immediately blamed the military losses on the colonial governors, especially Shirley, and suggested that the governor be recalled to England. Shirley and Johnson were in the midst of their ongoing argument concerning their individual authority to direct the colonial campaign, and Johnson, considered a hero, had Loudoun's ear!

Thereafter, Loudoun dismissed all of Shirley's former plans and replaced them with his own schemes. In November 1755, General John Winslow had been appointed by Shirley (then temporary commander-in-chief), to command the provincial troops in a second expedition against Fort St. Frédéric, New York. The Winslow family connections had allowed Shirley to recommend Winslow in 1748 for an appointment as a commissioned officer in the regular British army. This was quite a step up for a "colonial" and one that Washington had sought as a young man without success. In 1751, Winslow went off active duty, and, taking half pay, returned to Massachusetts to assist Shirley in the administration of the governor's properties. In 1754, Winslow had been promoted major general of militia and put in command of a force of 800 men, which was sent to the Kennebec River in Maine to build two forts, Fort Halifax (Maine) and Fort Western in response to the false rumor that the French were about to seize the carrying place between the Chaudière and the Kennebec. Although the 29-year-old Colonel Monckton was placed over the 52 year old Winslow in the expedition to Acadia, the older man played an important role at the capture of Fort Beauséjour in June 1755. Monckton was to lead 2,000 men that were principally raised at Boston, Shirley's regiment. This regiment was broken into two divisions; one was to be led by Winslow and the other by George Scott. The latter man enthusiastically embraced the deportation of the Acadians, and was praised for his daring and his energy during the campaign. For Winslow the business of rounding up and deporting civilians was "very disagreeable to my natural make and temper." Winslow wrote two important narratives of the Acadian operations: *Winslow's Journal - Bay of Fundy Campaign* (1755) and *Winslow's Journal – Fort Beauséjour*.[187]

Winslow was placed in command at Fort William Henry in upstate New York for most of 1756, and fought bitterly with Loudoun over his proposed integration of the provincial troops with the regulars. The argument was that the colonial army would operate much better as separate units with its own officers. The provincial soldiers had enlisted to serve only under their own officers, and feared the hard discipline, with floggings and hangings, that was part of the regular army. Their officers feared that the integration could result in them losing their rank, as they held it only by colonial commission. Loudoun would have none of it. The issue nearly developed into a mutiny of the provincial troops and a revolt of their officers, but Winslow eventually agreed to the integration under threats from Loudoun. It appears that after his military activities in 1757, Winslow, at the age of 53, determined to quit the army (the experiences with both Monckton and Loudoun had been bitter ones) and involve himself in Massachusetts' politics full time.

Along with Loudoun came an influx of regular British officers into the colonies. Among these were several officers who would figure prominently in the final stages of the war: General Daniel Webb, Major-General James Abercromby, Lieutenant Colonel George Munro, General Jeffrey Amherst, Brigadier-General Lord Augustus Howe, and Major-General James Wolfe.

Parallel with the development of rangers in the colonies was the development of regular light troops by the British. Colonel Thomas Gage is generally given credit for conceiving of the Light Infantry Regiment. Further developed by Lord Augustus Howe and Colonel Henry Bouquet, the Lights were expected to serve as scouts, skirmishers, and flankers as well as to stand in the battalion line. In the field, light troops carried only the basic essentials. While Howe, before his early death, eliminated many of the useless encumbrances from the light infantry field kit, Bouquet made effective changes in their training. General Braddock's successor, the Earl of Loudoun, was cognizant of the need for his men to fire both kneeling and lying down, to march in a manner suited to forests and mountains, and to take cover when ambushed. General James Wolfe had his men lay down under galling fire from Indians and Canadien militia before the walls of Quebec in 1759, and he used light troops to guard his flanks.

The attack on Ticonderoga in 1758 had been entrusted to Major-General James Abercromby, who was considered inept and infirmed at age fifty-one. The command was supposed to go to Lord Augustus Howe, brigadier-general and second in command of the forces under Abercromby, but the old general had precedence. Augustus Howe was a model soldier, young and highly regarded by the colonials. (His younger brothers General Sir William Howe and Lord Admiral 1st Earl Richard Howe would figure prominently in the Revolution). Augustus Howe placed himself in the hands of Major Robert Rogers and learned, firsthand, his methods of woodland warfare and ranger tactics. He insisted that the British army be sent to the frontier to learn to live and fight as rangers did. Regulars as well as provincials were made to cut down the tails of their regimental coats and fashion Indian leggings to ease their travel through the wilderness. Howe limited their equipment to weapons, canteen, a haversack, and a single blanket and bearskin. Even officers were required to follow these instructions, and it was remarkable to see his Lordship and his staff eating around the campfire like private soldiers. Also among the officers was Charles Lee, who was captain of the grenadier company of the 44th. He is best remembered to posterity as second-in-command of the United States troops during the Revolutionary War.

Colonel Thomas Ellison of the New York militia noted: "Both officers and men packed their bundles on their backs, and the colonel [himself] though an old man and afflicted with rheumatism marched on foot with his musket on his shoulder at the head of his men and waded through rivers crotch deep. ... Some of the men complained that their officers marched too hard for them." Had Howe's influence continued throughout the campaign, it might have proved more successful. Unfortunately, Howe, brave to the point of being oblivious to personal danger, went forward with a small party under provincial Major Israel Putnam to reconnoiter a possible line of attack from the rear of Fort Carillon. Near the rapids of the LaChute River they encountered a detachment of French and Indians numbering about 350 whom Montcalm had sent to harass the British. A sharp fight ensued and in the first moments Howe was killed by a shot to the chest. He was buried near the spot where he was killed in the virtual shadow of Ticonderoga. [188]

Abercromby foolishly ordered a direct assault on the lines surrounding Fort Carillon with disastrous effect. Montcalm, while concerned about the weak military position of the fort itself, conducted the defense of the outworks with spirit. Abercrombie ignored several viable military options, such as flanking the French breastworks, waiting for his artillery, or laying siege to the fort. The battle was the bloodiest of the war, with over 3,000 casualties suffered, of which over 2,000 were British and American. "No military campaign was ever launched on American soil that involved a greater number of errors of judgment on the part of those in positions of responsibility." [189]

Disaster had followed upon disaster: *Fort Necessity; Monongahela; Crown Point; Oswego; Ticonderoga;* and the destruction of *Fort William Henry*. The list of military routs and retreats was like a death rattle. The success in Acadia and on the shores of Lake George, forged largely by colonial troops, had seemingly faded. An expedition against Louisbourg in 1757 led by Lord Loudon had been turned back due to a strong French naval deployment, one of the few times in the 18th century that the British Royal Navy did not dominate. The reversals staggered the British public and frightened the colonials. The French also began the year of 1758 discouraged by the loss of many of their lesser posts in the preceding year especially the abandonment of Fort Duquesne. Yet they still held Fort Niagara at the western end of Lake Ontario, Fort Carillon at Ticonderoga, Crown Point, and the massive citadel of Quebec. The English campaign to reduce these important posts formed the core of British strategy in America.

However, the leadership in London, at least, had come to understand the problem. Under the renewed political leadership of William Pitt, 1st Earl of Chatham, it was resolved to try again with new field commanders. Pitt assigned the duty of capturing the fortress at Louisbourg in 1758 to Major General Jeffrey Amherst. To do the job he also dispatched 23,000 regulars. To oppose this impressive British force France grudgingly sent out only 7,000 troops. Pitt ignored tradition and seniority and promoted younger, first-class military men over more senior officers. The appointment to command the Louisbourg expedition was remarkable, not merely because Amherst was very junior in the army, but because all his operational experience had been on the staff. He had never commanded troops in action. Obtaining George II's sanction to grant to Amherst of the local rank of "Major General in America" was a delicate operation in which Pitt seems to have sought the aid of the king's mistress, Lady Yarmouth. The king finally agreed at the end of 1757.

The rank of "Brigadier in America" for James Wolfe was authorized at the same time. Amherst's other brigadiers were Charles Lawrence and Edward Whitmore. Of Governor Lawrence, the reader knows. The elderly Whitmore served without complaint in the rather unimportant position of Governor of Cape Breton Island, while his fellow officers, both younger and junior, covered themselves with glory in great victories. Major General James Wolfe was known for his training reforms of the British regulars but is remembered chiefly for his victory over the French at the Battle of Quebec in September 1759.

In June 1758 at the siege of Fortress Louisburg, a boatload of light infantry and rangers in Wolfe's division had found a rocky inlet protected from French fire and secured a beachhead on Gabarus Bay. Wolfe had redirected the rest of his division to follow. The dash and resolution of the advanced troops, and the leadership in particular of Wolfe and George Scott, turned into success what might have been a disaster. Wolfe noted: "Our attempt to land where we did was rash and injudicious, our success unexpected (by me) and undeserved. There was no prodigious exertion of courage in the affair. Our proceedings were as slow and tedious as the undertaking was ill-advised and desperate." This lodgment made the outer defenses of the French untenable and led ultimately to the fall of the fortress. Numerous warships were committed to the task under the command of the capable Admiral Edward Boscawen. Included among these was Captain James Cooke (later famed as an explorer of the Pacific) who served as chief navigator for the fleet. After Boscawen blockaded the Louisbourg harbor, Amherst and Wolfe successfully landed their troops very close to the spot where the colonials had landed in 1745. With the fortress besieged and with no hope of a relieving force breaking the blockade, the outnumbered French garrison surrendered within a few weeks. The loss of Louisbourg deprived Quebec and New France of naval protection, opening the Saint Lawrence to attack.

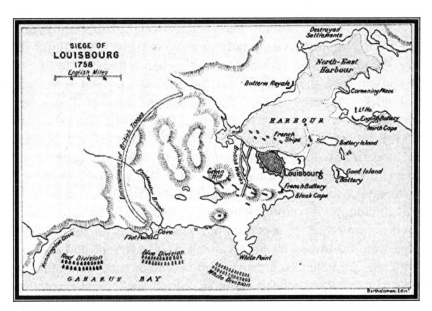

Situated on the fog-infested rocky southeast shore of Ile Royale, the enormous bastion and the fleet it sustained guarded the Gulf of St. Lawrence - key to the gateway to the heartland of the continent. The citadel served as a shield for New France and a dagger against New England. On the landward side, there was a ditch eighty feet in width and stone walls with four great bastions rising thirty feet into the air. Surrounded by moorland and marsh, the sea itself serving as a moat.

Wolfe had been the life of the siege, and although Amherst was called away with six regiments to support a planned operation against Ticonderoga, Wolfe wanted to press forward to Quebec immediately with the remainder of the army. He wrote to Amherst, with whom he was on good terms: "An offensive, daring kind of war will awe the Indians and ruin the French. ... If you will attempt to cut up New France by the roots, I will come with pleasure to assist." Another year was required, however, to marshal the forces needed to attack Quebec. Louisbourg was used in 1759 as the staging point for General Wolfe's famous Siege of Quebec ending French rule in North America. By the end of October 1760 the great citadel at Louisbourg that had taken 30 years and 50 million livres to build had been laid low, converted into a pile of rubble by the British engineers. [190]

Diplomacy by other means

It was during William Denny's first term as Governor of Pennsylvania that a plan proposed by Governor Morris, Denny's predecessor was carried out and "produced the most wholesome and pacifying effect on the Indians." A strong detachment from the militia was sent to Kittanning, along the Allegheny River, which was one of the largest Indian towns in Pennsylvania. Kittanning was the stronghold of Tewea (a.k.a. Captain Jacobs) and Shingas, the most active of the hostile Delaware chiefs. From this town they sent out strong parties of warriors to scourge the frontier. In an attempt to assert control over the western Delawares, a local Iroquois leader Tanacharison (the "Half-King"), dubbed Shingas the chief of the Delawares in an important treaty conference at Logstown in 1752. Shingas had proved difficult to control, while Tewea initially professed great friendship toward the British colonists, but was swayed by the French to think otherwise as the number of English settlers in his territory grew.

Undetected, three hundred Pennsylvanians marched on the native town and attacked from two directions. The Indians refused to surrender and were slaughtered. Led by Tewea because Shingas was absent, the Indians fought stubbornly and refused to surrender. As a result, the town was totally destroyed, Tewea and thirty or forty of his followers were killed, and the remainder of the band fled far to the west of Fort Duquesne. In consequence the fortress and the French garrison were placed between them and the English. A peace faction led by Shingas' brother Tamaqua soon gained ascendancy among the Delaware. Shingas kept a low profile thereafter and disappears from the historical record around 1764. By that time, Shingas and Tamaqua, who had advised accommodation with the British, began to lose influence to more militant Delaware leaders influenced by Neolin, known as the "Delaware Prophet."

Details of the attack follow from Colonel John Armstrong's report of September 14, written at Fort Littleton, to Governor Denny, describing the destruction of Kittanning on September 8: "It is impossible to ascertain the exact number of the Enemy killed in the Action, as some were destroyed by Fire and others in different parts of the Corn Field, but, upon a moderate Computation, it is generally believed there cannot be less than thirty or Forty killed and mortally wounded, as much Blood was found in sundry parts of the Corn Field, and Indians seen in several places to crawl into the Weeds on their Hands and Feet, whom the Soldiers, in pursuit of others, then overlooked, expecting to find and scalp them afterwards; and also several killed and wounded in crossing the River." [191]

Despite this widely celebrated success, Denny's tenure was largely one of internal dispute. He was considered in some quarters a "disgrace" and "in all respects a wretched governor." As an experienced military man, he might have been exactly the type of person needed to provide strong executive leadership during the French and Indian War, but Denny had neither the ability nor the courage to execute his instructions when challenged by the power-seeking Assembly. His first and most significant major crisis with the Quaker Assembly concerned the quartering of British troops in the fall of 1756.

Lord Loudoun was certainly less than honest when he "passed the buck" for quartering the British troops to Denny. The day following the enactment of the quartering act, Denny informed his council that he had been requested to obtain quarters for 500 soldiers and fifty officers. These troops, under the command of Lieutenant Colonel Henry Bouquet, constituted the first battalion of the Royal American Regiment. Moreover, in December 1756, Col. John Forbes of the British army had been commissioned "Brigadier General in America to command his Majesty's forces in the southern provinces." He assumed command early in the summer of 1758, and immediately began organizing an army much more formidable than that placed under Braddock three years before for the capture of Fort Duquesne. Loudoun had left Denny with no better authority than his own prerogative to be used against the time-honored English argument that no man should be forced to quarter except by law. Prior to 1756, the colonial legislatures usually appropriated funds to pay public housekeepers when troops were lodged with them for short periods. The real expense of the innkeeper was in providing a diet for the troops. If he chose not to feed the troops, he was paid nothing by the army for their quarters. This protocol as practiced in England was extended only to troops on the road, not to those in garrison. If the inhabitants of the colony thought it unfair, the governor declared, they could complain to Lord Loudoun.[192]

Christian Frederick Post, a Moravian missionary had long been known to the Indians, and had obtained among them the character of an honest man, whose word they might safely rely on. His two *Journals* of his diplomatic mission to the Indians in 1758 afford the reader "a fresh Instance of the Power of Religion, and a Sense of Duty, above Self-Interest, in inducing Men to undertake, and supporting the Mind in the most dangerous Enterprises for the Public Service." The second journal contains a continuation of his negotiations with the Indians of the Ohio, to withdraw them from the French interest, and bring about a peace, all on the orders of Denny. It also evidences the power of honesty above artifice in influencing the minds of others, calming the warlike passions, and reducing an enemy to reason and to peace. "Which methinks should incline even an Infidel wicked World, to countenance and support Piety and Virtue, that it may enjoy the Advantages of their public Usefulness, and reap the Benefits of their Protection," wrote Post.[193]

With the governor in discussions in Easton concerning peace with the northern tribes during 1758, Post was sent twice to Ohio to obtain a final conclusion of peace in the west. During his short absence from the Ohio between these diplomatic missions, the French had mostly recovered their influence with the Indians, and engaged some of them again to use the hatchet against the English, so that Post had fearful difficulties to encounter. Nonetheless, while Post was in discussion with the tribes General Forbes was making his way toward the forks of the Ohio with a massive army. Its objective was the capture of Fort Duquesne. The expedition methodically constructed a road across what is now southern Pennsylvania, then largely Indian territory. The Treaty of Easton concluded on 26 October 1758 caused the Lenape and Shawnee tribes in the Ohio Valley to abandon the French. When the expedition neared to within a few miles of Fort Duquesne in mid-November, the French abandoned and blew up the fort. This act further demoralized the Indians.

The message that Post delivered along with several strings and belts of wampum read in part: "Brethren on the Ohio, if you take the Belts we just now gave you, in which all here join, English and Indians, as we do not doubt you will; then, by this Belt, I make a Road for you, and invite you to come to Philadelphia, to your first old Council Fire, which was kindled when we first saw one another; which Fire we will kindle up again, and remove all Disputes, and renew the old and first Treaties of Friendship. This is a clear and open Road for you; fear therefore nothing, and come to us with as many as can be of the Delaware, Shawnee, or of the Six Nation Indians. We will be glad to see you; we desire all Tribes and Nations of Indians, who are in Alliance with you, to come." A large white Belt accompanied this message, with the Figure of a Man at each End and streaks of Black representing the road from the Ohio Country to Philadelphia, now a stark reality rather than a symbol.[194]

A ceremony was held in Easton, Pennsylvania between the British colonial governors of the provinces of Pennsylvania and New Jersey, and representatives of 13 Indian nations, including the Iroquois, who sent chiefs of three of their nations to ensure their domination of the Ohio Country; the eastern and western Lenape (Delaware), represented by two chiefs and headmen; Shawnee and others. Conrad Weiser served as an interpreter and arbitrator for the British colonial governments. Attorney General of Pennsylvania, Benjamin Chew attended the negotiations and documented the proceedings in his *Journal of a Journey to Easton* (printed by Ben Franklin in 1758). More than 500 Native Americans attended the outdoor ceremony and the lengthy negotiations to bring peace to the regions of Pennsylvania, New Jersey and the Ohio Country. A headman named Teedyuscung claimed to be the only person who could convince the French allied Indians on the western borders to stop their raids against the British. He also claimed that he represented the Six Nations of the Iroquois, the Shawnee, the Mohican, and the Christian Munsee. The Iroquois were not pleased that Teedyuscung claimed to negotiate on their behalf. Eventually Teedyuscung was left unsupported and unprotected, his people denied a home in the Wyoming Valley of Northeast Pennsylvania by the Iroquois envoys.

The treaty provided just enough ambiguity to allow for peace. Agents for Pennsylvania paid lip service to the old Iroquois claim that they "owned" the Ohio River Valley, while simultaneously accepting the right of the western Delaware and the other Ohio River Indians to speak for themselves in all future negotiations. Pennsylvania returned large blocks of land that the Iroquois had ceded a few years earlier. By the treaty, the Lenape ceded all remaining claims to land within the Province of New Jersey for the sum of one thousand Spanish dollars. They received payment immediately. The British colonial governors promised to recognize Iroquois and other tribal rights to their hunting grounds in the Ohio River Valley, and to refrain from establishing colonial settlements west of the Allegheny Mountains after the conclusion of the present war. This clause of the treaty contributed to the Crown's subsequent Proclamation of 1763, which later caused a serious rift to form between the government and the frontier inhabitants.

1759 – A Year of Success

As part of the new campaign strategy, Sir William Johnson had reached Fort Niagara with a besieging army in June 1759. This force was made up of two regiments of regulars, a battalion of Royal Americans, and 3,000 provincials. Johnson had also attracted 900 Iroquois to the English for this offensive, among them a large number of Seneca from western New York. Nonetheless, his attack, begun by Gen. John Prideaux, a British regular who was killed in the trenches, took the form of a formal siege. The

French had about one hundred Indian allies at the Fort who deserted when the British arrived. A French relief force under Capt. François de Marchand de Lignery attempting to reach the besieged French garrison fell into a British and Iroquois ambush led by Lt. Col. Eyre Massey. Forces under Charles Philippe Aubry from Fort Machault supported Lignery. The British knew of the French approach well in advance and constructed a breastwork across the road at La Belle-Famille about two miles south of Fort Niagara. In spite of a supposed knowledge of Indian ways, the French apparently advanced without taking normal precautions against ambush, and marched right into a prepared trap. It was the Braddock defeat in reverse. The British fired seven volleys, then advanced, firing at will. The French began a panicked retreat, in which the British Indians gave chase, according to one report, for as much as 5 miles. Massey later estimated that his men had each fired about 16 rounds in the action.

For the modern reader, 16 rounds may seem a small number when compared to the hundreds of rounds quickly expended by modern firearms, but this was not the case. The common regular soldier rarely carried more than 20 rounds in their cartouche boxes when going into an encounter, the rate of fire in a disciplined volley being two to three rounds in the first minutes of battle. Thereafter, musket fouling and the effects of enemy fire usually slowed the rate of fire considerably.

The subsequent capture of Fort Niagara on July 25 was a masterstroke for British arms because it cut off the entire French colony to the west from the rest of colonial Canada. The tactical details of the decisive ambush are preserved in three letters that Massey wrote to William Pitt. Johnson, who was conducting the siege and not present at the ambush, wrote an account of the action that gave equal credit to the regulars and to their Native allies. Before the action, the Seneca among the British native allies reportedly had told their French counterparts that they intended to remain neutral in the upcoming clash, and they wished that the French native allies would do likewise. Johnson admitted that he had no idea of the number of killed and wounded, but he did report that a French Jesuit Father Virot had fallen victim to the frenzied Iroquois. The priest had apparently been cut to pieces. To Massey's fury, Johnson's version of the operation reached the newspapers first. The British officer later claimed that the tribesmen behaved "most dastardly" by slaughtering the wounded and those who were trying to surrender. Sir Charles Hardy, Governor of New York considered the reduction of Fort Niagara of the utmost consequence, claiming that the loss of Niagara would "soon oblige the French to abandon their encroachments [in the Ohio country] as it will be scarce possible for them to support those forts with garrisons or supply them with provisions." [195]

Indeed, the French survivors and their allies retreated all the way to Detroit burning many of their western posts and forts. More importantly, French plans to counterattack the British at Fort Pitt collapsed when news that Niagara had fallen arrived. Ironically, the French posts in the west were like cannonballs supported by a very thin string of supplies. The capture of Niagara effectively cut off all of Canada to the west of Lake Ontario from the administrative heart of New France. The defeat also cut the heart out of the French-allied Indians who melted back into the forests.

The focus of British strategy now switched to Wolfe's campaign against Quebec. At the end of July 1759, however, an ill-advised attempt was made upon the French entrenchments at Quebec near the Montmorenci Falls. Wolfe had observed that the northern shore of the St. Lawrence River around Beauport, the most favorable site for the landing of troops, was strongly defended by the French, who had built entrenchments on high ground, redoubts and floating batteries. The British regulars supported by rangers, having landed from boats, became disordered as they tried desperately to cross the mud flats that lined the shore, and they could not bring a concerted effort to bear on the French positions. Wolfe, who was then in the heat of the action, immediately realized his mistake. The first troops advancing toward French lines were the thirteen companies of grenadiers and some 200 soldiers of the Royal Americans. More than 430 men lost their lives, including 33 officers, before the attackers could be brought off. General Wolfe was deeply moved by the disaster, and the French were equally buoyed by it, believing that with winter threatening the British campaign was winding to an end.

View of Montmorency Falls or Sault de Montmorence and of the Attack on the French entrenchments near Beauport by General Wolfe with the Army Grenadier on 31 July 1759. Drawn of the spot by Cap. Hervey Smyth. **Engraved by Wm. Elliot (1823).**

What French General Montcalm saw as he rode onto the Plains of Abraham at dawn on September 13 stunned him, however. Moving up-river at night on a six-knot tide beyond Quebec, Wolfe chose a small cove at the base of the cliffs called the Anse de Foulon as a landing place. Here the vertical walls of the valley seemed to be scaleable by a small party. The British light infantry scrambled up the woody precipice and overran a French guard post at the top. With very little loss, and a great deal of discipline and organization, Wolfe had moved his entire force to the Plains of Abraham by sunrise. An entire British army of 4,800 regular troops and two artillery pieces was drawn up in the best linear order facing the walls of the city with the Light infantry on the flanks and the Royal Americans held in reserve. Montcalm hurriedly called up his French Canadiens and allied Indians from the Charles River side of the city to support his regulars. He could have stayed behind the walls of the city, but Wolfe had set the stage for the type of battle that both he and Montcalm understood best: a standup European encounter between long lines of regulars on a fairly even and level piece of ground surrounded by rocky outcrops and bounded by the cliffside – a battle that would win the war!

The landings at Anse de Foulon (Quebec 1759). The cliffs are actually much steeper than they appear in this painting. Montcalm was reported to have said, "I see the enemy where they have no business to be. This is a serious affair!"

Brigadier General George Townsend made the following observations of the battle: "It is most certain that the enemy formed in good order and that their attack was very brisk and animated. ... Our troops reserved their fire till within forty yards, which was so well continued that the enemy every where gave way." Sir John Fortescue was less appreciative of the order demonstrated by the French, claiming that they came on the run, which at once broke their lines, and that they fired too soon. Of the British regulars he noted that the line fired like a single shot, repeated the feat, and followed with a charge of bayonets and claymores (Scottish swords) when the French fled the field.

Wolfe had been active along the lines and had received a wound in the wrist. Just as the enemy broke he was struck in the chest and groin by musket fire. He staggered and sat on the ground. Those around him came to his aid and sent for a surgeon, but Wolfe knew he was finished. Having been informed that the French were in rout, he gave a few barely coherent orders and died. Montcalm tried to bring order to the retreat, but he was borne along on horseback within the stream of panic-stricken soldiers. As he neared the walls of the city, a stray shot passed through his body. He kept his seat until he had ridden through the St. Louis Gate and then was placed in the house of the army surgeon. Montcalm was dying, heavy of heart and lost in the reflections of a defeated general. The battle lasted only fifteen minutes. The British lost about 660 killed, wounded, and missing in the siege, and the French most likely lost about the same number – the official reports by each side differ widely. One of only a dozen undisputedly decisive battles in world history was finally over. The great citadel at Quebec had fallen to the ill-fated Wolfe. Montcalm, possibly the best French general officer to serve in the colonial period, was dead, and France had effectively lost North America.

The supporting British Navy was forced to leave the St. Lawrence shortly after the capture of Quebec due to pack ice closing the mouth of the river. Before the ice left the rivers in April, the Chevalier de Lévis, Montcalm's successor as French commander, marched his 7,000 troops to Quebec. James Murray, the British commander, had experienced a terrible winter, as had his garrison of 4,000. On 28 April 1760, Lévis' forces met and defeated the British at the Battle of Sainte-Foy, immediately west of the city, but Murray remained in possession of the city until the Navy reappeared in the spring. At Montréal that September, Lévis and 2,000 troops confronted 17,000 British and American troops. The French capitulated on 8 September 1760, and the British took possession of Montreal. The Peace of Paris was signed in 1763.

By the provisions of the treaty, Havana and Manila, taken by the British Royal Navy were restored to Spain, which had belatedly entered the war as a French ally. In exchange Britain received Florida and all the Spanish territory east of the Mississippi River. Britain held on to Minorca in the Mediterranean, and the Grenada's, Dominica, Tobago, and St. Vincent in the Caribbean. France gave the Spanish all of Louisiana as compensation for their losses. (Louisiana would be returned to the French in the Napoleonic Era and sold to the United States in 1803).

The Year of Turmoil, 1764

Having won a transatlantic empire, the British immediately demonstrated their inability to govern it. The royal Proclamation of 1763 closed the frontiers to Anglo-colonial settlement, recognized the territorial rights of the tribes, and assured Catholics of their right to practice their religion. While the main provisions of the proclamation threaten financial disaster in America, the final provision threatened to resurrect a new religious war on the continent. It was widely believed by the frontier settlers — and not without supporting evidence — that the Jesuits were actively inciting the Catholic Indians against the Protestant English settlements.[196]

The siege of Fort Pitt by the Indians had marked the close of one colonial epoch and the beginning of another. The same year that had overseen the suppression of the Pontiac conspiracy had officially end of the long struggle between France and England for the domination of America. The two events released once more the westward surge of English settlement and the desire to do business on the frontier. Immediately, a new kind of conflict began. It is clear from subsequent events that at this point many Anglo-colonials became unhyphenated Americans. They rushed to remove the "Anglo" from their Anglo-Americanism. The careful reader of colonial history will discover that 1764 was not a good year in American colonial history. Nothing that happened was immediately overwhelming, but nearly everything that happened had awe-inspiring consequences. It was in fact a pivotal year in the relations between the colonies and the empire.

Colonial sensitivities were further assaulted when the line of the frontier proposed by the Proclamation of 1763 was "deliberately distorted" by Parliament into a permanent barrier to settlement in 1764. The "undeniable primary principle" of this line was to foster a market for British manufactures along the coastline and to prevent the development of any colonial industry in the interior. The boundary was so quickly drawn that it took no notice of previous settlements, grants or improvements. Many of the Scots-Irish and German immigrants that arrived late in the process of land acquisition with little money had moved through the settled areas to the frontier where they simply squatted on the land. It has been estimated that two of every three acres occupied on the frontiers were held with no legal rights other than the improvements made on them. Many families had a roof over their heads and were debt free, but they were also essentially penniless.[197]

Not a single shilling of indemnification was offered to the colonials in the proclamation for the losses they would sustain. Only land purchased from the tribes by the Crown would be recognized, and trade over the line was restricted to licensed merchants. The settlers and companies that had taken the earliest steps on the frontiers and made the largest investments of labor and money were now those most disadvantaged. Following the dictum that possession was nine tenths of the law, the governor of Virginia and several members of his privy council stressed that those who had abandoned their lands during the French war return to them immediately — even in violation of the Proclamation — or risk any hope of retaining them in the future.[198]

In a letter to William Crawford, a Pennsylvania surveyor, George Washington wrote concerning his own interests in circumventing the restrictive frontier policy as expressed in the Proclamation of 1763. "I can never look upon the Proclamation in any other light ... than as a temporary expedient to quiet the minds of the Indians. It must fall, of course, in a few years, especially when those Indians consent to our occupying those lands. Any person who neglects hunting out good lands, and in some measure marking and distinguishing them for his own, in order to keep others from settling them will never regain it." [199]

To add fuel to the unrest, the Sugar Act of 1764 required the payment in coin of all public debts and duties, and the Currency Act of 1764 effectively made all colonial paper money then in circulation worthless. All of the colonies except Massachusetts, which had redeemed most of its paper obligations, faced financial ruin as the value of their outstanding paper evaporated.[200]

Americans like Benjamin Franklin believed that a free flow of capital in the provinces would keep interest rates low and help facilitate trade. Although Parliament was actually attempting to formally stabilize the monetary systems of all the colonies, the colonists assumed that the coins paid in duties and taxes would be shipped to England, leaving them nothing in which to make the payments of trade balances. In fact, the British ministry intended to keep the coins in the colonies to help pay for the thousands of troops that it had authorized for colonial protection. Some of this would have found its way back into the colonial economy. However, the natural flow of hard currency (coin) under the system of mercantilism was purposely tilted toward the parent country, and the resulting balance of payments continually removed coins from the colonies.

A fear of the resultant drain of hard currency from North America gripped all the colonies, but it particularly affected the cash-dependent merchants of New England and the currency-starved frontier settlers. Colonials foresaw a future of perpetual debt unpayable regardless of how hard they labored or how successful were their businesses and farms. The fundamental problems surrounding the colonial monetary system were never rectified, and the cash provisions of the acts of 1764 remained in effect until the eve of the revolution serving as an undercurrent to the general discontent that the colonials had formed for the restrictions of British trade regulation.[201]

Americans soon began to realize that their own best interests were not always those of the Crown. James Otis, writing from the perspective of the seaboard colonials, noted, "The late acquisitions in America, as glorious as they have been, and as beneficial as they are to Great Britain, are only a security to these colonies against the ravages of the French and Indians. Our trade upon the whole is not, I believe, benefited by them one groat."[202]

Imagine also the surprise on the frontiers when, no sooner than the French war had ceased, the settlers witnessed a paradox — English merchants' wagons and pack trains under British licenses carrying arms and ammunition westward for sale to the same tribes who had destroyed their homes.[203] Matthew Smith and James Gibson responded to this circumstance for the frontiersmen in an open letter to Parliament. Called *A Remonstrance from the Pennsylvania Frontiersmen* (1764), the letter was published and widely read in the colonies. It stated in part:

> It grieves us to the very heart to see such of our frontier inhabitants as have escaped savage fury with the loss of their parents, their children, their wives or relatives, left destitute by the public, and exposed to the most cruel poverty and wretchedness [by the government]. ... We humbly conceive that it is contrary to the maxims of good policy, and extremely dangerous to our frontiers, to suffer any Indians, of what tribe so ever, to live within the inhabited parts of this province while we are engaged in an Indian war, as experience has taught us that they are all perfidious, and their claim to freedom and independency puts it in their power to act as spies, to entertain and give intelligence to our enemies, and to furnish them with provisions and warlike stores. To this fatal intercourse between our pretended friends and open enemies, we must ascribe the greatest of the ravages and murders that have been committed in the course of this and the last Indian war. ... We, therefore, pray that public rewards may be proposed for Indian scalps, which may be adequate to the dangers attending enterprises of this nature.[204]

At the end of the French war, the Grenville ministry in London had assured the colonials that the regulars in garrison on the frontier would be "a thin red line between kidnap, scalping, and massacre" and security for the white settlements now that the French were gone. The local militias and provincial regiments that had supported frontier expansion and protected the settlements for decades could retire their arms and live in peace with the tribes reassured by the intervening presence of the redcoats. However, Pontiac's uprising of 1763-1764 seemed once again to validate many of the negative convictions held by the colonials with regard to the regulars. Every British garrison in the Great Lakes region was taken by the Native warriors save two, Fort Pitt and Fort Detroit.

As a result the colonials tended to once again look down upon the regular British troops brought to the colonies to secure the borders. However, British colonel Henry Bouquet exhibited an exemplary understanding of Indian offensive tactics during the French and Indian War, which was confirmed by his signal victory at Bushy Run in 1763 during Pontiac's War. He wrote, "There were three basic principles in the Indians' method of fighting: first, fight scattered; second, try to surround; and third, give ground when hard pressed and return when the pressure eased."[205]

The woodland warrior of the 18th century exhibited a mixture of European and traditional Native accoutrements, but he maintained his cultural protocols.

At Bushy Run, Bouquet attempted a unique maneuver, which he described in a letter to his superior, General Jeffrey Amherst:

The savages growing every moment more audacious it was thought proper still to increase their confidence; by that means, if possible, to entice them to come close upon us, or to stand their ground when attacked. With this view two Companies of Light Infantry were ordered within the circle, & the Troops on their right and left opened their files and filled up the space; that it might seem they were intended to cover the retreat. The third Light Infantry Company, and the Grenadiers of the 42nd were ordered to support the two first Companies. This maneuver succeeded to our wish, for the few troops who took possession of the ground lately occupied by the two Light Infantry Companies, being brought in nearer to the center of the circle, the barbarians mistaking these motions for a retreat hurried headlong on, and advancing upon us with the most daring intrepidity galled us excessively with their heavy fire; but at the very moment of that certain success, they thought themselves Masters of the Camp, Major Campbell at the head of the two first Companies sallied out, from a part of the hill they could not observe, and fell upon their right flank. They resolutely returned the fire, but could not stand the irresistible shock of our men, who rushing in among them, killed many of them, and put the rest to flight.[206]

Although the back of the uprising was broken by the regulars of the Black Watch (42nd Highlanders), the British army seems to have been unable to fully secure the frontiers for more than two years. Gen. Amherst, in charge of the region, was recalled by the Board of Trade and replaced with Thomas Gage, now advanced to Major General.

The formal treaty between Pontiac and Sir William Johnson in July 1764 had hardly been a peace, much less a surrender. No lands changed hands, no hostages were taken, and no white captives were returned — all characteristics of previous agreements — and raids by disparate groups of recalcitrant warriors continued. Colonial confidence in British arms was severely shaken. The British regulars were humiliated, and the bureaucracy in London was embarrassed by the effectiveness of the Native American attacks.[207]

The Second Journal of Captain Thomas Morris, written in 1764 and found in *Miscellanies in Prose and Verse* (London, printed for James Ridgway, 1791), is of importance to historical students because of the light it throws upon conditions in the West at this critical moment, and the proof it furnishes that Pontiac's influence was still paramount among the Western Indians. Native hostility to British sovereignty over the West was deep-seated, and would take many years wholly to uproot. The journal also possesses considerable dramatic interest. Told in the first person by the chief participant, the thrilling incidents of repeated escapes from torture and death, the flight through the woods, and the final refuge at Detroit were fodder for novelists. The character of the man throws the incidents of this hazardous journey into still stronger relief. Here is no frontiersman like Weiser, Kenton, or Croghan, familiar with the hardships of the wilderness; no missionary seeking heavenly rewards; not even a bluff and practical soldier. Morris was a man of the great world, a fashionable dilettante, dabbling in literature and the dramatic art.

Morris came to America in 1758, as a lieutenant in the 17th Regiment of Infantry, in which he had been commissioned three years previous. Although this was Forbes' command, Morris saw service at Louisburg in 1758, and was with Amherst in the campaign around Lake Champlain in the following year. In 1761, he was promoted to a captaincy and assigned to the garrison of Fort Hendrick, at Canajoharie in the Mohawk Valley the home of the famous Mohawk chiefs, Hendricks and Brant. Doubtlessly he acquired there that knowledge of the Mohawk temperament that he exhibits in the opening pages of his journal concerning his mission to Ohio. "I was greatly delighted on observing the difference of temper betwixt these Indian strangers and those of my old acquaintance of the five nations," he wrote, "for it is certain that a reserved Englishman differs not more from a lively Frenchman than does a stern Mohawk from a laughing Chippewa."[208]

Initially fearing death at the hands of these recent French allies, Morris wrote: "Presently came Pontiac, and squatted himself, after his fashion, opposite to me. This Indian has a more extensive power than ever was known among that people; for every chief used to command his own tribe: but eighteen nations, by French intrigue, had been brought to unite, and choose this man for their commander, after the English had conquered Canada; having been taught to believe that, aided by France, they might make a vigorous push and drive us out of North America." When he mentioned that their father, the king of France, had ceded the Ohio Country to their brother the king of England, he was derided for telling a lie and assured that had the lie been received as other than propaganda he would have been killed. Morris' diplomatic mission had been greeted with contempt, not anger. Pontiac reportedly responded to Morris: "I will lead the nations to war no more; let them be at peace, if they choose it: but I myself will never be a friend to the English. I shall now become a wanderer in the woods; and if they come to seek me there, while I have an arrow left, I will shoot at them." At this meeting Pontiac had displayed a great belt of Wampum that was reportedly forty years old representing the alliance of two hundred and ten villages. Morris noted after this meeting: "A Huron woman however abused me because the English had killed her son. ... And as all the young Indians were determined to murder me, I was afterwards obliged to put on Indian shoes and cover myself with a blanket to look like a savage, and escape by fording the river into a field of Indian corn." No pursuit was made. After his adventures along the Maumee, related in this journal, Morris remained at Detroit for some time, and returned to England with his regiment in 1767.[209]

Hundreds of miles of ever shifting frontier settlements were not readily defensible against Indian raids, and the only effective strategy was retaliation so brutal as to deter further incursions. Colonial militias periodically organized punitive expeditions into the frontier regions. Since the Indians rarely chose to stand and fight, colonials learned to threaten and burn the natives' crops and villages. The Indians were thereby forced into an active defense of their families and homes that could be broken by trained soldiers. Recurrent hostilities and the need for repeated colonial forays into the border regions, with all of their political and economic consequences, posed a dilemma for colonial officials that they could never resolve. Nonetheless, a series of overwhelming victories by militia forces caused colonials to exaggerate their abilities in this regard.

At the beginning of 1764, the frontier border of the Middle American colonies was the Tuscarora Ridge, the western rim of the Conococheague valley. The old trading path along the ridge was sometimes called the Tuscarora Trail. There had been settlements and trading posts beyond it, but the Indians had wiped them out; the cabins that were not burned were abandoned. The valley itself had staved off massacre. When confronted with Indian attacks, the settlers in the West Conococheague settlements in the Alleghenies had either fled their homes for the safety of forts back east or took matters into their own hands in order to survive. Among those settlers that stayed to defend their homes were William Smith and James Smith of the so-called Black Boys, a core group of about 50 men who styled themselves as Rangers. James Smith had been captured by savages, ran the gauntlet, saw the prisoners of the Braddock massacre burned at the stake, lived five years as an Indian, escaped, and served through three wilderness campaigns. "His mind was a relief map of an unmapped wilderness. He knew the dialects of half a dozen tribes; he knew their folkways; he knew how they thought. He had 'relatives' in a hundred lodges."[210]

These frontiersmen not only stayed on the frontier, but they banded together to protect their homes and families by taking the fight to the enemy. They were not then considered lawless men or disloyal agitators, but they had ceased waiting for the pacifist provincial government of Pennsylvania or the redcoated battalions ensconced in their forts to come to their aid. These realities showed the impracticality of British plans for the management of the colonies, and disillusionment continued to build with each Indian raid that the regulars failed to prevent.[211]

Believing strongly that the British were allowing unscrupulous traders to supply the Indians with weapons and ammunition. Smiths' men set an ambush on Sidelong Hill on the Forbes' Road and stopped the pack trains and burned the supplies belonging to one Robert Callendar, who had obtained a license from Bouquet through the influence of George Croghan, the Royal Indian Agent. Croghan seems to have been less than innocent in this affair, even drawing the rebuke of Sir William Johnson for misrepresenting the nature and destination of the goods.

The attack by Allegheny frontiersmen on Fort Loudoun in 1764

Three hundred armed men under James Smith then marched to Fort Loudoun, where the traders led by a man named Ralph Nailer had fled, demanding that they be given up to the local justices of the peace for prosecution as violators of the Indian trade laws. Lt. Charles Grant of the 42nd Highland regiment commanded Fort Loudoun. Grant was an officious man, and he believed every distortion the traders told him concerning the confrontation over the goods. The permit the traders presented as a defense was from the commanding officer at Fort Pitt for the carrying of goods for the support of the troops not for trade to the Indians.

Three local magistrates were present led by William Smith. Justice Smith answered the permit by noting that no military officer's pass would do without a local magistrate's pass also. Grant acted arrogantly, dismissing the power of the civil authority in military matters. He neither accepted nor read the magistrates' legal warrants. They reminded Grant that there was a civil government in Pennsylvania, not a military one; that the road over which the traders traveled was a provincial road not a King's highway; and that the fort was a provincial fort not a Royal one, built and paid for by themselves. They would not have these used against them. The ultimatum of the magistrates might have sounded ridiculous to the commander of British regulars, but the presence of three hundred armed and grim-faced frontiersmen outside the fort caused Grant concern. However, it did not immediately convince him to turn over the traders to the magistrates for trial.

Restraint was not high on the list of frontier qualities, and the Black Boys thereafter opened fire upon the fort. Smith's rangers kept it up for two days and nights, so closely marking their targets that no one was permitted to go in or out, or even show his head above the parapet. The border marksmen, the deer hunters and the Indian fighters began to gnaw the edges of the loopholes into slivers. Firing was kept up on all parts of the fort, rifle and musket balls sending splinters of wood everywhere so that the sentries could not stand upright in the bastions. The protest was gaining reinforcements; Grant was not. The borderers came hurrying in from all directions, some just to join in the fun and spectacle. By nightfall Smith had another hundred rifles on his firing line. Amazingly no one was hurt save James Smith, who took a slight wound from the return fire early in the siege, but Grant was forced ultimately to abandon the post, marching out with military honors under arms with flags flying.[212]

A few days later, some of the valley men had their muskets and rifles confiscated by roaming British patrols. Some local men had a serious firefight with one of these patrols, which was forced to take refuge in a settler's cabin. Sergeant Leonard McGlashan of the 42nd was wounded, as was one of the locals, John Brown. McGlashan later related in a legal deposition that he was astounded at the time of the incident that these backwoodsmen actually meant to kill him!

Lieutenant Grant had stormed off to write a dispatch that sizzled with indignation. In it he informed his colonel that being under duress, he would keep the confiscated guns. And though all the rebels in the valley came against him, he would not surrender them. When the constable of the township ventured into Fort Loudon with a warrant, the commandant seized it and refused to give it up. He kept it all summer "with a design to make Use of it against Justice Smith, and thereby to prove that tho' he would give me no Redress for the gross Insult offered to me by those lawless Fellows who Carried me from my Post Prisoner into the Woods, and whom I met at his own House, and Complained of to him without Redress; Yet he had the Assurance afterwards to Issue Said Warrant with a Malicious design, as I had reason to believe, to persecute the poor Sergeant who had received hard usage for doing his Duty, And who I thought it Incumbent on me to Protect."[213]

Grant was ultimately forced to surrender the firearms to Justice William McDowell who, though neutral, returned them to their owners as illegal seizures. Grant later wrote: "Justice Smith, who was Sent for by the Governor [John Penn] ... has Returned, & in Consequence of the ... remonstrance, I'm informed. Stands in a fair light with the Governor. I am informed by good authority, that Mr. Allen, Chief Justice of this Province, has said, that if I should come to Philadelphia he should be obliged to arrest me by a Provincial Warrant, on account of my proceedings at this Post." Hence the lines of dispute were drawn between the military and civil governments of the colony — a dispute that would evidence itself later in the Constitution and Bill of Rights.[214]

Four years later — six years before Ethan Allen and Benedict Arnold stormed Ticonderoga — a band of these same borderers stormed Fort Bedford and took it from the soldiers of another British regiment (1769). Details of this fort during the inter-war years are sketchy and controversial, and Captain Lewis Ourry, in command of the fort at the outbreak of Pontiac's Rebellion, listed just twelve Royal Americans on his roster to guard the fort and more than 90 local families. It is clear that the British Army abandoned the fort sometime during this period. The specific location of the fort beyond being in Bedford, Pennsylvania has been lost to history, and several archaeological digs have failed to yield any solid evidence of the fort's exact site.

During the conflict nothing was really published about these encounters, they being considered localized matters. The events were eventually publicized when James Smith wrote his brief memoirs in 1799. These were reprint in 1870, but then basically nothing exists in print until a book was written describing the riots as the first armed uprising against Royal troops in the colonies by Neil Harmon Swanson.

The story of the West Conococheague rebellion was the subject of the 1934 historical narrative *The First Rebel* by Neil H. Swanson and it generated a screenplay five years later. The 1939 black and white film starring John Wayne and now called *Allegheny Uprising* competed poorly at the box office with the full color *Drums Along the Mohawk*, which was released just a week earlier starring Henry Fonda. In the United Kingdom, the Ministry of Information initially banned *Allegheny Uprising* for placing the British, already at war against Nazi Germany, in a bad light. *Unconquered*, a 1947 film based on a book by Swanson and starring Gary Cooper depicts the violent struggles between American colonists and Native Americans on the western frontier during the time of Pontiac's Rebellion, primarily around Fort Pitt. After serving as a company commander in the United States Infantry during the First World War, Swanson had worked as assistant city editor on a Minneapolis newspaper. As executive editor in Baltimore, Swanson directed news coverage at The Sun, The Evening Sun, and The Sunday Sun. The newspapers won three Pulitzer Prizes during his tenure. The author wrote the screenplay for *Unconquered* from Baltimore, barely keeping ahead of the production schedule set by Cecile B. De Mille while overseeing operations of the newspapers. In 1940, he authored *The Silent Drum*, a frontier novel, and in 1971, *The Forbidden Ground*, a novel concerning the struggle for a vast fur empire. Swanson, who was considered an expert on the War of 1812, wrote nine books.

Swanson wrote at the time of the film's release: "I, too, apprehend that a great part of this account of America's first rebel will be viewed as fable or romance. It is useless to deny that the life of James Smith is the stuff of which novels are made. James Fenimore Cooper would have fallen upon him with delight, for he was a leatherstocking and a deerslayer, and his career was a succession of dangers and audacities. The fact that James Smith has been almost completely overlooked for a hundred and fifty years, however, undoubtedly will make the truth about him hard to believe. ... Reduced to its simplest terms, the conflict on the Pennsylvania frontier was a conflict between ideas. It was man against money — the desire of ordinary men to live with security against the desire of capital to take profits where they could be found. It was human rights against property rights. ... Do courts exist to apply the law? Or should they interpret law in terms of changing circumstances and of the people's changing needs and wishes? That was a question on the frontier ... years ago. The frontiersmen answered it in their own way: they took the courts, and their own local magistrates led them in insurrection to defend their civil liberties and their security."[215]

The National Rifle Association (NRA) considers these incidents in May 1765 involving the citizens of the Conococheague Valley the first fight for the right to keep and bear arms in America. Moreover, the constitution of Pennsylvania was written to be even stronger than the Second Amendment to the Bill of Rights. Article I, section 21 of the Pennsylvania State Constitution states: "The right of the citizens to bear arms in defense of themselves and the State *shall not be questioned*." The Supreme Court of the United States has also reaffirmed the right of persons to use firearms to "defend their hearth and home." (*District of Columbia v. Heller*, 554 U.S. 570, 2008)

Other rebellious groups that formed in 1764, such as North Carolina's Regulators, revolted against corrupt colonial officials who took advantage of the local farmers and their lack of knowledge of property law when they became debt ridden due to famine and other unfortunate circumstances. The rebellion of the Regulators was no short outburst of colonial piqué, and some historians list it as a cause of the revolution. It lasted not months, but years, generally from 1764 to 1771, in which year it was brutally suppressed by the royal governor, William Tryon. Yet the so-called War of Regulation — intended to regulate and reform government abuse — was waged against local authorities, not the Crown, and evidence suggests that many of these authorities later became Loyalist leaders during the Revolution.

The core of the Regulator organization consisted of a number of radical Protestants, among them many Quakers, led by Herman (a.k.a. Harmon) Husband, a prosperous farmer originally from Maryland. Husband quickly became one of the main spokesmen for the farmers' movement, as well as its chief chronicler and ideologue. His powerful ideas about social justice and moral virtue were tremendously influential among these farmers who repeatedly petitioned the governor and the assembly over their grievances, tried to set up meetings with local officials, and brought suits against the dishonest sheriffs. When such legal measures had little effect, they refused to pay their taxes; repossessed property seized for public sale to satisfy debts; disrupted court proceedings; and finally resorted to arms.

Governor Arthur Dobbs was an associate of the Ohio Company that sought to speculate in land in the Alleghenies. In 1762, Dobbs purchased two 100,000-acre tracts in the counties that were to become the focus of Regulator activity. Some of the early settlers contested Dobbs' right to the land based on their being first to clear and plant it. Instead of paying modest fees to the colonial government for claiming vacant land, farmers were being required to buy the farms they and their families had created from the speculation company. They resisted Dobbs' efforts to survey his claims and blocked his attempts to eject them from their farms. They so scared county officials that none dared come to their neighborhood to serve legal papers. Although Husband was a Quaker convert, the majority of these farmers were Scotch-Irish Presbyterians with about twenty families of German and Swiss Pietists.[216]

Upon the death of Dobbs in 1765, Governor William Tryon had come to the province helped into office by Lord Hillsborough, an influential in-law who was a member of the Board of Trade and later secretary for the colonies. Tryon's out-of-hand dismissal of the farmers' grievances did much to escalate the conflict, and several demonstrations and mass meetings over the intervening years ended in counterproductive standoffs.

Historian of the movement, Marjoleine Kars noted how social and religious undercurrents affected the rise of this political revolution:

> The voices ... were not those of the learned ministers so ably captured by previous historians of religion. Instead, church minutes and the conversations among lay people recorded in the diaries of local Piedmont ministers revealed a world where farming men and women were deeply influenced by revivalist Protestantism and wrestled actively with crucial moral and political questions in their local communities. It seemed it could not be an accident that the Regulator Rebellion happened in the midst of this creative and subversive religious climate.[217]

Ultimately, the assembly passed a sweeping Riot Act that gave Tryon the authority and funds he needed to raise a military force and march against the Regulators. On 16 May 1771, about 1,100 provincial troops under Tryon confronted upward of 2,000 farmers on a field near Alamance Creek about twenty miles west of Hillsborough. A pitched battle ensued for upwards of two hours thereafter leaving two-dozen farmers dead, along with 9 colonial troops. More than 150 men on both sides were wounded and about a dozen were executed after the surrender, one by Tryon with a pistol.

For the Scotsmen among the Regulators the executions brought to mind the brutal aftermath of the Battle of Culloden in 1746. The brutality worked. At least 6,000 Regulators and sympathizers were forced to take an oath of allegiance as the victorious troops undertook a punitive march through the backcountry settlements. Some of the most dedicated Regulator leaders, including Husband, fled the province; other individual farmers remained defiant right up to the Revolution.

In 1773, after a decade of dispute with the frontier settlers and colonial agents, rumors spread through the colonies that it was the Crown's intention to secure an Act of Parliament that would vacate all American titles to land by annulling the former colonial patents, thereby causing all titles to land to revert to the Crown from which they would again have to be petitioned. These rumors were given increased credence when, by order of the King, Governor Josiah Martin closed the Royal land office in North Carolina. Although the Court of Claims continued to sit, applications for new entries, warrants, and patents were denied. Governor Martin issued a formal statement of denial to suppress this rumor, but in February 1775, two months before Lexington and Concord, the Royal land offices throughout the colonies closed forever.[218]

The Battle at Alamance Creek (1771) is often considered the first major armed conflict of the American Revolution.

XII. Cooper's Frontier in Fact and Fiction

Only a few dozen American novels were being written in the early decades of the 19th century leaving Cooper's works standing virtually alone as contemporary historical frontier fiction. In the last years of his life, Cooper wrote in *The Borderers* (1849) concerning the unique physical and psychological environment into which he placed his characters:

> They who dwell in the older districts of America, where art and labor have united for generations to clear the earth of its inequalities, and to remove the vestiges of a state of nature, can form but little idea of the thousand objects that may exist in a clearing, to startle the imagination of one who has admitted alarm, when seen in the doubtful light of even a cloudless moon. ... Accustomed as they were to the sight ... [and] excited by their fears, [they] fancied each dark and distant stump a savage; and they passed no angle in the high and heavy fences without throwing a jealous glance to see that some enemy did not lie stretched within its shadows.[219]

The struggle for control of North America was also a contest over which methods and rules of warfare would be used there. For centuries the Native Americans had fought among themselves in a conservative if seemingly inhumane manner using knives, clubs, and tomahawks made of wood and stone. The bow and arrow of the eastern woodland Indians of North America was unsophisticated and technologically inferior, not only to those developed by European and Asian cultures, but also to those found in South and Central America. Yet it was sufficient for hunting and making war. The Indians shifted from traditional weapons to firearms as quickly as they became available, but it has been pointed out that the Indians "never really mastered the white man's weapon." [220]

Also known as the Indian hatchet, the tomahawk was considered an essential piece of equipment on the frontier. So common was its use by both Indians and frontiersmen that it has come to symbolize the very concept of frontier warfare. During the 18th century, the terms tomahawk and hatchet were used to convey the very concepts of war and peace, as in "raising the tomahawk" and "burying the hatchet." Although the Indians sought out firearms and even carried pistols, they continued to rely on the tomahawk and knife for infighting. The origins of the tomahawk have often been misinterpreted to include only the formidable metal hatchet used by Native American warriors. In fact, Indians had no iron tomahawks before the period of European contact. They generally used massive wooden warclubs that were quite effective in disabling an opponent. Nonetheless, once they were made available, the Native Americans placed a high value on their iron-headed hatchets and war axes.

Nonetheless, the native war practices in terms of tactics, prisoners, and personal behavior on the field of battle changed little even with the introduction of firearms. The tactics employed by Native American warriors were simple and effective. They generally struck first without a formal declaration of war, using the basic offensive tactic of surprise. They commonly attacked isolated cabins and remote villages, often at dawn. They often attacked solitary farmers working in their fields after midday, and more than once fell upon farm carts driven by women or children. It was not unusual for an abandoned cart or riderless horse to serve as the first sign of a larger problem. The mutilated bodies of the victims were often found posed in gruesome caricature on the roadside or along the forested path. Most attacks, however, took the form of ambushes made in forested regions. These were especially effective against nonmilitary targets such as small parties of settlers or fur traders. The Indians' tactics evolved with time and with contact with Europeans. At the behest of the French, they abandoned their traditional practice of not fighting through the winter months to launch crucial forays against such targets as Deerfield, Massachusetts, and Schenectady, New York, the latter just a day's journey from Cooperstown.

Indian raids and conflicts were common throughout the colonial period as products of a clash of cultures. However, the affairs of European monarchs also affected the peace of the frontiers. The wars that characterized eighteenth-century Europe inevitably spilled over into America. The many conflicts that rocked Europe from 1688 to 1763 can safely be viewed as a single prolonged conflict. There were four distinct wars fought during this period, with France and England allied on opposite sides with the other states of Europe: (1) the War of the League of Augsburg, known in America as King William's War (1689-1697); (2) the War of Spanish Succession, or Queen Anne's War (1702-1713); (3) the War of Austrian Succession, or King George's War (in two stages in Europe between 1740 to 1748); and (4) the Seven Years' War, or the French and Indian War (1754-1763 in America; 1756-1763 in Europe). During six decades of Anglo-French conflict over the possession of North America, there were a series of woodland skirmishes, raids, massacres, and major battles that intimately affected the lives of colonials. None of these conflicts was decisive except the last. Not until several decades had passed did the English realize that their frontiers could best be secured by destroying the French presence in Canada. Thereafter, frontier settlers placed no limits on their cruelty and acted with brutal dispatch when dealing with their former Indian enemies-taking their lands and enslaving or killing natives when it suited them.

In the summer of 1689 as King William's War loomed over North America, Louis de Buade, Comte de Frontenac, was summoned to Versailles and ordered by King Louis XIV to proceed to New France for the second time as governor and to take up the conflict in the American theater. Frontenac carried with him orders that spelled out the king's optimistic plans for the invasion and capture of the English colony of New York. With 1,000 regulars, 600 militia raised from among the *habitants*, and as many Indian allies as he could attract to the enterprise, Frontenac was to proceed up the Richelieu River, traverse the lengths of Lakes Champlain and St. Sacrement (Lake George), march down the Hudson River, and take Albany by surprise.

Although the king thought the campaign could be concluded within a month of leaving Quebec, Frontenac, of course, was better informed of conditions in the forests of America. No meaningful army in the history of North America ever completely succeeded in carrying out the march from Quebec to Albany, although it looked so easy on paper. Nonetheless, Frontenac devised a plan of his own, and he proposed a raid on Schenectady, New York, deep in Mohawk territory, as the first step. He came very close to succeeding. To facilitate the movement of his troops along the ice, he set the timing of his raid for deepest winter 1690.

The tiny, palisaded village of Schenectady was founded in 1662 as a trading post above the lower Mohawk falls and rapids. On a bitterly cold night in February 1690, the gates of the palisade stood open guarded only by a pair of snowmen. The outlying houses and the interior blockhouse were dark. Shortly after midnight, a contingent of

Frenchmen, supported by their Indian allies, moved out from cover where they had been lying in wait for the village to grow silent. Every house was surrounded and at a signal the doors of every residence were driven in. The garrison in the blockhouse, caught quite by surprise, perished. The town was set ablaze and ransacked of all its valuables. Thirty-eight men and two boys were killed, while only two Frenchmen were reported killed by the defenders. Twenty-two women and children were marched off in the morning through the snow-filled forests toward Montreal, and a few older folk and small babies were left behind. One man, half dead, reached Albany on horseback to report the incident.

The bloody nighttime raid of Schenectady marked the beginning of seventy years of grim struggle between English and French colonials that inescapably involved the Native Americans of the region. One European power had purposely set the Indians against another for the first time.

Rumors of small bands of Indians stalking around the frontier communities of Northfield and Deerfield in Massachusetts abound before the winter of 1704. On the New England frontier Queen Anne's War was characterized by raids and skirmishes in the border regions, particularly in Maine. The event that came to characterize the plight of the frontier settlements in Queen Anne's War, however, was the raid against Deerfield, Massachusetts, on the Connecticut River in 1704. This operation almost mirrored the attack at Schenectady fourteen years earlier. More than one-third of the 300 residents of Deerfield were carried off in a midwinter raid, and between 40 and 50 of the remainder were killed.

The news of the Deerfield raid enraged the colonials, and later that same year, Caleb Lymen led a counterstroke on the Abenaki village at Cowass on the upper Connecticut River, driving the Indians to move their villages nearer to Canada. English expeditions like these were used throughout Queen Anne's War. They all shared the common characteristic of having the natives, who were their targets, evaporate into the forests at the approach of the colonial forces. The English saw nothing but deserted wigwams, and the Abenaki became adept at moving from place to place as they were pursued, leaving only a few cut-throats and bands of young warriors behind, which kept the country in constant alarm. Although the tactics employed by the colonials in combat generally failed to follow any particular pattern, these frontiersmen showed that they knew the arts of scouting, stealth, and ambush as well as any Native American.

Queen Anne's War was the longest of the frontier conflicts with France. French military successes near the end of the war (c. 1714) took place against the background of a changed political situation in Europe. As a result of a fresh British perspective on the European balance of power thereafter, Anglo-French talks began that culminated in the Treaty of Utrecht. There followed almost three decades of relative peace in Europe until 1740, but small conflicts continued to threaten the American frontiers. The earliest and most severe attacks were upon the New England Provinces in 1745; but the greatest annoyance to New York was experienced from the frequent parties sent out from Fort St. Frederick at Crown Point, which the French had strongly fortified in 1731.

Given hereafter are the encounters recorded in the Schenectady Collection of the Schenectady County Public Library for just one month in 1746. In May 1746, Gatienoude a Christian Iroquois of the Five Nations who had been settled near Lake Champlain for two or three years, left with five Indians of his village and the Sieur St. Blein (described as a cadet officer) to strike a blow in the neighborhood of Albany. This small party brought in one prisoner, but Gatienoude the leader of the party was killed and scalped by the English on the field of battle. A few days later, a party of eight Abenaki had raided in the direction of Schenectady returning with some prisoners and scalps. A week later a party of eight Iroquois of Sault St. Louis struck a blow near Albany and brought back six scalps. Sault St. Louis was an Iroquois mission, situated on the south bank of the St. Lawrence, about ten miles above Montreal. From 1667 to 1783 the Jesuits conducted the mission, and the residents were known as Caughnawaga. On 2 June 1746, a party of twenty-five warriors of the Sault and three Flatheads visiting from the west, who joined the former in the expedition, also attacked near Albany and returned with some scalps. A party of eighteen Nipissings raided nearby the next day. On 17 June 1746 – just one month from the first attack in May – a party of ten Abenaki went to make an attack at Kakecoute (probably at Schagticoke on the Hoosic River) and were defeated at the fort there. Their chief Cadenaret, a famous warrior, was killed, and the remainder returned with some scalps. These warriors were not able to bring away the dead because the bodies remained too near the fort. Finally, on 21 June a party of twenty-seven Iroquois under Sieur Parqueville an officer and Sieur Blein brought in some scalps and a prisoner that was on a scout to Saratoga. Such is the example of the energetic manner in which the French and their native allies made war upon the undefended frontier settlers who were taken by surprise and almost wholly unprepared for this type of war.[221]

A few miles west of Schenectady, some forty Dutch farmer-militiamen were ambushed by a French and Indian war party led by the Chevalier de Repentigny in 1748, locally called the battle of Beukendaal (Dutch for Beechdale). It was the only battle of King George's War (1744-1748) to take place in the Mohawk Valley or the Albany-Schenectady district. This was the third war to affect the colonial frontier. The bloody affray is sometimes called a massacre, but began as an ambuscade and developed into a combat between armed forces and had all the characteristics of a small battle. About 20 of the Schenectady militia were killed. The survivors barricaded themselves in the old DeGraaf frame house and fought off the enemy. This house may still be located by its cellar, and is marked as the site of this skirmish of the Colonial border wars.[222]

A raiding party of Canadian French and allied Indians, under the command of Le Sieur Chevalier de Repentigny, had entered the township of Glenville, Schenectady County, on the morning of 18 July 1748. They came upon Captain Daniel Toll with his black servant Ryckert and a man named Dirk Van Vorst who had gone in search of some stray horses at Beukendaal. Toll discovered his danger too late and was shot dead by the French Indians. Van Vorst was wounded and made a prisoner. Ryckert fled reaching Schenectady in safety with the dreadful news of the death of his master and the presence of the enemy.

The Schenectady militia and five or six young lads including Daniel Van Slyck went out to investigate under the command of Lieutenant John Darling. A second party led by Jacques Van Slyck, one of four brothers in the subsequent fight, trailed behind as other forces were being formed. The first party discovered the corpse of Toll and was lured into an ambush. The hidden enemy fired a volley and most of these Americans were shot down and killed, while several were captured.

Jacques Van Slyck and his party then came up and took refuge in the De Graff house where they tore the clapboards off from under the eaves, fired on the enemy, and successfully defended themselves by using the structure as a blockhouse. Fortunately as with most frontier raids the enemy had no artillery, which would have made the house untenable.

Adrian Van Slyck now came on the scene with a third party of New York levies. They were also fired upon. Adrian was killed and his men immediately turned around and fled to Schenectady.

Albert Van Slyck and Jacob Glen now came up with a fourth company, which reinforced the little band of defenders of the De Graff house. Their fire became too hot for the French raiders who fled into the woods, leaving the militiamen holding the field, surrounded by their dead and dying.

Meanwhile, Dirk Van Vorst, who had been captured when Toll was killed, was left under the charge of two young Indians when the fight began. They had tied him to a tree, so that they could go and watch the fight. Dirk then managed to get his hand into his pocket, took out his knife, cut his bonds, and escaped.

The survivors among the farmers brought their dead and wounded back to Schenectady, where the slain were laid out in a barn. A mounted messenger, who reached Albany in the evening, returned with an officer (Lieutenant Chew) and 100 Englishmen and 200 Mohawk Indians. These attempted a pursuit, but the enemy proved too far on the way back to Canada to be overtaken.

The American losses at Beukendaal were 20 killed, a number wounded and 13 made prisoner. Twelve of the killed were militiamen and eight were of the garrison. Seven prisoners were Schenectady militiamen and six were soldiers of the garrison. The loss of the enemy is not given in any of the accounts, but it is probable that it was small.

About 70 Schenectady militiamen and soldiers were in the encounter; probably not counting the levies that ran away. The enemy is supposed to have numbered over 100 Indians and some French. The Americans failed to win this encounter largely because they fed their forces into the fight in a piecemeal and unmilitary manner. The encounter at Beukendaal can serve as a prime example of the failure of the militia system when it was composed of untrained or under-trained men and led by inexperienced or incompetent officers. No family was safe unless protected by blockhouse or palisade; no man was exempt from military duty save by age or infirmity.

At the close of hostilities in 1748, Governor George Clinton sent an aide (Lt. B. Stoddert) and militia Capt. Anthony Van Schaick to Montreal to arrange for an exchange of Anglo-colonial prisoners. These two officers went into the Indian country to recover any captives that could be found, but returned with indifferent success. Several could not be found or could not be induced to return. Prisoners made by the Indians (especially laborers, slaves, or indentures) frequently preferred to remain in the free and easy life of the native villages rather than return to the drudgery and toil of the towns and farms settled by the English and the Dutch, or their descendants. Stoddert left Canada on the 28 June 1750 with twenty-four rescued prisoners. Only three of those captured at Beukendaal returned at this time.[223]

The Chevalier de Repentigny was an interesting personality on the frontier. In 1750, the Governor General of Canada granted to Repentigny a parcel of land on the northeastern end of Michigan's Upper Peninsula, at Sault Ste. Marie of six leagues (12 miles) frontage by six leagues in depth bordering on the St. Marys River below the rapids. Sault Ste. Marie was of little importance at the time, figuring merely as a stopping place for hunters, white and Indian, on their way to and from Mackinac Island, a strategic position for the commerce in furs on the Great Lakes. The Jesuits built a great mission on the island, St. Ignace, which drew many Indians to the French. The name of Michillimackinac (later abbreviated to Mackinac) was applied generally to the entire vicinity. The term Michillimackinac is the modern accepted spelling and definition for an old Ottawa term that is widely understood to mean "The Great Turtle" presumably named for the shape of Mackinac Island. This interpretation comes from an old written record of Michillimackinac from Antoine-Dennis Raudot, the Co-Intendant of New France in 1710.

De Repentigny visited the property in the fall of 1750. His first duty was to conciliate with the Indians, and he succeeded in completely withdrawing them from any alliance with the English. Indeed, the object of the grant was to thwart the English traders who were trying to gain favor with the natives. His attempt to fulfill the conditions of this grant was focused mainly on the building of a fort, what may be called the first one at Sault Ste. Marie. The French initially avoided the establishment of large military posts, but they built a number of so-called small posts or trading posts where the Indians brought their furs to barter for alcohol and the trinkets of civilization. De Repentigny employed a group of hired men during the whole winter cutting 1100 pickets of 15 foot length for his fort which was 110 feet square, and also the timber necessary for the construction of three houses, one of them 30 feet long by 20 feet wide, and two others 25 feet long and the same width as the first. Before the winter, he entirely finished the fort with the exception of a redoubt, which was to be 12 feet square and reach some distance above the gate of the fort. De Repentigny remained in Canada until shortly after the treaty of peace in 1763, and then returned to France. The Chevalier died in Paris in 1766, leaving certain French claimants among his heirs who in 1851 brought a suit against the United States claiming title to the parcel by inheritance. The grant now covered almost four counties. The case was decided against the Repentigny heirs.

Simon Girty was another interesting personality on the frontier. Born in 1741 in Chambers Mill, Pennsylvania, Native Americans had killed Girty's father at the opening of King George's War. His family had removed to Sherman's Creek in eastern

Pennsylvania thereafter. During the French and Indian War, the family, once again fearful of attack, sought refuge in Fort Granville. In 1755, a combined army of French soldiers and their native allies captured the fort, taking several British colonists captive including the teenaged Simon. He was first taken to Kittanning, a town belonging to the Delaware, but he eventually found himself traded to the Seneca who took him to the Ohio Country. There, he was adopted into the Seneca tribe. Girty seemed to enjoy his new surroundings, spending his late teens learning the language and customs of the Seneca.

In 1759, the "Ohio Seneca" signed a peace agreement with the English and agreed to return all captives. The natives returned Girty to his mother, and he spent the next several years as a struggling farmer. He also served as an interpreter for traders seeking furs from the Delaware natives in western Pennsylvania. With the outbreak of the American Revolution, both the British and Americans sought Girty's assistance. Each side hoped Girty's knowledge of native language and customs would help them secure alliances among the various tribes in western Pennsylvania and Ohio. The frontiersman first sided with the Americans, assisting General James Wood in 1775 in negotiations with the Shawnee, Seneca, Delaware, and Wyandot. Yet Girty did not take well to the structure of military life and frequently clashed with his superiors.

On 28 March 1778, the frontiersman left Fort Pitt and offered his services to the British military in Detroit. During the remainder of the war, Girty earned a reputation for his brutality. He supposedly had no misgivings about killing others or about watching them being tortured to death. Upon the American Revolution's conclusion, Girty continued to assist the natives in resisting American settlement of the Ohio Country. He played an active role in the defeat of General Arthur St. Clair and his army in 1791. He also participated in the Battle of Fallen Timbers in 1794. He thereafter escaped to Canada as a refugee.

Simon Girty was portrayed as a villain in many early history texts. *Simon Girty, the Outlaw, An Historical Romance* (1846), was a novel by Uriah James Jones portraying Girty as a renegade. Jones was a regular contributor to several big city newspapers and a writer of historical articles and sketches for magazines. In 1856, Jones also wrote *A History of the Early Settlement of the Juaniata Valley*, which book documented "the struggles, trials, and personal adventures of the pioneers [of Pennsylvania], as well as the many cold-blooded Indian massacres and depredations which spread desolation through the land, and laid waste the homes and firesides of so many who located in what was then a wilderness." The Indians inhabiting the valley, when the whites first invaded it, belonged to three or four tribes — the Delaware, Monsey, Shawnee, and probably the Tuscarora. The Conoy and Nanticoke settled in the valley in 1748. This mix of tribes led to their being collectivized by many period historians as Mingos. "Of all the savages in the valley, the Mingos were probably the most peaceably disposed, although it is a well-attested fact that they were a brave and warlike band. The fathers of the principal chiefs of the Mingos, settled in the Juaniata Valley, had been partially (if the term may be used) Christianized by the teachings of the Moravian missionaries." The number of white settlers gradually working their way to the west was so great, that it followed, as a matter of course, that the Juniata Valley was soon invaded by settlers.[224]

Caught between native nostalgia and concepts of white suppression, 20th century novelists generally made heroes of white adoptees into native society. *The Light in the Forest,* a novel first published in 1953 by author Conrad Richter, is about the struggles of a white boy, John Butler, who has been taken captive as a small child in Pennsylvania by the Lenni Lenape and has been fully assimilated into native culture. At the time, the book was thought to foster racial diversity, and was required reading in many high schools during the 1950s and 1960s. The story opens in the autumn of 1764 almost a dozen years after John's capture. The Lenape enter into a peace treaty with the British that requires that the Indians return any white captives. John, a teenager now called True Son, does not want to leave as he considers himself Lenape. He disdains white society. After returning to his white father's home, True Son refuses to recognize his blood relations, continues to wear his Indian clothes, and pretends that he no longer understands English. The white man's injustice and cruelty drive him back to the Lenape.

While all this is historical fiction, it is based on several real persons, places, situations, and events. Many genuine former captives eventually returned to their Indian families, and many others were never exchanged at all. A film based on the book was produced by Walt Disney Productions in 1958 and starred Fess Parker (Disney's Davy Crockett and TV's Daniel Boone) and James MacArthur (True Son), best known for the role in the 1960s and 1970s of Danny "Danno" Williams in *Hawaii Five-O*. The film version introduced the actress Carol Lynley as Shenandoe, a young indentured servant as a love interest for True Son. While the novel ends on a note of uncertainty, with True Son standing on a remote road and unsure where his future lies, the film returns him to his family, to Shenandoe, and, presumably, to a life on a plot of wilderness land his father has had deeded to him.

Another modern author, Allan W. Eckert, began writing American history as a teenager, eventually becoming an author of numerous books for children and adults. One of his children's novels was a runner-up for the Newbery Medal and seven of his 39 adult works were nominated for a Pulitzer Prize. His colorful frontier histories have been praised as more accessible than drier, more strictly factual, accounts, but he has sparked controversy within his historical narratives by using a novelist's technique to enhance dramatic events with "hidden dialogue." In this technique, he recreates historical conversations and thoughts in what some critics have considered to be "an entertaining blend of fact and fiction." Researched for seven years, *The Frontiersmen* (1968) was the first in Eckert's "The Winning of America" series. Herein Eckert recreated the real life of one of America's most outstanding heroes, Simon Kenton. Surviving the gauntlet and ritual torture, in 1778 Kenton was adopted into the Shawnee people. It was Simon Girty who rescued Kenton from the Shawnee in Ohio. Kenton's role in opening the Northwest Territory to settlement more than rivaled that of his friend Daniel Boone. By his eighteenth birthday, Kenton had already won frontier renown as a woodsman, Indian fighter and scout. His incredible physical strength and endurance, his great dignity and innate kindness made him the ideal prototype of the frontier hero. Possibly best known for his history of Tecumseh, Eckert's *Wilderness Empire: A Narrative* (1968) may be his best history / historic novel.[225]

In *The Wilderness War* (1978), Eckert begins in 1763 (where the second book in this series, *Wilderness Empire*, concluded with the English victory over the French in the French and Indian War) and continues through the American Revolution to 1780, by which time the Iroquois League had been ruptured and the Indians dispossessed of their homelands. This narrative history chronicles the march of the Sullivan-Clinton Campaign to destroy Iroquoia in 1779. Based on the numerous diaries, letters and official reports by the actual members of the expedition, it is a compelling account of the first major war waged by the nascent American government against the Indians and takes place primarily in eastern Pennsylvania and much of Cooper's central New York State.

Beginning in 1979, author Noel Gerson, who wrote the *Wagons West* series, initiated a second series called *White Indian* using the pen name of Donald Clayton Porter. Initially set in the late 1690s, it portrays the life of Renno, a child of settlers, who was raised by the Seneca to become a senior warrior. During a raid by Seneca warriors, a young couple named Jed and Minnie Harper are killed, and their infant son is carried off by a Seneca chief, who adopts the boy, names him Renno, and raises him to be a great leader among his people. The novels follow Renno as he eventually allies himself with the English while still maintaining his ties to the Seneca. The series ran for 28 books, most of them featuring descendants of the original Renno. The books continued to appear until the mid-1990s.

Although not considered "politically correct" in some circles, the penchant for authors to utilize the adoptive white captive as a protagonist is understandable. In his *Voyages*, Pierre Radisson, himself once a captive and an adoptee noted: "Nowhere on earth was a young man better treated than in the camps of warlike Indians. Life as he knew it there was without restraint." Radisson's adoptive family provided a feast for 300 persons on the occasion of his adoption. Ultimately, an elder woman of the native household would "address him as a son" and provide him gifts such as a blanket, leggings, or moccasins. His new "sisters" decorated him with bracelets and garters, and his "brothers" painted his face and arranged his hair with feathers and beads. During the feast, his new "father" made a mighty speech, presented him with a hatchet, and climaxed the ceremony by naming him after a dead son, who Radisson was replacing through adoption.[226]

Iroquois at play – La Crosse

Nowhere in white society could a young man in his teens experience the freedom and lack of restraint common to their Indian counterparts. Young boys were physically hardened and taught to be self-reliant. They were also taught a pattern of emotional restraint, social inhibition, and diplomatic reserve when they interacted with the world outside their own kinship group. It was from early reports of this characteristic among all woodland nations that the stereotype of the stoic, stone-faced, and detached Indian was formed. A Jesuit observer noted in 1710, "Whenever misfortune may befall them they never allow themselves to lose their calm composure of mind, in which they think that happiness especially consists." Yet, there were also consistent reports of great laughter, joking, and a keen sense of humor in the villages, and the individual's personal relationships were marked by gentleness, humanity, and genuine sociability. Such traits, common throughout the Northeast woodlands tribes, appear to have been culturally determined and transmitted through a careful program of education.[227]

Although Cooper's *Leatherstocking Tales* comprise America's introduction to the so-called "savages" of the unsettled frontiers, Cooper admittedly had very little first-hand experience with Native Americans. In *The Indian in American Literature*, Albert Keiser states that "the writer who more than anyone else impressed his conception of the Indian upon America and the world at large is James Fenimore Cooper." The Indians who Cooper described were those most contaminated by contact with white society and culture. The Northeast woodlands was one of the largest, most populous, and most stable regions supporting Native American life. In the Northeast region, family structure, kinship, and social organization; material culture and religion; governance and economics; and the ways of war, peace, and diplomacy were fairly precise and well defined, especially among the Iroquois. The region also had the largest number of literate observers in the 17th and early 18th centuries when Indian life was least contaminated by European contact. The Indians these early writers saw were most like the way Indians actually were.

The ruins of the forts at Ticonderoga and Crown Point were illustrated in a 19th century text.

However, the upstate region of New York – while beset by the almost constant threat of attack – was also perhaps the most heavily fortified by Europeans in all of North America in the colonial period. Dozens of substantial forts, scores of defensible blockhouses, and hundreds of fortified houses could be found in the region. Although a lone defense at the cabin door against the attack by even a small enemy force had no practical chance of success, men on the frontier remained reluctant to leave their homes in time of danger. Small groups of frontiersmen would rather "fort up" in a single defensible position than become part of a larger campaign. This reluctance was somewhat allayed because the laws governing the militia usually prohibited men from serving for long periods far from home or outside their own province or colony.

The forested frontier wastelands traveled by Hawkeye, the frontier hero in *The Last of the Mohicans*, took on the romantic image of scenery in Cooper's work, which was understood by his contemporaries who vacationed on the shores of Lake George roaming the dilapidated earthworks that had been Fort William Henry or who passed by steamboat up the lake to stony ruins of Fort Ticonderoga and Crown Point. Fort Edward and Fort Ann were located on the historic route linking the French and English colonies, and in 1823, the Champlain Canal was completed, linking the area to the outside world. Later the Delaware & Hudson Railroad established a depot at Fort Ann village.

The settlement blockhouse.

Farther west in the 1830s, the last remains of Fort Bull and the more substantial Fort Stanwix, located along the Oneida Carrying Place, a vital six-mile portage connecting the Mohawk River and the Wood Creek access to the Great Lakes, were covered over by increasing development, brought on by canals, railroads, and new industry allowing the Oneida Carry area of New York to flourish as the city of Rome. A modern recreation of Fort Stanwix built by the National Parks Service now resides in the center of the downtown area. From the 1840s, visitors to Old Stone Fort museum in the Schoharie Valley, arriving by coach from Albany on the plank road, had learned about the first Dutch and German settlers and their Indian neighbors, viewing artifacts that dated back to the early 1700s. A double-barreled rifle attributed to the legendary patriot marksman Timothy Murphy, who served there and remained after the revolution, was a highlight. But the same sense of place was largely lost on later generations of readers, television viewers, and movie enthusiasts. Cooper noted, "The history that most abounds in important incidents soonest assumes the aspects of antiquity. ... Thus, what seems venerable by an accumulation of changes is reduced to familiarity when we come seriously to consider it solely in connection with time." [228]

Scholars have attempted to better analyze the value of Cooper's "Leatherstocking Tales" by placing them in context among other forms of narrative. Yet he had a profound effect on how the colonial frontier period was viewed for more than a century because he appealed to the emotions of his readers, and aroused their imaginations and patriotism. All of Cooper's leatherstocking novels were written before the phrase "manifest destiny" was popularized (1845), yet the concept that Americans were foreordained by Providence to take possession of the North American continent was clearly recorded therein by him.

"On the Trail of the Captives." This illustration by F.O.C. Darley provides a good view of Indian-style leatherstockings and their attachment to the waistbelt.

XIII. Controversy

Among supporters of Americanism, Cooper should certainly be counted, but Cooper also shared many of the despicable Nativist (anti-immigrant) and racist views of his time. There are important differences between the benefits of Americanism and the evils of Nativism; and the reader should not bundle these concepts together. While Nativism is a despicable prejudice that targets people due to their ethnicity or place of origin, Americanism is a more inclusive attitude or conviction, which gives special importance to the culture and history of the United States and its people. It should be remembered that many persons who are today on the right side of history, in their own day may not have been considered nice people. Many of the persons of Cooper's time were not, in hindsight, politically correct in their utterances. Cooper's books were often related to current politics, and his methods of self-promotion often engendered an ill feeling between the author and the public.

The Whig press, in particular, was hostile in many of its published comments about him. Philip Hone, formerly an associate if not a friend of the author while a resident of New York, noted of Cooper in his diary in November 1838:

> There are two new works, *Homeward Bound* and *Home as Found*, which are reviewed, and the author most unmercifully scourged, in an able leading article of the *Courier and Enquirer* of this morning; a more severe, and, I add, a better written, castigation was never inflicted upon an arrogant, acrimonious writer than this. Mr. Cooper, spoiled at first by the kindness of his countrymen, and inflated by the praise of Europeans, who read his books without coming into personal contact with the writer, has returned to his own country full of malicious spleen against his countrymen, because, as I verily believe, he could not bully them into approving his dogmatical opinions, and liking his swaggering airs as well as the patriotic principles and unpretending deportment of his distinguished rival, Washington Irving. The works now published, of which copious extracts are made in the *Courier and Enquirer*, represent everything in this country in the most disparaging light; the misrepresentations are as gross, and the uncharitable temper as disgusting, as anything to be found in Basil Hall's, or Captain Hamilton's, or Mrs. Trollope's lying histories, and (what is more wonderful coming from such a quarter) the style of the works is puerile and the incidents ridiculous; more worthy of the talents of a silly girl than of the matured genius of the author of *The Spy* and *The Pioneers*.[229]

Cooper is sometimes accused of being insensitive to certain social issues like race and slavery largely in comparison to other social novelists like Charles Dickens or Victor Hugo. It should be noted by the reader, however, that all of Cooper's leatherstocking tales were written at least two decades prior to the American Civil War (1861). Cooper at his death in 1851 was largely unaware of the coming secession crisis. America was a different place then, and his attitudes towards the issues that brought on the Civil War were largely less developed than those of authors of his class who wrote after mid-century. This is not to excuse Cooper for his sometimes obnoxious posture and bearing. Cooper abundantly expresses the attitudes commonly held in his time toward Native Americans. He regularly refers to them as "savages" and "redskins." Magua is depicted as cunning and crafty, and it is implied that these are common characteristics of Indians.

Just as Hawkeye believes that revenge is an inherent Indian pursuit, Cooper's narrator comments that Magua was "goaded incessantly by those revengeful impulses that in a savage seldom slumber."

Cooper was not alone in his attitudes. An increasing number of 19th century writers maintained that the races constituted separate species with distinct origins and innate predispositions, the most desirable features being attributed to the white European race. Among the high-profile controversies of the antebellum period were race-based slavery and its abolition. Prior to the 1820s, many persons reflected the larger view of a "pre-cotton as king" economy that viewed slavery as a drag on profits. Before the widespread introduction of the Cotton Gin, indentured labor and wage labor were both more efficient and less expensive than maintaining a slave workforce. While it was true that the cotton gin reduced the labor of removing seeds, it did not reduce the need for slaves to grow and pick the cotton. In fact, the opposite occurred. The number of slaves rose in concert with the increase in cotton production. This startled many persons, like Cooper, who expected slavery to disappear of its own weight.

The State of New York where Cooper lived did not abolish slavery until 1827. Across the border, Pennsylvania had abolished slavery in 1780 through gradualism. Gradual emancipation had provided that children born as slaves could be freed on attaining maturity, having been given a skill or education in the interim so that they might provide for themselves. Similarly formed legislation had quietly obliterated slavery throughout the New England states by mid-century – the last being Connecticut in 1848. Having freed their slaves through the process of gradualism, many in the North exalted in their newfound righteousness and demanded that the nation immediately follow their lead.

Cooper's fiction was produced in an era of social and cultural transition, and it was hardly forward looking with respect to slavery and race. It was before 1827 that Cooper published the first three novels of the Leatherstocking series and before 1848 that he released the last two. He was an advocate, but his crusades of choice were the provision of a stable social order and an equitable distribution of public lands among the gentry, not slavery or secession. Moreover, he was writing fiction set in a period many decades earlier than his own time, a setting when slavery and other forms of involuntary servitude were commonly accepted. Indeed, wage labor was the odd-man-out among forms of bondage and indenture. The introduction of wage labor in the 18th century had been met with considerable resistance. Economist Adam Smith (*The Wealth of Nations*, 1776) had noted that where law did not regulate wages, employers often conspired together to keep wages low and rents high. Cooper was a vigorous commentator with respect to rents, and in a series of novels called the *Littlepage Trilogy*, he generally defended the large landowners of his own class along the Hudson River.

After the revolution, American settlers in great numbers moved into the lands west of the Appalachian Mountains. The first Land Ordinance of 1785 directed that the Northwest Territory be surveyed. The survey divided the area into sections with each section to be sold to the many land speculation companies owned by well-connected buyers who would act as brokers to the frontier class. The second ordinance, the Northwest Ordinance of 1787, established the system of governance for the territory. The 1803 Louisiana Purchase further opened up western lands to settlement. With sustained migration to the west and south, a number of these territories, as well as other areas, applied for statehood. Along with the expansion of the West came the liberalization of voting laws. Between 1812 and 1821, six western states entered the union with universal or near universal white male suffrage. The laws of the eastern states changed more slowly, but between 1810 and 1821 four of the older states dropped property restrictions on voting. By 1850, all the states except North Carolina had eliminated property qualifications. While the West was growing in power, there was a slow rise in the power of the urban working class. This brought a new challenge to America. Cooper was a somewhat reluctant participant in the Jacksonian revolution. This was partly because he was a man of divided opinions on the subject of expanded democracy.

Cooper also wrote directly about slavery, but he did so awkwardly and with such obvious discomfort that most readers politely averted their eyes to focus on something else. The slavery question arises only three times in all five leatherstocking texts. In his nonfiction, particularly in those works meant to explain the foundations of American civilization to a mid-19th century world uneasy over abolitionism, Cooper could not well avoid slavery. As a noted American citizen abroad, he tried to steer a middle course. Neutrality on any topic of *public* interest often doomed a *public* person to failure or at least controversy. America was in the throes of Jacksonianism, which changed the relationship among the social classes of free whites. In the Jacksonian era the white middle class took power and has struggled thereafter never to relinquish it. This change resulted in a group of leaders very different from the upper-class founding fathers – a group who would do anything to avoid being thought aristocratic or elitist.

American national politics between 1790 and 1845 was characterized by a remarkable silence about slavery punctuated by brief periods of intense debate, as in 1820 when the Missouri Compromise was fashioned. In 1836, Congress instituted a gag rule, in effect until 1844, barring all discussion of slavery in either house of government. Slavery again became a politically charged issue in the late antebellum period, especially after the Mexican War (1846-1848); and politicians fashioned the Compromise of 1850 to quell the fires. As the middle ground of compromise on such issues was eroded thereafter, only the extreme positions became viable. Slavery had produced a crisis for American political discourse having to do with property, equality, and the nature of man. The elaborate narrative of entitlement Cooper mobilized in his first frontier romances centered on precisely these categories, yet he was not present to see their evolution or ultimate outcome.[230]

Cooper died in 1851 almost a decade before slavery exploded into a civil crisis. In the year before his death, the year of the famous Missouri Compromise, he wrote:

> The American Union ... has much more adhesiveness than is commonly imagined. The diversity and complexity of its interests form a network that will be found, like the web of the spider, to possess a power of resistance far exceeding its gossamer appearance — one strong enough to hold all that it was ever intended to enclose. The slave interest is now making its final effort for supremacy, and men are deceived by the throes of a departing power. The institution of domestic slavery cannot last. It is opposed to the spirit of the age; and the figments of Mr. Calhoun, in affirming that the Territories belong to the States, instead of the Government of the United States; and the celebrated doctrine of the equilibrium, for which we look in vain into the Constitution for a single sound argument to sustain it, are merely the expiring efforts of a reasoning that cannot resist the common sense of the nation.[231]

Nonetheless, his critics have often cited passages in the Leatherstocking Tales as instances of Cooper's racism, but one of the most popular of these was the character Magua's speech concerning the belief of the Great Spirit's creation of red, black, and white men, which was simply a recitation of a widely held mythology among Native Americans. More importantly, few readers were going to agree with the speeches of Magua, in any case. In 1827, Cooper wrote a qualified defense of the constitutional legality of American slavery, but his concern was with explaining slavery's existence; while his purpose was in prophesying its ultimate disappearance in the natural course of time, rather than in condemning it. Slavery commanded a curious presence in Cooper's two works of political theory, *Notions of the Americans* (1828) and *The American Democrat* (1838). Yet references to slavery herein were digressive and had the quality of afterthoughts rather than the assurance of a fixed position.[232]

Nonetheless, Cooper repeated Magua's comment in *The Deerslayer* in 1841 in the person of Hurry Harry. He even dropped the N-word into the conversation though it was done in the uncouth manner that belonged to the habits and opinions of the frontier. "Here's three colors on earth: white, black, and red. White is the highest color, and therefore the best man; black comes next, and is put to live in the neighborhood of the white man, as tolerable, and fit to be made use of; and red comes last, which shows that those that made 'em never expected an Indian to be accounted as more than half human." But the author through Deerslayer immediately corrected him. "God made all three alike, Hurry."[233]

In 1850, there was held at Cooperstown a spirited public debate between Cooper, for colonization of freed blacks, and his friend Gerrit Smith, for immediate abolition. Smith was a social reformer, politician, and ultimately a financial supporter of abolitionist John Brown. Smith had been the Free Soil Party candidate for President of the United States. The question of slavery was given "able and exhaustive treatment by both debaters who spoke several hours." The audience listened with riveted attention. At its close the two gentlemen walked arm in arm to Cooper's home, where they dined together. The frontier novels were important in part because through them Cooper could air the contradictions surrounding slavery during a period when political discourse itself, including his own political writings, seemed at a loss to account for it.[234]

Perpetual race-based slavery even as practiced in colonial America was not recognized under English law. The official religious rationale for enslaving Africans and making war on Indians was that they were non-Christian heathens whose souls needed to be saved. Moreover, an increasing number of 19th century intellectuals and writers maintained that the races constituted separate species with distinct origins. Secretary of State John C. Calhoun arguing for the extension of slavery in 1844 said, "Here is proof of the necessity of slavery. The African is incapable of self-care and sinks into lunacy under the burden of freedom. It is a mercy to give him the guardianship and protection from mental death." This scientific classification of human variation was frequently coupled with racist ideas about the innate predispositions of different groups, always attributing the most desirable features to the white European race and arranging the other races along a continuum of progressively undesirable attributes (*hypodescent* assignment). Today, this is considered an example of rank pseudoscience, and part of the antebellum edifice of scientific racism. Most historians consider this attitude of racial and religious superiority a prototype of the so-called *White Man's Burden*, an idea advanced at the end of the 19th century during the expansive "age of imperialism."[235]

In the early 19th century, Jean-Baptiste Lamarck had proposed his theory of the transmutation of species, the first fully formed theory of evolution. In his book *Philosophie Zoologique* (1809), Lamarck referred to God as the "sublime author of nature." This attitude was clearly linked to the later rise of Social Darwinism – the application of Darwinian principles of "struggle" to society, often attributed to anti-philanthropic political agendas – not to be confused with the scientific principle as it was expounded in the second half of the 19th century (*On the Origin of Species,* 1859). The earlier theme was attributed to Erasmus Darwin, grandfather of the famed evolutionist Charles Darwin. The former physician was a friend of Benjamin Franklin and clearly anticipated the ideas of evolution in his most important work *Zoonomia* (1796). Social Darwinism was based on the discredited pseudoscience of *eugenics* first proposed in England by Sir Francis Galton, the cousin and later disciple of famed evolutionist Charles Darwin. Originally a hallmark of radical progressive intellectualism, but now generally associated with racist elements in society, eugenics was considered a method of preserving and improving the position of the dominant white racial group.[236]

Cooper, like the majority of his peers among intellectuals at the time, was a racist of this sort, but he was also noted as among the earliest American novelists to include African, African-American and Native American characters in his works. Many of the slave names he chose for his characters reflected simplicity and dignity: Johnson, Williams, Thomas, and Smith. The large majority of the slaves in his fictions have frivolous names meant to ridicule the aristocratic plantation culture of the South. Southern aristocrats seemed to favor naming their slaves from antiquity: in *Satanstoe* there are Pompey, Caesar, Juno, Cato, and Petrus; in *Red Rover* there is Scipio Africanus; in *The Pioneers*, Agamemnon; elsewhere, Cupid, Venus, Vulcan, Cassandra, and so on. Very early in *The Spy* we learn that Caesar, "the faithful old black ... has a double name: "Mr. Caesar Thompson, as he called himself." *The Red Rover* (1827) was one of Cooper's most popular novels all through the 19th century, but very nearly qualifies as the first abolitionist fiction in the American literary tradition. On the strength of this novel alone, Cooper might be called a forerunner of Harriet Beecher Stowe.[237]

In particular, Native Americans played central roles in the Leatherstocking tales. *The Last of the Mohicans* includes both the Native character Magua, who is devoid of any redeeming qualities, as well as Chingachgook, the last chief of the Mohicans, who is portrayed as noble, courageous, and heroic. However, Cooper's treatment of Native Americans was tenuous. Within his characterizations, Indians "by their very nature" were committed to forms of warfare, which whites called treacherous and cruel, and they would betray their natures were they to behave like European gentlemen. "The general character of the warfare pursued by the natives is too well known to require any preliminary observations," wrote the author, "but it may be advisable to direct the attention of the reader, for a few moments, to those leading circumstances in the history of the times, that may have some connection with the principal business of the legend. ... There is great obscurity thrown around the polity of the Indians." It should be remembered that not only were the Indian wars of recent decades still fresh in the minds of many readers but new encounters with Native Americans in the west were commonly being reported in the press while Cooper was writing.[238]

While categorizing his characters by race, gender, nationality, region, and social class in the manner of early Victoriana, Cooper clearly embraced cultural diversity and helped to create an image of America as a melting pot. "It has been objected to [concerning] these books," noted Cooper of his leatherstocking novels, "that they give a more favorable picture of the [Native American] than he deserves."[239]

The Indians of Cooper's novels were capable of inflicting and sustaining gruesome forms of torture, which they seemingly accepted as an honorable part of the ritual of warfare, but they railed at punishment, especially flogging, which they felt unmanned them. Hence both Magua and Wyandotté carried seemingly implacable hatreds for those who had them whipped. The first of these sought blood revenge, the second offered Christian forgiveness.

Even among other Indians the Iroquois were noted for their cruelty, cannibal feasts, and sickening torture of captives at the end of every successful war expedition, and time after time the fullest measure of their awful savagery was visited upon the devoted Jesuit missionary. There are stories that the neighboring tribes to the Iroquois would flee upon sight of just a small band of Mohawks, but these were not alone in these practices. There is ample evidence that most, if not all, of the Indians of northeastern America engaged in ritual cannibalism and torture. The Iroquois either vengefully tortured their prisoners to death or adopted them into the tribe. The bulk of the torture consisted of the careful use of flame upon the captive's body, which was excruciatingly painful and non-lethal if properly applied. The Iroquois tortured only men to death if they weren't adopted; they either quickly killed or adopted women and children. The Iroquois usually chose the captives who were adopted during their torture, specifically after they had run the gauntlet or were suffering the humiliation stage. Pierre Radisson exemplifies this when his adopted Iroquois parents drag him by the hair from the gauntlet in his second captivity.

Cooper more carefully recorded the relationship between frontier settlers and American Indians during King Philip's War (1675-1676) in *The Wept of Wish-ton-Wish* (1829), depicting a captured white girl who is cared for by an Indian chief and eventually returned to her parents after several years. Moreover, Cooper fashioned an oversimplified structure of intertribal relations and alliances for his readers. His work was highly regarded in the antebellum period because it derived from the principles of the American Revolution and the young American Republic, but it failed utterly to provide an accurate picture of the multi-national and multi-tribal complexities that existed on the colonial frontier.[240]

Captivity narratives were stories of people captured by enemies whom the reader generally consider "uncivilized." Colonial accounts of captivity were part of a well-established genre in Antebellum literature. Ann Eliza Bleecker's novel, *The History of Maria Kittle* (1793), is considered the first captivity novel; but, like Cooper's fictional work, it predated the most popular of the non-fiction captivity narratives that populated the bookshelves of the later 19th century. Cooper's book drew heavily on *The Redeemed Captive* (1707), Reverend John Williams' account of his captivity after the 1704 Deerfield Massacre and its aftermath during Queen Anne's War (1702-1713). Cooper's work was again released in 1849 as *The Borderers* among a flurry of mid-19th century captivity narratives.

"Magua leading the captives." Illustration by F.O.C. Darley for the 1859-1861 edition of Fenimore Cooper's novel "Last of the Mohicans."

XIV. The Intrusion of Politics

Cooper had lived for several years in Europe (1826-1833). The French Revolution of 1830 saw the overthrow of King Charles X, the French Bourbon monarch, and the ascent of his cousin Louis Philippe. On the appeal of the Marquis de Lafayette, leader of the republican forces in the French Chamber of Deputies, Cooper had been drawn into the Finance Controversy of 1831-1832 that followed the somewhat questionable election of Louis Philippe as king. The entire episode marked the shift from one constitutional monarchy to another. Although he was neither an economist nor a politician, Cooper yielded to the appeal, and involved himself in an internal political controversy in France. In Europe, entrenched reactionary regimes were accustomed to look with disdain on American ideas and institutions.

Cooper's 1831 novel, *The Bravo*, had been one of his darkest, as was intended. He wrote it for an American public, and his clear intention was to send America a message about itself. But he published it in France. At the center of Cooper's story was the State Inquisition in Venice. It was a feared and secretive body, both powerful and malevolent. Herein Cooper reminded and warned his American audience, that Republics have "frequently been prostituted to the protection and monopolies of privileged classes." His real target was not the defunct Venetian Republic or that of the French, but an economic aristocracy that might increasingly be found in the America of the 1830s. Comparing national traits became at times an unfortunate habit with Cooper.[241]

Cooper's message, which was not well received in America, was that there were many forms of aristocracy, and one of them arguably already existed in America, in the form of the unrestricted corporation. Cooper's America in the 1830s was increasingly subject to a government that he believed was under the control of self-perpetuating moneyed institutions. The directors of these institutions were not inherently evil, but like the antagonists of his novel they had been insidiously led to equate the interests of their corporations, and their personal finances, with those of the nation and of its morality. Cooper was greatly surprised by the rancor of the criticism. He wrote in his defense:

> Several months previously to the occurrence of the late French revolution [of the 1830s], I had had abundant occasion to observe that the great political contest of the age was not, as is usually pretended, between the two antagonist principles of monarchy and democracy, but in reality between those who, under the shallow pretence of limiting power to the *elite* of society, were contending for exclusive advantages at the expense of the mass of their fellow-creatures. ... I knew that there existed at home a large party of *doctrinaires*, composed of men of very fair intentions, but of very limited means of observation, who fancied excellencies under other systems much as the ultra-liberals of Europe fancy perfection under our own; and, while I knew what I was doing was no more than one nail driven into an edifice that required a million, I thought it might be well enough to show the world that there was a writer among ourselves of some vogue in Europe, who believed that the American system was founded on just and durable principles. ... When the fact was sufficiently established, that a critique on an American book, which appeared in an American journal, and as an American production, came in truth from a country where the writer of the work was openly assailed for party purposes, it created a strong presumption of foul play.[242]

It was while in Europe that Cooper had become political. In *A Letter to His Countrymen* (1834), among several works that he published on his return to Otsego Hall, Cooper expressed a sharp criticism of American culture immediately unleashing a furor in the press. For Cooper the purpose of democracy was to keep the upper classes from getting more than that to which they were constitutionally entitled. Cooper argued that there were three factors endangering democracy – public opinion, demagoguery, and the press. He believed that the corruption of these things made political liberty, equality, individual rights, and justice more abstract notions rather than true pillars of society. "The demagogue is usually sly, a detractor of others, a professor of humility and disinterestedness, a great stickler for equality as respects all above him, a man who acts in corners, and avoids open and manly expositions of his course, calls blackguards gentlemen, and gentlemen folks, appeals to passions and prejudices rather than to reason, and is in all respects, a man of intrigue and deception, of sly cunning and management." He also claimed that the press was easily corrupted and capable of spreading inaccurate information at any time. Not surprisingly, the press retaliated and his name appeared in newspaper editorials almost daily portrayed as a villain who sought to undermine America. So bitter were the accusations against him that he soon found himself spending an inordinate amount of time in courthouses defending himself against what he saw as libelous allegations.[243]

A good friend and one of the most prominent and influential Nativist leaders was none other than Samuel Morse, inventor of the telegraph. In 1834, Morse published 12 letters in the *New York Observer*, entitled "A Foreign Conspiracy against the Liberties of the United States;" and a year later he wrote a new series for the *Journal of Commerce*, "Immigrant Dangers to the Free Institutions of the United States through Foreign Immigration." In 1836, he ran for New York City mayor on the Nativist ticket, but lost.

In an 1836 letter, Cooper, a supporter and defender of Morse, revealed the depth of his own Nativist feelings. In the following stinging statement, Cooper for the first time identified the supposed enemy of America by name and, more importantly, linked the presence of immigrants to the deterioration of the nation, an issue that would occupy him thereafter. He further suggested, as others would later in the century, that certain cultures might be incompatible with democratic principles:

> The foreigners have got to be so strong among us that they no longer creep but walk erect. They throng the presses, control one or two of the larger cities, and materially influence public opinion all over the Union. By foreigners, I do not mean the lower class of Irish voters, who do so much at the polls, but the merchants and others a degree below them, who are almost to a man hostile in feeling to the country, and to all her interests, except as they may happen to be their interests.[244]

Cooper's comments upon America were often discussed by him and thoroughly summarized in *The American Democrat* (1838). Originally intended as a textbook on the American republican democracy, this work analyzed the social forces that shaped, and could ultimately corrupt such a system. In democracies, "the tyranny of majorities is a greater evil than the oppression of minorities in narrow systems," wrote Cooper. "Whenever the government of the United States shall break up, it will probably be in consequence of a false direction having been given to public opinion." Yet despite the persistency with which Cooper insisted upon making his points of view understood — an insistence often ill-timed and irritating — his stand was almost always met with hostility from his critics or was misunderstood. [245]

In the late 1840s, Cooper returned to his campaign of public attacks on his critics and enemies in a series of novels called the *Littlepage Trilogy* where he defended landowners along the Hudson River, lending them social and political support against rebellious tenant farmers in the anti-rent wars that marked this period. In one of his later novels, *The Crater*, an allegory of the rise and fall of the United States, authored in 1848, his growing sense of historical doom was exemplified. At the end of his career he wrote a scornful satire about American social life and legal practices called *The Ways of the Hour*, authored in 1850.

XV. The Illustrations

In 1856, Felix O.C. Darley was commissioned to illustrate the complete works of James Fennimore Cooper. Over his career, he had produced nearly 350 drawings for Cooper's works. It is impossible to know what the author would have thought of these. His death predated the first of them by five years. Hence, the illustrations may reflect Darley's understanding of Cooper's text and allusions rather than the author's image of the scenes. Yet Darley was noted as particularly good at doing scenes from Indian life.

Later in the century, images like these would be reproduced photographically onto a steel die. Prior to this, the appeal and final look of printed illustrations was dependent on the engraver's ability to interpret the artist's tones and shading with manually incised lines. Henry Fox Talbot is usually credited with the first workable process for converting a grayscale image into a varying structure of stark black and white that resulted in a reasonably durable printing plate. The so-called *halftone process* allowed photographs, complete with their "half-tone" intermediate shades of gray or color, to be reproduced in ink on paper by means of a printing press, like text. The process was too precise for cheap newssheets, but it was a sensation for making book illustrations and maps. With the Cooper project of 1856, the artistic license of the engraver was essentially eliminated. Darley was Victorian America's most prolific and accomplished illustrator before the Centennial. He helped forge the American identity. His work is found in the publications of Cooper, Dickens, Irving, Longfellow, Poe, Stowe, and Clement Moore.

Halftone daguerreotype of noted illustrator Felix O.C. Darley

After moving to New York, his work began to appear in magazines such as *Harper's Weekly* and in books by various publishers. Darley signed a contract with Edgar Allan Poe in 1843, to create original illustrations for his upcoming literary journal *The Stylus*. Due to Poe's failure to sign subscribers and find financial backers and contributors, *The Stylus* was never actually produced, but Darley provided illustrations for the final installments of the first serial publication of Poe's award-winning tale "The Gold-Bug" later that year. Darley provided the drawings for the first fully illustrated edition of Irving's *Rip Van Winkle*, an edition of *The Sketch Book of Geoffrey Crayon,* and lithographic illustrations for Irving's *The Legend of Sleepy Hollow.* He made 500 drawings for Benson J. Lossing's *History of the United States* (1867).

Cooper was a friend of many influential painters in his day, including Thomas Cole and Asher Durand. His texts were replete with lush descriptions of natural imagery and detailed scenes of the landscape. During his life, Cooper almost challenged artists to paint his native, wild scenes. One artist who answered the challenge to paint the "native" landscape was N.C. Wyeth considered by many to be America's most influential and enduring illustrator. During his lifetime, Wyeth created over 3,000 paintings and illustrated 112 books, twenty-five of them for *Scribner's*, which is the work for which he is best known. The first of these, *Treasure Island*, was one of his masterpieces and the proceeds paid for his studio. Wyeth's longest sustained period of concentration on a single set of pictures was spent working on *The Last of the Mohicans*. Further, Wyeth earned more for his work on *The Last of the Mohicans* than he earned on any other edition for Scribner's. He was paid $3,500 for his work, which represented a 40 percent increase over his eight previous years. Wyeth's illustrations have become the standard for representing Cooper's work. A curiosity should be pointed out that in all of Wyeth's illustrations the white characters are brightly colored and all the Indians are treated with earth tones. Uncas is large, manly, almost heroic in stature, but like other Indians faces or looks away from the audience. Despite his stature, however, his coloring and positioning still keep him from being represented as favorably as the whites. Bumppo, who walks in two very different worlds, and is considered a hero in both, is represented no differently from Chingachgook, with whom he stands in the background.[246]

XVI. Notes on Native Americans

Native American sources of information regarding their history, culture, or way of life are available and interesting, but they must be used with certain qualifications. While generally accurate as to the description of events, the sources are widely scattered chronologically and limited in absolute number. Moreover, Indian sources have proven to be imprecise with regard to the order and chronology of events. Events were more important to Indian traditions than dates, and it is left to the modern historian to delineate dates from events rather than vice-versa. Unlike the scholar Sequoia of the Southeastern Cherokee, the Native Americans of the northeast woodlands developed no system of narrative writing that might have catalogued a reliable description of their pre-contact culture in their own words. Almost all the surviving impressions of their lifestyle in the 17th and 18th centuries were recorded through the backward-looking and not-so-unbiased filter of European observation.

It is fruitless to involve oneself in endless arguments concerning the proper or improper use of terms such as *tribe, band, nation, or Indian* as if the Native people of a former time might suffer insult through their improper use. The Indians used none of these, usually referring in their own language to persons of their own kinship group as "the people" or "the real People" as did the Lene Lenape of the Delaware Nation. These terms are simply white attempts to bring order and structure to their studies of Native American life. Such classless societies tend to stress the gender roles, status positions, and rank of their individual members rather than the continuation of a royal house or the permanent subservience of the populace to a single bloodline. In a tribal society there were usually few high ranking or high status positions, and the vast majority of the tribe were simply ordinary members who found their place within the kinship group through everyday living. The latter were often ranked by their abilities or their reputations, but in no case were they considered lower class or inferior persons.[247]

Chieftainship was not a generally accepted political concept among Native Americans. Before the arrival of whites, a chain of separate but interrelated Algonquian-speaking communities flourished along the Atlantic seaboard from Chesapeake Bay to the Gulf of St. Lawrence. These groups rarely achieved anything beyond local unity, but the relative weakness of the early European settlements made local native leaders like Metacomet, Powhattan, or Massasoit seem like potentates. European observers, in cases like these, often impressed their own ideas of chieftainship on the political structure of the Native Americans that they faced. The term *chief* was not altogether inappropriate, however. The clans of Scotland, Wales, and Ireland had recognized *chieftains*, and Native American governance was seemingly characterized by a personal and interactive relationship between the political head and the people that was very similar to the Celtic understanding of the role of a chieftain. Moreover, it seems certain that it was the French who first brought their own Gallic concept of traditional *chieftainship* into use when dealing with the nations of the woodlands. Frenchmen often used the concept of a chief as a "generic tag for any Indian who showed signs of having influence in his own society." This idea of *chieftainship* was foreign to most Indian concepts of leadership, law, and military or political organization.[248]

The Europeans who made early contact with the native population noted unique differences among the *tribes* – a term commonly used by anthropologists with regard to

Native American societies. The *tribe* may be defined as the constellation of small communities, or bands, composed of major groupings of kinspersons who came together with some regularity for the social or religious purposes of the group. Descent groups within these communities – what most people would call *family trees, kinship groups,* or *clans* – often comprised the nucleus of a tribe. They provided a framework for social organization and bound persons together into a self-conscious body that was self-sufficient, self-sustaining, and politically independent. Tribes could be groupings with a strict class structure and hierarchy like a *chiefdom*, or they could be less stratified and conglomerate – exhibiting an absence of clearly defined social strata with separate and distinct, but unequal levels.

Presentation medals (peace medals) were the visible marks of chieftainship to which the French resorted to designate those persons they considered chiefs, and they became such a characteristic part of Euro-Indian politics that the British adopted them as a sign of alliance and the Americans in later decades as symbolic of peace. Most Indian leaders welcomed the medals because they bestowed influence on the recipient. The chiefs so designated became a conduit for the gifts given by the French to the Algonquians, and according to Indian logic, a good chief was recognized for his liberality in distributing presents. "Accumulating wealth meant little to Algonquians, but the status and influence that came from bestowing goods on others meant much." Europeans often referred to these persons as medal chiefs.[249]

Some of the young men who had gained status and reputation through war or other deeds were overlooked as the medals were commonly distributed to the elders of the tribal council. This tended to create a fragile and unnatural political structure within the village or tribe that the French needed to control through careful management and constant compromise. The French diffused this situation somewhat by distributing brass and silver *gorgets* to warriors in recognition of their high military reputations, a practice also adopted by the British. The gorget was a metal plate worn by most European officers as a part of their uniform. It had a lima bean or kidney shape, was four to eight inches long, and was suspended below the throat from a cord or ribbon worn around the neck. The gorget mollified the warriors somewhat without confirming the status of chieftain upon them. Pontiac, the Ottawa leader known in Algonquian as Obwandiyag, led a serious uprising of Great Lakes tribes against the British in 1764 although he was only a warrior of considerable reputation. Joseph Brant (Thayendanegea) was initially a minor war leader among the Mohawk, but he was able to rally a majority of the Iroquoian-speaking tribes to the side of the British during the American Revolution.

The Delaware of the Northeast Woodlands were generally organized into chiefdoms based on consensus and compromise rather than authority or mandate. The Indians of New England and Long Island recognized village leaders called *sachems,* or *Sagamores* — the latter name made more common by its use in the novels of Cooper. The character Chingachgook speaks a line that holds the title, saying, "When Uncas follows in my footsteps, there will no longer be any of the blood of the sagamores, for my boy is the last of the Mohicans." This leadership role among the Algonquians was usually hereditary and may have moved through matrilineal generations with both men and women holding political power.

Kinship formed the bonds between bands and villages; set apart clans, phratries, and moieties (if there were any); and sometimes defined the tribe itself. Kinship obligations required certain patterns of behavior on the part of the individual toward others and toward the wider community, and vice-versa. Respect, deference, support, education, counsel, revenge, and loyalty all originated in kinship. The discussion of Native American kinship systems requires the use of some unfamiliar terms that are quite specific. The *clan* was a kinship group that claimed descent from a common ancestor even if that ancestry could not be proven. If the supposed common ancestor was non-human, the term *totem* might be used, but this was rarely done as the word had other meanings as with small sacred objects. A *sept* is an Anglo-Scottish word for a division of a family, especially a division of a clan, used almost exclusively with Celtic clans. A *phratry* was a kinship group consisting of two clans claiming a common ancestor. There could be several phratries in a societal structure, and in some cases, one of the foundational pair may have extinguished itself leaving a single clan as a phratry. The term *moiety* (from a French word for *half*) was used to describe societies that were divided exactly into two and had only two descent groups. Sky–earth and peace–war moieties were not uncommon.

Historian Allan W. Eckert has documented the "septs" of the Shawnee in his narrative *The Frontiersmen* (1968), but he warned that there were numerous spellings and pronunciations of the five sept names:

> Although the Shawnee septs were individual entities and governed themselves, each was an important branch of the Shawnee tribe as a whole and each had a distinct office or duty to perform for the benefit of the tribe. The Peckuwe sept, for instance, had charge of the maintenance of order or duty and looked after the celebration of matters pertaining to Shawnee religion. ... The Maykujay clan controlled matters pertaining to health, medicine and food. The Kispokotha sept, on the other hand, was in charge of all circumstances of warfare, including the preparation and training of warriors. ... But the two most powerful septs were the Thawegila and Chalahgawtha, which had charge of all things political and all matters affecting the entire tribe. These two septs were equal in power and from one of them the principal chief of the Shawnees had to come. The chiefs of the other septs were subordinate to the principal chief in all matters of importance to the tribe but, in circumstances pertaining to their own jurisdiction, they were independent chiefs. The Thawegila, Kispokotha and Peckuwe septs were closely related morally and politically, while the Maykujay and Chalahgawtha septs always stood together, as they had in times past during occasional instances of tribal dissension.[250]

Individual Iroquois tribes were usually divided into three clans: Turtle, Bear, and Wolf. A clan mother and a group of clan matrons headed each clan. The Seneca, like their Huron cousins, initially had eight matrilineal clans. Like the Shawnee, the Seneca/Cayuga alliance and Mohawk/Oneida alliance often opposed one another with the Onondaga serving as moderators in their confederacy. Before the formation of the Iroquois confederacy, Turtle, Bear, and Wolf were in one phratry, and Hawk, Deer, Snipe, Crane, and Eel were in another. Phratries were super-groupings of clans used for ceremonial and social purposes. After the confederacy, the Turtle-Bear-Wolf phratry remained, but the other changed to Hawk, Little Snipe, and Great Snipe. The Deer, Duck, and Eel clans seemingly disappeared and may have been absorbed into others. No representatives of them appeared at any council after the time of confederation. All of the original Huron clan names have been lost in the dustbin of history, but they are thought to have paralleled those of the Seneca. The Huron also organized into phratries, and the names of these have survived: Bear, Cord, Rock, and Deer.

The Iroquoian-speaking peoples were more settled in their village lifestyle than their Algonquian neighbors who tended to wander from campsite to campsite. Although the Iroquois may have traveled annually to hunt in the grasslands or fish in waters far removed from their homes, they were much more sedentary than the Algonquians, who tended to roam over large areas in small bands of 8 or 10 marital units totaling 50 to 60 adult persons. The latter groups may have found this organization more efficient for hunting and gathering, but it was less effective in making a wartime defense. The Iroquoian-speaking peoples lived in villages having substantial populations, sometimes numbering several hundred. Iroquoian culture was organized around an annual cycle of extensive agricultural activity, established political institutions, and permanent, fortified villages. The daily life of most woodland Indian women centered on the production of their three main crops — maize, beans, and squash. The women cultivated the fields and gardens that surrounded the village. An observer noted "a considerable Indian town inhabited by the Seneca. ... The low lands on which it is built, like all the others, are excellent, and I saw with pleasure a great deal of industry in the cultivation of their little fields. Corn, beans, potatoes, pumpkins, squashes appeared extremely flourishing."[251]

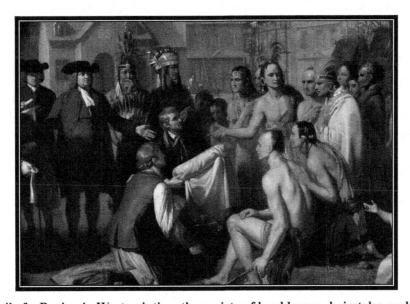

In this detail of a Benjamin West painting, the variety of headdresses, hairstyles, and "costume" among the Delaware is clearly portrayed. The painting depicted 1701 peace negotiations between William Penn and Lenni Lenape. West painted *Penn's Treaty with the Indians* in 1772.

Most Native American men could not be persuaded to use one-piece trousers, "for they thought these were a great hindrance in walking." [252] Jean-Bernard Bossu reported that the male war leaders even in winter went "naked, like the other warriors, and the scars on their bodies distinguished them from their men and take the place of military commissions."[253] This report seems extreme, the 18th century concept of *nakedness* being somewhat different than today, but the men certainly had a great aversion to the wearing of breeches, "for to that custom, they affix the idea of helplessness and effeminacy."[254]

They wore instead a slip of cloth or dressed skin known as a breechclout (loincloth) that was about a half-meter wide and a meter and a half long.[255] This they passed between their legs and under a conveniently broad belt or cord tied around their waists. A French soldier noted, "The two ends of the loincloth are folded over in front and in back, with the end in front longer than the one in the back."[256] Another observer noted that the breechclout was "like a short apron or skirt." [257]

As trade increased between Natives and Europeans, a great number of the male Indians began to dress in European-style jackets and vests mixed with loincloths, Indian leggings, and native footwear. Blankets worn in the style of a wrap or toga often made up part of male native wear. The women were not so quick to give up their traditional clothing styles, but they readily replaced skins and woven grass with colorful skirts and wraps of wool broadcloth.[258] John Knox, a contemporary journalist (1769), gave a very full account of the construction and use of leggings and described the adoption of these useful and necessary items. "The legs are preserved from many fatal accidents that may happen by briars, stumps of trees, or under-wood ... in marching through close, woody country." [259]

The moccasin is the quintessential Native American accoutrement. Several styles of moccasin construction have been identified as being that of Algonquian, Iroquoian, or other tribal type. A one-piece construction, "an ancient form," seems to have been favored by many tribes. In the eastern areas of Canada, a separate top, or vamp, covered the instep and was sewn to the body of the shoe with a thick puckered seam. In the Great Lakes region, both styles seem to have been used. A more complicated design, requiring three pieces and often attributed to the Iroquoian peoples, had a separate sole of tough leather to which the sides of the moccasin were stitched with deer sinew. There was a seam along the top of the foot and at the heel. This style also had flaps that turned down over the ankle hiding the leather thong that tied it to the ankle. A British observer noted, "They make their shoes for common use out of skins of the bear and elk, well dressed and smoked, to prevent hardening; and those for ornament out of deer-skin, done in the like manner." It was also noted that the natives frequently went without moccasins but usually wore their leggings even when bare-footed.[260]

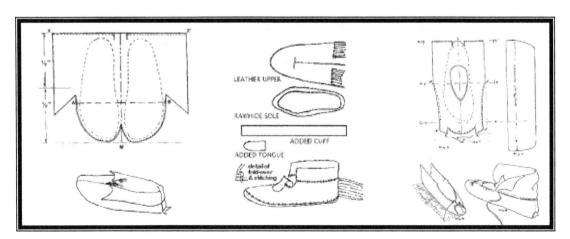

An illustration of some of the many types of moccasins.

The war bonnet composed of a trailing double-line of feathers – familiar to school children as a symbol of native American dress – was an item used by the Plains Indians, not by those of the woodlands. Nonetheless, there is strong evidence that woodland Indians adorned their heads in some fashion. James Adair, who studied several woodland tribes from 1735 to 1744, described the men as fastening several sorts of beautiful feathers to a lock of hair on the crown of their heads, "frequently in tufts; or the wing of a red bird, or the skin of a small hawk. And every Indian nation when at war trim [decorate] their hair after a different manner through contempt of each other. Thus we can distinguish an enemy in the woods so far off as we can see him."[261]

NORTH AMERICAN TRADERS AND INDIANS.
Gauthier and Faden's Map of Canada, 1777.

As to headdresses among the Algonquian, naturalist William Bartram found a "very curious diadem or band, about four inches broad ... encircling their temples." This was decorated with stones, beads, wampum, porcupine quills, and a large plume or feather "of crane or heron" set in the front peak.[262] Many Iroquoian peoples wore similar caps. On the other hand Peter Kalm, who traveled among the Huron, found that they wore no hats or caps whatever, and when among the Abenaki, he reported women who had "funnel-shaped caps."[263] Colonel James Smith who spent some time in western Pennsylvania with the Caughnawaga noted the use of red handkerchiefs in place of hats.[264] Finally, John Knox who traveled among the Micmac tribe of northeastern Canada noted the use of a turban-like headgear by both males and females.[265]

After returning from a long time on the warpath, Pierre Radisson noted that his Mohawk foster sisters "cleaned him up, dressed his hair ... put feathers on his head, and tied up his hair with beads." He also noted that the "typical Iroquois headdress" consisted of "a cap with an upright silver band, like a crown. This was adorned on the top with a cluster of white feathers, and a single eagle plume tilted backward from the forehead. The feather was so fastened in a tube that it would revolve and turn in the wind."[266]

Some among Native peoples were alike in virtually every visible material characteristic save language, and it has been estimated that in North America alone there were from 500 to 1000 mutually unintelligible languages and dialects. The widest diversity of these was among the nations of the prairie and mountain west. Mid-way through the 16th century Europeans had no inkling of the vast diversity that would greet them one hundred years hence, and the majority of New World nations had received no word of the collision of cultures that had taken place. [267]

Nonetheless, the descriptive literature that was created by these Europeans was remarkable. It ranged from personal letters and private diaries first scribbled in the forests or written aboard ships to adventure journals and captivity narratives published for the consumption of a mass of 19th-century readers. Unfortunately, the catalogue of observations also includes a number of questionable documents dictated in the boudoirs of Europe and illustrated with more imagination than factual detail often by persons who had never visited America. Certainly, those writers closest to the events deserve the most attention from historians and researchers.

When Cooper was a boy, many among the Six Nations Iroquois were yet a power in the Mohawk Valley, then the highway to the western lands beyond. "And they are now remembered in the names of the principal lakes and streams of the country that once was theirs. The boy was face-to-face with the grim warriors, braves, and chieftains that the man, Fenimore Cooper, translated into his pages." Yet, even the most careful of the on-site observers were biased in their reporting. "Indeed, to later observers the interpretations offered by members of one society for the practices of another can appear ludicrous." This book will attempt to work through the centuries of distortions and stereotypes in order to expose the truth.[268]

XVII. The Scourge of Frontier Warfare

The wars that characterized eighteenth-century Europe inevitably spilled over into America. The many conflicts that rocked Europe from 1688 to 1763 can safely be viewed as a single prolonged conflict. It was a period in which trade generally replaced religion as the fundamental motive for most of the political and social upheavals, and it was during this period that France and Britain fought for control of the North American continent. Both English and French colonists on the frontier were inescapably involved in their own local conflicts during these intermittent wars, and both sides allied themselves with Native American tribes. Consequently, European colonists fought not only among themselves, but also with native allies and antagonists.

There were four distinct wars fought during this period, with France and England allied on opposite sides with the other states of Europe: (1) the War of the League of Augsburg, known in America as King William's War (1689 - 1697); (2) the War of Spanish Succession, or Queen Anne's War (1702 - 1713); (3) the War of Austrian Succession, or King George's War (in two stages in Europe between 1740 and 1748); and (4) the Seven Years' War, or the French and Indian War (1754 - 1763 in America; 1756 - 1763 in Europe). Many Anglo-colonials on the frontiers considered these the First through Fourth Indian Wars, respectively, because they never saw a regular French soldier ranged against them – only Native warriors and mixed race Franco-Native Métis. During six decades of Anglo-French conflict over the possession of North America, there were a series of woodland skirmishes, raids, massacres, and major battles that intimately affected the lives of colonists. None of these conflicts was decisive except the last.[269]

The specter of a continuous European-style war fought in the forests of North America was removed by the ultimate British victory over the French in 1763. Yet until 1764 the Crown had seemingly chosen to govern its colonies in British North America with what amounted to benign neglect. Thereafter their governance can rightly be termed as bordering on despotic — a word used by many Americans including Thomas Jefferson. Among some of the supporters of the Crown, however, it was suggested that the frontier country had fallen into rebellion from an earlier point. Backward looking authors were often able to find the seeds of rebellion in the years before the Proclamation of 1763, and they endowed their characters and stories with threads of precognition that seemed appropriate in hindsight. Some resurrected Bacon's Rebellion of 1675 as a symbol of a unique Americanism, but this was a crisis between a royal governor and his elite counsel over Indian policy, not an early struggle for independence.

The first resistance of Americans against British governance took place among the Conococheague Valley settlements on the Allegheny frontier along the Pennsylvania-Maryland border in 1764. The first rebel blood was shed there, and the first American victory over British arms was won there, ten years before the fights at Lexington and Concord. Some of the factors that spawned the Boston Tea Party were more than a decade in the making with the Proclamation of 1763, which largely affected the frontiers immediately, and the Stamp Act of 1764, which affected everyone in 1765, generally being assigned as points of departure between colonial acquiescence and active resistance to Royal governance. The enervating Sugar Act and the Currency Act of 1764, the restrictive Townshend Acts of 1767 and 1769, and the despised East India Company Act and the Tea Act of 1773 followed.

XVIII. Scenery as History

James Fenimore Cooper released *The Pioneers*, the first published of the *Leatherstocking* series, in 1823. The series featured Natty Bumppo, a resourceful Anglo-American woodsman allied with the Delaware Indians and their chief Chingachgook. Fourth in the five-volume narrative, the story setting in *The Pioneers* dates from the 1790s. Bumppo (a.k.a. Deerslayer, Hawkeye, and Pathfinder) was also the main character of Cooper's most famous novel, *The Last of the Mohicans* (1826). Written in New York City overlooking the Long Island Sound from a cottage in Astoria, Queens where Cooper and his family lived from 1822 to 1826, the latter book became one of the most widely read American novels of the 19th century. It was set in 1757.

Four of Cooper's novels were set in Otsego County, distributed over twenty years of his literary career: *The Pioneers* of 1823; *Home As Found* of 1838; *The Deerslayer* of 1841; and *Wyandotté* of 1843. This was a world that, in an almost literal sense, his father had created. Shortly after the American Revolution, the government had opened up some of the former Iroquois lands in New York for development. Cooper's father, William had purchased several thousand acres along the headwaters of the Susquehanna River in 1788, and he had selected and surveyed the site of Cooperstown on Lake Otsego. James was born in New Jersey in 1789 and moved with his family to Otsego Hall at age one. It was here that James became acquainted with the Indians of central New York State, the arts of wilderness survival, and the frontier prototypes who visited the Cooper home with their long rifles and wilderness tales. He went to Yale at age 13, failed out due to misbehavior, joined the merchant marine and navy, and in 1808 received his commission as a midshipman. At age twenty, he inherited the estate of his father, and at age twenty-one, he married Susan De Lancey the daughter of a wealthy Loyalist family from the Revolution. They had seven children, five of whom lived to adulthood.

**The shoreline of Glimmerglass (Lake Otsego) scene of *The Deerslayer*.
Illustration by F.O.C. Darley.**

In 1826, Cooper moved with his young family to Europe. Like others of his class, he enjoyed the fascinations of its cities and toured the Continent. Yet little did he know that his novels would help to open a trade in tourism in his beloved New York. In 1834, he had decided to reopen his family mansion, Otsego Hall, in remote Cooperstown. It had long been closed and falling into decay because he had been absent in Europe for nearly a decade, but the area had its own fascination. Susan Fenimore Cooper noted of the lake known as the Glimmerglass when she was a girl: "There was a romantic mystery hanging over the Lake at that time – a mysterious bugle was heard in the summer evenings and moonlight nights, now from the Lake, now from the wooded mountain opposite Fenimore. 'There is the bugle!' my Father would call out, and all the family would collect on the little piazza to listen. I remember hearing the bugle frequently, and being aware, in a baby fashion, of the excitement on the subject. No one knew the performer. It was some mysterious stranger haunting the mountain opposite Fenimore, for several months."[270]

Even today the little village of Cooperstown, 100 miles to the east of the central fire of the Iroquois at Onondaga Lake and 75 miles west of Albany, remains best known only for the author and its Baseball Hall of Fame. Most of the historic pre-1900 core of the village is included in the Cooperstown Historic District, but Otsego Hall is no more. Once known as the "Village of Museums," in the latter part of the 19th century Cooperstown also boasted the Indian Museum, the Carriage and Harness Museum, the Woodland Museum, the Farmers' Museum, the Fenimore Art Museum, The Hyde Hall Mansion and Museum, the Ommegang Brewery and Museum, and the New York State Historical Association's (NYSHA) library. Many of these are still in operation.

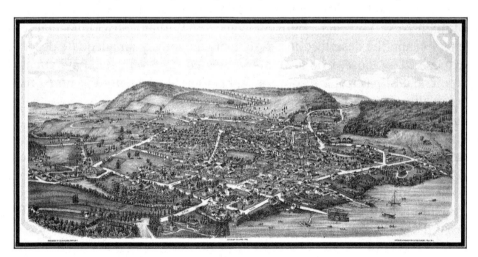

Cooperstown on Lake Otsego as it appeared in 1890

In 1810, much of what happened in New York was in the east — the Catskills, Albany, and the Mohawk and Hudson River valleys — with the western part of the state still largely unsettled. In the six counties between the Pennsylvania border and Lake Ontario there were less than 24,000 residents. No towns had more than 6,000 persons and most were less than half that size. Slow to develop as a colony, New York quickly became the most dynamic state in the newly independent American republic. By 1820, New York had become the most populous state in the nation. Most of the newcomers settled in northern, central, and western New York, which dramatically shifted the distribution of the state's population. In 1820 three-fourths of the state's people lived in the newer counties to the north and west of Albany. Washington Irving's popular *Sketch Book* had drawn upon the Knickerbocker legends of the Dutch settlers of the east making the Hudson River Valley the haunt of painters and poets. James Fennimore Cooper wrote about early frontier life in the west and attracted a new group of readers and history enthusiasts.

The novels of Cooper, located by the author in this region of Cooper's own childhood, produced a great demand among readers to visit the places mentioned in the adventure tales derived from the Colonial Period and the Revolution. The ruins of the forts at Lake George, Ticonderoga, and Crown Point competed for the vacation dollars of antebellum sightseers with Balston Spa and Saratoga Springs in New York. Yet it is impossible to tell with precision, which came first: the interest of the readers or the interests of the author.

In his Leatherstocking saga, Cooper sought to capture the romantic enchantment of the bygone wilderness. His focus was on the features of the natural environment. In his early novels, he emphasized the rugged verticality of the rocky terrain, a ragged landscape, marked by dramatic peaks and chasms. In the later ones he seemingly looked more to the interior of wooded groves, the filtered light and shadows enhancing the romantic effect. Cooper's travels in Europe from 1826 to 1833 may have provided the catalyst for the transformation in his representation of landscape.

During his visits to Otsego during the 1760s and 1770s, Richard Smith, an amateur naturalist as well as a land speculator, was astonished by the abundant, large, and diverse plant life, especially on the fertile bottoms beside the rivers and larger streams. Traveling in 1794 through New York, an Englishman named William Strickland marveled, "The whole scenery cannot be described in words that can convey an adequate description nor can it be conceived by those, who have not witnessed it." Smith also paid attention to the economic potential of particular resources. In his journals, he carefully noted the types of timber, the quality of soils, and, especially, the potential sites to harness the power of flowing and falling water.[271]

Contemporary with Cooper's writing was a remarkable rise in the science of geology. James Hutton is often viewed as the first modern geologist. In 1785 he presented a paper entitled *Theory of the Earth* to the Royal Society of Edinburgh. In his paper, he explained his theory that the Earth must be much older than had previously been supposed in order to allow enough time for mountains to be eroded and for sediments to form new rocks at the bottom of the sea, which in turn were raised up to become dry land. Hutton published a two-volume version of his ideas in 1795. Mineralogy was frequently taught in medical courses, but a few professors began to offer systematic lectures on the new technique of field geology. One of these was John Walker, Regius Professor of Natural History at the University of Edinburgh from 1779 to 1803, whose students went on to become leading scientists in nineteenth century Scotland, England, Ireland, Africa, and America. Walker developed a sophisticated theory of the earth based on evidence gathered from geochemistry and human history.

In *The Prairie* Cooper implicitly accepts this concept of terrestrial antiquity, if only for fictional purposes, when he says that that the wastelands beyond the Missouri would appear to a poet as having once been a seabed from which the water had departed.

William Maclure, then living in Philadelphia, produced the first geological map of the U.S. in 1809. In 1807, Maclure commenced a geological survey of the United States. Almost every state then in the Union was traversed and mapped by him, the Allegheny Mountains being crossed and recrossed some 50 times. With a body of teachers and scientists, Maclure joined Robert Owen's utopian colony at New Harmony in 1824.

Curiosity about the geology of New York dates back to the late 1700's. The proximity of the region to the established schools of higher education in the East; the natural diversity of its geological structures; and the need to assess the substructure for the construction of canals and railroads caused geologists to frequent the area. Ordovician and younger rocks make up the central and western portions of the state, which encompass the Ontario Lowlands and Allegany Plateau. Lake Ontario and the Adirondack Mountains form the northern boundary, the eastern margin is formed by the Hudson Lowlands and Taconic Mountains, and to the west terminates at the shore of Lake Erie. The structure of this region is fairly simple, but the black coal-like appearance and slightly combustible nature of the shales were of interest to the coal industry. Gas seeps in creek beds motivated early explorationists to study the rocks and find use for them. The first known commercial shale gas well was drilled in 1821 in the town of Fredonia, Chautauqua County, New York near a gas seep along Canadaway Creek.

One of the great unresolved scientific mysteries concerns an extensive body of evidence for extraordinary catastrophic flooding events in the very recent geological history of North America. Evidence for megascale flooding at the end of the most recent ice age, is not limited to North America or to Central New York, but has been documented from all over the world.

New York City and Long Island mark the southernmost boundary of an ice sheet that mantled much of North America. The Laurentide ice sheet advanced and retreated repeatedly over a period of 60,000 years. The last advance reached maximum 22,000 years ago, extending from southeastern Alberta across what are now the Great Lakes to the east coast. The ice may then have been more than a mile thick. The Hudson River sluiced through a deep gorge that cut through the plain and emptied into the Atlantic. The end of the last ice age was a time of extreme and rapid climatic change. The natural cycle of global warming accelerated 10,000 years ago, triggering rapid changes in plant and animal life witnessed by Paleo-Indian hunters possibly within a single lifetime.

A glacial lake called Lake Albany was formed 15,000 years ago when water melting from the edge of a glacier was dammed by glacial debris. This body of water occupied the Hudson River Valley from Poughkeepsie to Glens Falls until the natural dam gave way and the water drained away. Floodwaters rushed down the Hudson River Valley; past modern Manhattan, Brooklyn, and Staten Island; through an earthen dam where the Verrazanno Narrows Bridge now stands; and across another hundred miles into the North Atlantic. Glacial Lake Iroquois was a prehistoric lake that existed at the end of the last ice age approximately 13,000 years ago. The lake was essentially an enlargement of the present Lake Ontario that formed because the St. Lawrence River downstream from the lake was blocked by the ice sheet near the present Thousand Islands. Trapped behind the Adirondack Mountains and a tremendous ice sheet, glacial Lake Iroquois was three times the size of modern Lake Ontario. This body of collected melt water covered all of Cooper's world save the tallest peaks. Then, 13,000 years ago, a natural ice dam probably located near the northern end of today's Champlain depression collapsed. This lake also drained to the southeast, through a channel passing near present day Rome, New York. The Rome Sand Plains has several sand ridges that geologists think were formed at this time. The channel then followed the valley of the Mohawk River to the Hudson River. The water level in Lake Iroquois dropped 400 feet in the equivalent of a geological instant, revealing the extent of Cooper's world. Hence the cycle of global temperature change formed the creative setting for some of the world's best-known frontier novels.

In the 1800's, curiosity among scientists over the formation, movement and effects of glaciers began to grow. Scientists were extremely intrigued and eager to study and uncover the history of the earth, focusing on any visible patterns. The glacial evidence is prevalent nearly everywhere in the region of Cooper's tales, so much so that glaciologists are able to reconstruct the glacial formation, movement, thickness, and effects simply by observing the geological evidence the ice sheet has left behind. For example, hills were modified by glacial erosion into a hog backed form that changed the topography of the region. Where a glacier once covered the land can now be see distinct horizontal layers, as in most sedimentary rocks. However, the layers tend to slope gently in one direction and sharply downward in the other with near vertical cliff faces ripped away by the ice, the latter indicating the direction of the flow of the massive sheet. Giant kettles were cut in the stone of the bedrock by swirling melt water and the abrasive action of sand and gravel. Glacial eskers, long winding ridges of stratified sand and gravel, were thought to have formed within ice-walled tunnels by streams that flowed within and under glaciers. In New York, State Route 104 runs from west to east along a ridge of the old shoreline of Lake Iroquois.

Tourists visited Glens Falls and Cooper's Cave in the late 19th century.

It is certain that in 1824, Cooper and his friends were exploring a Cave on an island at Glens Falls, New York that was formed in this manner. Here the Hudson River was called *Muhheakunnuk* or, "river that flows two ways" by the Mohicans for the tidal flow that forced salt water into the river causing it to stand still periodically, and even reverse its flow. Cooper incorrectly refers to the "Falls at Glen's" in his novels, but Colonel John

Glen of Schenectady did not come into this section of the region except during his services as a quartermaster in the French and Indian Wars, and he had no proprietary rights at the falls until about 1775. Cooper, therefore committed an anachronism, when he might easily have used either of the two Indian names for the location, "Chepontuc" or "Kayandorossa," with equal good effect. Several limestone rocks form islands in the rapids here, the biggest island contains a small cylinder cave with an impressive elliptic shape that is open on both ends. Most of the time the cave is dry, but at high water levels water flows through it.

One of Cooper's companions, Edward Stanley, a future Prime Minister of Britain, later noted in his diary, "Cooper was much struck with the scenery which he had not seen before; and exclaimed 'I must place one of my old Indians here' – *The Last of the Mohicans* was the result." Three other young British aristocrats accompanied Stanley, all the young men being engaged in a relatively new activity: tourism. Like other rich young Englishmen of the time, they were touring the strange new American Republic that had broken away from Britain just fifty years before. Stanley's own great grandaunt Lady Charlotte Stanley had eloped with British General John Burgoyne, who had surrendered his entire army in 1777, just a few score miles away. The party of tourists made its way to Lake George, passing over the toll bridge at Glens Falls and along the passable but sandy road that ran by Meadow Run and Bloody Pond. The tourists included on their itinerary the well-known sites of the upper Hudson Valley: Albany and the Great Falls of Cohoes, the Mineral Water springs and revolutionary battlefield of Saratoga, Lake George and its relics of the French and Indian Wars, Ticonderoga and Lake Champlain. On their return trip they paused for half a day at Glens Falls and explored Hawkeye's Cave.[272]

Cooper included the cave in a long section of *The Last of the Mohicans* in which he instructs the reader and his female characters in the geology of the scene:

The cavern had two outlets ... a deep, narrow chasm in the rocks, which ran at right angles with the passage they were in ... and entered another cave, answering to the description of the first, in every essential particular. 'Such old foxes as Chingachgook and myself are not often caught in a barrow with one hole,' said Hawkeye, laughing ... 'The fall was once a few yards below us, and I dare to say was, in its time, as regular and as handsome a sheet of water as any along the Hudson. ... Providence first placed them at, but where, it seems, they were too rebellious to stay. The rock proved softer on each side of us, and so they left the center of the river bare and dry, first working out these two little holes for us to hide in. ... If you had daylight, it would be worth the trouble to step up on the height of this rock, and look at the perversity of the water. It falls by no rule at all; sometimes it leaps, sometimes it tumbles; there it skips; here it shoots; in one place 'tis white as snow, and in another 'tis green as grass; hereabouts, it pitches into deep hollows, that rumble and crush the earth; and there aways, it ripples and sings like a brook, fashioning whirlpools and gullies in the old stone, as if 'twas no harder than trodden clay. The whole design of the river seems disconcerted. First it runs smoothly, as if meaning to go down the descent as things were ordered; then it angles about and faces the shores; nor are there places wanting where it looks backward, as if unwilling to leave the wilderness, to mingle with the salt.'

Today, reaching the shores of Lake George by car, the modern tourist finds the restored Fort William Henry (1953), a tourist attraction surrounded by a car park. To readers and tourists in the 1820s, however, it was a sacred ruin, a symbol of a bitter betrayal, defeat, and massacre that had happened within living memory – much like the *USS Arizona* Battleship Memorial at Pearl Harbor serves for WWII today. On the visit to Lake George that inspired *The Last of the Mohicans*, his companions informed Cooper that French Canadien Catholics called it the Lake of the Holy Sacrament (Lac du St. Sacrement). According to the Englishmen in the party, Catholics supposedly believed that only its waters among all those in America were pure enough for the holy rites, great quantities being exported abroad to be used for that purpose.

When asked why he called Lake George "Horicon" in his novel in later years, Cooper replied, "The French name was too complicated, the American too commonplace, and the Indian too unpronounceable to be used in a work of fiction." Cooper was accused, however, of repeatedly employing unpronounceable Indian names. According to Mark Twain, one could hardly pronounce "Chingachgook" without coming out with "Chicago." The lake had two names, namely, *Andiatarocte*, given it by the Indians according to the Jesuit Father Isaac Jogues, and meaning "the place where the lake contracts," and *Caniderioit*, suggesting that it was "the tail of the larger lake" (i.e. Champlain), supposed to be a Mohawk term.[273]

Cooper chose to call the lake "Horicon." A Lake George Steam Packet - 1844

Connections

The historic town of Horicon was first settled around 1800, and in 1838 incorporated parts of the lakeside towns of Hague and Bolton at which tourists of Cooper's time could find steamboat landings. These provided day tours of the lake and passage to the many guest cottages that lined its shores. For the dedicated tourist, the steamboats traveled down (north) the lake to the La Chute River with its impressive falls and connections by coach to the ruins of Ticonderoga. The first Lake George steamboat was launched in 1817, and it was a peculiar creature by modern standards constructed on the canal-boat lines that characterized the vessels of the time. Following the Civil War, the Lake George Steamboat Company became part of the Delaware and Hudson Railroad System, serving as a link from New York City to Canada. A railroad branch ran from Glens Falls to Lake George.

As an unintended consequence of the Erie Canal (1825), Central New York became one of the few places in America where readers could become tourists and experience the historic frontier without major inconvenience. With little effort, fans of Cooper's works could stand, eat, sleep, and ride into the very scenes that the author had described. The Erie Canal itself became a destination for most visitors to the region. Between 1820 and 1850, many travelers came from Europe to America, including the Marquis de Lafayette (revolutionary hero), Charles Dickens (author), Fanny Kemble (actress), Jenny Lind (singer), Frances Trollope (novelist), Edward Stanley (a future Prime Minister), Basil Hall (naturalist), Thomas Hamilton (soldier / tourist), and many more. The flurry of British travelers who came to America roughly between 1820-1840 to assess the new republic seemed to have a preconceived anti-American agenda, insinuating a cultural inferiority that was partially behind the new assertion of American literary nationalism.

In 1810, Charles Jared Ingersoll began an American counter offensive in *Inchiquin's Letters* by responding to European charges of American physical, moral, social, political, and cultural deficiency. Robert Walsh continued the cultural counteroffensive in *An Appeal from the Judgments of Great Britain Respecting the United States of America* (1819). In "English Writers on America," an essay in the *Sketch Book* (1819-20), Washington Irving attempted to address the resultant hard feelings on both sides of the Atlantic by diplomatically discussing English cultural aggression and the correspondent American reaction. Cooper's own publication *Notions of the Americans* (1830) was a continuation of the cultural war. Although written while he was resident in Europe, it was among the first descriptions of the waterway and encouraged others to focus on that subject in their works. In *Gleanings in Europe*, published in 1837 and dealing with his travels in England, Cooper was still responding to British criticisms of America especially those of Basil Hall.

After a visit, Nathaniel Hawthorne wrote of the canal and its potential as a subject for artists in his "Sketches from Memory, By a Pedestrian" that appeared in the *New England Magazine* in 1835. In fact, several landscape artists painted the canal and the Mohawk Valley thereafter. These included Luman Reed, Thomas Cole, Asher Durand, Thomas Doughty, Alexander Wyant, George Inness, and many artists of the so-called Hudson River School. A volume entitled *American Scenery,* written by Nathaniel Parker and illustrated by William Bartlett, included almost 140 prints of various places in the region based on a two-year trip the author and illustrator undertook. They spent an entire summer on the canal in 1836.

During possibly the most significant period in the nation's history, the construction of the Erie Canal across New York ranks along with the Louisiana Purchase as one of the most significant events of the Antebellum Period. Its construction impacted westward expansion, industrial development, and the flow of commerce. But it also helped New York City to develop into the world's dominant commercial center and port of entry displacing Boston and Baltimore as the principal ports on the Atlantic as well as far away Mobile and New Orleans on the Gulf as exporters of American produce. Cooper noted in this regard: "As to the notion of there arising any rival ports, south, to compete with New York, it strikes us as a chimera. New Orleans will always maintain a qualified competition with every place not washed by the waters of the great valley; but New Orleans is nothing but a local port ... not the mart of America. New York is essentially national in interests, position, and pursuits. No one thinks of the place as belonging to a particular State, but to the United States.[274]

In 1817, Governor DeWitt Clinton decided that work on the 365-mile Erie Canal would first begin on a 94-mile middle section from Utica west to the Seneca River. In 1825, the opening of the Erie Canal formed a convenient transportation link between the cities of the Northeast, the headwaters of the Ohio River, and via the Great Lakes to all the Midwest as far away as the Indian lands in Wisconsin and Minnesota. The parade marking the opening of the Canal included carpenters, millwrights, merchants, cabinetmakers, and many other workers who had good paying jobs because of it. In 1833, John B. Jervis began a canal system to extend the Chenango River and connect the waters of the Susquehanna from Chenango Point to the Erie Canal, which ran through the Mohawk Valley, ultimately connecting with Lake Erie through the Wood Canal.

Travel between Manhattan and Lake Erie prior to the opening of the Erie Canal required a combination of land and water transport and took about 50 days, costing approximately $150, a large fraction of the average family income. Shipping from Seneca Lake to Albany cost $100 per ton and from the Niagara River to Albany half as much again. In its first year of operation 19,000 vessels passed through the Erie Canal. Manufacturing in the western part of the state increased by 262% between 1820 and 1840. Thereafter, shipping costs on the canal fell to $32 per ton, and passenger fares along some stretches cost as little as $5. Its financial success provided an impetus for imitation, and man-made watercourses soon connected separate lakes and streams into a vast and efficient waterborne transportation web. Along the riverbanks and lakeshores a mix of mostly New Yorkers, Pennsylvanians, and New Englanders created the first great urban centers of the American Midwest.

Westward expansion along the growing system of canals and the successful navigation of the Western rivers by steamboats made a number of inland ports equally important. St. Louis, in particular, served as a central hub for river traffic. Detroit, which had been a disappointment as a fur trading post to its French founders in the 17th century, took on a revitalized importance as a commercial center as emigrant farmers entered the region via canal barge and river steamboats. The existing pattern of trade with the Western territories and the Midwest shifted from a predominately north-south direction into a west-east orientation. By 1840, inland cities like Buffalo, Cleveland, Chicago, Milwaukee, and Detroit had emerged as important centers serving the Great Lakes Region. Buffalo, at the western terminus of the Erie Canal, underwent a remarkable transformation from a frontier trading outpost to a virtual metropolis in just a few decades.

Prior to the arrival of Europeans, the Mohicans had a number of settlements along the Hudson River at the confluence with the Mohawk River near Troy. The fur trade with these Indians made Troy not only one of the most prosperous cities in New York, but one of the most prosperous cities in the entire country. Ultimately it rose as an industrial center, was the transshipment point for meat and vegetables from Vermont, which were sent by the Hudson River to New York City, and as the head of the tides at the great falls in the Hudson River, sloops and steamboats filled its wharfs on a regular basis. This trade was vastly increased after the construction of the Erie Canal, with its eastern terminus directly across the Hudson at Cohoes. Along the canal or connected to it, towns like Syracuse, Rochester, Ithaca, Utica, and Rome became cities with hotels, inns, and attractions.

Ruins were significant symbols of the impermanence of human institutions and inseparable from a cyclical idea of history that renders all evils not learned in its study inevitably repeatable. The stone ruins of Fort Ticonderoga on Lake Champlain, in particular, changed hands a number of times and finally were sold to a man named William Pell in 1820. He built a steamboat landing, a guest cottage, and a floral garden on the property for day visitors attracted to their romantic or gothic character. The 40-acre landscaped area along with the formal garden near Fort Ticonderoga was shown on old British maps as the King's Garden. The King's Garden — renamed the Garrison Garden — maintained features from each of the many historical eras that had shaped it. The completely renovated site, fort and gardens, remains a time capsule of history and horticulture today.

Until the construction of the canal, travel westward through the "leatherstocking region" for both people and goods was by stagecoach or cart, and it was slow and expensive. The coaches were cumbersome vehicles with the body slung on thick leather straps. Eight to twelve first-class passengers rode inside and the second-class fares rode on top. The common four-horse team pulled them at top speed over the roughly graded highway or turnpike and occasional stretches of log or "plank roads." In 1819, the Newburgh & Geneva Mail Stage left Geneva every Tuesday, Thursday, and Saturday afternoon and ran through Ithaca near Cayuga Lake, Owego, and Chenango to Newburgh west of the Genesee River in three days skirting the southern tips of the Finger Lakes and passing along the Tioga River and the New York headwaters of the Susquehanna River — the very heart of ancient Iroquoia. The fare was $12 and included overnight accommodations equal to any other line of stages.

The stagecoach was the only public conveyance in the region prior to the advent of the canal packet in 1825.

State Route 5, a 135-mile corridor that traverses New York State from east to west paralleling the Mohawk River, is a visitor's dream-come-true today, and it was a major stagecoach route to history 200 years ago. This road was officially known as the "Great Genesee Road" and is one of the earliest state roads in New York. In 1797, an all-turnpike stagecoach route over good quality roads was available from Albany to Canandaigua, and the western extension to Buffalo soon followed suit. On or near this route, tourist could find the homes of Sir William Johnson, his nephew John Johnson, General Nicholas Herkimer; Forts Plain, Klock, Dayton, and Stanwix (a.k.a. Schuyler) among almost 100 other period forts and blockhouses; Oriskany battlefield, the Cherry Valley, German Flats, and Fox Run battle memorials; the remains of Indian castles and Jesuit missions, and many other historic sites; hot, mineral, salt, and sulfur springs for the health, and Little Falls, Trenton Falls, Niagara Falls, caves, caverns, and natural wonders for the adventuresome; and, of course, Cooperstown (the Village of Museums). Fishing, boating, swimming, shooting, hiking, and hunting were available virtually everywhere.

In 1786, the Legislature had granted to Isaac Van Wyck, Talmage Hall, and John Kenny, all Columbia County men, the exclusive right "to erect, set up and carry on, and drive stage wagons between New York and Albany on the east side of the river, for a period of ten years, forbidding all opposition to them under penalty of two hundred pounds." John Butterfield had built a plank road through the area from Albany to the west - which experience helped him greatly when he came to establish the Overland Mail. He was also one of the first to realize the importance of North-South roads as well as the migratory East-West roads of the time, and he established a stage line from Utica south, connecting with other lines at Mt. Pleasant, to New York via Newburgh, and Philadelphia via Easton, PA. In the early days of Lakeville, where the stage route from Geneseo to Canandaigua crossed the route from Dansville to Rochester, the center of the town was filled with large hotels and other buildings. A daily line of stages provided public communication with all points, and carried the mails with regularity and dispatch. A line from Rochester to Bath, accommodated all the principal places in the county, and made connection with a Philadelphia and Washington line, and also with lines running to Buffalo, Lewiston, Utica, and Albany. The famous Ridge Road, opened in 1816 and described as the "Appian Way of Western New York," was one of the most popular stagecoach routes east and west near the south shore of Lake Ontario. By 1845 there were as many as ten stagecoaches each way daily on the Ridge Road and branch lines running to various communities both to the north and south.

Fanny Kemble, a very young and celebrated English actress journeying to Utica in 1832, found that she disliked her experience in the stagecoach. She could not conceive of a "more clumsy or wretched conveyance" as she was "bumped, thumped, jolted, shaken, tossed, and tumbled over the wickedest roads cut through bogs and marshes and over ruts, roots, and protruding stumps with the over hanging branches scratching at the window." She continued, "Oh, these coaches! English eye hath not seen, English ear hath not heard, nor hath it entered into the heart of Englishmen to conceive the surpassing clumsiness and wretchedness of these leathern inconveniences." Oddly her American companions on the coach, including several young women, seemed quite unaffected by these inconveniences laughing and talking at the very top of their voices incessantly.[275]

Kemble made two trips in 1832; one from New York, by steamboat, stagecoach, and horse-drawn railroad car, to Philadelphia; the other by canal boat from Schenectady to Utica. The steamboat was described as very large and commodious, and "in fact, the ground floor, being the one near the water, is a spacious room completely roofed and walled in, where the passengers take their meals, and resort if the weather is unfavorable. At the end of this room, is a smaller cabin for the use of the ladies, with beds and sofa, and all the conveniences necessary." She fondly remembered her second journey by canal, and her diary entries are presented here as a means of comparison:

> We proceeded by canal to Utica, which distance we performed in a day and a night, starting at two from Schenectady, and reaching Utica the next day at about noon. I like traveling by the canal boats very much. Ours was not crowded, and the country through which we passed being delightful, the placid moderate gliding through it, at about four miles and a half an hour, seemed to me infinitely preferable to the noise of wheels, the rumble of a coach, and the jerking of bad roads, for the gain of a mile an hour. The only nuisances are the bridges over the canal, which are so very low, that one is obliged to prostrate oneself on the deck of the boat, to avoid being scraped off it; and this humiliation occurs, upon an average, once every quarter of an hour. ... The valley of the Mohawk, through which we crept the whole sun shining day, is beautiful from beginning to end; fertile, soft, rich, and occasionally approaching sublimity and grandeur, in its rocks and hanging woods. We had a lovely day, and a soft blessed sunset, which, just as we came to a point where the canal crosses the river, and where the curved and wooded shores on either side recede, leaving a broad smooth basin, threw one of the most exquisite effects of light and color, I ever remember to have seen, over the water, and through the sky. ... We sat in the men's cabin until they began making preparations for bed, and then withdrew into a room about twelve feet square, where a whole tribe of women were getting to their beds. Some half undressed, some brushing, some curling, some washing, some already asleep in their narrow cribs. ... At Utica we dined; and after dinner I slept profoundly.[276]

Among the early accounts of canal travel was a description of Lafayette's travels in America in 1824 and 1825, which included a brief trip on the Erie Canal, written by his personal secretary, Auguste LeVasseur. The book was first published both in French and English editions in 1829. Although LeVasseur was often critical of America and American culture, he was highly complimentary of the voyage on the canal. "We had been able to travel, since leaving Lockport, for nearly 300 miles on the canal, and had been able to judge of the beauty and utility of this great channel of communication." LeVasseur also described the beauty of Niagara Falls, Rochester, Syracuse, Rome and Utica and New York in general as follows: "This journey confirmed us in the opinion, that no part of America, or, perhaps, the whole world, contains so many wonders of nature as the state of New York."[277]

Upper class travelers, artists, tourists and journalists wrote most of the accounts of first class canal travel by passenger *Packet* boats, but some narratives survive from the early immigrants who used *Line* barges. The *Line* barges hauled cattle, wheat and other agricultural products from the Midwest to the Eastern Seaboard. Each could carry 75 tons equivalent to 2500 bushels of wheat. On the westbound trip, which had the right-of-way, the *Line* barges offered a low cost passage for the immigrants because freight and produce generally passed in the opposite direction. The barges on the Erie Canal traveled seven days a week, twenty-four hours a day at an average speed of two to three miles per hour. The maximum speed on the canal was four miles per hour – any faster speed was thought to cause damage to the bottom and sides of the canal ditch by the excessive movement of water. For this reason steamboats were banned from use. Repair crews were situated every ten miles on the canal to make emergency repairs and to deter the speeders.

A lock system was necessary as there was a rise in elevation of 568 feet from the Hudson River to Lake Erie along its 363-mile length. Many of the locks were encountered in the ascent of the Niagara Escarpment. At Lockport, five locks raised each barge a total of 60 feet. Erie Canal engineer, Nathan Roberts, devised a double set of five locks, which were necessary so that boats could continue their passage either up or down the Niagara Escarpment en route to Buffalo or Albany. Construction began by hand in 1823. The system at Lockport was considered a modern engineering wonder.

The main purpose of the Erie Canal was to move freight, not passengers. Yet passengers were attracted to it despite some inconvenience. A description of the arrival of canal barges in Buffalo, quoted from a Genesee farmer in the *Rochester Daily Advertiser*, 9 June 1832, shows what followed its opening:

> Canal boats filled with emigrants, and covered with goods and furniture, are almost hourly arriving. The boats are discharged of their motley freight, and for the time being, natives of all climates and countries patrol our streets, either to gratify curiosity, purchase necessaries, or to inquire the most favorable points for their future location. Several [river] steamboats and vessels daily depart for the far west, literally crammed with masses of living beings to [populate] those regions. Some days, near a thousand [persons] thus depart. As I have stood upon the wharves and seen the departure of these floating taverns, with their decks piled up in huge heaps with furniture and chattels of all descriptions, and even hoisted up and hung on to the rigging; while the whole upper deck, and benches, and railing, sustained a mass of human bodies clustering all over them like a swarming hive - and to witness this spectacle year after year, for many months of the season, I have almost wondered at the amazing increase of our population, and the inexhaustible enterprise and energy of the people! What a country must the vast border of these lakes become! And Buffalo must be the great emporium, and place of transit for their products and supplies. [278]

An antique stereopticon card showing the Flight of Five Locks at Lockport.

Travel on the canal was remarkably smooth especially when compared to the jostling of a coach, and it was often distractingly quiet – quiet enough to attract itinerant musicians who worked the packets between towns for gratuities. Thomas S. Allen wrote a popular song in 1905 at a time when the Erie Canal barge traffic was converted from mule power to diesel engines, raising the speed of traffic but loosing some of the 19th century mystique. The tune is sadly nostalgic for former days:

> ♪ *I've got a mule, her name is Sal.*
> *Fifteen miles on the Erie Canal.*
> *She's a good old worker and a good old pal.*
> *Fifteen miles on the Erie Canal.*
>
> *We've hauled some barges in our day*
> *Filled with lumber, coal, and hay*
> *And every inch of the way we know*
> *From Albany to Buffalo.*
>
> *Low bridge, everybody down.*
> *Low bridge, for we're going through a town.*
> *For you'll always know your neighbor,*
> *You'll always know your pal,*
> *If you've every navigated on the Erie Canal.* ♪

Yet not everyone found canal travel limited to a smooth glide and a musical interlude on the waterway. The public barges used by migrants were often filled to overflowing with nowhere to sit among freight and livestock. An English engraver, Thomas Woodcock traveled on the canal in 1836 and kept a record of his journey:

> The Bridges on the Canal are very low, particularly the old ones. Indeed they are so low as to scarcely allow the baggage to clear, and in some cases actually rubbing against it. Every Bridge makes us bend double if seated on anything, and in many cases you have to lie on your back. The Man at the helm gives the word to the passengers; "Bridge," "very low Bridge," "the lowest in the Canal," as the case may be. Some serious accidents have happened for want of caution. A young English Woman met with her death a short time since, she having fallen asleep with her head upon a box, had her head crushed to pieces. Such things, however, do not often occur. [279]

Capable passengers often got off and walked ahead along the canal track way gathering local fruit, especially apples, which they brought on board in big sacks. When the boat caught up, they readied themselves on the first convenient bridge and then hopped down on the deck as the boat passed underneath. Knud Knudsen from Numedal, Norway noted that there were sixty-four towns or cities along the canal, some two or three times as large as Christiania, Norway's capital. Each had a half-dozen or more churches, and many smaller towns had one or two. Another Norwegian traveler, O.L. Kirkenberg noted that the canal often stank, and dead animals, including mules, were found floating in the yellow, slimy water. He claimed that cholera broke out during his journey and that several persons later died.[280]

Grain-Boat on the Erie Canal.

Many subsidiary projects also came into operation. The Genesee Valley Canal rapidly approached a finished state in some of its parts by 1840. It was to run from the Erie Canal on the south side of Rochester south-southwest along the Genesee River valley. It afforded ample and cheap facilities for transporting the abundant products of the region: fresh farm produce, shoes, furs, firearms, hard cheese, salt, and flour. The whole canal was opened for navigation in 1862 running to Olean on the Allegheny River and to Mill Grove on the river just north of the Pennsylvania state line.

The canals were generally closed in the winter, sections drained and repaired, or expanded, but commercial "sleighs" with long rectangular bodies were used to move both people and product along their frozen surfaces. Moreover, sledges moved blocks of winter ice for summer cooling to the cities under licenses from the many canals that had been created in the region. The ice trade, also known as the frozen water trade, was a major 19th-century industry, previously centering on the New England and Maine coast. It involved the large-scale harvesting, transport, and sale of natural ice for domestic consumption and commercial purposes. Ice was cut from the surface of ponds, streams, and canals to be stored in icehouses before being sent on by ship, barge, or railroad to destinations around the world. Sawdust was a free waste product of the lumber industry used to insulate the ice. Known as Boston's "Ice King", Frederick Tudor was the founder of the industry in 1806. Tudor's business centered on the shipment of ice from Massachusetts to such tropical destinations as Martinique, Cuba and other Caribbean ports. In 1855, a total of 75,000 tons of ice from the canal and Hudson River was sold in New York City. To meet rising demand by 1880, approximately 135 commercial icehouses had been constructed between Manhattan and Albany, providing 2.5 million tons of ice to the New York City market. As the natural ice industry grew, small locally owned companies were absorbed and consolidated into large corporations, such as the American, National, and Knickerbocker Ice Companies.

From early in their history, railroads competed with canals. In 1841, the State refused a request to substitute a railroad for part of the Genesee Valley Canal, but in 1877, it was abandoned in favor of the Genesee Valley Canal Railway. The first common carrier railroad in the northeast was the Mohawk & Hudson Railroad, which began operating in

1831 to replace the stagecoaches between Albany and Schenectady. A second line, the Saratoga & Schenectady Railroad, opened the next year. Early in the spring of 1838, steam engines replaced the horses that had been used on the Lockport and Niagara Falls Horse Tram or "strap railroad." The one or two car trains pulled by the "tea kettles on wheels" traveled only slightly faster than the stagecoaches to reach Niagara Falls. These railroads provided ease of access to the vacation hotels, mineral springs, underground caves, and spas of the Central New York foothills and Hudson River-Lake George-Lake Champlain corridor, which provided the scene of Cooper's works.[281]

Transportation of passengers, produce, and freight was greatly enhanced by the expansion of railway mileage and the development of more powerful locomotives. The Oswego and Syracuse Railroad route was surveyed during the summer of 1839, and the company was fully organized and operating by 1848. The line ran a total distance of 36 miles from Syracuse on the Erie Canal to Oswego on Lake Ontario where steamboat connections could be had. The O&S R.R. consolidated with the Syracuse, Binghamton and New York Railroad in 1853, and in 1862 the passenger depot in Syracuse was located at the New York Central Railroad passenger depot. The New York Central System, like many Eastern railroads, resulted from mergers, consolidations, and leases from many smaller lines. One by one, railroads were incorporated, built, and opened westward from the end of the Mohawk & Hudson to include the Utica & Schenectady, Syracuse & Utica, Auburn & Syracuse, Auburn & Rochester, Tonawanda (Rochester to Attica), and Attica & Buffalo railroads. By 1841 it was possible to travel between Albany and Buffalo by train in just 25 hours. In 1851, the state passed a law absolving the railroads from paying tolls to the Erie Canal corporation. The Hudson River Railroad then opened a line from New York City to Rensselaer and a connection to the New York & Erie R.R. at Albany with a terminal on Lake Erie. By 1851, the trip from Albany to Buffalo had been reduced to a little over 12 hours.

An illustration of the Erie Canal as it passed through Schenectady, New York

Western New York was a site of intense religious revivalism during the middle of the 19th century. Due possibly to the ease of travel offered by the Erie Canal and an expanding rail system, the region became extremely popular and was related to other reform movements of the period such as abolition, women's rights, and utopian social experiments. The term "burnt over district" was coined by Reverend Charles G. Finney, who referred to a "burnt district" to denote the area in central and western New York State that had been so heavily evangelized as to have few persons left to convert with the fire of the Lord. Whatever the cause, the Genesee region in particular certainly had more than its share of cults and true believers as wave after wave of religious revival spread across the region.

Besides being the geographical origin of Mormonism, the region was home to the immediate Second Coming cult espoused by William Miller (Millerism), the Free Methodism of Benjamin T. Roberts, the Millennial Kingdom of John Humphrey Noyes called the Oneida Society, the Fourierist utopian socialist movement, a Shaker community, and several Pietist enclaves. It was chosen by local feminist Elizabeth Cady Stanton who organized the Seneca Falls Convention there, which was devoted to women's suffrage and rights, and later was the home of several religious camps including one at Lake Chautauqua, which gave its name to an entire religious movement.

Besides the Hudson River, the major rivers of the northeastern Atlantic seaboard in this region were the Delaware and the Susquehanna. All three rivers found their headwaters in the mountains east and southeast of the Great Lakes. Two separate Susquehanna River Basin watersheds drain portions of south-central New York State: The Upper Susquehanna Watershed and the less extensive Chemung River Watershed. The tributaries of the Delaware and Susquehanna rivers are almost completely entangled in this region. Dominated by the flatter hilltops and valleys, the major tributaries of the Chemung River are the Tioga (flowing north from Pennsylvania), Cohocton, and the Canisteo Rivers.

Cooper presented a picture of America struggling in its infancy. He acknowledged that his books were meant to provide a "descriptive tale" of the area of upstate New York in which he lived as a boy. He wrote, "They who will take the trouble to read it may be glad to know how much of its contents is literal fact, and how much is intended to represent a general picture. ... But in commencing to describe scenes, and perhaps he may add characters, that were so familiar to his own youth, there was a constant temptation to delineate that which he had known, rather than that which he might have imagined." [282]

Cooper's was a prime example of how Anglo-Protestant civilization was being realized in the new world. Cooper wrote of two irreconcilable forces, his admiration for the untamed wilderness and the individual living in harmony with it; and his love for a developing social structure on the frontier that was conquering and taming the wilderness. Yet religion was not the guiding force of morality in Cooper's wilderness. Americans sought to impose Christianity on the indigenous peoples of America in the form of Jeffersonian ideals of "Republican motherhood" and natural morality. Cooper transformed the hideous and desolate wilderness of the Bible into a secularized yet still sacred frontier along which contending cultures collided.

A generation after Cooper, the historical works of Francis Parkman, including seven volumes written between 1865 and 1892, left an indelible stamp on all subsequent writing about the period of the French and English colonial wars. His research was prodigious and subsequent researchers have detected very few errors or omissions. Almost all of Parkman's narratives go unchallenged by modern historians. However, it is clear that Parkman, a Harvard trained Unitarian, harbored anti-Catholic, anti-Native American, and pro-British prejudices in his writings that have largely gone uncorrected. His opinions have also been reflected in popular literature and the cinema. Nonetheless, Parkman's reports of factual events were detailed and exhaustive, and his work remains a foundation for all future study in this area. Many of the interpretations discussed by Cooper or Parkman involve either the various romantic myths of individualism and wilderness within the setting of a Cooper novel or the role of imperial power and ecclesiastical authority that Parkman was creating or perpetuating in his writings. In *Studies in Classic American Literature*, Lawrence discussed the portrayal of Bumppo in Cooper's *The Deerslayer*: "You have there the myth of the essential white America. All the other stuff, the love, the democracy, the floundering into lust, is a sort of by-play. The essential American soul is hard, isolate, stoic, and a killer."[283]

Parkman described how he believed the Catholic faith manifest itself in New France. For him two forces governed the lives of these Canadian settlers. One was the specter of death haunting them from the fringe of the woods in the skulking form of the Iroquois. The other was the Roman Catholic Church and its perceived war with the protestant religion. Parkman devoted one of the seven volumes that composed his monumental study of this period solely to the Jesuit order in New France. As a religious order, the Jesuits were widely feared and hated in Europe even by other Roman Catholic orders because of the control they were able to exert over political and economic events. Yet Parkman's descriptions were based on his visit to Quebec in the last half of the nineteenth century, and while historians laud his exhaustive research and the meticulous preparation of his manuscripts, the facts present a slightly different picture of religious life in New France in the seventeenth century from those that he gleaned 200 years later. Parkman's works were so well received that by the end of his lifetime histories of early America and stories set therein had become the fashion.

In *The Master of Ballantrae: A Winter's Tale* (1889), for example, a book by the Scottish adventure author Robert Louis Stevenson, the title character, James Durie is an 18th century Scottish rebel and sometime pirate who obtains passage to Albany, New York striking out across land for Canada where he hopes to find sanctuary among the French, who supported the final Scottish Rising of 1745-1746. Stevenson went out of his way to place his main characters in the forests of New York, tortuously sending them from Scotland to the South Pacific, to America and India, and back to Scotland before ending the story again in the American wilderness.

The Master of Ballantrae is possibly Stevenson's darkest work rivaling even the psychoanalytical interplay of good and evil in *The Strange Case of Dr. Jekyll and Mr. Hyde* (1886). Stevenson had searched in vain for several years for a place of residence suitable to his ill state of health, and he chose Saranac Lake, New York. Stevenson and his family occupied the west wing of a cottage from October 1887 to April 1888, and he began the novel while he was recovering from a lung ailment.

During the inland journey to Central New York described in the novel, Durie takes along an Indian trader who dies of a fever leaving the Master hopelessly lost. In the end, he buries his pirate treasure in the wilderness. Having miraculously arrived in New

France some years later and now on his own deathbed, he reveals where the treasure is hidden. A small party sets out to find the treasure, but they fall foul of hostile Indians, and all but two of the white men are killed. "I think it was the third day that we found the body of a Christian, scalped and most abominably mangled, and lying in a puddle of his blood; the birds of the desert screaming over him, as thick as flies," notes the book's narrator. "Whether they were French or English Indians, whether they desired scalps or prisoners, whether we should declare ourselves upon the chance, or lie quiet and continue the heart-breaking business of our journey: sure, I think these were questions to have puzzled the brains of Aristotle himself." In the story, these two survivors encounter the very real Anglo-Colonial diplomat and Indian agent Sir William Johnson, who lived in the region with the Iroquois. Further attempts by Durie's brother to recover the treasure end in a tragedy so gloomy, pessimistic, and filled with Asian mysticism that it caused some readers to reject the novel as not sufficiently realistic.

XIX. A Want of Common Language

The cultures of Native America were as remote from antebellum Americans as they are from us today — possibly more so because modern researchers have the advantages of archeology, historiography, hindsight, and computer-based Internet information. Nonetheless, the Indian nations residing in the woodlands of the northeast quadrant of the North American continent and those living in the adjacent coastal and piedmont regions almost certainly had been among the most familiar to Euro-colonials for more than two centuries. From the tribes of the northeast woodlands came "great hunters, fishermen, farmers and fighters, as well as the most powerful and sophisticated Indian nation north of Mexico [the Iroquois Confederacy]." [284]

In the 17th and 18th centuries, little or nothing was known of the nations of the plains, the deserts, or the western mountains. The Indians themselves were in transformation — largely due to the invasion of whites and their European culture, but also due to a changing natural environment and an unusually long period of climatic cooling. The problems associated with this climate anomaly (known as the Maunder Minimum, c. 1645-1715) were universal, even affecting Europe and the early colonists. Hence the many references to extreme wintry conditions on the early frontier. The Indians, perforce, were in varying stages of a complex system of adaptation throughout much of the 17th and 18th centuries, and observers saw them at different points during their transformation. Being hunter-gatherer societies, many nations relocated during this period and intertribal relations were in flux.

The Iroquois desire for hegemony extended in all directions from their Central New York homeland in Iroquoia. These included the drainage basin of the Great Lakes and Ohio River to the West, the valley of St. Lawrence to the Northeast, the Lake George-Lake Champlain corridor to Canada as far to the East as the Connecticut River, and the southern flowing valleys of Hudson, Delaware, and Susquehanna Rivers to the Atlantic Ocean. All of these areas originated in or touched on Iroquoia, and they were closely related geographically to a pattern of villages and tribal territories that extended throughout the Eastern Woodlands. In the 1640s, the Iroquois developed a grandiose strategy aimed at controlling all the interlacing tributary systems that might provide transportation by canoe for any rival tribe carrying furs to the Europeans. It is remarkable that they seem to have so influenced events at critical times in the history of European colonization, thereby making decisive events of even simple strategic moves.

During the period of the dispersal of the Huron, Erie, and other tribes, the power of decision was passing from the Indians to the colonists. Onondaga remained the center of all Iroquois councils, but by 1677 Albany had become the place were treaty negotiations with the English were to take place. This circumstance placed the Mohawks, who were nearest to Albany, at a distinct advantage over the other member nations of the Iroquois Confederacy in terms of their influence. Here the English and the Mohawks formed a special alliance and seemingly unshakable friendship that would last throughout the colonial period. The French, on the other hand, had refused to negotiate in central New York, forcing the Five Nations to come to Montreal or Quebec where they were all equally disadvantaged. [285]

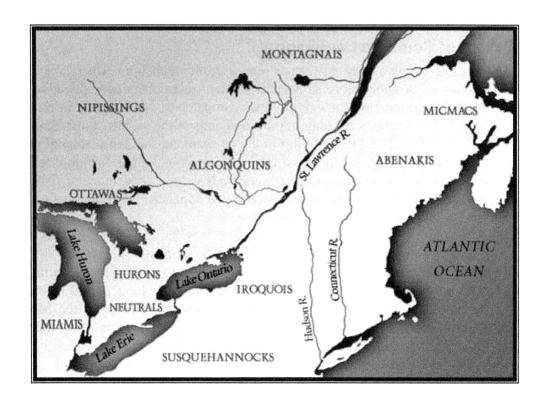

In order to better serve their Indian allies, the French made Fort Niagara a fortified outpost in 1726. It became one of the most significant outposts and trading centers in the region. It was built near the western end of Lake Ontario and ultimately controlled the fur trade coming from the Great Lakes. For the Seneca, who lived nearby, the fortified trading post built by the French at Niagara had attracted their trade, and even Sir William Johnson became unsure of their loyalty. Ironically, the French posts in the west were like cannonballs supported by a very thin string of supplies from the east that held the French allied tribes together. If the string were broken the posts would fall of their own weight. The capture of Niagara in 1759 by Johnson, his provincial troops, and his Mohawks effectively cut off all of Canada to the west of Lake Ontario from the administrative heart of New France. The defeat also cut the heart out of the French-allied Indians who melted back into the forests. Farther west, the Ojibwa family was the most populous of Algonquian-speaking nations. It included the Ojibwa, Ottawa, Chippewa, Mississauga, and Pottawatomie. In the course of time they would drive the Iroquois out of the territories they had conquered during the dispersal north of Lake Erie and west of present-day Cleveland.[286]

The fall of Quebec to General Wolfe and his regulars confirmed all the English victories of 1759 and led directly to the fall of Montreal and all of French Canada with it. The struggle for North America was over. In the Peace of Paris (1763), France lost almost all its possessions in North America. The British won a great worldwide empire in the Seven Years War, but their grip on North America was a tenuous one. Moreover, the Indians initially envisioned the peace with the British in the same terms as those that had defined their alliance with the French and the former members of the French alliance were seemingly willing to acknowledge at least a token Iroquois hegemony in the Northeast region. Yet, the British seemed incapable of fulfilling paternal obligations as the Indians viewed them, and they almost instantly asserted mastery over the Indians by building and garrisoning forts in Indian country in contravention of the propaganda they had disseminated among the tribes during the conflict. If the British did not act as fathers and had given up their role as truth-speaking brothers to act like conquerors, then they might very well be enemies capable of plotting the destruction of the Indians.

The accumulated effects of almost a century of colonial neglect, widespread prejudice against provincials, and a growing hatred of British regulars would cause the Anglo-American colonists to sever their ties with Britain in 1775. Consequently all of the people living in the region – white and native – became mixed together in an unavoidable network of strategies, counter-strategies, field tactics, and political gambits.

Then, in the first decade of the 19th century, the explorations of Lewis and Clark opened the Louisiana Territory introducing to Americans the Native nations of the plains, mountains, and Pacific coast. Aside from an unfriendly confrontation with the Teton Sioux, these nations were largely peaceful and the Corps of Exploration received extensive help from the various tribes they met. During the course of the expedition, contact was made with at least 55 different native cultural groups. Other groups, such as the Crow (Absaroke), almost certainly saw the explorers from concealment without themselves ever being seen. Some groups were encountered only through individual members, while others were met in formal councils. Still other Native Americans participated in the expedition by literally saving its members from starving and losing their way as they crossed the continent. Some like the Mandan, Hidatsa and Nez Perce forged friendships and alliances whose written descriptions in the journals still resonate with good will after 200 years.

One of the long-standing paradigms dominating the study of the Northeast woodlands in Cooper's time was that there were only two great linguistic stocks of native peoples who were in constant conflict over control of the same region: the Algonquian and the Iroquoian. In his introduction to *The Last of the Mohicans*, Cooper wrote:

> [The Native American] language has the richness and sententious fullness of the Chinese. He will express a phrase in a word, and he will qualify the meaning of an entire sentence by a syllable; he will even convey different significations by the simplest inflections of the voice. ... Philologists [experts in language] have said that there are but two or three languages, properly speaking, among all the numerous tribes, which formerly occupied the country that now composes the United States. They ascribe the known difficulty one people have to understand another to corruptions and dialects. The writer remembers to have been present at an interview between two chiefs of the Great Prairies west of the Mississippi, and when an interpreter was in attendance who spoke both their languages. The warriors appeared to be on the most friendly terms, and seemingly conversed much together; yet, according to the account of the interpreter, each was absolutely ignorant of what the other said.[287]

The classification titled "Native American languages" is geographical rather than linguistic, since those languages do not belong to a single linguistic family, or stock, as the Indo-European or Afro-asiatic languages do. Besides Iroquoian and Algonquian, there were several linguistic stocks of native peoples identified in Cooper's time: Muskhogean, Timucan, Siouan, and Caddoan among them. As a result of European conquest and settlement, perhaps two thirds of the many indigenous American languages had already died out or were dying out, but others flourished. Nonetheless, tribes related by language could be found among any hypothetical geographic or regional divide between political or tribal entities making Cooper's simplistic division of Iroquoian and Algonquian a regional rather than continental one. John Heckewelder, a Moravian missionary and staunch advocate of the Delaware Indians, quite clearly established the language dichotomy later employed by Cooper, at least in terms of its application to the Indians of the Northeast woodlands. In an *Account of the History, Manners, and Customs of the Indian Nations ...* (1819), the missionary also categorized the woodland nations into two types: the "noble savage" and the "savage fiend." Yet he might as well have divided them into pro-English and pro-French factions, or savage friends and savage enemies.

General Lewis Cass, Governor of Michigan Territory from 1813 to 1831 and certainly familiar with Native Americans of the Great Lakes region, led a party of scientists, soldiers, woodsmen, and Native Americans into the wilderness of western Michigan Territory in 1820 – the very center of Huronia, the cultural counterpoint to Iroquoia in New York. The project to map the region and locate the source of the Mississippi River is known as the Lewis Cass Expedition. The source of the river was then unknown, which resulted in an undefined border between the United States and British North America. In addition, a survey of the Indians of the region – their numbers, tribes, customs, and loyalties, whether to the United States or Great Britain – was made, sites for future forts were selected and purchased, and a geological survey was taken of possible mineral riches.

Henry Schoolcraft's book concerning the expedition, *Narrative Journal of Travels ... from Detroit ... to the Sources of the Mississippi River*, sold 1,200 copies within a few months of its publication in 1821. Cass noted with some irritation that Cooper should have crossed the Alleghenies to see Indians rather than having followed the work of the unreliable Heckewelder:

> The effect of Mr. Heckewelder's work, upon the prevailing notions respecting Indian history, is every day more and more visible. It has furnished materials for the writers of periodical works, and even of history; and is one of the most beautiful delineations of American scenery, incidents, and manners for which we are indebted to the taste and talent of an eminent novelist. *The Last of the Mohicans* is an Indian of the school of Mr. Heckewelder, and not of the school of nature. ... The most idle traditions of the Indians with him [Cooper] become sober history; their superstition is religion; their indolence philosophic indifference or pious resignation; their astonishing improvidence, hospitality; and many other defects in their character are converted into corresponding virtues.[288]

Meanwhile, unbeknownst to early white observers who attempted to record the Native languages that they encountered, it seems that the Indians, rather than being "untutored" or "in a perpetual infancy as to language or reason," had taken the practical expedient of simplifying their language for their European contacts. Modern linguistic analysis of surviving documents, grammars, and dictionaries from the early contact period show that the natives were deliberately fashioning a *pidgin dialect*, or over-simplified language, that allowed for communications and facilitated trade. It seems certain that in this regard the Indians were treating the Europeans as children, or simpletons, incapable of mastering the many nuances and subtle qualities of their native tongue.[289]

Some Europeans realized that they were being offered something less than a full knowledge of the language spoken among the natives themselves, and others assumed that the natives wished to keep the Europeans largely in the dark so that they could speak freely in front of them without their understanding what was said. Such simplifications seemingly satisfied 19th-century anthropologists, historians, and a general public following in the newspapers the forcible crusade to remove the Indians from "public lands."

Admittedly, Iroquoian was a distinct language (not a dialect) from Algonquian. Moreover, Algonquian was one of the most widespread linguistic stocks, but it comprised more than 50 distinct tribal languages. In 1846, Congress commissioned Henry Rowe Schoolcraft, an American geographer, geologist, and ethnologist, for a major study of Native America. Schoolcraft had noted of these two groups, "Regard [them] in whatever light we may, it is impossible to overlook the strong points of character in which they differed. Both were dexterous and cunning woodsmen, excelling in all the forest arts necessary to their condition, and having much in their manners and appearance in common. But they spoke a radically different language, and they differed scarcely less in their distinctive character and policy. The one was mild and conciliating, the other fierce and domineering. ... The Iroquois ... interposed themselves between New England and the Algonquin sub-types, and thus cut off their communications with each other. This separation was complete." The finished study, known as *Indian Tribes of the United States*, was published in six volumes from 1851-1857.

Recent studies have suggested that there may have been up to 500 distinct native languages (not dialects) used north of present-day Mexico. A single band or village might limit their everyday speech to a small number of dialects in common use among local tribes speaking the same root language. Due to the patterns of intermarriage, trade, and politics, however, it seems reasonable that many native communities were multilingual as often as they were language-specific.

As an example, the word "Manhattan," which today is clearly understood to mean the island in New York harbor, has been translated as "island of many hills" from the Lenape language, yet other derivations are possible including from the Munsee dialect of Lenape: *manahachtanienk* ("island of drunkenness"), *manahatouh* ("island of bow wood and arrows"), or simply *menatay* ("island"). The island of Manhattan and most of Brooklyn belonged to the Canarsie (who were Lenni Lenape). In fact, a group known to early explorers as Manhattans (Island People) occupied the wooded and rocky island that is now a borough of New York City, but as their was no such discrete band or tribe, this name may have been descriptive of the place rather than the people. The Algonquian root *munnoh* or *manah* means *island*. There was also a native tradition that the region actually belonged to the Raritan (also Delaware), who had removed their entire population in the pre-contact period from Manhattan to New Jersey.

There were a number of functional site types represented in the archaeological record. In this period these included spring fishing camps along major streams, fall open air hunting camps, rock shelter habitations, shellfish collecting and processing stations, burial sites, quarry and workshop sites were stone tools and *wampum* were manufactured, and villages occupied for a portion of the year. While many Indian families erected temporary bark huts called wigwams (*we-gi-was*), but others chose to return each season to a convenient rock shelter. This was usually an overhanging rock ledge facing away from the prevailing wind that afforded protection from wild animals and was near a source of potable water. A small central fire and a few boughs properly arranged about the shelter could make a warm and cozy habitation, even in a rock crevice. Evidence unearthed by archeologists suggests that some rock shelters were used continuously for several generations. Such habitations often left their mark in place names: Indian Rocks, Indian Cliffs, or Indian Ledge for instance. Most Archaic sites are small and contain evidence of later cultures living in the same area, but they lack traces of substantial dwellings or houses, fortifications, storage pits, or graves.

In 1609, Manhattan Island contained several seasonal villages that were used only for hunting and fishing. Not many paces from the paved portion of the modern pedestrian path in Inwood Park in upper Manhattan, there is still a rock shelter, which was excavated in the early 20th century. Archeological evidence of sturgeon scales and shells taken from food pits excavated elsewhere on the island of Manhattan in the 1920s suggests that the rivers swarmed with fish. In the shallows along the shores of the East River and on Long Island opposite were oysters, clams, and scallops in incredible numbers that grew to immense proportions.[290]

The Canarsie, residents of the western end of Long Island across the bay from Manhattan, were clearly a sub-tribe of the Delaware nation. The remaining 10 or so tribes on Long Island viewed the Pequot of Connecticut across Long Island Sound as their overlords. Indians on Long Island called their home *Meht-anaw-ach* (or ear shell country) for the availability of conch shells and giant quahog clams. The Dutch recorded the Indian name of Long Island as *Sewanhacky* (or Land of Shells).

It was often declared with great authority that like the Iroquois league of the Six Nations, so the Delaware, the Mohican, and the Munsee were but one confederacy. But this was not strictly true. The Lenape and Wappinger spoke using very similar Delaware root languages — similar enough that a Wappinger speaking in the Munsee Delaware tongue and a Lenape would mostly understand each other. Robert Bolton, in his *History of the County of Westchester From its First Settlement to the Present Time* (1848), noted that in political terms the Wappinger were divided into between seven and nine main groups or chieftaincies and numerous subgroups and bands. These were the Siwanoy, Kitchawanc, Wechquaesgeek, Rechgawawank, SintSink, Nochpeem, Wappinger, Tankiteke, and Uncowa. To the Dutch and English, the majority of the groups were known collectively as the River Indians. The Siwanoy of present-day Westchester County, New York claimed much of the mainland coast of Long Island Sound from the Norwalk archipelago in Connecticut to the mouth of the Bronx River as part of the Wappinger Confederacy, but they did not actually occupy the vast shoreline. The Wappinger knew the Putnam-Westchester County area as *Laaphawachking*. The name reportedly translates as the "place of stringing," which apparently refers to Native American wampum manufacturing that occurred in the area.[291]

In 1640, the Dutch in New Netherlands under Peter Minuet had famously entered into a good-faith transaction for Manhattan with Seyseys, chief of the Canarsie, who were only too happy to accept valuable merchandise in exchange for an island that was actually occupied, if not owned by another band. The Dutch then negotiated a separate agreement with ambassadors of the Siwanoy to purchase the entire coastline west of the

Norwalk River to the East River. The English at Norwalk made a similar agreement, at approximately the same time, with other chieftains of the Siwanoy living to the east of the Norwalk River (the New England side) for rights to overlapping portions of the same shoreline. No one — not the Dutch, not the English, not the Indian chiefs who had received payments for the land — thought to inform the actual overlords of the region or the hapless natives that actually used the valuable seashore that their rights to be there had been bartered away. The effect of the dislodgement of the fishing population of the waters of the New York area was to drive these people back into the forests, where their conditions of livelihood were radically changed. Ironically, the mainland shoreline of Long Island Sound, so easily bartered away, is today called the "Gold Coast" because of the value of its real estate. Today the cities of this coastal region are commonly considered among the best places in the United States in which to live.

Wampum

Regardless of their linguistic stock, the Indian nations highly valued wampum as a decoration, as a medium of exchange, and as a device for recording traditions and agreements. *Sewan* (loose beads) were made in flat disks of clam or oyster shell and as cylindrical beads, in either white or dark blue (sometimes called black), taken from the conch (welck) or the quahog clam, respectively. When strung together the sewan were called *wampum,* which term came from the Algonquian Indian word *wamp-umpe-ag* for white string of shells (*wamp*–white, *umpe*–shell string, *ag*–representing the plural).

It seems certain that in the pre-contact period wampum was not considered money or currency of any sort among the Indians. Rather, it was regarded as a highly appreciated gift or token that represented a significant demonstration of good faith and friendship. When a conference resulted in a treaty or agreement, a string or belt of beads was presented as a physical embodiment of the understanding, and when given as part of a condolence ceremony, it represented the heart-felt sympathy of the giver. In a culture that relied on oral memories rather than writing, these beads were very important as symbols.

In 1762, Sir William Johnson recorded a meeting with the Mohawk at his home in New York. Several strings and belts of wampum were exchanged. William Marsh his secretary recorded the following ways in which the wampum was used:

Sir William after entering the Council Room, got Abraham, a Mohawk Chief, to perform the Ceremony of Condolence on the Death of the Bunt's Sister (as mentioned yesterday) and gave 3 Strings of wampum. He likewise, with a black Belt of Wampum, leveled the grave of the deceased Sister of the Bunt, that it might no longer be seen, or give her Relations any farther concern. Gave a black Belt. The ceremony being Ended, Sir William told them He was ready to hear what they had to say. ...

A Belt with five Squares — Brother; This Belt, or Covenant Chain, was given to Us Several years ago by Nine Governments hereon represented, and His Majesty King George at the Top, Assuring Us then that they were, and would remain our Friends; insomuch, that if any Nation, either French, or Indians, or others, should quarrel with Us, they would rise, and Assist Us; at the same time assuring Us, that the Great King would protect Us in the possession of our Lands. — They then also showed a Space in said Belt, which they desired We would Fill with as many Nations of Indians, as we could bring into their, and our Alliance. This Belt We only show you, to let you know that, we constantly look at it, and repeat the purport of it to our old and young, so as never to forget the Promises you then made, as We are determined inviolably to abide by those made on our Side.[292]

The flat-disk sewan seem to have been the earliest form of wampum, and they were highly valued as decoration. They were a convenient form for use on dresses and shirts, or for incorporation as decorations in the hair. The long cylindrical wampum beads were more difficult to produce, but they were more easily adapted to use in necklaces or when stitched together. In the form of belts, wampum was exchanged upon the occasion of ceremonies or tribal conferences. It was possible to vary the pattern of dark and light beads on the belts to form a pictograph as a memorial of events or agreements, but the idea that they could be read like hieroglyphs is generally incorrect.

The tribes that resided on the Northeast Atlantic coast seem to have had a monopoly on the raw materials needed to make sewan, but its use and production did not extend to the tribes of the southern Atlantic coastal regions until whites put a currency value on it in the 17th century. For a long period, which extended up to the time of the American Revolution in some places, this was set at three black beads or six white beads to the English penny. Although the size of the bead was set at 60 to the English foot, the most common unit of exchange for strings of wampum found in period documents was the fathom (six feet). Using these values, the English considered the Indians of Long Island, Narragansett Bay, and Block Island to be rich.

While both the flat white and dark sewan disks could be fashioned from almost any shell material, the conch and quahog were exclusively used to produce the highly valued cylindrical beads. The conch—actually the Knobbed Atlantic Whelk—has a spiral core or column around which the shell grows. When the thin shell wall is broken out, the column can be drilled down its length and made into cylindrical white beads that can be shaped and ground smooth with a stone. Archeologists have found these conch shells in various stages of development at Indian campsites, especially in the area of Oyster Bay on the north shore of Long Island. The Algonquian-speaking Indians on Long Island called the place *Meht-anaw-ach* (or earshell country) for the availability of conch shells and giant quahog clams. Only white beads could be made from the conch. The more rare and more valuable blue beads, known as purple or black, can be made only from the thick blue portions of the quahog that occurs near the hinge of the shell. Quahog were available in almost any season, but Adriean Van der Donck, an early Dutch visitor to the area, was under the impression that the conch was "cast ashore from the sea" only twice a year.

The Indian tribes that inhabited the coastal regions surrounding the sheltered waters of Long Island Sound were particularly blessed with vast quantities of the raw materials for making sewan in the form of unbroken shells. The shores of Shelter Island, Gardiner's Bay, and Oyster Bay were littered with archeological evidence of widespread sewan manufacture, and it seems certain that the Indians that lived there traded the beads and disks that they made to other nations in the interior as a commodity, perhaps in exchange for flint and chert. By gift, trade, or barter wampum produced on the Northeast Atlantic coastline found its way as far west as Wisconsin and the Dakotas, and as far south as Virginia and the Carolinas.

Obsidian, a form of volcanic glass, had been traded for wampum for at least 5,000 years. The fractured surfaces of obsidian can be razor sharp. It was used in the making of knives, arrowheads and spearheads, fishhooks, jewelry, masks, and even mirrors. It is slightly softer than quartz flint and harder than manufactured glass. Obsidian was often thought to have mystical powers such as driving out demons. Native Americans traded obsidian throughout the Americas over remarkable distances, which evidence the interconnected nature of Native America. Each volcano and in some cases each volcanic eruption produces a distinguishable type of obsidian, making it possible for archaeologists to trace the origins of a particular artifact even from across a continent. Samples of obsidian uncovered in Florida had their origin in Washington State. Moreover, dozens of obsidian projectile points from the coastal mountains of the Pacific Northwest have been found as far east as New York. The "fingerprint quality" of obsidian makes it possible to identify its specific source and track down the movement of both prefabricated blanks and finished objects over considerable distances. [293]

Certain tribes exchanged lithic (stone) materials through broad-based trade networks focused on sources as far away as Michigan and Minnesota. Archeological evidence of trade items brought into New England included mica and quartz crystals from the Carolinas, galena from Missouri, flint from Illinois, obsidian from the Rockies, and copper from the Great Lakes. The woodland nations resident in Kentucky, Tennessee, and the Ohio Valley also seem to have participated in these exchanges. The volume of the trade items found suggests a widespread and vigorous intertribal trading system.

Trade is an integral and indispensable part of the human evolution and human behavior, since it paves the way for innovation and progress through social interaction. People learn new ideas, new attitudes or new techniques from other people. Nonetheless, obsidian (like other materials from outside the Northeast) was a rare item in the woodlands, found predominantly in high-status and ritual contexts having in all likelihood passed through many hands through the mechanism of trade.

On the French River north of Lake Huron was a stretch of rapids and falls known as the Sault de Calumets where the Indians looked for stones that could be made into tobacco pipe bowls (calumet). Red stones were considered the most sacred of all those available for making the calumet. Both the Potawatomi (People of the Sacred Fire) and the Mascoutah (People of the Fire) were noted for dealing in these materials. The red pipestone – a soft, reddish, iron-rich form of a mineral known as Catlinite – was eroded from underground sources in Minnesota, but it could also be found in Tennessee. Bluestone (blue-green Catlinite) generally came from the Appalachian Mountains. A salmon alabaster pipestone shaded from pink to white could be found in quarries in southern Manitoba. Black pipestone, actually a marbled white on black, came from South Dakota and was widely used by Plains Tribes for ceremonial pipes.

It was also noted that most of the Indians wore copper jewelry. "Some of the copper is very red and some of a paler color, none of them but have chains, earrings, or collar of this metal." Instead of viewing copper as a utilitarian object for every day use, they seemingly regarded it as sacred, and reportedly preserving pieces of it wrapped up in skin in their lodges for many years. Although the Jesuit fathers frequently mention the existence of copper and even use the term "mines" within the mineral region of Lake Superior, it is clear from the general tenor of their narratives that they neither saw nor knew of any actual mining in the technical sense of that word. The attention of the fathers was not particularly called to the subject of mineralogy, and although they were learned men, their knowledge of geology must have been very limited. There is nothing to show that the Indians wrought copper from mines at that time.[294]

Native North Americans had no copper smelting technology, but copper can be found in flakes, nuggets and ribbons. The metal would have been found in nature without need for smelting techniques and shaped into the desired form using heat and cold hammering techniques without chemically altering it by alloying it. In South America the case was quite different. Indigenous South Americans had full metallurgy with smelting and various metals being purposely alloyed. Evidence exists of copper trading routes throughout North America among native peoples, proven by isotopic analysis. Archaeologists generally agree that "prestige goods" made of obsidian, copper, or marble can be significant factors in assuming that those who possess one of them also holds a high position in society.[295]

The Rockaway and Canarsie tribes of the western end of Long Island (present-day Brooklyn, New York) doubtlessly traded the finished shell beads, sewan, and strings of wampum with other tribes, and examples from that area have been found as far west as the western-most Great Lakes and as far north as Hudson's Bay. Thousands of beads have been unearthed in Iroquoian villages in central and western New York, which may indicate their use as part of the tribute paid to them by the coastal tribes. It is known from the *Pennsylvania Colonial Records* that in 1712 the Delawares spoke to the Governor and Council at White Marsh and showed thirty-two wampum belts, which they were about to take north to Iroquoia as tribute. The evidence of wampum belts in this case indicates that each of the thirty-two belts of wampum was accompanied by a message that the sender expressed in one form or another of words spoken by a woman. It was also reported by men such as Conrad Weiser that records had been handed down by early "wampum keepers," the equivalent of ancient Indian archivists. In 1743, Weiser recounted how at a special meeting of the Onondaga Council a message from Virginia was delivered in this manner through a wampum keeper.

The Ceremony of the Dead, or the condolence ritual, was widespread among the tribes of the Northeast woodlands. Iroquois tradition has it that Deganawida, the peacemaker, gave Hiawatha the five basic rituals of the Condolence Ceremony on the occasion of his daughter's death. Most common people followed these rituals, and each required the giving and exchanging of strings of wampum between the mourners and the consolers. These exchanges happened throughout the rituals, but in the last two, the progression was completed as the mourners returned all the strings to the consolers. This signified what we would call closure. As an example, the text associated with the offer of a string of wampum might be: "When a person has suffered a great loss caused by death, his throat is stopped and he can not speak. With these words, I remove the obstruction from your throat so that you may speak and breathe freely." This was not unlike the practice among Christians of lighting a candle for the dead or having a mass celebrated by a priest. Hiawatha expanded the condolence ritual to include fourteen burdens, or acts that needed to be followed for the healing of those who were in mourning. These expanded principles became the Condolence Council Ceremony that was used for the death of a chief or the loss of another important person.[296]

XX. Contamination

The effects of cultural and biological contamination were largely a product of geography with the coastal tribes and those nations living on navigable rivers being contacted first, and those in the interior remaining largely unaffected. For instance, the Erie nation, who populated the region around the Great Lake named for them, seemingly had no European visitors prior to their dissolution as a viable nation in the 1650s at the hands of the Iroquois. The Erie were first mentioned in 1615 when Etienne Brule, an interpreter and guide for Samuel de Champlain, met a group of them near Niagara Falls, a natural obstacle to the inland progression of European style vessels. Even the Natives in their canoes had to transfer their loads across a difficult seventeen-mile portage to move from Lake Ontario to Lake Erie. The only detailed knowledge of the Erie nation comes from the records of the French Jesuits who took them in after they had been dispersed. In 1680, the last small group of Erie Indians surrendered to the Iroquois in southern Pennsylvania. Therefore, nothing of their cultural pattern, or lifeways, is known with certainty, although they appear to have been a highly numerous nation.

In 1637, the Erie nation was supposedly weakened by epidemics including smallpox. This was almost a decade before the Iroquois launched their regional war of extermination. Smallpox spreads through direct contact with an infected person or contaminated objects such as clothing, blankets, or furs. The virus also can be carried in the air in enclosed settings. Almost without exception, oral traditions among affected tribes continued to claim that whites were to blame for spreading the smallpox disease. Smallpox and the fur trade seemingly combined in one of history's most tragic pairings. The disease was possibly transmitted to the Erie through their allies the Susquehannock, an Iroquoian language nation of the Northeast Woodlands who populated the lands bordering the Susquehanna River and its branches from the north end of Chesapeake Bay in Maryland across Pennsylvania into southern New York. These also were to be devastated by smallpox.

Almost completely forgotten today, the Susquehannock were one of the most formidable tribes of the mid-Atlantic region at the time of white contact. They have also been described as aggressive, warlike, imperialistic, and bitter enemies of the Iroquois. They may also have warred with the Mohican from the central Hudson Valley. The Susquehannock absorbed many Erie among them, but succumbed to Iroquois conquest in the 1670s. In the aftermath, the Iroquois seemingly allowed the resettlement of some of the semi-tributary Lenape in the area formerly belonging to the Susquehannock, as it was near the western boundary of the Lenape's former territory, known as Lenapehoking or Scheyischbi, or "the place bordering the ocean." Europeans seldom visited Susquehannock villages, and by 1700 there were fewer than 300 persons of partial Susquehannock descent living among the Iroquois and Lenape. Most of these were the mixed-nation offspring of captives or hostages.

When Cooper or Parkman wrote of the region, the Susquehannock and the Erie as distinct tribes along with the less numerous Petun, Wenro, and Neutrals were gone, the survivors of Iroquois aggression being scattered to the west and south. What little is known about them has come from the Huron by way of the Jesuits. Many of these homeless migrants, taking refuge among the Jesuit missions of the Ohio, Wisconsin, and Canada, became known on the frontier as Mingo (a Delaware name suggesting *stealthy*), or Wyandot (an Algonquian word meaning *villagers*). Eventually, a distinction was made between White Mingo (Conestoga) residing in the Delaware Valley and the Black Mingo (probably a remnant of the Erie) who lived farther to the west. Pennsylvanians during the 1700s preferred the name Conestoga derived from *Kanastoge* (place of the immense pole), the name of a native village in Pennsylvania. Historians have been forced, therefore, to assume much about these cultures from the lifeways of their neighbors.

The Jesuit Relation for 1671 has the following passage regarding refugees: "Four nations make their abode here [Jesuit mission of St Francis Xavier at Green Bay, Wisconsin], namely, those who bear the name Puans (the Winnebago), who have always lived here as in their own country, and who have been reduced to nothing from being ... exterminated by the Illinois, their enemies; the Pottawatomie, the Sauk, and the Nation of the Fork (la Fourche) also live here, but as strangers (or foreigners), driven by the fear of Iroquois from their own lands which are between the lake of the Hurons and that of the Illinois." According to tradition, the Pottawatomie, Chippewa, and Ottawa were originally one people. The Pottawatomie are described in the early journals as "the most docile and affectionate toward the French of all the savages of the west." Sir William Johnson, however, complained in 1772 of robberies and murders committed by them through the intrigues and jealousy of the French traders and priests. The Pottawatomie were well disposed toward Roman Catholicism, siding actively with the French down to the peace of 1763. They then supported the rising under Pontiac, and in the Revolution in 1775 took arms against the United States. They continued hostilities until the treaty of Greenville in 1795. They again took up arms in the British interest in 1812, and made final treaties of peace in 1815. Between 1836 and 1841, they removed beyond the Mississippi.[297]

In 1738, a major disaster struck the Cherokee when their towns were swept by an epidemic of smallpox. At the time, the Cherokee Chief Oconostota accused the British of deliberately planting smallpox germs in the trade goods that they had shipped to the Cherokees. There is evidence that a captain at Fort Pitt (then the western frontier) did give two infected blankets and one infected handkerchief to Indians in June of 1763. In a letter to Colonel Henry Bouquet dated July 7, 1763, Lord Jeffrey Amherst writes, "Could it not be contrived to send the Small Pox among those disaffected tribes of Indians?" Bouquet wrote back, "I will try ... with some blankets that may fall in their hands, and take care not to get the disease myself." The strategy proved particularly effective among the Ohio tribes who had little immunity having missed the naturally occurring 1757-58 epidemic among the French allied tribes contracted during the capture of Fort William Henry in New York.[298]

It has often been repeated that the Cherokee were given blankets infected with smallpox from a hospital in Tennessee during the Cherokee removal (Trail of Tears) of the 1830s, but there is no historical basis for this story. In fact, there is no evidence of a major smallpox outbreak along the trail, the Cherokee population having been given some immunity through several documented epidemics in previous years. The story seems rather to be a modern conflation of the earlier British attempts at biological warfare with American guilt concerning its racial politics.

Between 1837 and 1838, a major devastating smallpox epidemic swept the Upper Missouri region infecting the Mandan, Hidatsa and Arikara tribes. Francis Chardon, a mid-level trader and clerk with the American Fur Company, in his "Journal at Fort Clark

1834–1839," wrote that the Hidatsa (Gros Ventres) said the steamboat brought the smallpox. William Fulkerson, an Indian agent onboard, and Chardon both tell of an Indian sneaking aboard the vessel and stealing an infected blanket from a sick passenger. Chardon appears to have been compulsive about tracking such things, from the number of rats killed each month in the storehouses to the number of daily Indian fatalities during the 1837 small pox epidemic. In the earliest detailed study of the western fur trade, *The American Fur Trade of the Far West* (1902), Hiram M. Chittenden used Chardon's account to blame the American Fur Company for the epidemic in passing, but he was vastly more concerned with the availability of alcohol to the natives in the form of "ardent spirits." Chittenden was typical of the Progressive era of American history with a strong belief in social reformation and the divine mission of the Anglo-Saxon race to save the heathen Indian race from itself.

R. G. Robertson in his book *Rotting Face: Smallpox and the American Indian* (2001) places blame on the captain of the vessel for failing to enforce a quarantine once the epidemic broke out. Robertson claims an estimated 20,000 natives died, doing more damage to the Northern Plains tribes in one year than all the military expeditions ever sent against American Indians. Yet the Mandan were first plagued by smallpox in the 16th century before white contact and had been hit by similar epidemics every few decades. The great smallpox epidemics of 1780 through 1781 and 1801 through 1802 crippled the Indian nations and altered tribal hegemony across the upper Missouri. Admittedly, the fur trade was the primary means by which smallpox reached the Indians of the interior, but it traveled primarily with middleman traders who were themselves Native Americans. There was no reason for the fur companies to desire the removal of the Native population, who worked for nothing while providing pelts to the trading stations. Moving inland from the Atlantic coast and northward up the Mississippi and Missouri rivers, smallpox diffused along tribal trading networks, far in advance of the first white traders.[299]

There were approximately 1,600 Mandan living in the two villages at that time. The disease effectively destroyed the Mandan settlements. Almost all the tribal members died. Estimates of the number of survivors vary but most sources put the number at 125 persons. The survivors banded together with the nearby Hidatsa in 1845, and were joined with the Arikara in 1862. With the second half of the 19th century, there was a gradual decrease in the holdings of the Three Affiliated Tribes (the Mandan, Hidatsa and Arikara). By the beginning of the 20th century, the U.S. government estimated that the Native American population of the continent had been reduced by approximately 65 percent through starvation, exposure, fevers, epidemic diseases, and wholesale massacres.

Intertribal Warfare

The Iroquois Confederacy to the east and the Hurons and their related cantons to the west inhabited the geographical center of the Northeast woodlands at the time of white contact. Among these the Mohawk were the staunchest allies of the English, while the Huron were most likely to support the French. According to Cooper in *The Last of the Mohicans*: "Magua [the treacherous antagonist of the story] was born a chief and a warrior among the red Hurons of the lakes … till the people chased him again through the woods into the arms of his enemies. The chief, who was born a Huron, was at last a warrior among the Mohawks," an idea rejected by Hawkeye as implausible. "Magua slept hard in the English wigwams. ... The spirit of a Huron is never drunk; it remembers forever!" The Huron and Mohawk, though related, were implacable enemies.[300]

Prior to the dispersal of the 1640s, all of the Iroquoian speaking peoples lived in centralized villages and stockaded towns (sometimes called "castles" in Dutch and English documents). The orderly layout of these settlements in streets and pathways inside a stockade, when compared to the randomness of the camps of other tribal nations, lent an air of permanence and civilization to them that was reflected in the journals of those Europeans who observed them. Whole extended clan families dwelled in the long cylindrical structures built to accommodate large extended families, all of them able to trace their descent to a common female ancestor. The Clan Mother title was usually passed on to her female relatives. Long houses were built for families who intended to stay in one place. Once a decade, a nation might decide to relocate once the farming land and resources in that particular area had been exhausted.

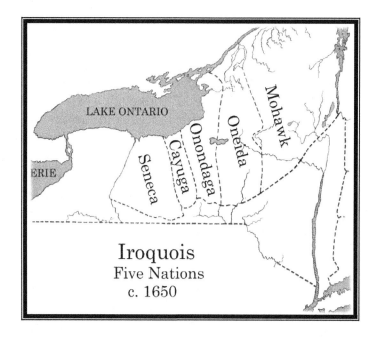

The several confederated tribes of Iroquois inhabiting present-day central New York were possibly the most influential natives in the history of the region. Generally known as "the Iroquois," which in Algonquian means rattlesnake, the Iroquois Confederacy included the Seneca, Cayuga, Onondaga, Oneida, Mohawk, and later the Tuscaroras. These tribes considered themselves *Haudenosaunee* (people of the long house), and were formed into the strongest of the political and military confederacies in the region, known either as the Five Nations, or Six Nations (after 1722). The longhouse, with various roof styles, was closely associated with the Iroquois, but many groups in the Northeast also used it. It was a permanent, multifamily residential structure that usually housed a single clan or kinship group. The number of longhouses and their placement in a village was often a measure of the kinship structure of the community.

In the 1970s, certain archeologists uncovered a number of sites near St. Johnsville, New York belonging to a pre-contact Indian culture called the Owasco. These people seemingly maintained a material culture that may have affected the New York Iroquois. The Owasco were almost certainly the first natives in the region to cultivate corn on a large scale. Moreover they produced cordmarked pottery, triangular projectile points, clay elbow pipes, bone harpoon points, and other items similar to those found among the Iroquois at the time of contact. One of the most convincing pieces of evidence in this regard were posthole marks that showed that the Owasco lived in large oblong or rectangular houses similar in size and structure to the longhouses of the Iroquois. Nonetheless, anthropologists have recently registered strong reservations concerning any cultural continuity other than a casual one between the Owasco and the Iroquois. It is unlikely that this tribe considered itself *Haudenosaunee.*

Today, anthropologists generally refer to the last prehistoric culture to dominate North America before European contact as the Late Mississippian culture, a defunct mounding building civilization. Thriving from about a.d. 800, the Mississippian culture seemingly spanned a huge region from Wisconsin and Minnesota in the north, through Georgia to the south, and westward into the Great Plains. Divided into three distinct cultural periods Early (a.d. 800–1200), Middle (a.d. 1200–1500), and Late (a.d. 1500–1700), the Mississippians may have introduced the cultivation of maize (corn) throughout the eastern woodlands, but Indian traditions recorded after European contact seem to bolster the idea that the practice of extensive agriculture was imported from outside the region rather than developed from within it. The Late Mississippian period (beginning about a.d. 1500) seems to have remained quite dynamic. Bow and arrow technologies seemingly improved, hunting efficiency increased, and maize, beans, and squash were introduced to supplement native seeds, nuts, and roots as sources of food. These factors tend to give a view of the Mississippian culture as one in expansion, not one in collapse. Once again, the Indians first contacted by Europeans seem to have been as much in the dark as they with regard to the identity of these people.

As to the size of their enterprise, Native American agriculture was either extensive or rudimentary. Iroquoians with their permanent villages tended to produce the latter. Large fields with corn hills in the tens of thousands often covered more than 30 acres — the spaces between the corn hills averaging a little more than a yard apart. The corn hills were created and kept clear of weeds by the application of simple hand tools alone. Almost no cultivation was necessary after the corn plants had gained some height because they outstripped the growth of the weeds. Moreover, the ears could hang for a long time and could be picked at leisure. Unlike the grains favored by the whites, corn also required no threshing or winnowing. Early accounts of the extent of Indian agriculture noted adjoining fields numbering in the hundreds of acres interspersed with orchards, berry banks, rows of sunflowers, and vines right up to the edge of the forests. On the other hand, many natives kept small garden plots from a few tens of meters square to the size of an acre or two.

Unlike many cultural groups, the spiritual Haudenosaunee rarely tried to force their beliefs on anyone and generally allowed their people to follow their own beliefs without criticism. The Caughnawagas, (a.k.a. French Praying Indians or French Iroquois), were often counted as Mohawks. Originally from Ossernenon near Auriesville, New York (where Jesuit Father Isaac Jogues met his martyrdom), the Caughnawagas had separated from their Iroquois relatives in the historical period mainly due to their adoption of Catholicism, but they maintained a kinship bond with the more English leaning Mohawks. When the hostility of the pagan Iroquois in their territory frustrated the object of the French to attach the former to their interests, the Jesuits determined to draw their converts from the confederacy and to establish them in a new mission village near the French settlements on the St Lawrence. Driven out by an informal form of social segregation, some 600 Caughnawaga Christians moved to La Prairie, and 160 more moved to the Lac des Deux Montagnes mission near Oka on the Ottawa River. A few dozen more joined their Catholic Huron cousins at Lorette. In 1676, they were removed from this place to Sault St. Louis, where the Jesuit mission of St Francois du Sault was founded. The majority of the emigrants came from the Oneida and Mohawk, and the Mohawk tongue, somewhat modified, became the speech of the whole of this village. Women converts often led these migrations. They thereby drew their kin with them and spread family connections in ways that would affect trade and war for generations.[301]

Through the alliances that it made, or refused to make, the Iroquois Confederacy unintentionally determined which European nation would rule the region. There is no doubt that an Iroquois League (Haudenosaunee) was fully established sometime between 900 and 1570 and that it was composed of four major language-sharing confederacies led by the Attiwandaronk (Neutrals), Susquehannock, Hurons, and Iroquois, respectively, and supported by their sub-groups. According to tradition, the League was formed through the efforts of two men, *Deganawida*, sometimes known as the Great Peacemaker, and *Hiyonwantha*, a name later appropriated by Henry Wadsworth Longfellow as *Hiawatha*. Legend has it that the sage Deganawida blotted out the sun as part of his program to convince recalcitrant cantons to join the league. A total solar eclipse visible in the region in 1451 may set the actual date of the formation of the Iroquois League to the later part of this range. Native tradition suggests that at the time of the league's creation most of the individual tribes were residing in those regions in which whites found them during the period of initial European contact.

Longfellow's poem (1855) was a work of American Romantic literature, not a historical representation of Native American oral tradition. Longfellow had originally planned on following Henry Schoolcraft in calling his hero *Manabozho,* the name in use at the time among the Ojibwa of the south shore of Lake Superior for a figure of their folklore. He chose instead Hiawatha a historical figure associated with the founding of the League of the Iroquois. Longfellow insisted that he gave chapter and verse for these legends. The chief value of the poem was that the tales were Indian legends as he heard them from non-Iroquoian sources like the Ojibwa Chief *Kahge-ga-gah-bowh* during his visits to Longfellow's home; and from Black Hawk and other Sac and Fox Indians Longfellow had encountered on Boston Common – all natives of the western Great Lakes region where no Iroquois nations had resided.[302]

The Huron and their associated cantons (Bear, Cord, Rock, and Deer) had moved into the inter-lake region of present-day Ontario, while the Five Nations settled in the Finger Lake region of central New York. There is evidence that the Rock and the Deer cantons came into Huronia from the middle and upper St Lawrence valley, and they may have been the people first seen by Jacques Cartier as residing near the prominence that would become Quebec City. These same villages — about a dozen in all — had completely disappeared when Champlain explored the area, having been replaced by roving bands of nomadic Algonquian-speaking hunters such as the Montagnais and the Nipissings. Historians have called these missing natives the Laurentian Iroquois, and both Huron and Mohawk traditions claim them as their own. Yet neither has a legend that convincingly explains the disappearance. They simply appear to have been expelled some time between 1541 and 1608. A solution has been suggested in this regard that the Five Nations Iroquois were traditionally hostile toward most of these surrounding Iroquoian peoples. Of course, they were also hostile to the surrounding Algonquian peoples and the members of their own confederacy before its formal founding.

Tribal legends lend support to the existence of warring factions among the Haudenosaunee in the late prehistoric period. It has been suggested that the Iroquoian-speakers were "the most divergent" of all the language groups residing in the Northeast woodlands. Not only was their linguistic foundation different from that of the other resident nations of the region; but also they practiced a more extensive form of agriculture, followed a different method of determining familial lineage (essentially matrilineal v patrilineal), and practiced a number of unique ceremonies, including ritual cannibalism.

The Five Nations Iroquois Confederacy also changed the face of Native America in the 17th century through their use of trade agreements, coercive diplomacy, and unrelenting warfare against both Iroquoian and Algonquian rivals. The intertribal conflicts of the mid-17th century, known as the Great Dispersal, were total wars prosecuted with means that often bordered on genocide primarily by the Mohawk and Seneca — the eastern and western doorkeepers of the confederacy and possibly the most actively aggressive Native tribes in the region. Most of these attacks were made at a time when white Europeans were barely hanging on in coastal settlements such as Jamestown, Plymouth, Albany, Montreal, or Quebec. The result of this series of conflicts radically shifted the pre-contact mix of indigenous peoples in the region and in many cases restructured it beyond our ability to know what it had been.

In 1625, with the encouragement of the Dutch, the Mohican attacked the eastern-most village of the Mohawk, probably Schaunactada, which was situated near present-day Schenectady, New York. As both sides were still using traditional weapons, the attack and defense was little more than a skirmish by European standards. Daniel van Krieckebeeck, Dutch commander of Fort Orange, probably thinking that his guns would help the Mohican to overpower the Mohawk, accompanied a group of Mohican with four or five soldiers on a subsequent raid in 1626. A few miles from the fort, the party was set upon by the Mohawk who seem to have caught them in a storm of arrows from ambush. In the ensuing fight, the commander and at least three of his soldiers were killed along with upward of two dozen Mohican. Little more can be known about the extent of the so-called Mohawk–Mohican War because the Native American nations involved kept no written records and because there was no further involvement of Europeans. According to a detailed native tradition, however, the last major battle of the war was a decisive one. The Mohawk and Mohican forces were arrayed against one another on an island in the Hudson River. The island has not been definitely identified, but such set-piece gladiatorial encounters were not unusual in Native American warfare. Champlain had blundered into a similar affair between the Mohawk and a force of Montagnais at Crown Point in 1609 and had won only the undying enmity of the Iroquois for the French.

According to the account, the Mohican were winning the island contest until a group of Mohawk sprang from ambush, launching a furious flanking attack and killing many Mohican warriors. The Mohicans then sued for peace. The surviving Mohican took refuge at Schagticoke on the Hoosic River in New York or moved into New England. Jonas Michaeleus, minister of the Dutch Reformed Church in New Amsterdam, wrote in

1628, "The Mohicans have fled and their lands are unoccupied." Nonetheless, the Mohawk continued to harass the Mohican refugees in their villages in southwestern Vermont and western Massachusetts for many years. The immediate effect of the Mohawk–Mahican War was a rapid destabilization of the balance of power that had existed among the native tribes of the region. For their part, the French were disappointed at the increased power of the Mohawk who were their implacable enemy.[303]

Before the English arrived, the Pocumtucks shared a lifestyle, language, and culture similar to that of the Mohicans, Wappingers, Abenaki, and Nipmucks that shared parts of the Connecticut River valley with them. As late as 1638, they seem to have been a healthy, strong, and generally amiable people who lived alongside their neighbors in a natural state of equilibrium. In 1664, the Pocumtucks hosted a great conference concerning Dutch and English trade that included representatives of the Mohawks and several local Algonquian tribes. The Pocumtuck having been slighted by the Mohawk at the meeting attacked and murdered the entire Mohawk delegation of almost two dozen persons killing among them an important Iroquois leader named Saheda. In retaliation, the Mohawks sent a large war party to the Pocumtuck village at present-day Deerfield, Massachusetts. As Europeans took no part in the conflict, no independent account of the ensuing battle remains, but the result according to Indian tradition was that the Pocumtucks fell into a set-piece ambush and were utterly destroyed. The few survivors of the tribe scattered to be absorbed into other bands of Algonquian speaking peoples, and their fertile and cleared lands were abandoned and opened to English settlement. Possibly the largest Indian force resident in the Connecticut Valley was no more. The agent of this change was neither contagious infection nor the unfettered greed of white expansion, but rather the politics of submission, negotiation, alliance, and domination to be found among the Indians themselves.

The Susquehannock, an Iroquoian speaking people, were noted as a redoubtable enemy of the Seneca, who had previously fought with them but had failed to achieve any decisive results. Although they inhabited a large region of present-day Pennsylvania, the Susquehannock were a far-ranging people who sent hunting and war parties west into the Ohio River valley and well north of Lake Ontario. The Seneca and the Susquehannock continually annoyed one another during these small excursions in an attempt to patrol the borders of their respective territories and to stave off the likelihood of a clandestine buildup of invasion forces.

The Mohawk, reassured by their successes in the so-called Beaver Wars of the 1640s, had ventured into the northern borderlands of Susquehannock territory in the winter of 1651–1652 to attack the village of the Atrakwaeronons, who may have been one of more than a dozen bands associated with a loosely formed Susquehannock confederacy that dominated the mid-Atlantic region from the Potomac River in northern Virginia to the southern New York border with Pennsylvania. Although the Susquehannock maintained almost two dozen fortified villages and may have numbered between 5,000 and 7,000 persons, they took fright at reports of 500 to 600 captives being taken on their northern border by the Mohawk. They quickly began their own preparations for war with the Five Nations at that time. Periods of ill-feeling, discomfiture, and open conflict were to continue between the Susquehannock and their northern cousins over the next quarter century.

Little is known of the First Susquehannock War. From 1652 until 1658, the Mohawk and the Susquehannock warred on each other by means of small itinerant raiding parties. The Mohawk failed to force either the surrender or the dispersal of the Susquehannock by these means, but the two nations joined together with the Dutch diplomatically in 1660 to settle a dispute with the Esopus Indians of the Hudson Valley. It is quite certain that the Susquehannock were receiving firearms from the Swedish colonists in the Delaware Bay, and they were reported to have fitted their villages with several small cannon from this source.

In 1663, however, more than 800 Iroquois warriors — drawn from the Seneca, Cayuga, and Onondaga — opened a fierce attack on the main stronghold of the Susquehannock. This was the first encounter of the Second Susquehannock War. Almost 700 Susquehannock, supported by 100 Delaware allies, massed to repel the attackers. The proximate cause of the outbreak of a second major conflict between the Seneca and the Susquehannock in 1663 is obscured by the same lack of direct evidence that affects the study of all the intertribal wars of the 17th century. However, it seems clear that the causes of the conflict were rooted in the interdiction of the fur trade in the Susquehanna River valley. Throughout the 1660s, the Susquehannock had increasingly harassed the Seneca as they tried to move furs across the region that is now the New York–Pennsylvania border. The Seneca carried their beaver skins to Albany "with great inconvenience and by long and perilous routes" with the Susquehannock laying ambushes for them all along the way.

Allied to the Susquehannock were the remnants of the Erie (hereafter known as the Mingos), the Delaware and the Shawnee — the last making their first appearance in the historical period as an aggressive force in intertribal warfare. The Shawnee at this time may have been members of a closely knit single tribe. However, in the 18th century, they represented a confederation divided into five semi-autonomous groups that included the Chillicothe, Hathawekela, Kispoko, Mequachake, and Piqua (all with various spellings). The leadership of this confederation seems to have come from the first two of these groups. In an attempt to win concessions by diplomacy rather than might, the Seneca sent 25 representatives to the Susquehannock village to treat with the defenders. They were seized and burned at stakes raised upon the stockade in full view of the besieging Iroquois army. The Seneca retreated in frustration.

The sudden retirement of the Susquehannock from their tribal territory has been explained in various ways. The Iroquois were supposed to have badly beaten the Susquehannock sometime between 1672 and 1675, although no historian has been able to identify the battle or the campaign that was supposed to have taken place, even in terms of a tribal tradition. It is altogether possible that a decisive battle between the Iroquois and Susquehannock in the wilderness might go unrecorded, yet, it is almost as certain that the reason for this is that the event never happened. The Iroquois themselves were uncharacteristically silent about any such victory. Certainly, had it taken place, they would have bragged about it.

Maryland's governor, Sir Charles Calvert had called the Susquehannock diplomats to a conference at Mattapinie (St. Mary's City) in the winter of 1675. To his surprise all the Susquehannock appeared, rather than just a few representatives, and after some tedious debate they agreed to remove their villages from Piscatawa to the general vicinity of present-day Washington D.C. on the Potomac River. There is also some evidence that the

Susquehannock may have sought refuge in New York as protection from the colonial governments of Maryland and Virginia, especially during the period of Bacon's Rebellion of 1676 when the Piscatawa and Mattawoman of the Delaware Confederacy had aided the colonial militia in the pursuit of a band of renegade Doeg Indians. Word of the near extermination of the followers of Metacomet (King Philip) in New England in that same year may also have caused the Susquehannock to seek a certain level of anonymity by residing among their Delaware neighbors. An Indian informant of the English noted, "The Susquehannock laugh and jeer at the English saying they can do what mischief they please [because] the English can not see them."[304]

The colonial authorities were anxious that the Susquehannock remain apart from the Delawares lest they increase the power and influence of the latter. In 1677, most of the Susquehannock retired to Iroquoia to be under the protection of New York colony, but 26 families joined the Delawares. This effectively destroyed the tribal integrity of the Susquehannock people, and gave the Delawares, due to their adoption of a minority of the tribe, command of the property rights below the falls of the Susquehanna River that William Penn recognized in 1683 when forming the colony of Pennsylvania. The Iroquois seemingly received the territorial rights of the Susquehannock above the falls. The Susquehannock were thereafter "reduced to anonymity among their Iroquois and Delaware hosts."[305]

Unlike the Iroquois, who seem to have formed a strong sense of central governance and tribal integrity, the Algonquian peoples, like the Mohicans and Delawares who populated Cooper's tales, were most often divided into many small *bands* or *villages* throughout the region. Bands were small groups with limited lines of shared descent that lived and traveled together. The Mohican lands initially extended from Lake Champlain south nearly to Manhattan Island and on both sides of the Hudson River, west to Schoharie Creek and east into Massachusetts, Vermont, and Connecticut. The Munsee, part of the Lenni Lenape (true men), settled near the headwaters of the Delaware River just west of the Mohicans and were sometimes known as the River People. The work of the devoted Moravian missionaries in eastern Pennsylvania in the 17th and 18th centuries forms an important part of the history of these tribes. A significant group of Lenape, many of them converted Christian Munsee later lived in several mission villages in Ohio established by Moravian missionaries.

The position and status of the Delaware nation during this and subsequent periods is a topic of some debate. The Iroquois, when dealing with the whites, often referred to the Delaware as their "nephews" or as "women," and there is no record of the Delawares dealing directly with the colonial government of New York. Some historians have taken this as a symbol of Delaware subservience to the Iroquois. Yet the Delawares dealt with the officials of Pennsylvania independent of the Iroquois, and formulated agreements without asking their permission or sanction. Certainly the Delawares served as mediators time and again in disputes between neighboring tribes and between the tribes and the Dutch.[306]

The Delaware were accorded the respectful title of "grandfather" by all the Algonquian tribes, a recognition of ancient ancestry accorded as a courtesy. The Nanticoke, Conoy, Shawnee, and Mohican claimed close connection with the Delaware and preserved the tradition of a common origin. Tributary nations were often called *younger brothers* or *children,* terms that connoted a protective familial relationship.

Protectors of long standing and close relationship were often called *uncles,* a term which also reflected a mutually respectful kinship-like relationship.

The Delaware of New Jersey, Pennsylvania, and surrounding areas considered themselves Lenni Lenape (true men), yet the Iroquois more than once called these Delaware "women" at grand councils implying to the whites present that they held sovereignty over them. Both the Delawares and many historians find this claim dubious. Cooper, through his hero Deerslayer, noted of the controversy: "That matter is not rightly understood — has never been rightly explained. ... the Mengwe fill the woods with their lies, and misconstruct words and treaties. I have now lived ten years with the Delawares, and know them to be as manful as any other nation, when the proper time to strike comes." [307]

Contrary to opinions revolving around Cooper's use of the term *Mohicans* in the title of his most famous novel, both the terms *Mahican* and *Mohican* refer to the same people and are equally correct. The Mahican version of the term is most common in Dutch documents of the period. Conversely, the name *Mohegan* refers to a tribe living between the Connecticut and Thames Rivers who were more closely tied to the Pequot of eastern Connecticut. At the time of European contact, the Mohegan and Pequot were a unified tribal entity living in the lower Connecticut region, but the Mohegan gradually became independent. Under the leadership of a *sachem,* incidentally named Uncas (*Wonkas* – the fox), the Mohegan became a separate tribe. European colonists defeated the Pequot in 1637. In reward for their aid against their erstwhile cousins, the English gave Pequot captives to the Mohegan; but as a nearly landless people, the Mohegan gradually lost their tribal status.

The Mohicans and the Delaware were cousins (both being Lenni Lenape). They suffered attacks by the Iroquois similar to that perpetrated on the Pocumtucks. As the fur trade with the Albany Dutch expanded and furs became more difficult to find, tensions developed between the Mohicans and the Mohawks. The Mohicans were eventually driven from their territory west of the Hudson, and settled at their major village at Stockbridge, Massachusetts. Almost two dozen Stockbridge Mohicans were killed in a single encounter of the Revolution fighting for the patriots in the Bronx on a bluff overlooking the Van Courtlandt mansion. Driven to near extinction, the Mohicans accepted a grant of land in Central New York near the Oneida nation, who also fought for the Patriots in the Revolution.

Unlike the Iroquois, who seem to have formed a strong sense of central governance and tribal integrity, the Algonquian peoples were most often divided into many small *bands* or *villages* throughout the region. Bands were small groups with limited lines of shared descent that lived and traveled together. They were often patrilineal, and they rarely came together with other bands for group activities. Documents from the period refer to both villages and bands promiscuously, and the true nature of any tribal organization among the Algonquians in the early contact period remains uncertain. Such small groups existed among the Chippewa and the Cree sub-groups of the Ojibwa of the western lakes region that they exhibited little in the way of overall leadership or tribal organization. Their cousins, the Ottawa, seem to have had more settled villages and a better organization than other Ojibwa peoples. Yet the actual level of isolation among the Algonquian groups is almost impossible to determine because they generally lacked a political structure with cohesive and long-lasting institutions similar to the Central

Council of the Iroquois at Onondaga. Rather they lived in a society in which obedience to central authority was neither a societal expectation nor a cultural virtue. Nonetheless, if a particular native community was under a definite political leadership, the term *band* seems more appropriate in sociological parlance than either the term *tribe* or *village*. This observation has "stirred some controversy" among anthropologists, but "it has a certain general validity." [308]

Recent historians and modern Native Americans recognize several loosely confederated groupings of Indians that existed in the Northeast region in the 17th century other than the Iroquois. These were based on the political or defensive alliances they formed during the nascent contact period or during the Great Dispersal (1649–1653). They included the Wabanaki (or Northeastern) Confederacy, the New England Confederacies (separated by three dialects: Pequot, Wampanoag, and Narragansett), the Delaware Confederacy (the French called them Loups), the Illinois Confederacy (a group of 12-13 tribes of the upper Mississippi River valley), the Ojibwa (Chippewa, Ottawa, and Cree, or Three Fires) Confederacy, and a loose confederacy of Iroquoian-speakers generally formed around the Huron survivors of the dispersal. In the late decades of the 17th century, a strong alliance of confederated tribes from the Great Lakes region was formed at the instigation and with the continued support of the French. This Algonquian alliance was essentially anti-English and anti-Iroquois, and formed the nemesis of Cooper's protagonists. The Shawnee, sometime allies of the Seneca, were an Eastern Woodland tribe originally pushed from their ancestral land to Ohio by white encroachment. They were also the last to leave their homelands there for Missouri and Oklahoma in 1831.

Among other particulars concerning Native Americans, early European writers attempted to precisely represent Indian speech patterns and language both because of their anthropological interest in the topic and because of the purely practical aspects of improving cross-cultural communications and trade. Yet, the nature of Native American speech made the recording of it difficult. In 1641, John Elliot translated the Bible into the native dialects of Massachusetts and set about teaching the Native Americans to read it. French Jesuit Sabastien Rasles (sometimes spelled Rale') spent more of his life living among the Abenaki than he did in European society. He learned their language and was so trusted by the Indians that he was allowed to speak at their most solemn councils. Cooper attempted to overcome this disability by endowing his Native American characters with a remarkable ability to speak passable English or French.

Most genuine Indian dialects were polysynthetic; that is, many stem words were fused together into one until the thought was transmitted. Sometimes words of 10 to 15 syllables were needed to determine a single thought. This may be illustrated by the Algonquian word *takusar-iartor-uma-galvar-nerpa* (Do you think he really intends to go to look for it?) The phrase is made of several elements: *takusar* (he looks after it), *iartor* (he goes to), *uma* (he intends to), *galvar* (he does so, but), and *nerpa* (do you think?) Such a language, composed of up to 2,000 stem words such as these, has a fathomless number of derivatives. The distribution of Algonquian dialects is uncertain because most of them were scantily or poorly recorded. The language reached out to the Blackfoot, Cheyenne, and Arapaho nations of the Great Plains, and had two widespread geographical vernaculars in the Northeast woodlands.

XXI. Wilderness

It was the Spaniards who first called America a wilderness, a world where civilized man was an alien presence; a world that lacked the control and order common in the Old World from which they had come; and most importantly, a world without the stamp of more than a thousand years of Christianity. One remarkable characteristic of this New World wilderness was the constant presence of the native population. Yet opinion varied among European intellectuals as to whether the natives of North America were children of the devil who might be exterminated and whose land might be appropriated without remorse, or simple heathens whose spiritual salvation was the responsibility of all good Christians. This type of thinking affected Native-European relations to a marked extent.

Beyond the geopolitical boundaries of European claims and counterclaims, of sovereignty and possession, was a frontier of culture, spirituality, and economic exchange. In their frontier outposts, the Dutch, Spanish, French, and English came to take what riches the continent offered. They also came to settle, to build, and to develop the land, but with the less noble desire to own the land and to impose on the New World wilderness their own view of civilization. Many times the native inhabitants were treated with appalling disregard and cruelty. Under the pressure of expanding settlement into their traditional surroundings, the Indian population often relinquished any disputed territory, simply giving way to white encroachment by relocating to an adjoining region. At other times, they fought to hold or regain what was theirs.

The frontier region, which is the focus of this book, was the interface between the older American wilderness and European-style civilization. To the Europeans, it teemed with undomesticated and unfamiliar beasts, and even its indigenous peoples seemed perplexing, uninhibited, and violent. The frontier was both a place and a process. It was not a clear line along which contending cultures collided, but rather a disrupted region in which explorers, traders, missionaries, colonists, and native peoples came into contact and interacted. The frontier population altered the wilderness of North America and planted the seeds of religious, economic, and political change that would sprout over the next two centuries into a young American Republic.

Among these seeds were the weeds of persistent hostility found among Europeans-rooted in deep and genuine religious and political antagonisms formed during the Protestant Reformation. These dominated much of the thinking and politics of many generations of settlers on the colonial frontier. Many early colonists attempted to transplant the emotionalism of the religious and theological controversies raised by the Protestant Reformation in Europe to the colonies in America. The Catholic kingdoms of Europe, which had little success in stopping the Protestant movement that swept their domains in the sixteenth century, were not going to allow "heretics" to infect their holdings in the New World. Protestants held similar antipathetic feelings toward Catholics of all nationalities, distrusted them, and believed that they represented the anti-Christ.

The Spanish found America rich in gold. Yet the search for the fur trade, rather than the search for gold, proved the driving force behind much of the exploration and settlement of North America, and it dramatically altered Native American culture, material possessions, economic activity, and society. It was the abundance of furs in the northeast quadrant of the continent and the almost inexhaustible market for them in Europe that produced some of the most far-reaching changes in North America. In the northeast quarter of the continent the English, Dutch, and French established trading posts in the interior ever nearer to the source of the furs, and here the final struggle for control of the North American continent took place.

While the frontier population viewed Indians as obstacles to progress, potential adversaries, or mere nuisances, they perceived other Europeans (even those of their own nationalities) as competitors vying for the same trade agreements, arable land, and geographically strategic positions. European politics and warfare continually spilled over into the American wilderness, making those who populated the frontier regions dread enemies for no reasons other than those of their rulers many thousands of miles away. Consequently, many colonial governments tried to establish military and economic alliances with the native population. This inadvertently introduced great suffering and unspeakable terror to the frontier experience.

The most enduring and harmonious relationships with the Native American population were formed by the French, who attempted with some success to peacefully coexist with the Indians, living with them, marrying into their families, and converting them to Christianity. However, the native possessors of the land sometimes proved resistant or even aggressive in the defense of their rights. Many attempted to stand their ground and repel the European invaders. This was especially true when native peoples encountered the Spanish, who enslaved them and used them as laborers and beasts of burden everywhere they went. Finally there were the English, who sought to remove the Indians from the land by treaty, contract, bargain, or force. It can be said with some justification that the French embraced the Indians, the Spanish crushed them, and the English displaced them.

XXII. Rangers

Almost all the colonies used rangers. Only Pennsylvania and New York seem to have neglected the establishment of a formal corps of these paid frontiersmen to watch their outlying borders. Of course New York relied on the ubiquitous Mohawk of William Johnson. Robert Rogers raised and commanded the famous Rogers' Rangers that fought for the British during the French and Indian War. This militia unit primarily from New Hampshire also operated in the disputed Lake George and Lake Champlain regions of New York. The pacifists in Pennsylvania absolutely refused to take any steps toward creating military units, even defensive ones. Ultimately the non-Quaker settlers of Pennsylvania paid the price of pacifism with their blood on the western frontiers. Virginia, on the other hand, established a system of paid, mounted rangers of almost 1,000 men.

Over the continued objections of Quakers in the legislature, Benjamin Franklin had tried for eight years to establish volunteer militia companies in Philadelphia (called associators so that the word "militia" would not offend any pacifist sentiments). He even penned a pamphlet — *Plain Truth* — printed in 1747 in both English and German to reach the widest audience. In the autumn of 1755, the violence that militarists and pacifists alike dreaded took on the form of an unremitting terror of Indian attack. With armed colonists displaying the mutilated bodies of victims on the capital steps and frontier families huddling together in their homes in the face of imminent capture, torture, or death, the assembly finally gave in to Franklin's long-standing proposal for an unpaid volunteer force in the form of the colony's first Militia Act.

Edmond Atkin, a prosperous Charleston merchant familiar with the Indians of the southeastern frontiers, was made an Indian agent for the southern colonies by the Board of Trade and asked to submit a plan for the defense of the Carolina borderlands during the troubled times of 1755. One of Atkin's proposals was the creation of an extensive line of forts on the frontier to provide not only safe havens, but also trading posts and warehouses for presents and trade goods for the natives. In combination with these he suggested the formation of two troops of rangers from among "men used to the woods" to be paid by the provincial fund. Two rangers were "to be quartered at all times at each fort, in order to carry expresses. And the rest to be employed ranging on the back of the settlements of the several provinces in such manner as shall be found most convenient for their protection. For which purpose they should carry some dogs with them, the more effectually to discover skulking Indians by their scent. Whereby the Indians will be terrified, and the back settlers rendered quiet and safe in their plantations." His later counterpart for the southern colonies was John Stuart, who served as a militia captain in the Anglo-Cherokee War (1759-1761), and who had been captured by the Cherokee, ransomed, and returned to South Carolina.[309]

The New England colonies established a similar but less extensive system of rangers along their northern borders in the French and Indian War to protect the outlying settlers from the ravages of sudden attack. The best-known group of rangers were those raised by Robert Rogers from among the tough woodsmen of the New Hampshire frontier. Through his mastery of the forests Rogers was to become one of the great romantic legends of the eighteenth century. To make continued long-range penetrations possible, the British high command had previously ordered Rogers to recruit and train six companies of Rangers, nearly a thousand men. It had also called upon him — an unlettered son of the New Hampshire wilderness — to indoctrinate young British officers in the techniques of wilderness fighting. To accomplish this Rogers set up a guerrilla-warfare training school on the shores of Lake George and supplemented on-patrol instruction with a tersely written manual. Rogers' Rangers could rival any Indian war party in ambush, murder, and scalpings. Like chameleons, they combined Indian moccasins and leggings with uniform coats that were sober green in spring and faded to an almost perfectly camouflaged green-yellow by fall. They were seemingly impervious to weather, bivouacking in the snow, silently flashing past French outposts in winter on ice skates, and penetrating their lines on snowshoes.

As word of the Rangers' exploits spread, Rogers became the colonies' most romantic combat hero. Newssheets from Virginia to Maine printed his dispatches verbatim. London print shops blossomed with portraits of Rogers, and every Englishman from royalty to commoner rejoiced in the Rangers' daring accomplishments. Rogers' own hairbreadth escape during the Battle on Snowshoes, fought near Lake George in 1758, caused colonial recruits to flock to him. It soon became evident that no British army, provincial or regular, could move safely through the wilderness without a protective screen of rangers.[310]

Although Rogers' Rangers seem to have provided good service to the British regulars, their status as something between regulars and frontiersmen had drawbacks. Many regular British officers considered rangers chronically unruly, undisciplined, and overpaid. Ironically, these officers seem to have harbored a special resentment against Rogers, who was personable, charming, and a natural leader, simply because he was a provincial officer. British army officers who served in North America during the Seven Years War never tired of reminding one another that the American colonists made the world's worst soldiers.

Rogers' Rangers were important during the colonial period, but they left their mark on American culture as well. The rangers' effective attack on the Abenaki Indian mission at St. Francis in 1759 and their heroic return through the wilderness have become the stuff of novels and of classic cinema and television. The rangers so captured the imagination of Americans that their name was given to the special striking forces of World War II, and Captain Rogers' detailed instructions for his volunteer rangers, written in 1758, still serve as the basis for the irregular tactics used by the Special Forces of the U.S. Army today. Almost exactly 200 years later, *Northwest Passage,* a 26-episode half-hour adventure TV series (1959) about rangers in the French and Indian War, derived its title and the main characters, including Rogers, from the 1937 novel and 1939 film of the same name by author Kenneth Roberts.

Battling on Snowshoes

There were two significant winter encounters between the Rangers and French forces in the region of Lake George. In the winter of 1757, the real Rogers and several companies of his rangers were stationed at Fort William Henry at the southern end of Lake George and at Fort Edward on the landing on the upper Hudson River. Rogers led a scouting expedition from Fort Edward on January 15, stopping at Fort William Henry to acquire provisions, snowshoes, and additional soldiers. The next day, 86 men, among them rangers and provincial troops, headed down the snow-covered frozen surface of Lake George on snowshoes continuing north to Lake Champlain at a point between Fort

Carillon (Ticonderoga) and Fort St. Frédéric (Crown point). On January 21, Rogers sent Lieutenant John Stark and some men to intercept a French supply sled thinking it was alone rather than part of a convoy. Once attacked, the leader of the supply convoy immediately sent word to Carillon of the presence of the Rangers. Concerned that the escaped sleds would raise the alarm, Rogers immediately ordered a return to their last camp.

The French fort, however, sent out a party of about 90 regulars under the command of Capt. de Basserode, accompanied by about 90 Canadian militia and Ottawa Indians. The Indians were under the command of the Métis leader Charles Langlade. Rogers' men then walked into an ambush. Stark, who was bringing up the rear of the ranger column, established a defensive line on a rise that gave covering fire as the rangers retreated to that position. Roger's had establish among his men the concept of a fighting retreat in which half his force retreated some distance in good order while the remainder fired upon the enemy. These then set up a firing line that allowed their comrades to retreat in order through them in turn. This tactic could be kept up for some time. The enemy, observed Rogers, would then be obliged "to pursue you, if they do it at all, in the face of constant fire." In addition outlying rangers should move from high ground to high ground to watch for hostile movement ahead and in the rear. "If the enemy pursue your rear, take a circle till you come to your own tracks and there form an ambush to receive them," he advised. The fight lasted several hours until dark, when neither side could see the other, the men escaping in small groups and ones and twos. The French numbering two to one reported, nonetheless, that they were at a disadvantage, since they were without snowshoes and in snow up to their knees; hence the name of the battle. It is remarkable that the Native forces would have been without snowshoes, however.[311]

This impression from 1884 of the opening attack in the Battle on Snowshoes illustrates the tactics of the Rangers.[312]

On 23 March 1758, a second battle was similarly fought on snowshoes. Rogers led a band of about 180 rangers and regulars out from the ruins of Fort William Henry, which had been destroyed the previous autumn, to scout French positions down the Lake (i.e. North). The French commander at Fort Carillon (Ticonderoga) had been alerted to their movement, and sent a force up the Lake consisting mostly of Indians to meet them. The British scout was originally planned for 400 men, but the commander at Fort Edward (Lt. Colonel William Haviland) had reduced the number to 180, even though he had reason to believe the French knew of the expedition. The French had captured a man (a civilian suttler) from an earlier expedition by Israel Putnam's Connecticut rangers, and it was suspected that he had informed his captors of the British plans.

Haviland had previously clashed with Rogers and incurred the wrath of the ill-tempered provincials, who wanted no part of British discipline, but the Rangers continued as part of his command until the surrender of Montreal in 1760, when Haviland was made a colonel commandant in the Royal Americans (60th Foot). With the rangers in the vanguard, Haviland played a significant role in completing the conquest of Canada. Around this time, Haviland had invented a kind of slide rule "that permitted an officer to quickly determine the number of men to be detached from each company of a regiment, or from a regiment in a larger force, if a draft was made against it, consisting of two circular wheels, one within the other, made of ivory, about three inches across, with useful information on regimental organization etched into the back, which was possibly the first mechanical administrative aide ever invented for officers serving in the field." Called the Haviland, the instrument was being manufactured by Anthony Lamb in London in 1760. It is not known if Haviland's fascination with such administrative matters informed his decisions in the case of Rogers' scout. Certainly the colonel was tinkering with the idea at the time. John Stark noted of Colonel Haviland's decision: "This officer … was one of those sort of men who manage to escape public censure, let them do what they will. He ought to have been cashiered for his conduct on that occasion. He was one of the many British officers who were meanly jealous of the daring achievements of their brave American comrades." [313]

Putnam's earlier reconnaissance had revealed that there was an estimated 600 Indians encamped near Fort Carillon in winter 1758. Haviland considered Rogers force to be sufficient for the reconnaissance. Rogers wrote later: "What could I think to see my party, instead of being strengthened and augmented, reduced to less than one half the number at first proposed? I must confess it appeared to me (ignorant and unskilled as I then was in politicks and the art of war) incomprehensible; but my commander doubtless had his reasons, and is able to vindicate his own conduct." Meanwhile Ensign Oliver de la Durantaye and Ensign Jean-Baptiste de Langry (a.k.a. Langy) had each been sent out with considerable forces of Indians and Canadiens to find Rogers. The two French groups had ultimately joined forces, but Durantaye's company was about 100 yards ahead of Langry's when Rogers' force of 180 men spotted them and opened an ambush. Durantaye's force broke and retreated in disarray. Rogers and about half his men gave chase, critically failing to reload their muskets, while leaving their packs with the others who stopped to collect scalps. The pursuing party of Rangers now fell into an ambush by Langry near a location today known as Roger's Rock, a shear rock face rising from the waters of Lake George north of the present town of Hague and also north of Roger's Rock State Park. [314]

Rogers' descendant, Mary Cochrane Rogers wrote of the encounter in *A Battle Fought on Snow Shoes* (1917):

Once more they began their toilsome march, one division headed by Major Rogers, the other by Captain Buckley; a rivulet at a small distance was on their left, and a steep mountain on their right. They kept well to the mountain, for the Major thought that the enemy would travel on the ice of the rivulet since it was very bad traveling on snowshoes. When they had gone a mile and a half a scout from the front told Rogers that the enemy was approaching on the bed of the frozen stream — ninety-six of them — chiefly savages. The Rangers, concealed by the bank of the rivulet, immediately laid an ambush, gave the first fire and killed above forty Indians whom they scalped on the spot. The rest retreated, followed by about one-half of the Rangers, who were exulting over their victory, only to be suddenly confronted by more than six hundred Canadians and Indians fresh from Fort Ticonderoga, under Durantaye and De Langry, French officers of reputation, who were fully prepared to meet four hundred Rangers, of whose movements they had been apprized both by the prisoner taken and by the deserter from Putnam's men. Rogers ordered a retreat, which he gained at the expense of fifty men killed; the remainder he rallied and drew up in good order.[315]

Short of ammunition because they had removed their packs, the Rangers soon had to fight off their attackers with hatchets, musket butts, and scalping knives. Twice the French tried to outflank the Rangers, but each time they were thwarted by a small reserve that Rogers had cunningly concealed in the trees to his rear. A body of two hundred Indians was discovered ascending a hill on the right, in order to gain the rear of the Rangers. Lieutenant (Henry) Phillips, with eighteen men, reached it before them and drove them back. Phillips and his men, laying aside their snowshoes and putting on skates, had glided down the lake, as an advanced guard. Phillips, ultimately surrounded by the Indians, surrendered under promise of good quarter, but a few minutes later he and his whole party were tied to trees and hacked to death in a most barbarous manner.

Lieutenant Crafton of the Cadet Company, with fifteen men, had been ordered to anticipate a similar movement in another quarter. In the fierce fighting, the British troop was decimated, with more than 120 casualties. Rogers was injured twice during the battle, once to the head and once to the hand, and was said to have saved himself during the fight by jumping from the huge rock face 400 feet into the snow below. The French believed that Rogers was killed in this action, as he was forced to abandon his regimental jacket, which contained his commission papers, during his escape from the scene.[316]

The men, having lost their knapsacks in the initial encounter, passed an extremely cold night, without fire or blankets. Rogers returned to Fort William Henry with only 48 men and six wounded. Reports of casualties among the French were 6 killed and 24 wounded. Reports of Native casualties are so inconsistent as to be meaningless. The French listed Native casualties as ten killed and seventeen wounded. Rogers' report of the event estimated the French-Indian force at 700, with one to two hundred casualties. Most commentators find these statistics dubious, but Rogers certainly spent the remainder of the year rebuilding his corps of Rangers.

As they retreated Rogers had ordered his captives slain so that his men might move more freely. Even France's savage mercenaries were perturbed by the ruthlessness of the Rangers, who often adopted the Indians' custom of hatcheting and scalping prisoners. Being "behind enemy lines" Rogers considered this legitimate under the laws of warfare.

Yet this was not his finest hour. In this case Rogers seems to have violated his own *Rules for Rangers* (No. 5): "If you have the good fortune to take any prisoners, keep them separate, till they are examined, and in your return take a different route from that in which you went out, that you may the better discover any party in your rear, and have an opportunity, if their strength be superior to yours, to alter your course, or disperse, as circumstances may require."

In the *Narrative of Ranger Private Thomas Brown* (1760), in which Captain Rogers is referred to by his later rank of Major, Brown describes the ambush and some of the horrors of the fight. It is a wonder that Private Brown survived his ordeal:

> The Major thought it best to return to Fort William Henry in the same path we came, the snow being very deep. We marched in an Indian file and kept the prisoners in the rear, lest we should be attacked. We proceeded in this order about a mile and a half, and as we were ascending a hill, and the center of our men were at the top. The French, to the number of 400 [sic] besides 30 or 40 Indians, fired on us before we discovered them. The Major ordered us to advance.
>
> I received a wound from the enemy (the first shot they made on us) through the body, upon which I retired into the rear, to the prisoner I had taken on the lake, knocked him on the head and killed him, lest he should escape and give information to the enemy.
>
> As I was going to place myself behind a large rock, there started up an Indian from the other side. I threw myself backward into the snow and it being very deep, sunk so low that I broke my snowshoes (I had time to pull them off, but was obliged to let my shoes go with them). One Indian threw his Tomahawk at me, and another was just upon seizing me; but I happily escaped and got into the center of our men, and fixed myself behind a large Pine, where I loaded and fired at every opportunity. After I had discharged 6 or 7 times, there came a ball and cut off my gun just at the lock. About half an hour after, I received a shot in my knee. I crawled again into the rear, and as I was turning about received a shot in my shoulder.
>
> The engagement held, as near as I could guess 5 1/2 hours, and as I learned after I was taken, we killed more of the enemy than we were in number. By this time it grew dark and the firing ceased on both sides, and as we were so few the Major took the advantage of the night and escaped with his well men, without informing the wounded of his design, lest they should inform the enemy and they should pursue him before he had got out of their reach.[317]

An officer later captured by the French, quoted by Mary Cochrane Rogers and recorded in *Journals of Major Robert Rogers* (London: 1765), noted in a long letter to the commandant of Fort Edward in 1758:

> I shall not be particular; only to do this justice to those who lost their lives there, and to those who have escaped, to assure you, Sir, that such dispositions were formed by the enemy (who discovered us long before), it was impossible for a party so weak as ours to hope for even a retreat. Towards the conclusion of the affair, it was cried from a rising ground on our right, to retire there; where, after scrambling with difficulty, as I was unaccustomed to snow-shoes, I found Capt. Rogers, and told him that I saw to retire further was impossible, therefore

earnestly begged we might collect all the men left, and make a stand there. Mr. ——, who was with him, was of my opinion, and Capt. Rogers also; who therefore desired me to maintain one side of the hill, whilst he defended the other. Our parties did not exceed above ten or twelve in each, and mine was shifting towards the mountain, leaving me unable to defend my post, or to labor with them up the hill. In the meantime, Capt. Rogers with his party came to me, and said (as did those with him) that a large body of Indians had ascended to our right; he likewise added, what was true, that the combat was very unequal, that I must retire, and he would give Mr. —— and me a Sergeant to conduct us thro' the mountain. No doubt prudence required us to accept his offer; but, besides one of my snow-shoes being untied, I knew myself unable to march as fast as was requisite to avoid becoming a sacrifice to an enemy we could no longer oppose; I therefore begged of him to proceed, and then leaned against a rock in the path, determined to submit to a fate I thought unavoidable.[318]

Wounded prisoners were not always so lucky, with Capt. Spikeman of the Rangers scalped alive. Rogers himself was originally reported to have been killed. One group of Rangers surrendered, only to be killed and scalped when a scalp was discovered in a pocket of one of the men. Accounts of these battles are found in Burt Loescher, *The History of Rogers' Rangers*, in Francis Parkman's classic *Montcalm and Wolfe*, and in Lawrence Henry Gipson's *The Great War for the Empire: The Victorious Years, 1758-1760*, as well as in John Cuneo's biography, *Robert Rogers of the Rangers*.

Raid on St. Francis in 1759

Excavations of archeological sites known to have been Jesuit missions to the Native tribes in New York and New England have turned up brass rings and silver or brass crucifixes that were handed out by the missionaries among the Indians. Although the Jesuits felt that these items helped them win converts, it is quite certain that many native Americans wore these tokens as mere decorations, not knowing their religious meaning and regarding them as any other amulet or charm. Similarly the Indians often believed that the priests, by "throwing water upon [their] heads," subjected them to the will of the governor of Canada and exercised a special spiritual power over them.

New Englanders dismissed the French missionary activity as mere subversion of native allegiance and displayed little understanding of the dedication of the Jesuits to the conversion of souls. It was widely believed by the English settlers – and not without supporting evidence – that the Jesuits of New France actively incited the Indians against the English frontier settlements because of their Protestantism. The missionaries were accused of bringing presents of powder, ball, and guns to the tribes and of announcing the support of the French government for their raids. The French civil authorities viewed the Jesuit missions as the equivalent of outposts guarding the main avenues to New France. In fact, most were situated just far enough from the border of English settlement to make it difficult for the English to attack them by surprise.

There were a number of the villages composed of native American converts to Catholicism well located to serve this purpose. The earliest Catholic mission in what was to become New England was founded in 1613 on Desert Mountain Island, Maine. This was almost immediately destroyed by Englishmen, and the priests were carried off to Virginia. Two important Abenaki missions were located at Penobscot (1633) on the

Maine coast and Norridgewock (1646) on the Kennebec River. Both villages supported missions kept by the Jesuit fathers. Penobscot was one of the farthest outposts of the French influence at the end of the seventeenth century. Abenaki villages were also located at Trois Rivieres, and on the St. Francis River.

St. Francis was a particularly active launch point for war parties planning attacks on the English settlements, as the river opened a practical route by canoe to the New England border. Many of the Abenaki of Maine removed themselves to the St. Francis mission of Father Jacques Bigot as early as 1683, making it one of the most successful strongholds of Catholic Indians in New France. The mission housed, besides the Abenaki, a large number of related Algonquin Indians who were refugees from King Philip's War (1675) in New England, and a smaller population of Christian Caughnawaga Indians of Iroquoian lineage. A great deal of intermarriage had taken place among the Algonquian refugees and the Abenaki. The inhabitants of St. Francis soon acquired among the English a reputation as devout Catholics and unshakable allies of the French. This flourishing mission was attacked in 1759 by a force of rangers under the command of Colonel Robert Rogers and completely destroyed. Its church with all its records were burned and an estimated 200 warriors were killed.

On the morning of October 4, 1759 after a careful and undetected approach to the mission, Rogers and about 140 men entered the village, slaughtered many of the inhabitants where they lay, shot down many who attempted to flee, and then burned the village. Rogers reported killing as many as 300 people, while French reports placed the number closer to thirty, mainly women and children. One of Rogers' men was killed, and seven were wounded.

Lord Jeffrey Amherst's orders to Rogers had included the following: "Remember the barbarities that have been committed by the enemy's Indian scoundrels on every occasion, where they had an opportunity of showing their infamous cruelties on the King's subjects, which they have done without mercy. Take your revenge, but don't forget ... it is my orders that no women or children are killed or hurt." The village itself was eventually rebuilt.[319]

The journals of the retreat of the expedition from French controlled territory provide only a fragmented picture of what occurred to those of Rogers' force as they eluded the pursuit. The journal kept by Rogers was relatively terse concerning the trek to the Connecticut River over steep mountains and through swamps. Clearly the march was attended with terrible fatigue and hunger. The men reported eating bark, roots, mushrooms, and fragments of flesh from animal skins. Robert Kirkwood supposedly told how Rogers killed one of the prisoners, an Indian woman, butchered the remains, and divided them among his men. Another widely reported account of cannibalism (by Lieutenant George Campbell) suggested that his party of men came upon the previously scalped remains of a woman trapped among the logs on a small river. The reports of cannibalism seem extreme, as an English army officer, Thomas Mante, who proved to be spy in the pay of the French government recorded them. The British probably knew of Mante's role as a double agent. In 1774, they finally ceased to pay him.[320]

After nine days of difficult travel, the group led by Rogers reached the appointed rendezvous, but no food or aid was to be found. Rogers took the disappointment in stride, and leaving most of his emaciated company behind, he and three men descended the Connecticut River on rafts to Fort Number Four. He was reportedly barely able to walk.

Supplies were immediately dispatched upriver. Rogers and his men were treated as heroes. The *New Hampshire Gazette* published the exploits and raised Rogers' popularity, even while he still worried about the fate of all of his men. Once in London in 1764, Rogers added new luster to his reputation with the publication of his military *Journals* and *A Concise Account of North America*. Both books were highly successful, but the *Concise Account* had a special appeal for the British public, because it described regions of the continent previously occupied by the French. There is little doubt that Rogers used this audience to forward his pet project: an expedition to discover a northwest passage through the Great Lakes of America to China. For the cost of £32,000 he proposed to lead an expedition on a three-year trek to the Pacific. Although the king favored the project, he judged it too expensive. Instead, he appointed Rogers the first royal governor of Fort Michillimackinac at the salary of £183 a year. In the following months, however, the subtle and devious pressures brought to bear by Thomas Gage and William Johnson were too much for Rogers. Preoccupied with paying off his enormous debts, Rogers took little interest in the Revolution, but aligned himself with the Loyalists. He sailed to New York, only to be captured by an American privateer and incarcerated, this time as a prisoner of war. "He returned to London with the defeated British armies to live out the remainder of his days in a haze of alcoholic penury."[321]

On the Pennsylvania frontier where he had settled and was determined to live, John Brady was among those who joined the provincial forces as a ranger to battle the Indian marauders. On 18 April 1760, Brady received his first commission as Ensign. He fought until the Peace of 1763. However, the Indian threat on the frontier did not end with the end of the French and Indian War. In 1764, Pontiac's War began where the French and Indian War had left off. The Ottawa leader Pontiac persuaded the tribes, which had been the French allies, to unite to continue battling the British. John Brady was commissioned as a Captain in the Second Battalion of the Pennsylvania Regiments. He actively fought against the Indian forces that were attacking and killing many frontier families in Bedford and Cumberland Counties, Pennsylvania.

Captain Samuel Brady, John's son, had been with an independent militia engaged in the battles of the revolution in New York and New Jersey, but had earned his name as a scout in the Ohio country under Daniel Brodhead and "Mad" Anthony Wayne. Brady's Rangers often found themselves in extremely dangerous situations deep in Indian land. Indians had murdered Sam Brady's father and a brother. Sam Brady acquired a reputation of near mythical proportions from his many exploits against the Indians. His jumps across streams when pursued are legendary. One took place near Kent State University in Ohio and is now memorialized by a bronze plaque. A second jump over a stream in Pennsylvania was measured and said to have been 23 feet from bank to bank. Considering these jumps were made carrying a rifle, bullet and powder bag, tomahawk and knife, they were remarkable and exemplify a superior physical prowess.

The Brady homestead was perilously close to the leading edge of the frontier of that time, the Susquehanna River. Samuel's Scotch Irish maternal grandfather, James Quigley, came to America from Ireland in 1730. He settled on 400 acres of frontier land, in what is today, Hopewell Township. The Indians dominated the other side of the Susquehanna. The Indians resisted settler encroachment on their territory by routinely crossing the Susquehanna to raid the settlers. The settlers just as routinely crossed the Susquehanna to pursue the raiding war parties to retaliate and sometimes to rescue captives taken by the

Indians during these raids. In this ongoing skirmishing, both sides committed unspeakable atrocities on the other, which drove a long-lasting cycle of revenge for revenge brutalities between the settlers and Indians.

No family of pioneers was more conspicuous in the early history and settlement of the country than the Brady's. Both John Brady and his son Sam have been identified as models for Cooper's character Natty Bumppo. These are sometimes joined to other legendary Indian fighters. Two of these were Peter and Wendell Grove, whose father and brother were also murdered by Indian terrorist bands. Thomas Bevington obviously was an excellent rifleman, as he was selected to serve in one of three elite detachments placed under Colonel Daniel Morgan. All 578 of the latter were frontiersman, and were needed to prevent the Indians from ambushing the opposing American forces. To their fellow soldiers these men were sometimes known as "Long Shirts," as they were issued a long, fringed hunting shirt.[322]

Forting Up

While the colonial authorities in the coastal cities made plans to take the war to the French by attacking Acadia, Montreal, or Quebec, the initial response of the frontier population to unsettled conditions in the border regions was to "fort up." On the frontier a distinct type of structure evolved to meet the needs of the various communities for protection against human enemies. These local safe-havens became known as garrison houses, stronghouses, blockhouses, and sometimes (euphemistically) forts. The design and use of these structures was often a balance of unwarranted fear and misplaced optimism, of strategy and counterstrategy, and of isolation and community effort.

The colonists seem to have used many terms interchangeably when speaking or writing about them, but the term blockhouse seems to have been saved for a square structure of strongly laid-up logs or timbers with a second floor overhanging the first. The door, if located on the first floor, was heavily barred; if on the second floor, it was accessed by a ladder, hinged at the sill of the door, which could be pulled up like a drawbridge. Walls built of timber, with gates securely bolted and barred at night, usually surrounded blockhouses; families whose homes were not considered defensible slept in blockhouses in times of crisis. In the morning, if all was safe, they went back to their own houses again. Blockhouses were also incorporated into military strong points within or near a fort.

Another answer that evolved to address the need for a secure local retreat was the garrison house. In each settlement enclave one or two stoutly built houses would be chosen as sites for refuge and local defense. Most of these were private residences given over to the public defense in times of crisis. Examples are DePuey's Fort, a stone building surrounded by a stick-pole stockade located at Shawnee in Pennsylvania, the Old Stone Church in Schoharie, New York, and the group of reconstructed timber garrison houses at Charlestown, New Hampshire, known as Fort No. 4.

Garrison houses were often built of thick wood, either round logs or squared timbers, as this was the most convenient and abundant material available. Buildings laid up in field stone and mortar, or of dressed blocks of limestone, sandstone, or granite, were less frequent but infinitely more defensible against fire. For the same reasons slate roofs were desirable, but wood shingles were more common. In any case, the roof of a garrison house was usually lightly built, but the attic floor was constructed of strong timbers covered with a thick layer of sand or ashes. This ingenious strategy allowed the attic to act as a fire stop for the rest of the building if the roof was fired. Garrison houses could be of one or two stories, and it was not uncommon for the second floor to overhang the first. This allowed the defender to shoot down along the wall of the first floor or to pour water on brushfires laid up against the sides of the building.

One necessary characteristic of a good garrison house was a well or large cistern inside the house, or one that was easily accessible by the defenders if outside. The stone trading post built by the French at Fort Niagara had an internal well, even though the entire volume of Lake Ontario was no more than twenty feet from the door. This allowed the defenders access to water for drinking and firefighting without exposing themselves to attack. As the Indians lacked artillery and relied on fire as their primary means of reducing defensive structures, such an arrangement almost certainly allowed the defenders to outwait all but the most determined siege. Public funds were often appropriated for the fortification of private residences in times of impending crisis. In 1754, Virginia voted funds to build several military posts and to fortify with stockades several garrison houses. At the same time Benjamin Franklin and his supporters were able to press the Quakers in the General Assembly to fund a series of improvements to preexisting garrison houses along the Delaware and Susquehanna Rivers. These forts, actually little more than stockaded homes, were about ten miles apart, allowing settlers to flee in times of unrest. They were useless in a sudden attack.

When planning an attack the enemy usually intended to throw the entire weight of their force on an unsuspecting village and allow terror and confusion to do the rest. The best time for such an attack proved to be at dawn when the inhabitants were first stirring and getting about their chores. A number of circumstances could combine to foil this strategy. The most common of these was that the village had been placed on alert either by a warning from the patrolling rangers or by a chance sighting of the enemy before they were able to ready their attack.

The enemy's presence could be given away quite accidentally by the scattering of wildlife, cattle, and hogs from the woods as they were frightened by large groups of men pushing forward toward the village. Additionally, the eagerness of some of the Indian scouts, in particular, to waylay the first inhabitants with whom they came in contact, raising a scalping halloo (battle cries) and firing upon the terrorized settlers, often served as a first warning to the rest of the village. It was important for survival on the frontier that settlers learn to act upon these implicit warnings immediately. If the attack was truly sudden, or if the unsuspecting settlers were busy in the fields, they might be forced to literally run from their homes for the refuge hoping that the marauding band would not cut them off. The few who did so owed their safety to fleetness of foot.

Undefended houses were easily taken, but the assailants usually met with a rough reception at the garrisons or the blockhouses. However, being in the blockhouse was not a guarantee of safety. In the village of Dover, New Hampshire, the colonists had built five blockhouses, distributed so that the villagers could reach them with little trouble. On the evening of 27 June 1689, all five were considered impregnable, and the inhabitants went peacefully to their beds inside at the usual early hour. Secure in the strength of their barred doors, but mainly because it was raining, they failed to set even one sentinel over the village. However, the town had been under the surveillance of a band of Indians raiding from the Androscoggin and Kennebec Rivers for some days. By morning, all but one blockhouse had been taken either by guile or direct attack during the night. After a stout defense the final blockhouse surrendered rather than watch their fellows, now captives, dispatched before their eyes. Twenty-three persons were killed, twenty-nine more were taken captive, and half a dozen houses and some mills were burned.

According to their diaries and journals, the English seem to have been easily convinced of their inability to withstand a determined attack, and they were often more willing to surrender to groups of assailants led by French officers than to those composed of only native warriors. However, the Frenchmen, often outnumbered by their Indian allies and practically unable to check their vengeance for the losses accumulated in the assault, sometimes allowed the terms of a surrender to be "shamefully violated." Instead of finding the promised protection of the French, the survivors were often "abandoned to the fury of the Indians." At Casco Bay, for instance, the defenders held out for four days before surrendering to the French officers in charge. Following the capitulation, the French simply stood by while the Indians killed more than 100 English of all ages from among the captives.

XXIII. Captivity Narratives

It has been estimated that one in eleven of frontier farmsteads were attacked and "burned out" during the struggle for control of North America. Certainly captives could be made anywhere. Because of the competition and proximity between Montreal and Quebec in New France and the most populous English settlements in North America, the French and their Indian allies most frequently took colonists in New England captive. Conservative estimates run into the thousands of persons, many of them women and children. Traditionally, historians have made limited use of certain captivity narratives, which were regarded as racist propaganda. They have regarded the genre with suspicion because of its ideological underpinnings. Nonetheless, the narratives provided the excitement of escapist literature. American captivity narratives were usually based on true events, but they frequently contained fictional elements as well. Ann Eliza Bleecker's novel, *The History of Maria Kittle* (1793), is considered the first captivity novel.

Perhaps the most famous of what have come to be known as the captivity narratives is Captain John Smith's *General Historie* (1624). One of the earliest accounts, this was written for a European audience. Like similar works it offered its readers firsthand information, if sometimes distorted, about the Native American tribes (Indians) in the New World. More significant in a literary sense, however, were the numerous accounts of captivity, written mainly by or about Puritan and Quaker women that persisted well into the first quarter of the nineteenth century. These writings were as much spiritual autobiographies as descriptions of extraordinary events experienced by ordinary people. They often described journeys of religious salvation through suffering and despair with nothing more than one's saving faith. They epitomized the spiritual trial and redemption theme, which reinforced certain religious beliefs seeking signs of Providence at work in the world. They were widely read during the 18th and 19th centuries.

Mary Rowlandson's captivity narrative, *The Sovereignty and Goodness of God, Together with the Faithfulness of His Presence Displayed* (1682), was the second of only four works by women authors published in seventeenth-century New England and went through four editions. Prominent clergyman Increase Mather saw the value of attaching a providential meaning to the captivity and redemption experience and included an account of Mary's ordeal in his own *Essay for the Recording of Illustrious Providences* (1684). Other popular captivity narratives from the late 17th century include Cotton Mather's *The Captivity of Hannah Dustin* (1696–97), a famous captivity narrative set during King William's War, and Jonathan Dickinson's *God's Protecting Providence* (1699). Rev. John Williams' *The Redeemed Captive Returning to Zion* (1707), like other narratives of this time, seemed almost to be a spiritual allegory of divine favor, but it included a clear condemnation of Roman Catholicism. The theme of providential intervention was often heightened by the religious titles of these works. Elizabeth Hanson's Quaker narrative, *God's Mercy Surmounting Man's Cruelty* (1728) continued in the footsteps of Rowlandson and Williams. Each of these was popular at the time of their first printing and each was reissued during the Antebellum Period — Williams' work having six editions in the 19th century. As such they formed a connection between the First Great Awakening and the religious revival of the Second.

By the 19th century, captivity narratives had become more secular. The stories became more a recounting of an extraordinary experience. They also, at times, became a vehicle for spreading propaganda against the Indians who were perceived as the enemy at the time. Naturally, these accounts also must be read through the possibly jaundiced eye of the writer, whose position was seldom that of ethnographer and who may have easily misinterpreted or misunderstood the actions of his or her captors. Those accounts in which white captives came to prefer and eventually adopt a Native American way of life — and there were many — challenged the general antebellum assumption concerning the superiority of white culture. Keeping in mind the purpose for which they were written, however, these accounts can provide a good deal of insight into the Antebellum Period. Some of the more popular narratives from the period are:

—John R. Jewitt (1803-1805), *A Narrative of the Adventures and Sufferings of John R. Jewitt,* the only survivor of the crew of the ship *Boston,* during a captivity of nearly three years among the natives of Nootka Sound, also known as King George's Sound, British Columbia.

—Robert Adams (1816), *The Narrative of Robert Adams,* an American sailor who survived shipwreck off the Barbary Coast of North Africa and was held a slave under brutal conditions by "Moorish" pirates.

—John Ingles (1824), *The Story of Mary Draper Ingles and Son Thomas Ingles,* abducted by Indians and later escaped. Mary (whose child was murdered) made a harrowing trek over hundreds of miles of rough terrain to return home after killing her abductors.

—Mary Jemison (1824), *A Narrative of the Life of Mrs. Mary Jemison.* An American teen captured by the Senaca, Jemison married and remained with them in western New York.

—John Tanner (1830) *A Narrative of the captivity and adventures of John Tanner,* thirty years of residence among the Indians. Captured by the Shawnee in present-day Kentucky at age ten, Tanner grew up among the Ojibwa nation, becoming fully acculturated and learning their language. He married an Indian woman, guided Europeans in the Northwest, and worked as an interpreter at fur trading posts.

—Rachel Plummer (1838), *Rachael Plummer's Narrative of Twenty One Months Servitude as a Prisoner Among the Commanchee Indians.* An Anglo-Texan woman of Scots-Irish descent, she was kidnapped at the age of seventeen, along with her son. This was the first narrative about a captive of Indians published in the Republic of Texas, and it was a sensation not just there, but in the United States and even abroad.

—Sarah Ann Horn (1839), *A Narrative of the Captivity of Mrs. Horn, and Her Two Children, with Mrs. Harris, held captive by the Camanche Indians.* Having immigrated from England in 1833, Horn, her husband and two sons were attacked near Loredo. She was held for 15 months and never again saw her family.

—Olive Ann Oatman Fairchild (1858), *The Captivity of the Oatman Girls Among the Apache and Mohave Indians.* The sisters captured by Apache in Arizona in 1851, were then sold to Mojave Indians. Mary died in captivity, reportedly of abuse and starvation. Olive was ransomed in 1856. The book, written by Rev. Royal B. Stratton, sold 30,000 copies, a best-seller for that era. It remained in print continuously until 1903.

—Matthew Brayton (1860), *The Indian Captive, A Narrative of the Adventures and Sufferings of Matthew Brayton in His Thirty-Four Years of Captivity Among the Indians of North-Western America.* Brayton was seven years old when he was captured by Wyandotte warriors from his father's farm in northern Ohio, and he endured thirty-four years in captivity before returning to his family in 1859. He spent most of his captivity with tribes in northwestern Canada and Alaska. In 1862, he enlisted in the Michigan Cavalry Brigade and fought in America's Civil War. He died in battle at Murfreesboro, Tennessee and is buried in Stones River National Cemetery.

These captivity narratives were often used as part of the culture's definition of what a "proper woman" should be and do when captured, which usually insinuated some form of suicide, especially if she became pregnant. Women were depicted as outside their normal gender roles under such circumstances, creating surprise and even shock in the reader. There were salacious hints of improper sexual treatment, forced marriage, or rape. The captivity stories also perpetuated stereotypes that were part of the on-going conflict between these native groups as the settlers moved westward. In a society in which men were expected to be the protectors of women, the kidnapping of women was viewed as an attack on and affront to the males in the society, as well.

In 1956, John Ford directed the Hollywood film, *The Searchers*, a drama about a man's search for his niece, his dead brother's daughter who as a child was taken captive by the Comanche in the West. Starring John Wayne and Jeffrey Hunter, the film based on the 1954 novel by Alan Le May was primarily about their search rather than her captivity. It was influential because of the multiple psychological layers seen in the character portrayals and the fact that it attacked many of the stereotypes of the former century through the interaction of Wayne's with Hunter's character, a loyal foster brother of the missing girl. Some critics view it as Wayne's best work in the western film genre. It was named the greatest American western by the American Film Institute in 2008. The Writers Guild of America ranks Frank S. Nugent's screenplay for *The Searchers* among the top 101 screenplays of all time. Nugent wrote screenplays for several more of Ford's westerns including *3 Godfathers*, *She Wore a Yellow Ribbon*, *Wagon Master,* and *Fort Apache*. Nugent has been credited with providing Ford with more sophisticated male-female relationships than his other scripts and tempering the racism so endemic to the western genre's portrayal of Indians.

Several film historians have suggested that *The Searchers* was inspired by the actual 1836 kidnapping of nine-year-old Cynthia Ann Parker by the Comanche. She spent 24 years with the tribe, married a war chief, and had three children one of which was the leader known as Quanah Parker. Cynthia was rescued against her will by Texas Rangers in 1860. She had difficulty in understanding her status as having been redeemed from a life among the savages, and spent the remaining 10 years of her life refusing to adjust to life in white society. James W. Parker, her uncle, spent much of his life and fortune in what became an obsessive search for his niece, just like Ethan Edwards in the film. Quanah Parker was designated the chief of the Comanche by the federal government and was one of the founders of the Native American Church movement of the 1880s, which employed *peyote* in its prayer rituals.

About the Author

A hardened and shameless scribbler of historic nonsense, who for more than thirty years has taken his meals in front of his laptop, astride his saddle, or beside the campfire.

James M. Volo, PhD. has been teaching science and writing history for almost five decades. He is a widely published historian of daily life and military topics, and a physics professor with a curiosity concerning the military sciences in which he has a Masters degree. Dr. Volo was chosen to be a contributor to the 150th anniversary Essential Civil War Curriculum Project (2013). He is the author of several reference works regarding military, social, and cultural history, and has served as an historical consultant for TV and cinema productions including the PBS production *Liberty! The American Revolution* (1997), the A&E TV miniseries *The American Revolution* (1994), and the Universal Pictures movie *Sweet Liberty* (1986). An avid horseman and horse owner, he has appeared in a number of Civil War productions. He was featured in the *New York Times* (31 March 1991) for his article "Slavery in Connecticut" done for the National Endowment for the Humanities, and he hosted a segment on the C-SPAN TV series *Democracy in America, the Alex De Tocqueville Special* (1997-1998). Among his three dozen full-length published works are *The Boston Tea Party, Foundations of Revolution* (2012), *Daily Life in Native America* (2007), *Blue Water Patriots: The American Revolution Afloat* (2006), *Daily Life in Civil War America* (1998, 2010), *Family Life in the 19th Century* (2007), the *Popular Culture of the Antebellum Period* (2004), *Daily Life During the American Revolution* (2003), *Daily Life on the Old Colonial Frontier* (2002), *Daily Life in the Age of Sail* (2001), and the *Encyclopedia of the Antebellum South* (2000). Several of these are co-authored with his wife Dorothy Denneen Volo, PhD. He is presently teaching at Sacred Heart University in Fairfield, Connecticut. This volume is part of the **Traditional American History Series** begun in 2013 that concerns the history of American liberties and American Exceptionalism. "We can only hope that other historians carry on this kind of valuable research and writing." - The Journal of Southern History

Citations

[1] The Adirondack Mountains in New York are sometimes considered part of the Appalachian chain but, geologically speaking, they are a southern extension of the Laurentian Mountains of Canada.

[2] James Fenimore Cooper, The Last of the Mohicans, Introduction.

[3] James Fenimore Cooper, The Last of the Mohicans, Chapter 3.

[4] See Robert E. Ritzenthaler and Pat Ritzenthaler, The Woodland Indians of the Western Great Lakes (Garden City, NY: The Natural History Press, 1970), 18. See also: Timothy B. Wheeler, (8 May 2015). "Once nearly wiped out, shad stage an uneven comeback in the Chesapeake Bay." *Baltimore Sun*. URL: baltimoresun.com.

[5] Letter of Daniel Brodhead to Major General John Sullivan, August 6, 1779; reported in Frederick Cook, Journals of the Military Expedition of Major General John Sullivan Against the Six Nations of Indians in 1779 with Records of the Centennial Celebrations (Auburn, NY: Knapp, Peck & Thompson, 1887), 307.

[6] Stanley Vestal, King of the Fur Traders, The Deeds and Deviltry of Pierre Esprit Radisson (Boston: Houghton Mifflin, 1940), 98–99.

[7] John Charles Phillip Von Krafft, Journal of Lieutenant Von Krafft (New York: Arno Press, 1968) 103.

[8] Rien Aerts, (1995). "The advantages of being evergreen." *Trends in Ecology & Evolution* 10 (10): 402–407.

[9] James Fenimore Cooper. Pathfinder; or, the Inland Sea (Kindle Locations 190-193).

[10] Ibid.

[11] Quoted in George T. Hunt, The Wars of the Iroquois, A Study in Intertribal Trade Relations (Madison: University of Wisconsin Press, 1972), 63.

[12] Richard White, The Middle Ground, Indians, Empires, and Republics in the Great Lakes Region, 1650–1815 (New York: Cambridge University Press, 1991), 105-106. See also Clarence M. Burton, ed., The City of Detroit, Michigan, 1701-1922, (n.p.: The S. J. Clarke Publishing Company, 1922), 49.

[13] Scott Manning Stevens, "The Historiography of New France and the Legacy of Iroquois Internationalism." *Comparative American Studies* (2013) **11** (2): 148–165.

[14] Evan T. Pritchard, No Word For Time, The Way of the Algonquian People (Tulsa: Council Oaks Books, 1997), 11–12.

[15] The six were Sasquesahanough, Quadroque, Attaock, Tesinigh, Utchowig, and Cepowig. Proceedings of the Council of Maryland for 1636-1667, pp. 421, 550.

[16] Pages and Pictures from the Writings of James Fenimore Cooper, *with Notes by Susan Fenimore Cooper* (New York: W.A. Townsend and Co., 1861), Introduction.

[17] See James Fenimore Cooper, Second Preface to *The Deerslayer* (1850). URL: http://pinkmonkey.com/dl/library1/book0619.pdf

[18] James Grossman, *James Fenimore Cooper* (Stanford: Stanford University Press, 1949), 24.

[19] Leslie A. Fielder, "James Fenimore Cooper: The Problem of the Good Bad Writer," (1997). Cooper Seminar at the State University of New York College at Oneonta (SUNY Oneonta). URL: http://www.oneonta.edu/~cooper/articles/suny/1979suny-fiedler.html

20   Allan W. Eckert, *The Frontiersmen* (Winning of America Book 1) (p. 44-45). Jesse Stuart Foundation. Kindle Edition.
21   See cooper's preface to the 1832 edition.
22   D.H. Lawrence, "Studies in Classic American Literature" in <u>The Shock of Recognition</u>. ed. Edmund Wilson. New York: Doubleday, 1943.
23   Mircea Eliade, *The Sacred And The Profane: The Nature Of Religion*, trans. Willard R. Trask (New York: Harcourt, Brace & World, 1959), 148. Original computer graphic by J.M. Volo.
24   Sidney Smith, "Who Reads an American Book?" Great Epochs in American History. URL: http://www.usgennet.org/usa/topic/preservation/epochs/vol5/pg144.htm
25   James Fenimore Cooper, <u>The Pioneers</u> (Albany: State University of New York Press, 1980), 291-94.
26   "Historical Introduction," <u>The Red Rover, A Tale</u>, ed. Thomas and Marianne Philbrick (Albany: State University of New York Press, 1991), xvi-xix.
27   The tavern belonged to Stewart Lewis. James Fenimore Cooper, <u>The Letters and Journals of James Fenimore Cooper</u>, ed. James Franklin Beard (Cambridge: Harvard Univ. Press, Belknap Press, 1960), 1:16.
28   David Herlihy, <u>The Black Death and the Transformation of the West</u> (Cambridge: Harvard University Press, 1997), 10.
29   Eckert, *The Frontiersmen*, 120.
30   Susan Fenimore Cooper, <u>Small Family Memories</u> URL: http://www.oneonta.edu/external/cooper/biographic/memories/1883susan.html
31   Susan Fenimore Cooper, <u>Small Family Memories</u> URL: http://www.oneonta.edu/external/cooper/biographic/memories/1883susan.html
32 The University of Pennsylvania Library holds something like 1,110 English novels from the period, the University of Illinois approximately 1,000, and the University of Virginia about 1,200. See Julie Shaffer.
33   Barbara Sicherman, <u>Well Read Lives: How Books Inspired A Generation of American Women</u> (Chapel Hill: The University of North Carolina Press, 2010), 34.
34   Dorinda Outram, *The Enlightenment* (Cambridge University Press, 1995), p. 24.
35   Franz Potter, "Writing for the Spectre of Poverty, Exhuming Sarah Wilkinson's Bluebooks and Novels," URL: http://www.romtext.org.uk/articles/cc11_n02/
36   See <u>Letters for Literary Ladies</u> URL: http://digital.library.upenn.edu/women/edgeworth/ladies/ladies.html#letter-4
37   Jane Austen, *Northanger Abbey*. Great Literature Online. 1997-2013 URL: http://www.classicauthors.net/austen/northanger/northanger5.html
38   Susan Fenimore Cooper, <u>Small Family Memories</u> URL: http://www.oneonta.edu/external/cooper/biographic/memories/1883susan.html
39   J. Thomas Scharf, <u>History of Westchester County, New York</u> (1886), Kindle Location 4211.
40   See Beard, op cit, 332. See also Cooper *Hunt's Merchants' Magazine*, I (July, 1839), 2.
41   Page Smith, <u>The Nation Comes of Age</u>, vol. 4 (New York: McGraw-Hill Book Co., 1981), 783–784.
42   William Cecil Headrick, "A Study of Social Stratification With Reference to

Social Class Barriers and Social Class Rigidity" (1941). URL: http://www.thehistorybox.com/ny_city/society/printerfriendly/nycity_society_colonial_rigidities_article0002.htm

[43] George Peter Murdock, *Social Structure* (London: The Free Press, 1949), 102. Available on line. URL: http://www.archive.org/stream/socialstructurem00murd/socialstructurem00murd_djvu.txt

[44] J. Thomas Scharf, History of Westchester County, New York (1886), 91.

[45] Much of the Cooper estate had been part of an earlier grant to the Bayard family. When Nicholas Bayard chartered his purchased land, the original 4000 acres suddenly and fraudulently became a tract forty miles long and thirty miles broad on both sides of the Schoharie Creek, some 768,000 acres! Queen Anne later granted the same land to a colony of Palatine settlers, who moved to the Schoharie valley in 1713 and were promptly challenged by Bayard's heirs. Unable to prevail against the settlers the Bayards sold the land to the "Seven Partners" who eventually managed to force the Palatine settlers to pay quitrents or leave the land.

[46] Harry Edward Miller, "The Spy on Neutral Ground." *The New England Magazine* (1898), 18.

[47] Dorothy Denneen Volo and James M. Volo. Daily Life During the American Revolution (p. 209). Kindle Edition.

[48] There is no known connection between the Morris family of Morrisania and several other well-known Morris families in America, as that of Robert Morris, the financier of the American Revolution, of Anthony Morris of Philadelphia, or Col. Roger Morris of the British Army.

[49]

[50] Claude Halstead van Tyne, Loyalists in the American Revolution (Ganesvoort, NY: Corner House Historical Publications, 1999), 182.

[51] Jennifer J. Baker, Securing the Commonwealth: Debt, Speculation, and Writing in the Making of Early America (Baltimore: Johns Hopkins University Press, 2005), 67.

[52] Volo and Volo. Daily Life During the American Revolution (p. 303). Kindle Edition.

[53] Allen Johnson, ed., et al, The Dutch and English on the Hudson (New Haven: Yale UP, 1919), Chapter III.

[54] Ibid.

[55] Hofstadler, 11-12.

[56] James M. Volo, "The Acquisition and Use of Warlike Stores During the American Revolution, Part II," *Living History Journal*, No. 15 (Fall 1986), 10.

[57] The idealized equation for the formation of the byproduct glycerin and sodium stearate from stearin (the triglyceride of stearic acid) and lye follows. However, the limited solubility of sodium hydroxide means that the more soluble potassium hydroxide (KOH) was often preferred.:

$(C_{18}H_{35}O_2)_3C_3H_5 + 3\ NaOH \rightarrow C_3H_5(OH)_3 + 3\ C_{18}H_{35}O_2Na$

[58] Original Henry M. Paynter article from *Invention & Technology*, Fall 1990; David Maxey's corrections from *The Pennsylvania Magazine of History & Biography*, Jan/Apr 1998 and from the *Journal of the Patent & Trademark Office Society*, March 1998. URL: http://www.me.utexas.edu/~longoria/paynter/hmp/The_First_Patent.html

59   James Fenimore Cooper. The Pioneers (Kindle Location 26625).
60   William Cooper, "Guide to the Wilderness." (Dublin, Ireland: 1810)
61   James Fenimore Cooper. Pathfinder; or, The Inland Sea (Kindle Locations 282-284).
62   See Susan Fenimore Cooper, op cit.
63   Benjamin Franklin, "Positions to Be Examined Concerning National Wealth," in John Bigelow, ed. *The Complete Works of Benjamin Franklin* vol. 4 (Ulan Press, 2011).
64   Ralph Birdsall, "Fenimore Cooper in Cooperstown," Proceedings of the New York State Historical Association Volume XVI, pp. 137-139. URL: http://www.oneonta.edu/~cooper/articles/nyhistory/1917nyhistory-birdsall.html .html
65   Tocqueville, *Journey to America*, 322.
66   Basil Hall quoted in Adam McNall, *Agricultural History of the Genesee Valley*, 83.
67   "Preface to *The Leather-Stocking Tales*." The American Tradition in Literature. Vol. 1. George Perkins, ed. (New York: McGraw-Hill, 1990).
68   Thomas L. Philbrick, Cooper in Europe: The Travel Books (3rd Cooper Seminar at SUNY, 1980). URL: http://www.oneonta.edu/~cooper/articles/suny/1980suny-philbrick.html
69   C. Hartley Grattan, The Three Jameses: A Family of Minds (New York: New York University Press, 1962), 239.
70   Henry Adams, The Education of Henry Adams (New York: Modern Library, 1999), 70.
71   Alexandra Lee Levin, "Miss Knight Abroad," *American Heritage* 11, no. 3 (April 1960): 15.
72   Levin, "Miss Knight Abroad," 15.
73   Mark Twain, *The Innocents Abroad* (New York: Penguin Putnam, 1980), 2–3.
74   Tuckerman, Bayard, ed., The Diary of Philip Hone, 1828-1851 (Kindle Locations 1428-1431). New York, Dodd, Mead.
75   See James Fenimore Cooper, New York (Kindle Locations 80-82). Prior to his fatal illness in 1851, Cooper was engaged upon this historical work, to be entitled "The Men of Manhattan," only the Introduction to which had been sent to the press. The printing office was destroyed by fire and with it the opening chapters of this work. Fortunately a few pages had been set up and are the only parts of this work available.
76   The Letters and Journals of James Fenimore Cooper, ed. James F. Beard, 6 vols. (Cambridge, Mass., 1960-68), II, 180. See also: Cooper, The American Democrat (Penguin Classics, 1989), 185.
77   James Grossman, Cooper and the Responsibility of the Press (*New York History*, Vol. 35, No. 4, October 1954, 512-521). URL: http://www.oneonta.edu/external/cooper/articles/nyhistory/1954nyhistory-grossman.html
78   Cooper to Thomas Warren Field, 4 November 1848, in Beard, *Letters*, V, 388.
79   David Kaser, Books and Libraries in Camp and Battle: The Civil War Experience (Westport: Greenwood Press, 1984), 3.
80   Fanny Trollope, Domestic Manners of the Americans (p. 24).Kindle Edition.
81   See Benita Eisler, ed., The Lowell Offering: Writings by New England Mill

Women, 1840–1845 (New York: W. W. Norton & Co., 1977), 31.

[82] Charles Dickens, American Notes (London: 1850), 4250. Kindle edition. See also Charles Dickens. Speeches: Literary and Social (Kindle Locations 1179-1182).

[83] Schollander Wendell and Wes Schollander. Forgotten Elegance, The Art, Artifacts, and Peculiar History of Victorian and Edwardian Entertaining in America. (Westport, CT: Greenwood Press, 2002), 217.

[84] Sir Walter Scott, The Fair Maid of Perth (New York: Harper, 1831), 9. The actual quote reads: "Yes—respect; and who pays any respect to me?" said the haughty young lord. "A miserable artisan and his daughter, too much honored by my slightest notice, have the insolence to tell me that my notice dishonors them."

[85] See Robert H. Abzug, Cosmos Crumbling: American Reform and the Religious Imagination (New York, 1994) and John G. West Jr., The Politics of Revelation and Reason: Religion and Civic Life in the New Nation (Lawrence, Kansas, 1996).

[86] T. L. Haines and Levi W. Yaggy, The Royal Path of Life; or, Aims and Aids to Success and Happiness (Chicago: Western Publishing House, 1876), 91.

[87] James Fenimore Cooper, Wyandotte (1843).

[88] Christopher Hibbert, Queen Victoria: A Personal History (London: HarperCollins, 2000), 123.

[89] Kay S. House, Cooper's Females (SUNY, 1978). URL: http://www.oneonta.edu/~cooper/articles/suny/1978suny-house.html

[90] See Chuck ZeitVogel, "Gender Power and Social Class ... Cooper." URL: http://www.oneonta.edu/external/cooper/articles/other/2004other-zeitvogel.html

[91] James Fenimore Cooper, The Complete Leatherstocking Tales: All 5 Books (Kindle Locations 12127-12130). Waxkeep Publishing. Kindle Edition. See also Kindle Locations 11898-11899.

[92] James Fenimore Cooper. Pathfinder; or, the inland sea (Kindle Locations 214-215).

[93] Jaime Javier Rodríguez, The Literatures of the U.S.-Mexican War: Narrative, Time, and Identity (University of Texas Press, 2010).

[94] "Review of Red Rover." *The North American Review* (University of Northern Iowa) 27 (60): 139–154. July 1828.

[95] Unpublished: The Papers of William Mather (1889) in the George Arents Research Library at Syracuse University. See Constance Evans, ed. URL: http://www.oneonta.edu/external/cooper/articles/other/1989other-evans.html

[96] Donald A. Ringe, "Cooper's Mode of Expression," (1978). Cooper Seminar at the State University of New York College at Oneonta (SUNY Oneonta). URL: http://www.oneonta.edu/~cooper/articles/suny/1978suny-ringe.html

[97] Richard Morton, "Perception and Reality: the Novelist, the Deerslayer and the Reader." Presented at the Cooper Panel of the 1990 Conference of the American Literature Association in San Diego. URL: http://external.oneonta.edu/cooper/articles/ala/1990ala-morton.html

[98] L. Chandler Ball, "The Real Natty an Elder Brother," *Proceedings of the New York State Historical Association*, Vol. XVI (1917), pp. 187-192. URL: http://www.oneonta.edu/~cooper/articles/nyhistory/1917nyhistory-ball.html

[99] See Richard Morton.

[100] D.H. Lawrence, "Studies in Classic American Literature" in The Shock of Recognition. ed. Edmund Wilson. New York: Doubleday, 1943.

[101] James Fenimore Cooper, 1850 Preface to *The Deerslayer*, *The Deerslayer; or, The First Warpath* [1841]. (Albany: State University of New York Press, 1987), 11.

[102] James Fenimore Cooper, The Complete Leatherstocking Tales: All 5 Books (Kindle Locations 13923-13927). Waxkeep Publishing. Kindle Edition.

[103] Common Sense ideas as developed by such philosophers as Thomas Reid and Dugald Stewart were principally responsible for making the "Scottish philosophy" of morality predominant in early 19th-century. See: William Owen URL: http://www.oneonta.edu/~cooper/articles/suny/1997suny-owen.html See also: Drew Gilpin Faust, Mother of Invention: Women of the Slaveholding South in the American Civil War (Charlotte: University of North Carolina Press, 1996), 154.

[104] Twain, chapter 46.

[105] Mark Twain, *Life on the Mississippi* (1883), chapter 46.

[106] Jane Austen, *Northanger Abbey*. Great Literature Online. 1997-2013 URL: http://www.classicauthors.net/austen/northanger/northanger5.html

[107] Saintsbury, 115.

[108] Eustace Chesser, *Shelley and Zastrozzi: Self-Revelation of a Neurotic*. (London: Gregg/Archive, 1965).

[109] Rudyard Kipling, *American Notes* (1891). URL: http://www.chicagohs.org/fire/queen/pic0521.html

[110] Volo and Volo, 2004: 216.

[111] Lydia M. Child, The Mother's Book (Boston: Applewood, 1831), 93-94.

[112] V. M. Rice, Code of Public Instruction (Albany: State Printing Office, 1856), 325.

[113] Stanley J. Kunitz, ed., British Authors of the Nineteenth Century (New York: Wilson, 1936), 105-106.

[114] Edna Kenton, *Simon Kenton: His Life and Period, 1755-1836* (Garden City, 1930). Herein she recorded a circumstance quite similar to that reported in as reported in Allan W. Eckert, *The Frontiersmen*, 166-168.

[115] *The American Journal of Psychology* Vol. 3, No. 1 (Jan., 1890), 124.

[116] See Antiquarian Books, http://home.navisoft.com/blackstn/crime.htm; and E. A. Duyckinck, Cyclopedia of American Literature (Detroit: Gale Research, 1965).

[117] Kunitz, 511-512.

[118] Ibid., 383-384.

[119] James Fenimore Cooper, The Chainbearer, or The Littlepage Manuscripts (New York: D. Appleton and Company, 1845, reprinted 1883), 138-139.

[120] Barbara Mann, "James Fenimore Cooper and God," James Fenimore Cooper Society Miscellaneous Papers No. 30, May 2013, pp. 7-9. URL: http://external.oneonta.edu/cooper/articles/ala/2013ala-mann.html

[121] James Fenimore Cooper, The Wept of Wish-Ton-Wish (1871), 32.

[122] Emanuel Spenser, "Glimpses of Log-cabin Life in Early Ohio." Magazine of American History, Vol. 24 (August 1890), 101-111.

[123] Keiser, 37.

[124] Peter Martyr as quoted in David J. Weber, The Spanish Frontier in North America (New Haven: Yale University Press, 1992), 38.

[125] The US Supreme Court case *Johnson v. M'Intosh* (1823) made "discovery doctrine" explicit in US law. The court denied individuals permission to buy land from American Indian tribes.
[126] Richard White, The Middle Ground, Indians, Empires, and Republics in the Great Lakes Region, 1650–1815 (New York: Cambridge University Press, 1991), 111–112.
[127] Stephen Aron and Jeremy Adelman, From Borderlands to Borders: Empires, Nation-States, and the Peoples in between in North American History The American Historical Review (1999) Vol. 104, 3: 814-841.
[128] David A. Copeland, "Fighting for a Continent: Newspaper Coverage of the English and French War For Control of North America, 1754-1760." URL: http://www.earlyamerica.com/review/spring97/newspapers.html
[129] Dinwiddie, *Papers*, 1:83–85.
[130] See "Editorial Note," Founders Online, National Archives (2015). URL: http://founders.archives.gov/documents/Washington/01-01-02-0004-0001. Source: *The Diaries of George Washington*, vol. 1, *11 March 1748–13 November 1765*, ed. Donald Jackson. (Charlottesville: University Press of Virginia, 1976), 162–173.
[131] *The Maryland Gazette, March 21, 1754 and March 28, 1754.*
[132] Educational Resources, Mount Vernon. URL: http://www.mountvernon.org/educational-resources/primary-sources-2/article/the-journal-of-major-george-washington/
[133] Stephen Aron and Jeremy Adelman, From Borderlands to Borders: Empires, Nation-States, and the Peoples in between in North American History, *The American Historical Review* (1999) Vol. 104, 3: 814-841.
[134] Andrew Gallup, ed., Memoir of a French and Indian War Soldier: Jolicoeur Charles Bonin (Bowie, MD: Heritage Books, 1993), 216.
[135] Samuel Adams Drake, The Border Wars of New England, Commonly Called King William's and Queen Anne's Wars (Williamstown: Corner House, 1973), 52-53.
[136] Richard White, The Middle Ground, Indians, Empires, and Republics in the Great Lakes Region, 1650–1815 (New York: Cambridge University Press, 1991), 63.
[137] John W. Shy, "A New Look at Colonial Militia." William and Mary Quarterly 35 (1963), 187.
[138] Allen W. Eckert, Wilderness Empire (Toronto: Bantam Books, 1980), 196-107.
[139] John K. Mahon, "Anglo-American Methods of Indian Warfare, 1676-1794," The Mississippi Valley Historical Review 45 (1958), 255.
[140] Stanley Vestal, King of the Fur Traders, The Deeds and Deviltry of Pierre Esprit Radisson (Boston: Houghton Mifflin, 1940), 98–99.
[141] Samuel Adams Drake, 15.
[142] John Ferling, Struggle for a Continent: The Wars of Early America (Arlington Heights, IL: Harlan Davidson, 1993), 98-99.
[143] James Fenimore Cooper, The Complete Leatherstocking Tales: All 5 Books (Kindle Locations 9102-9108). Waxkeep Publishing. Kindle Edition.
[144] Nicholas Birns, "The Unknown War: *The Last of the Mohicans* and the Effacement of the Seven Years War in American Historical Myth." (2005 Cooper Seminar). URL: http://exterma;.oneonta.edu/cooper/articles/suny/2005suny-birns.html

[145] Arthur G. Bradley, Fight with France for North America (New York: E.P. Dutton, 1902).
[146] Marc Lescarbot, Nova Francia: A Description of Acadia, 1606, H. P. Biggar, ed. (London: Harper & Brs., 1928), 156-157.
[147] Ibid.
[148] Cecil B. Williams, Henry Wadsworth Longfellow (New York: Twayne Publishers, Inc., 1964), 155.
[149] Frank H. Severance, An Old Frontier of France (New York: Dodd, Mead and Company, 1917). Kindle Locations 170-171.
[150] See James M. Volo, From Whence the Silver, The Role of Money in Colonial America, Traditional American History Series, No.3 (CreateSpace Independent Publishing Platform, 2014).
[151] Both can be found in Andrew J. Wahll, ed., The Braddock Road Chronicles, 1755 (Bowie, MD: Heritage Books, 1999), 349.
[152] Rueben Gold Thwaites, ed., Tomasz Mentrak, electrical transciptor, The Jesuit Relations and Allied Documents 1642-1643, Vol. 24, URL: http://puffin.creighton.edu/jesuit/relations/relations_24.html
[153] Major-General Johnson, September 3, 1755, to Governor George Clinton. Volo and Volo. Daily Life on the Old Colonial Frontier (p. 298). Kindle Edition.
[154] Volo and Volo, Family Life in Native America, (Westport: Greenwood, 2007), 295-296.
[155] Alan Gallay, ed., Colonial Wars of North America, 1512–1763: An Encyclopedia, (New York and London: Garland Publishing, Inc., 1996), 363.
[156] C.E. Potter, The History of Manchester (New Hampshire), (C. E. Potter, Publisher, 1856).
[157] Volo and Volo, Family Life in Native America.
[158] Henry N. Stevens, ed., The Battle Near Lake George in 1755, A Prospective Plan with an Explanation thereof by Samuel Blodget (Cornell University Library, 1911), 4.
[159] Reported in Armand Francis Lucier, ed., French and Indian War Notices Abstracted from Colonial Newspapers: 1754–1755 (Bowie, MD: Heritage Books, 1999) vol. 1. See also Francis Parkman, *Montcalm and Wolfe,* (New York: Atheneum, 1984), 244.
[160] Donald Grant Mitchell, et al, eds., Luke Gridley's Diary of 1757 (Hartford Press: The Case, Lockwood & Brainard Company, 1906), 8.
[161] Henry N. Stevens, viii.
[162] Ibid., 13-15.
[163] Ibid., 2.
[164] Biography of Ephraim Williams by Ebenezer Fitch (1802). URL: http://archives.williams.edu/ewilliamsexhibit/officer/officer.html
[165] Letter of Abigail Dwight, 10 November 1755, Williams College Archives. URL: http://archives.williams.edu/ewilliamsexhibit/bms/transcript04.html
[166] James M. Volo and Dorothy Denneen Volo. Daily Life on the Old Colonial Frontier (p. 3). Kindle Edition.
[167] Sir Charles Hardy, January 16, 1756, to the Board of Trade, found in E.B. O'Callaghan, ed. Documents Relative to the Colonial History of the State of New York,

V7 (Albany, NY: Weed, Parsons, 1855), 4.
[168] James Fenimore Cooper, The Complete Leatherstocking Tales: All 5 Books (Kindle Locations 9581-9583). Waxkeep Publishing. Kindle Edition.
[169] See Francis Parkman, Montcalm and Wolfe (New York: Atheneum, 1984), 281-282.
[170] Parkman, Montcalm and Wolfe, 226.
[171] Ian K. Steele, Betrayal: Fort William Henry and the Massacre (New York: Oxford University Press, 1990), 97.
[172] Ibid.
[173] Quoted in Francis Russell, The French and Indian Wars (New York: American Heritage Publishing, 1962), 94.
[174] James M. Volo and Dorothy Denneen Volo. Daily Life on the Old Colonial Frontier (p. 292). Kindle Edition.
[175] See "Plain Truth" URL: http://www.revolutionary-war-and-beyond.com/plain-truth-by-benjamin-franklin-november-17-1747.html
[176] Samuel Adams Drake, The Border Wars of New England, Commonly Called King William's and Queen Anne's Wars (Williamstown, MA: Corner House, 1973), 2.
[177] Report of the Commission to Locate the Site of the Frontier Forts of Pennsylvania (1916), Thomas Lynch Montgomery, Ed., (Clarence M. Busch, State Printer of Pennsylvania, 1896), 300.
[178] The Project Gutenberg EBook of The Virginians, by William Makepeace Thackeray (1857). Kindle Locations 120; 1144.
[179] A letter to Sir Robert Napier from Braddock, April 19, 1755, found in Andrew J. Wahll, ed., The Braddock Road Chronicles, 1755 (Bowie, MD: Heritage Books, 1999), 354.
[180] James M. Volo, and Dorothy Denneen Volo. Daily Life on the Old Colonial Frontier (The Greenwood Press Daily Life Through History Series) (p. 288). Kindle Edition.
[181] Pamela Kline, "General Edward Braddock." URL: http://www.revolutionary-war.net/edward-braddock.html
[182] E.C. Stedman and E. M. Hutchinson, comps. A Library of American Literature: An Anthology in Eleven Volumes. 1891. Vols. I–II: Colonial Literature, 1607–1764.
[183] James Webb, Born Fighting, How the Scots-Irish Shaped America (New York: Broadway Books, 2005. Kindle Edition), 335.
[184] Gentlemen's Magazine (London: November 1756) Report of the Battle of Oswego. RL: http://www.rarenewspapers.com/view/545003
[185] Battle of Oswego 1756 and the Captivity of Benjamin Taylor (2012). URL: http://minerdescent.com/2012/12/08/battle-of-oswego-1756/
[186] Parkman, 271.
[187] Winslow's Journals, The Collections of the Nova Scotia Historical Society (1882-1884); V. 4, p. 178-80; and V. 3, p. 125. URL: http://www.blupete.com/Library/History/NSHS.htm
[188] James M. Volo and Dorothy Denneen Volo. Daily Life on the Old Colonial Frontier (The Greenwood Press Daily Life Through History Series) (p. 303). Kindle Edition.

[189] Lawrence Henry Gipson, <u>The British Empire before the American Revolution</u>, Volume 7 (New York: Knopf, 1965), 232.

[190] Quoted in Francis Parkman, <u>Montcalm and Wolfe</u> (New York: Atheneum, 1984), 296-297.

[191] C. Hale Sipe, *The Indian Wars of Pennsylvania* (Telegraph Press, 1929).

[192] Ibid.

[193] *The Second Journal of Christian Frederick Post* (London: 1759), *iv-v*.

[194] *The Second Journal of Christian Frederick Post* (London: 1759), 37-38.

[195] Stephen Brumwell, <u>Redcoats: The British Soldier and War in the Americas, 1755-1763.</u> (New York: Cambridge University Press, 2002), 254.

[196] Father Sabastien Rasles (sometimes spelled Rale') spent more of his life living among the Abenaki than he did in European society. He clearly incited the tribe to war on the English settlements.

[197] Hofstadler, 11-12.

[198] Samuel Eliot Morison, <u>Sources and Documents Illustrating the American Revolution 1764–1788 and the Formation of the Federal Constitution</u> (New York: Oxford University Press, 1965), 8.

[199] Edward Redmond, "George Washington: Surveyor and Mapmaker." <u>Annals of the Association of American Geographers</u> 23, no. 3 (September 1941): 147. URL: http://memory.loc.gov/ammem/gmdhtml/gwmaps.html

[200] All of Massachusetts' paper was redeemed by 1773.

[201] John C. Miller, <u>Origins of the American Revolution</u> (Boston: Little, Brown and Company, 1943), 269.

[202] Samuel Eliot Morison, <u>Sources and Documents Illustrating the American Revolution 1764-1788 and the Formation of the Federal Constitution</u> (New York: Oxford University Press, 1965), xx.

[203] Neil Harmon Swanson, <u>The First Rebel: Being a Lost Chapter of Our History and a True Narrative</u> (New York: Farrar & Rinehart, 1937), 54-55.

[204] Morison, 11.

[205] James M. Volo and Dorothy Denneen Volo. <u>Daily Life on the Old Colonial Frontier</u> (The Greenwood Press Daily Life Through History Series) (p. 205). Kindle Edition.

[206] Letter of Colonel Henry Bouquet to General Jeffery Amherst (6 August 1763). URL: http://bushyrunbattlefield.com/history/henry-bouquet/

[207] John Keegan, <u>Fields of Battle: The Wars for North America</u> (New York: Vintage Press, 1997), 135.

[208] *The Journal of Captain Thomas Morris*, (1764) and found in *Miscellanies in Prose and Verse* (London, printed for James Ridgway, 1791), 304-305.

[209] Ibid.

[210] Neil H. Swanson, *Allegheny Uprising* (Original title: *The First Rebel*. New York: Farrar – Rinehart, 1937), 113.

[211] The word "Conococheague" is translated from the Delaware Indian or Unami-Lenapi term *òk'chaxk'hanna*, which means "many-turns-river."

[212] Swanson, 366.

[213] Swanson, 114.

[214] Swanson, 247.
[215] Swanson, Introduction.
[216] Marjoleine Kars, <u>Breaking Loose Together: The Regulator Rebellion in Pre-Revolutionary North Carolina</u> (Chappel Hill: University of North Carolina Press, 2002), 594.
[217] Marjoleine Kars, 98-101.
[218] Margaret F. Hofmann, "The land grant process in North Carolina," <u>The Colony of North Carolina, 1735-1764</u>. Accessed June 2011, URL: http://www.pipesfamily.com/landgrant.htm
[219] James Fenimore Cooper, <u>The Wept of Wish-Ton-Wish</u> (1871), 40.
[220] John K. Mahon, "Anglo-American Methods of Indian Warfare, 1676-1794," <u>The Mississippi Valley Historical Review</u> 45 (1958), 255.
[221] <u>A History of the Schenectady Patent in the Dutch and English Times; being contributions toward a history of the lower Mohawk Valley</u> by Jonathan Pearson, and others, edited by J. W. MacMurray (Albany: J. Munsell's Sons, 1883), 290-303.
[222] Nelson Greene, ed., <u>History of the Mohawk Valley: Gateway to the West 1614-1925,</u> Vol. I, (Chicago: The S. J. Clarke Publishing Company, 1925), 545-547.
[223] See Greene, 547.
[224] Uriah James Jones, <u>History of the Early Settlement of the Juniata Valley Embracing an Account of the Early Pioneers, and the Trials and Privations Incident to the Settlement of the Valley</u> (Kindle Locations 42-44).
[225] <u>Publishers Weekly</u> review (1992) of *A Sorrow in Our Heart: The Life of Tecumseh.*
[226] Stanley Vestal, <u>King of the Fur Traders, The Deeds and Deviltry of Pierre Esprit Radisson</u> (Boston: Houghton Mifflin Company, 1940), 19–20.
[227] Louise S. Spindler, "Women in Menominee Culture," in <u>The North American Indians, A Sourcebook</u>, ed., Roger C. Owen (Toronto: Collier-Macmillan Limited, 1971), 598.
[228] James Fenimore Cooper, <u>The Complete Leatherstocking Tales: All 5 Books</u> (Kindle Location 110). Waxkeep Publishing. Kindle Edition.
[229] Hone, Philip, (Kindle Locations 5764-5776).
[230] Ezra F. Tawil, (Brown University), "Romancing History: *The Pioneers* and the Problem of Slavery," 1997 Cooper Seminar at the State University of New York College at Oneonta (SUNY Oneonta). URL: http://www.oneonta.edu/~cooper/articles/suny/1997suny-tawil.html
[231] Cooper, New York (Kindle Locations 150-153).
[232] James D. Wallace, <u>Cooper and Slavery</u>. Presented at the Cooper Panel of the 1992 Conference of the American Literature Association in San Diego. URL: http://external.oneonta.edu/cooper/articles/ala/1992ala-wallace.html
[233] James Fenimore Cooper, <u>The Complete Leatherstocking Tales: All 5 Books</u> (Kindle Locations 646-647). Waxkeep Publishing. Kindle Edition.
[234] Mary E. Phillips. James Fenimore Cooper (Kindle Locations 2221-2224).
[235] Herbert A Aptheker, *American Negro Slave Revolts*, was published in 1943.
[236] Erasmus Darwin, <u>Zoonomia</u> (Project Gutenberg) XXIX.4.8
[237] James D. Wallace, opcit.

[238] Thomas S. Gladsky, Cooper's Other Americans: Cultural Diversity and American Homogeneity. Presented at the Cooper Panel of the 1992 Conference of the American Literature Association in San Diego. URL: http://external.oneonta.edu/cooper/articles/ala/1992ala-gladsky.html

[239] See James Fenimore Cooper, Second Preface to *The Deerslayer* (1850). URL: http://pinkmonkey.com/dl/library1/book0619.pdf

[240] James Fenimore Cooper. The Wept of Wish-Ton-Wish (Kindle Locations 22-24).

[241] Mary E. Phillips. James Fenimore Cooper (Kindle Locations 1672-1673).

[242] Hugh MacDougall, The Bravo – Cooper's Message to America. Papers from the 2009 Cooper Seminar at SUNY (No. 17). URL: http://external.oneonta.edu/cooper/articles/suny/2009suny-macdougall.html

[243] James Fenimore Cooper, "On Demagogues," The American Democrat (1838).

[244] Cooper. The Wept of Wish-Ton-Wish (Kindle Locations 22-24).

[245] Hugh MacDougall, The Bravo – Cooper's Message to America. Papers from the 2009 Cooper Seminar at SUNY (No. 17). URL: http://external.oneonta.edu/cooper/articles/suny/2009suny-macdougall.html

[246] James Donahue, Representing Cooper's Landscape: The N.C. Wyeth Illustrations. Papers from the 2005 Cooper Seminar at SUNY. URL: http://external.oneonta.edu/cooper/articles/suny/2005suny-donahue.html

[247] William A. Starna, "The Pequots in the Early Seventeenth Century," in Laurence M. Hauptman and James D. Wherry, eds., The Pequots in Southern New England, The Fall and Rise of an American Indian Nation (Norman: University of Oklahoma Press, 1990), 40-41.

[248] Colin G. Galloway, Dawnland Encounters, 170.

[249] Richard White, The Middle Ground, Indians, Empires, and Republics in the Great Lakes Region, 1650–1815 (New York: Cambridge University Press, 1991), 183.

[250] Allan W. Eckert, The Frontiersmen (p. 6). Jesse Stuart Foundation. Kindle Edition.

[251] Albert E. Stone, ed., Letters from an American Farmer and Sketches of Eighteenth-Century America by J. Hector St. John de Crevecoeur (New York: Penguin Classics, 1986), 377.

[252] Peter Kalm, *Peter Kalm's Travels in North America*. (New York: Dover Publications, 1964), 560.

[253] James F. O'Neil, ed., 31. Quoting Jean-Bernard Bossu.

[254] James F. O'Neil, ed., 2-3. Quoting James Adair.

[255] Having the hair or fur removed by scrapping after soaking in a vat of oak bark, the leather was softened by rubbing in the brains of deer mixed with rotten-wood powdered into a powder.

[256] James F. O'Neil, ed., 29. Quoting Jolicoeur Charles Bonin.

[257] Peter Kalm, 556.

[258] Peter Kalm, Peter Kalm's Travels in North America (New York: Dover Publications, 1964), 560.

[259] James F. O'Neil, ed., 19. Quoting John Knox in An Historical Journal of the Campaigns in North America from 1757-1760 (first published 1769).

[260] James F. O'Neil, ed., 2. Quoting James Adair.

[261] Ibid.
[262] James F. O'Neil, ed., 77-78. Quoting William Bartrum.
[263] Peter Kalm, 563.
[264] James F. O'Neil, ed., 16. Quoting Col. James Smith.
[265] James F. O'Neil, ed., 19. Quoting John Knox.
[266] Stanley Vestal, 20-21.
[267] Alvin M. Josephy, Jr., ed., The American Heritage Book of Indians (New York: American Heritage Publishing, 1961), 110.
[268] See: Mary E. Phillips. James Fenimore Cooper (1905: Kindle Locations 393-395); and Richard White, The Middle Ground, Indians, Empires, and Republics in the Great Lakes Region, 1650-1815 (New York: Cambridge University Press, 1991), 56.
[269] James M. Volo and Dorothy Denneen Volo. Daily Life on the Old Colonial Frontier (pp. 269-270). Kindle Edition.
[270] Susan Fenimore Cooper, op cit.
[271] Richard Smith. "Journal," July 26, 1773, in Huntington, "Old Time Notes," (Transcript, New York State Historical Association), 353; William Strickland, *Journal of a Tour in the United States of America, 1794-1795* (New York: New-York Historical Society, 1971), 139.
[272] Hugh C. MacDougall, The Book that Made Glens Falls Famous: An Introduction to James Fenimore Cooper's *The Last of the Mohicans.* URL: http://www.oneonta.edu/external/cooper/articles/informal/hugh-glensfalls.html
[273] See: A.W. Holden, "The Frauds of History," address delivered before the Warren County Teachers Association at the Central House, Lake George, February 20, 1855; and also Anthony F. Hall, "Toponomy, or the Study of Place Names," Lake George Mirror Magazine (2011) URL: http://www.lakegeorgemirrormagazine.com/2011/03/24/toponomy-or-the-study-of-place-names/
[274] Cooper, New York (Kindle Locations 123-127).
[275] A Journal of a Residence in America (Henry Holt, 1835). URL: http://www.jmisc.net/jm970415.htm
[276] Ibid. See also Volo and Volo, (2004), 306-307.
[277] A. LeVasseur, Lafayette in America, (1829), 199.
[278] See "Early Norwegian Immigrants on the Erie Canal," Norway Heritage. URL: http://www.norwayheritage.com/articles/templates/voyages.asp?articleid=150&zoneid=6
[279] Ibid.
[280] Ibid.
[281] Alan Taylor, "Fenimore Cooper's America," History Today 46, no. 2 (February 1996): 21-27.
[282] Thomas Berson, "James Fenimore Cooper's frontier: *The Pioneers* as history," A treatise submitted to Florida State University (2004), 1. URL: http://diginole.lib.fsu.edu/cgi/viewcontent.cgi?article=1892&context=etd
[283] Quoted in Richard Slotkin, Regeneration Through Violence : The Mythology of the American Frontier, 1600-1860 (University of Oklahoma Press, 2000), 466.
[284] James A. Maxwell, ed., America's Fascinating Indian Heritage (Pleasantville, NY: Reader's Digest Association, 1978), 111.

285 Francis Jennings, 166.
286 Francis Jennings, 111.
287 James Fenimore Cooper, The Last of the Mohicans, Introduction.
288 Albert Keiser, The Indian in American Literature (New York: Octagon Books, 1978), 106-107.
289 Harold F. McGee, 24.
290 Martha J. Lamb, History of the City of New York, I, 53, 187.
291 Robert Bolton, History of the County of Westchester From its First Settlement to the Present Time (New York: Alexander S. Gould, 1848).
292 (Sir) William Johnson, The Papers of Sir William Johnson (Albany: University of the State of New York, Kindle Location 9698).
293 W. Andrefsky, Jr. Lithics: Macroscopic Approaches to Analysis (United Kingdom: Cambridge University Press, 2000), 41-42. Obsidian, a glassy textured material, has been known in literature since Pliny's Natural History and named after a Roman Obsius who recognized it as a distinct form in Ethiopia.
294 Charles Whittlesey, Ancient Mining on the Shores of Lake Superior (Philadelphia, 1862), 2.
295 Robert Ellis Cahill, New England's Viking and Indian Wars (Danvers, MA: Old Saltbox Publishing, 1987), 21-22; M. Mauss, The Gift: The Form and Reasons for Exchange in Archaic Societies (New York, London: W.W. Norton, 1990), 71; and S.R. Martin, Wonderful Power: The Story of Ancient Copper Working in the Lake Superior Basin (Great Lakes Books Series. Wayne State University Press, 1999), 136.
296 Volo and Volo, (2007) 157.
297 Jesuit Relations, 1671, 42, 1858.
298 "Smallpox Blankets," Cherokee Heritage Documentation Center. (2015) URL: http://cherokeeregistry.com/index.php?option=com_content&view=article&id=407&Itemid=617
299 R. G. Robertson. Rotting Face: Smallpox and the American Indian (Kindle Locations 52-53). Kindle Edition.
300 Cooper, James Fenimore (2013-04-14). The Complete Leatherstocking Tales: All 5 Books (Kindle Location 10818, 10843). Waxkeep Publishing. Kindle Edition."
301 Ian K. Steele, Warpaths, Invasions of North America (New York; Oxford University Press, 1994) 121-122.
302 William M. Clements, "Schoolcraft as Textmaker," *Journal of American Folklore* (1990) 103: 177-190
303 Shirley W. Dunn, The Mohicans and their Land, 1609–1730 (Fleischmanns, NY: Purple Mountain Press, 1994), 99.
304 Francis Jennings, The Ambiguous Iroquois Empire, (New York: W. W. Norton & Company, 1986), 164.
305 Francis Jennings, 159.
306 Francis Jennings, 160-161.
307 James Fenimore Cooper, The Complete Leatherstocking Tales: All 5 Books (Kindle Locations 187-190). Waxkeep Publishing. Kindle Edition.
308 Robert E. Ritzenthaler and Pat Ritzenthaler, 47.
309 Wilbur R. Jacobs, ed., The Appalachian Frontier: The Edmond Atkins Report and

Plan of 1755 (Lincoln: University of Nebraska Press, 1967), 82.

[310] Jake T. Hubbard, "Americans as guerilla fighter: Robert Rogers and his rangers," American Heritage (August 1971) Vol. 22 No. 5. URL: http://www.americanheritage.com/content/americans-guerrilla-fighters-rorert-rogers-and-his-rangers

[311] Ibid, 4.

[312] Francis S. Drake, *Indian History for Young Folks* (1884). URL: http://www.heritage-history.com/index.php?c=read&author=drake&book=indians&story=_front

[313] "Suitable for Gentlemen of the Army," *The Journal of the American Military Institute*, Vol. 3, No. 4 (Winter, 1939), 263-264. See also Caleb Stark, ed., *Memoir of Gen. John Stark*, 454.

[314] Mary Cochrane Rogers, A Battle Fought on Snow Shoes (Kindle Location, 272).

[315] Mary Cochrane Rogers, 34-35.

[316] Hubbard, 3.

[317] "Right Rangers, Wrong Fight," Walking the Berkshires (October 2007). URL: http://greensleeves.typepad.com/berkshires/2007/10/right-rangers-w.html

[318] Mary Cochrane Rogers, 111.

[319] Francis Parkman, The Works of Francis Parkman, (Boston: Little, Brown, 1910) Volume 9, 264

[320] See Stephen Brumwell, White Devil (Cambridge, MA: DaCapo, 2004).

[321] See Hubbard.

[322] Belle McKinney Hays Swope, History of the Families of McKinney-Brady-Quigley, Newville, Pennsylvania (Chambersburg, Pennsylvania: 1905), 140.